THE OWLS
OF NORTH AMERICA

Karl E. Karalus
1971

THE OWLS
OF NORTH AMERICA
(NORTH OF MEXICO)

*All the Species and Subspecies Illustrated in
Color and Fully Described*

PAINTINGS AND DRAWINGS BY
Karl E. Karalus
TEXT BY
Allan W. Eckert

WEATHERVANE BOOKS · NEW YORK

This 1987 edition is published by Weathervane Books,
distributed by Crown Publishers, Inc.,
225 Park Avenue South, New York, New York 10003,
by arrangement with Allan W. Eckert and Karl E. Karalus

Design by M. Franklin Plympton

Printed and bound in Hong Kong

LIBRARY OF CONGRESS CATALOGING-IN-PUBLICATION DATA

Karalus, Karl E.
The owls of North America.

Reprint. Originally published: Garden City, N.Y. :
Doubleday, 1974, c1973.
Bibliography: p.
Includes index.
1. Owls—North America.   2. Birds—North America.
I. Eckert, Allan W.   II. Title.
QL696.S83K37 1987   598'.97'097   87-8187
ISBN 0-517-63220-9
ISBN 0-517-65380-X (Deluxe Edition)
h g f e d c b

For their many years of
unstinting effort
in every conceivable manner
on our behalf,
the authors
dedicate this book
with heartfelt appreciation
and deepest love
to our wives,
HELEN C. KARALUS
AND
JOAN D. ECKERT

Contents

Color Plates

(Plates appear after page number)

Acknowledgments

In a volume of this scope the aid of numerous people, professional scientists and laymen alike, becomes necessary. The authors have been most fortunate in receiving aid in various ways from a great many people—too many, in fact, to attempt listing them all here individually. To those who have been of such assistance, we wish to acknowledge with sincere appreciation their efforts on our behalf.

Especially are we indebted to the vast number of scientists, researchers, students, ornithological investigators, and skilled observers who have, over scores of years, added to man's knowledge of the owls through their records, reports, and findings. Without the cumulative work done by these people, published in such ornithological periodicals as *The Auk, Bird Lore, The Condor, The Wilson Bulletin, Oölogist,* and others, along with articles, papers, and books they have written and upon which we have drawn heavily, a work such as ours would not have been possible. Their contribution has been of inestimable value, yet to mention all of them individually here or in the text would be in one respect a monumental task and, in another, a decided distraction to the readability of this work. Therefore, while principal sources for this work are listed at the back of the book, the authors have preferred to keep the text itself reasonably free of matter which is chiefly extraneous or incidental to the text.

There are, however, certain individuals who have contributed large amounts of their time, energy, and scientific knowledge to aid us, and these people in particular deserve specific recognition. For their continuing extended efforts to help during the production of this volume; for their aid and advice in such matters as evaluation and taxonomy, the loan and identification of numerous preserved specimens, the providing of textual materials, the use of collections and facilities, and for their personal encouragement of us in this project, the authors express their most profound gratitude to the staff of the Department of Ornithology, Field Museum of Natural History, Chicago, Illinois—Dr. Emmet R. Blake, Curator of Birds and member of the American Ornithological Union Check-list Committee; Dr. Melvin A. Traylor, Jr., Associate Curator of Birds; and their very able assistant, Miss Dianne Maurer.

To Dr. William Beecher, Director, and his staff at the Chicago Academy of Sciences, Chicago, Illinois, we express thanks for the use of numerous study skins and textual materials, and for their aid and advice in other matters concerned with the production of this work.

For his advice and assistance in providing information, specimens, materials, and facilities, as well as for his helpful comments on both artwork and manuscript, our appreciation to E. J. Koestner, Director of the Dayton Museum of Natural History, Dayton, Ohio, and his extremely co-operative staff.

For their cheerful and more than willingly given aid and advice throughout production of the manuscript and art, and for their directional comments from both literary and scientific standpoint, the authors are indebted to husband-and-wife ornithological biologists Dr. Dorothy C. Saunders and Dr. George B. Saunders, formerly of the United States Fish and Wildlife Service and presently in retirement at Englewood, Florida.

For his superb photographic work on owls as an aid to our project, and for the portrait work done by him in connection with this volume, our sincere appreciation to Richard Muntjanoff of Aurora, Illinois.

KARL E. KARALUS *and* ALLAN W. ECKERT

Introduction

Owls are marvelous birds.

They are incredible in the acuteness of their senses of sight and hearing and remarkable in their ability to fly with utter soundlessness. They are admirable in their ferocity and courage and always fascinating in their habits.

Yet, because owls are essentially birds of the night and thus far less often seen than birds of the day, they are also decidedly creatures of mystery. On a world-wide basis, probably no other bird throughout the history of mankind has been so deeply revered, so greatly feared, so thoroughly respected, or so soundly hated. No other bird has been so fundamentally misunderstood or so much the subject of superstition and fancy. For some cultures the owl has been the symbol of war or death, stillbirth or tragedy; for others it has been the symbol of wisdom or prophecy, truth or omniscience, and was frequently represented in emblem, effigy, symbol, or ornament. Even today the "wise old owl" is more commonly represented in statuary, posters, art, bookplates, advertising, architectural design and—most especially—jewelry than any other bird in the world, surpassing even the eagle.

In the preparation of the paintings for this book, every known species and subspecies of owl on the North American continent north of Mexico was very closely studied and, wherever possible, the actual type specimens of the owls were used, i.e., the individual museum bird skins upon which the original descriptions were based. Often this led to difficulties, especially where accurate portrayal of the coloration and markings was concerned. A museum collection of owl skins might well contain twenty or thirty specimens of the same subspecies, yet with some birds very dark and others very light and the remainder in gradations of considerable degree between them. Which bird, then, from this spectrum of choices, should be used to exemplify the species? In all cases, the authors and various helpful museum personnel studied all available birds very carefully and then selected as a model what seemed to be the bird with a plumage most representative of the subspecies to which it belonged. Often this would not be the type specimen from which the race was originally described.

Where text was concerned there were similar difficulties. It was important to include all known aspects of the life histories of each subspecies of the eighteen North American owl species north of Mexico. Since owls, as a scientific order (Strigiformes), have many similar characteristics and these become progressively more abundant as the classification is narrowed down through family, genus, species, and subspecies, repetition was most likely to occur. It was necessary to avoid this problem, yet without undermining the value of the description for each subspecies. To do so, the most prominent, familiar, or representative owl of each of the eighteen species has been selected for major description. The subspecies falling under that species designation are described only insofar as they *differ* from the representative subspecies that is described in detail.

A word about "subspecies" is advisable here. The terms race, subspecies, and geographic variation are basically synonymous. Yet, the term "race" has come to be considered a somewhat looser term than "subspecies," which itself has become rather identified with man-established boundaries which do not necessarily conform to natural or ecological boundaries. Subspecies are rarely constant in coloration, markings, and characteristics in the same sense that there is a constancy to species determination. The geographic variations—races or subspecies—are rarely separable into distinctly bounded geographic areas. Variation of a species on any continent is almost invariably continuous in smooth clines of intergrades and intermediates and therefore not neatly separable. Yet, to establish some sort of order, the subspecific scientific names become a necessity, however lacking they may be in the clarity one would hope to ascribe to them. This in itself was a problem of considerable moment when it came to a determination of which geographical variations should be included in a book purporting to describe all continental subspecies of any one order of birds.

The matter of taxonomy is more often than not a decidedly sticky issue. In some cases owls that were accepted as legitimate species, or subspecies, some years ago may now be part of another species, or themselves broken into more extensive subspecies. Further, subspecies continue to be named and described and often it becomes difficult to keep pace.

It is not the province of this book to establish new races of owls, nor to eliminate races whose validity may be in question. Rather, after considerable research, discussion with authorities far more able in these matters, and exhaustive study of specimens from all over North America, the authors have included those subspecies (or races) with characteristics which seem truly to set them reasonably well apart from others. Undoubtedly there will be some question as to whether this owl or that should have been included or, for that matter, excluded. Admittedly, the authors are not taxonomists and perhaps, for the purposes of this volume, advantageously not. Judgment, as a result, has not been colored or biased for a personal belief, as has sometimes stigmatized otherwise distinguished works previously published.

For the species and subspecies to be included in this volume, the authors have utilized the most recently published American Ornithological Union Check-list (*The A.O.U. Check-list of North American Birds,* Fifth Edition, 1957) as the most reliable foundation. The eighteen owl species we include are all accepted species in that Check-list. Of the fifty-nine subspecies we include, which make up those eighteen species, fifty-two are described in the 1957 Check-list. Some of the seven that are not will quite likely be included in the new edition of the A.O.U. Check-list now in preparation. A possible example is the Ontario Horned Owl (*Bubo virginianus scalariventris* Snyder), which was not described until 1961.

The date and location listing accompanying each color plate of the owls indicates the place and date where the specimen owl was taken which the artist used as a model for accuracy in preparing the paintings for this book. Many of these, obviously, were birds from museum collections, although a few were collected by the artist and author while this work was in progress.

As an aid to the lay reader in understanding some of the possibly unfamiliar anatomical terms used in this volume, there are three "topographic" owl sketches— upperparts view, underparts view, and side view—with all visible portions of the anatomy and plumage named. These sketches immediately follow this introductory section. In addition, there is a Glossary of Terms at the back of the book.

For a more thorough understanding of the art and text, it will be of value to briefly discuss here the use of the various descriptive headings for each of the major owl discussions to follow. Naturally, wherever owls as an order are similar in habit or physical attribute, this factor will be made clear. The headings themselves and what they include are as follows:

COMMON NAME

The most commonly used and generally accepted English name of the subspecies under discussion will be the one used to designate each of the fifty-nine birds included.

SCIENTIFIC NAME AND ORIGINAL DESCRIPTION

Here will be given the genus, species, and subspecies scientific name of each owl. For example, the Rocky Mountain Screech Owl is in the genus *Otus,* the species *asio,* and the subspecies *maxwelliae.* This particular bird was first scientifically described by ornithologist Robert Ridgway. Therefore, under this heading it would appear as: *Otus asio maxwelliae* (Ridgway). Following this, data concerning the original scientific description are given. If the owl in question has had previous scientific names which were abandoned through reclassification or revision of nomenclature, the most commonly used former name (or names) will be given here.

In some cases it will be noted that the name of the describer of the bird, appearing after the scientific name, is shown in parentheses, and in other cases it is not. This is intentional and follows the standard nomenclature practices for scientific naming. Where the name of the describer is not given in parentheses, it means that the original description of the bird still remains valid today; but where parentheses enclose the describer's name, it means that the species or subspecies under discussion has been reclassified or revised since the original description of the bird was written.

OTHER NAMES

Often an owl will be better known in a specific area by a name other than its standard English name. Such a name may be a local name, nickname, regional name, or foreign name. Under this heading will be listed in alphabetical order those names and the reason for such designation.

FOOT STUDIES OF VARIED OWLS

1. Barred Owl (*Strix varia*) depicting how middle toe will sometimes turn to one side while the owl is in relaxed perching posture. (From subspecies *georgica.*)
2. Screech Owl (*Otus asio*) with foot three-quarters open for grasping, just prior to striking prey. (From subspecies *naevius.*)
3. Horned Owl (*Bubo virginianus*) in alert standing pose on perch, with reversible toe sideways rather than in more customary rearward-pointing position. (From subspecies *occidentalis.*)
4. Horned Owl (*Bubo virginianus*) individual talon study. (From subspecies *pacificus.*)
5. Burrowing Owl (*Speotyto cunicularia*) in normal ground-perching posture. (From subspecies *floridana.*)
6. Elf Owl (*Micrathene whitneyi*) with foot one-quarter open for grasping prey. From subspecies *idonea.*)
7. Barn Owl (*Tyto alba*) with foot fully open for snatching prey. (From subspecies *pratincola.*)
8. Snowy Owl (*Nyctea scandiaca*) with foot fully open for coming to perch.

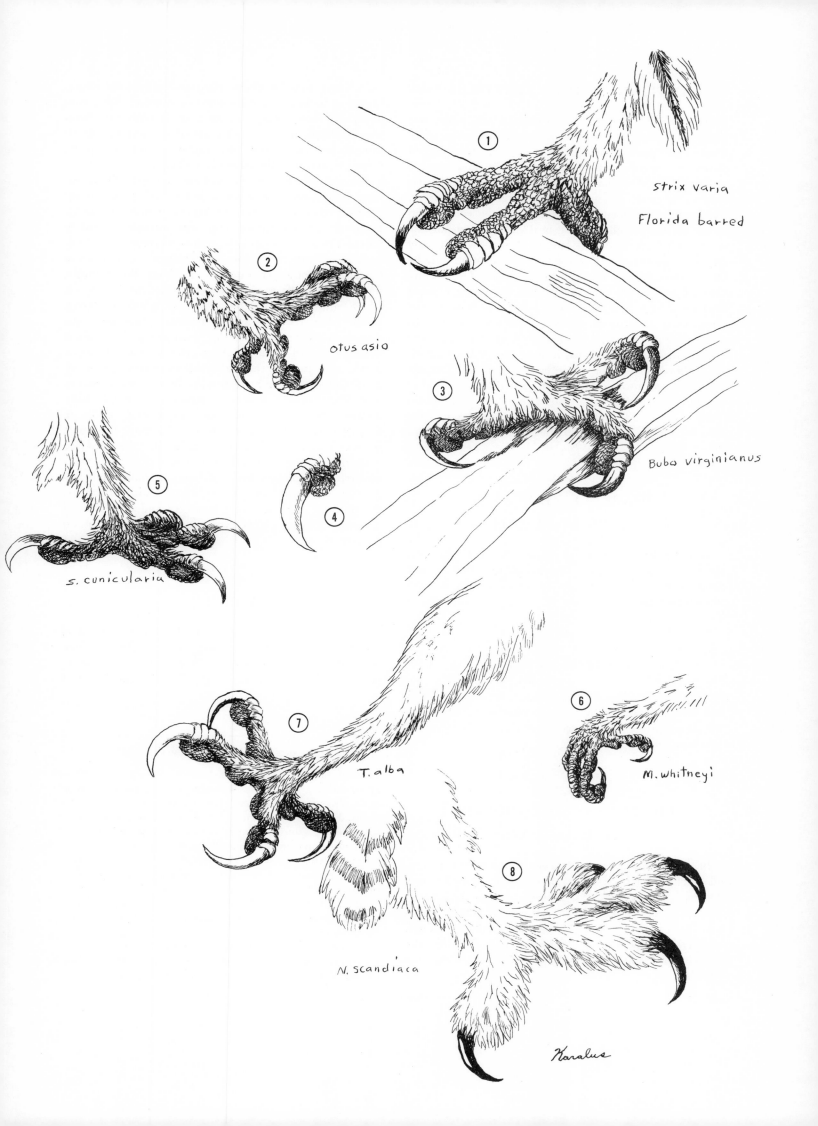

① strix varia
Florida barred

② otus asio

③ Bubo virginianus

④

⑤ s. cunicularia

⑥ M. whitneyi

⑦ T. alba

⑧

N. scandiaca

Karalus

DISTINGUISHING FEATURES

Here will be included the aspects which make this particular owl unique and recognizable in its own right. Under this heading as well, for each of the eighteen major descriptions, will be listed the owl's rank in over-all maximum size among the eighteen different species. When one speaks of one owl being larger than another, the statement is open to conjecture. Is the comparison based on the weight of the bird? Does it mean the wingspan? Is it the total length of the owl? If only one such measurement is used, the conclusion can be very misleading. For example, although the Great Gray Owl surpasses both the Snowy Owl and Great Horned Owl in total length, yet those latter two surpass the Great Gray Owl in wingspan and in body weight. In attempting to resolve this matter of relative size, the authors have discovered that a quite acceptable rank-in-size calibration can be achieved by a simple formula which takes into consideration all three factors of weight, total length, and wingspan. (See Comparison Table 1.) It is through use of this formula that the relative rank-in-size by species has been ascertained.

SHAPE AT REST AND
SHAPE IN FLIGHT

The characteristics which make the particular owl species recognizable as it is perched or while on the wing, whether in good light or in silhouette, are described under these headings.

FLIGHT PATTERN

This describes the characteristic movements of wings and body during flight—the undulation or levelness, the directness or indirectness that the owl in question normally exhibits while flying.

WEIGHT AND MEASUREMENT
CALIBRATIONS

Because of the greater accuracy of the metric system, all weights have been calibrated in grams, carried to one decimal place. As an aid, however, to the lay reader unaccustomed to metric calibrations, all gram weights have been parenthetically transposed to ounces through use of the standard basic formula of multiplying the number of grams by 0.035 to arrive at the weight in ounces.

In linear measurements, all have been initially calibrated in millimeters, carried to one decimal place. Also as an aid, these measurements in millimeters have been transposed to inches through use of the standard basic formula of multiplying the number of millimeters by 0.0394 to arrive at the length in inches.

Normally, to reverse the process and get millimeters from inches, one multiplies inches by 25.4; and to get grams from ounces, one multiplies ounces by 28.35. However, all calibrations here were initially carried to four decimal places, and the results therefore figure out accurately from millimeters to inches and from grams to ounces, but not as accurately so vice versa. For example, the Snowy Owl's average weight in grams is 1,659.8, which multiplied by 0.035 gives a figure of 58.093, which when reduced to one decimal place gives the weight in ounces as 58.1. Yet, multiplying 58.1 ounces by the standard figure of 28.35 gives a result of 1647.1 grams, thus making the end result in grams appear inconsistent. The same holds true for linear measurements. The Snowy Owl's average wingspan is 1,610.6 millimeters, which when multiplied by 0.0394 results in 63.45764 inches or, reduced to one decimal place, 63.5 inches. Yet, multiplying 63.5 inches by the standard conversion figure of 25.4 gives a result of 1,612.9 millimeters, which makes the end result in millimeters appear inconsistent. Such inconsistencies are, of course, the result of not carrying the ounces and inches to six or seven decimal places, which would serve no useful purpose here.

WEIGHT

All weights indicated are for birds that were alive (or freshly dead) when weighed. Such weights are given in grams and parenthetically in ounces. For each species is included the average weight for the species as a

---

HEAD AND SKULL STUDIES OF VARIED OWLS

1. Head (above) and skull (below) of Screech Owl (*Otus asio*), showing the greater symmetry of skull formation than in the other species pictured. (From subspecies *asio*.)
2. Head (above) and skull (below) of Horned Owl (*Bubo virginianus*), showing greater cranial development than in other species pictured. (From subspecies *virginianus*.)
3. Head (left) and skull (right) of Barn Owl (*Tyto alba*), showing elongation of both beak and skull in this species as compared to the typical owls also pictured. (From subspecies *pratincola*.)
4. Facial studies of the Great Horned Owl (*Bubo virginianus virginianus*).

Note the difference and asymmetry of the auricular (ear) cavities of the three species depicted. The ear cavities are located just above the jaw hinge on each.

① Otus asio

② Bubo virginianus

③ Tyto alba

④

Haralue

whole, plus the minimum, average, and maximum weights of both male and female birds. Included as well is this particular owl's rank in maximum weight among the eighteen species. (See Comparison Tables 3, 4, and 5 for relative maximum, average, and minimum weights of all eighteen species.)

LINEAR MEASUREMENTS

All measurements given under the headings of Total Length, Wingspan, Individual Wing Length, Tail Length, and Beak Length are given in millimeters, and parenthetically in inches, based on a stated number of birds measured for this purpose. Total Length is the length of the outstretched bird from tip of beak to end of tail. (See Comparison Tables 6 and 7.) Wingspan is the distance from the outermost outstretched limit of one wing in a straight line to the outermost outstretched limit of the other. (See Comparison Tables 8 and 9. Individual Wing Length is the straight-line measurement of the individual wing from the carpal joint (also called wrist or bend-of-wing) to the outermost tip of the longest primary feather. (See Comparison Tables 10 and 11.) Tail Length is the straight-line length of the longest extent of the tail, from the point where the longest rectrix enters the flesh to its outermost limit. (See Comparison Tables 12 and 13.) Beak Length is the length of the upper beak, measured with calipers in a straight line, from the tip to the cere, but not including the cere. (See Comparison Tables 14 and 15.)

LEGS, FEET, TALONS

This heading includes the specific characteristics involved, such as plumage, markings, color, strength, and other aspects. It should be noted here that among all owls there are four toes on each foot, two of which point permanently forward, one of which points permanently backward, and a fourth which is reversible and may point in either direction or sideways. The authors, in a close study of over 4,000 photographs of perched owls where the feet were visible, discovered that 95.90 per cent of the owls photographed were perched with two toes forward and two toes backward; 2.17 per cent were perched with two forward, one backward, and one sideways; and 1.93 per cent were perched with three toes forward and one backward.

EYES AND VISION

Color of the irides and visual ability of each species are noted, as well as any peculiarity, ocular or visual, of the species. The eyes of all owls are most unusual and their vision is remarkable, night or day. Although even the largest North American owls weigh only a fiftieth of an average-weight man, their eyes are as large as human eyes. The eyes of humans have smooth muscles, but the eye muscles of owls are striated fibers which provide for amazingly rapid changes in focus. Also, unlike humans with one plane of focus at a time, the owls have two fovea for simultaneous focus at objects near and far. Their eyeballs are set in a tube-shaped or conelike bony structure, and the lens and cornea portion of the eye is very large in comparison to the rest of the eye, thus allowing for incredible light-gathering and light-concentrating ability—about 100 times that of the human eye. As a further aid in detecting prey and, even more particularly, in avoiding obstacles during night flight through interlaced branches of trees, there is an odd, rather comblike organ in the back of the eye which acutely sharpens perception. In addition to both upper and lower eyelids, all owls have a nictitating membrane which usually is translucent. (In the Barred Owls [*Strix varia* sp.] this "third eyelid" is opaque.) This membrane helps protect the eyeball from damage during struggles with prey, and some claims are made that it also acts as a shield against damage from brush while the bird is flying through heavy cover, but evidence to support this claim is not substantive. There is an almost complete lack of ability to roll the eyeballs in their sockets; thus, to see in different directions or up and down, the owl must turn, raise, or lower its entire head. In doing so, it often gets into what humans consider as being amusing and seemingly impossible positions, further descriptions of which follow under specific owl headings.

EARS AND HEARING

The hearing of owls is very probably among the most acute in the animal world. It is said, quite likely with accuracy, that some species of owls can hear the footfalls

OWL PELLETS

Feeding habits of owls can be determined quite accurately by dissection and analysis of regurgitated pellets of undigestible material—fur, feathers, bones, teeth, claws, chitin, skulls, etc.—found usually at or near nesting sites or favored roosting sites of owls. Extensive studies have been conducted on tens of thousands of pellets collected, which were regurgitated by North American owls, especially Barn Owls, Screech Owls, and Great Horned Owls.

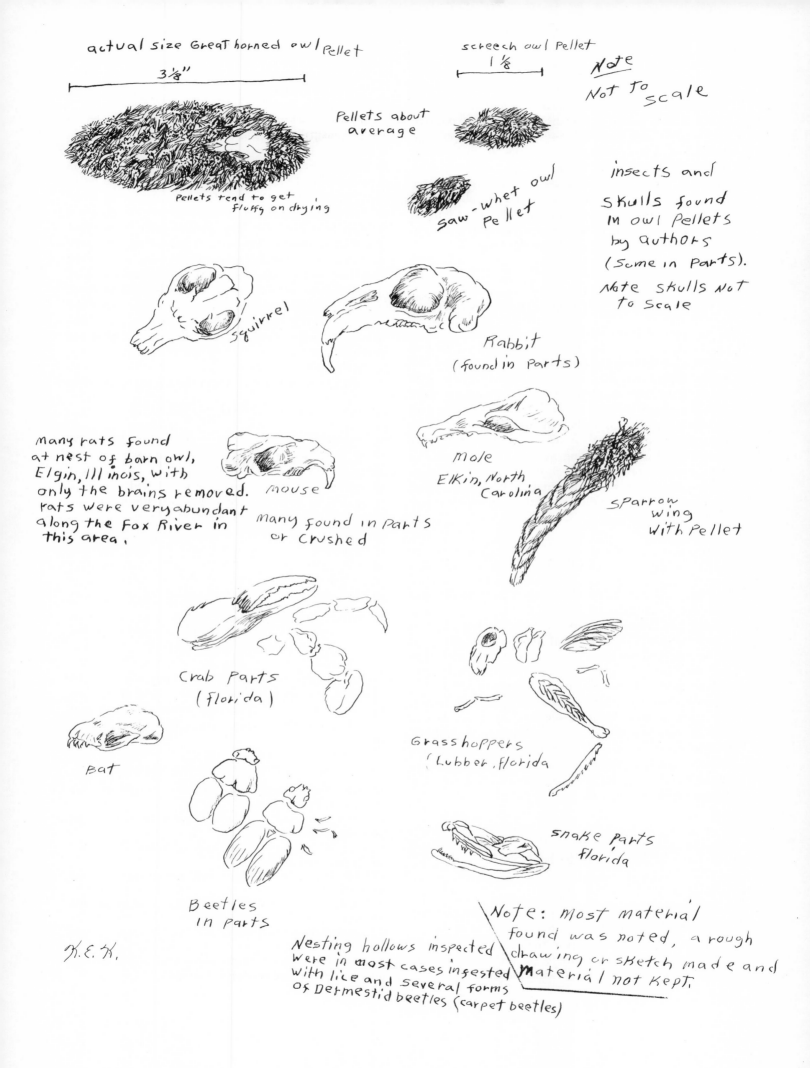

actual size Great horned owl Pellet

|——— 3⅛" ———|

screech owl Pellet
|— 1⅛ —|

Note
Not to scale

Pellets about average

Pellets tend to get fluffy on drying

saw-whet owl Pellet

insects and skulls found in owl Pellets by authors (some in Parts). Note skulls not to scale

squirrel

Rabbit (found in Parts)

many rats found at nest of barn owl, Elgin, Illinois, with only the brains removed. rats were very abundant along the Fox River in this area.

mouse

many found in Parts or crushed

Mole Elkin, North Carolina

Sparrow wing with Pellet

Crab Parts (Florida)

Bat

Grasshoppers (Lubber, Florida

Beetles in Parts

snake Parts Florida

K. E. K.

Nesting hollows inspected were in most cases infested with lice and several forms of Dermestid beetles (carpet beetles)

Note: Most material found was noted, a rough drawing or sketch made and material not kept.

of a beetle in the grass at a distance of well over 100 yards and the squeak of a mouse for half a mile. Not only can they hear well, but in many cases asymmetrically placed and sized ear cavities allow for pinpoint location of a most remarkable nature—to such extent that a sightless owl can fly directly to, and grasp with its talons, prey that it cannot see. For more on this, see the discussion under this heading for the Barn Owl (*Tyto alba pratincola*) and the Saw-whet Owl (*Aegolius acadicus acadicus*). Ear construction and the auditory sense of each species fall under this heading.

EAR TUFTS, PLUMAGE, ANNUAL MOLT

Not all owls have ear tufts, which are simply erectile head feathers and have nothing whatever to do with the sense of hearing. Whether or not they have these tufts is material included under this heading, along with specific information regarding plumages and the annual molt that is undergone by all species to a greater or lesser degree. An interesting general factor about the flight feathers of most owls is that they have a saw-toothed fluting on the leading edges of those feathers, permitting almost soundless to entirely soundless flight.

VOICE

Some owls tend to be rather silent most of the year and not even especially vocal during the breeding season, but there are others—such as the Barred Owls (*Strix varia* sp.)—whose vocal abilities are little short of incredible. They have a wide repertoire of calls they can utter and, in addition, many owls are extremely ventriloquistic. It is often most difficult to attempt to reproduce in writing the sound that a bird makes, especially an owl. What sounds a certain way to one listener may sound considerably different to another. Where a call lends itself to a form of transliteration, effort is made to reproduce the call in written form under this heading for the specific owl, along with the reason for the call if this is known.

SEXUAL DIFFERENCES: SIZE, COLOR, VOICE

Under this heading, whatever sexual differences are known in these aspects are listed. Almost as a general rule, the female owl is larger than the male and, in many cases, her voice tends to be higher. Sometimes there is a difference in coloration to some degree.

MORTALITY AND LONGEVITY

Although owl-banding programs have increased in recent years, there is still somewhat a dearth of information for many species in this respect. Mostly it has become necessary to rely on information supplied from zoos about their captive birds—cause of death, death rate, length of life, and related matters—and while this serves as something of an indicator, it does not necessarily reflect what may actually occur under normal wild conditions. Whatever is known regarding the mortality and longevity of the owls is included under this heading for each species. It is interesting to note that a captive owl in Europe was rather well reported to have lived for 68 years and that another unverified report noted that one had lived for over 100 years. The first is altogether possible; the second is doubtful but perhaps not impossible.

COLORATION AND MARKINGS: ADULT AND JUVENILE

Reasonably comprehensive written descriptions fall under this heading and help to augment what is visually apparent in the Color Plates of the fifty-nine owl subspecies. The reader should bear in mind that what is written or painted is closely representative of the coloration and marking of the species in question, but great degrees of variation in these physical characteristics can and do occur in virtually all species. Where juvenile colorations and markings are concerned, they are noted in order to establish the difference between an adult owl and an immature one of the same species.

GENERAL HABITS AND CHARACTERISTICS

Here the traits which make of the owl what it is are discussed, and each species has habits and characteristics which set it well apart from other species, as well as making it distinct from the other races within its own species.

PORTRAIT STUDIES OF VARIED JUVENILE OWLS

1. Great Horned Owl (*Bubo virginianus virginianus*) approximately five weeks old.
2. Northern Spotted Owl (*Strix occidentalis caurina*) approximately one month old.
3. Saw-whet Owl (*Aegolius acadicus acadicus*) approximately nine weeks old.
4. Long-eared Owl (*Asio otus wilsonianus*) approximately six weeks old.
5. Eastern Screech Owl (*Otus asio naevius*) three days after hatching.
6. Eastern Screech Owl (*Otus asio naevius*) approximately two weeks old.
7. Great Horned Owl (*Bubo virginianus virginianus*) approximately three and one-half to four weeks old.

Great horned ①

spotted owl ②

③

Young Long-eared owl ④

'screech Three days old ⑤

screech owl about second week ⑥

Young Saw-whet owl
dark parts uniform deep
slaty-brown or rich
burnt sienna.
specimen about
2½ weeks old
Elk Grove,
Illinois

Great horned owl
very young - fourth week ⑦

Juvenile studies

K.E.K.

HABITAT AND ROOSTING
ENEMIES AND DEFENSES
HUNTING METHODS
AND CARRYING OF PREY
FOOD, FEEDING HABITS, WASTES

These headings are reasonably self-explanatory, and for each of the eighteen species under discussion, specific information is provided regarding type of terrain favored, how and where roosting is done, the foes of the owl and its ability to protect itself, how it secures and carries its prey, what it eats, how it eats and how it disposes of its wastes. Most owls, for example, when prey is small enough, swallow it whole and later regurgitate compact pellets containing the bones, fur, feathers, teeth, and other indigestible materials. But some owls carefully dissect their prey, much as a hawk does when feeding. These and other matters related to the above headings are discussed in detail for each of the species.

COURTSHIP AND MATING
ANNUAL BROODS, NEST,
NESTING HABITS

Under these headings are included the courtship activities and mating habits of the species, along with specifics regarding their nests and nesting habits. Although owls are almost universally single-brooded, sometimes they do lay second or even third sets of eggs in a single year.

EGGS

Under this heading for each species is listed not only the number of eggs laid per nesting and the color, shape, texture, and size of the eggs, but the interval of time elapsing between the laying of one egg and the next, and the dates when egg-laying occurs in various geographic areas of the bird's distributional range. (See Comparison Table 2 for average egg size of all eighteen owl species in North America north of Mexico.)

INCUBATION AND BROODING
CHARACTERISTICS

It is interesting to note that most owl eggs in a nest do not hatch at the same time. In fact, it may be more than two weeks from the hatching of the first egg until the hatching of the last, depending upon when actual incubation was begun. These and other matters pertaining to the heading above are discussed for each species.

YOUNG AND FAMILY LIFE
CHARACTERISTICS

From hatching, through early development until the time they leave the nest, and even beyond, the young birds and their family life are discussed under this heading.

DISTRIBUTION IN NORTH AMERICA

The distribution of each subspecies is described in detail in the text, as explicitly as possible, and for each there is an accompanying North American distributional map. Where the maps are concerned, some owls have a more southerly winter range than their breeding range. Such winter ranges tend to fluctuate greatly as to distance and regularity of occurrence and these variations are discussed under the heading above as well as under the heading for Migration. Breeding range on the distributional maps is indicated by shading; the southerly range, if any, is indicated by more darkly shaded areas.

MIGRATION

Many owls do not migrate at all; others simply move from higher elevations in mountainous areas to lower elevations for the winter. Some, such as the Snowy Owl (*Nyctea scandiaca*), are quite erratic in their migrations, reaching cyclic peaks of movement about every four years, depending to some extent upon severity of the winter and availability of prey. Often there is scarcely any migrational movement at all. Characteristics in regard to migration are described here.

ECONOMIC INFLUENCE

North American owls are generally, with but very few exceptions, highly beneficial economically and ecologically. Why this is so is discussed under this heading.

Because owls are indeed primarily birds of the night, and therefore much more difficult to observe and study than the diurnal orders, a great deal still remains unknown about their natural history. Yet, they are no longer so distinctly the birds of mystery that they were through so many centuries. It is the hope of the authors that *The Owls of North America* will help to dispel the myths and superstitions that have accumulated about owls and that this presentation of art and text will bring a greater appreciation and understanding of just what an owl is, what it does, and its place in our world today.

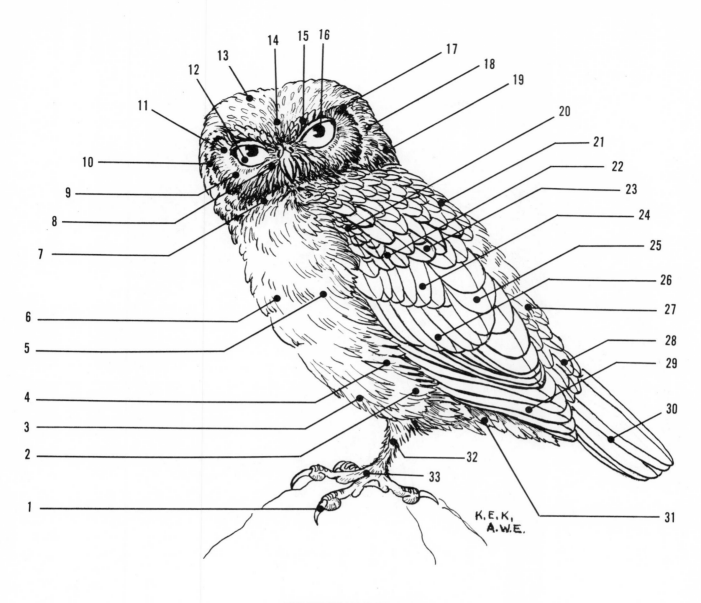

THE TOPOGRAPHY OF AN OWL

(Side View)

1. Talon
2. Thigh
3. Belly
4. Flank
5. Side
6. Breast
7. Malar Region
8. Lores
9. Facial Disk
10. Auriculars (Ear Coverts)
11. Outer Eye Corner

12. Iris
13. Crown
14. Forehead
15. Superciliary (Eyebrow)
16. Pupil
17. Facial Rim
18. Side of Head
19. Hindneck (or Nape)
20. Lesser Coverts
21. Back
22. Middle (or Median) Coverts

23. Scapulars
24. Greater Coverts
25. Tertials
26. Secondaries
27. Rump
28. Upper-tail Coverts
29. Primaries
30. Rectrices (Tail)
31. Undertail Coverts
32. Tarsus
33. Foot

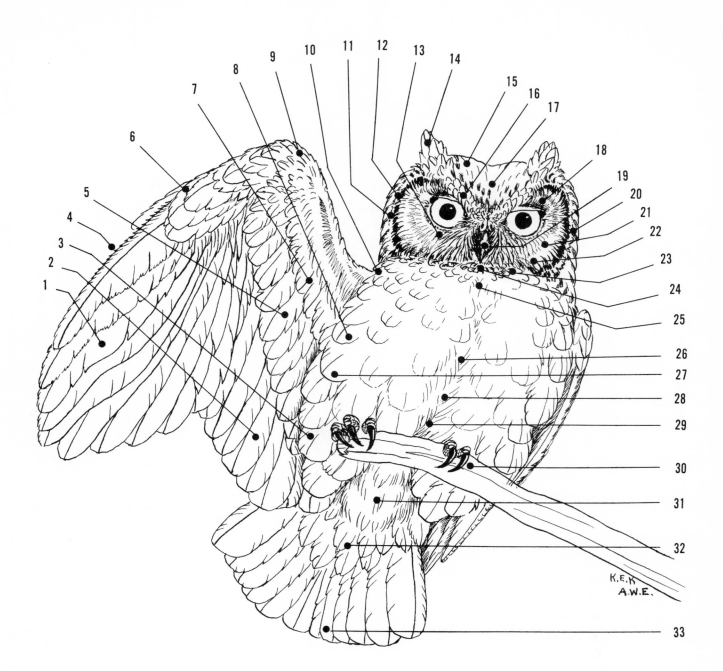

THE TOPOGRAPHY OF AN OWL

(*Underparts*)

1. Primaries
2. Secondaries
3. Flank Feathers
4. Fluting
5. Greater Coverts
6. Alula
7. Lesser Coverts
8. Axillaries
9. Carpal Joint (or Wrist)
10. Shoulder
11. **Ear**

12. Facial Rim
13. Suborbital Area
14. Ear Tuft
15. Crown
16. Superciliary (or Eyebrow)
17. Forehead
18. Supraorbital Area
19. Culmen (Beak)
20. Side of Head
21. Facial Disk
22. Malar Region (Lower Cheek)

23. Collar
24. Chin
25. Gular Area (or Throat)
26. Breast
27. Side
28. Median (or Center) Line
29. Belly
30. Talon
31. Vent (or Cloaca)
32. Undertail Coverts
33. Rectrices (or Tail Feathers)

THE TOPOGRAPHY OF AN OWL

(*Upperparts*)

1. Outer Toe
2. Talon
3. Primaries
4. Middle Toe
5. Tarsus
6. Greater Coverts
7. Flutings
8. Middle (or Median) Coverts
9. Alula
10. Throat
11. Malar Region (Lower Cheek)
12. Chin
13. Lower Beak (or Mandible)
14. Culmen (Upper Mandible)

15. Rictal Bristles
16. Cere (Nostrils)
17. Forehead
18. Superciliary (or Eyebrow)
19. Crown
20. Auriculars (or Ear Coverts)
21. Facial Rim
22. Ear Tuft
23. Occiput (or Back of Head)
24. Ear
25. Hindneck (Nape)
26. Side of Head
27. Carpal Joint (or Wrist)
28. Facial Disk

29. Shoulder
30. Neck
31. Lesser Coverts
32. Back
33. Scapulars
34. Lower Back
35. Secondaries
36. Rump
37. Heel
38. Upper-tail Coverts
39. Inner Toe
40. Rectrices (or Tail Feathers)
41. Hind Toe
42. Foot

SPECIES AND SUBSPECIES OF

THE OWLS

OF NORTH AMERICA

(NORTH OF MEXICO)

SPECIES

ORDER:	STRIGIFORMES
FAMILY:	TYTONIDAE
SUBFAMILY:	TYTONINAE
GENUS:	*Tyto* (Billberg)
SPECIES:	*alba* (Scopoli)

SUBSPECIES

---

pratincola (Bonaparte)   BARN OWL

BARN OWL

(COLOR PLATE I)

SCIENTIFIC NAME AND ORIGINAL DESCRIPTION

Tyto alba pratincola (Bonaparte). Original description: *Strix pratincola* Bonaparte, *Geographic and Comparison List,* 1838, page 7. New name for *Strix flammea* Wilson, *American Ornithology,* Volume VI, 1812, page 57, plate 50, figure 2, based on a specimen from Pennsylvania without specific locale designation. Former scientific names: *Strix flammea, Strix flammea americana, Strix flammea pratincola, Aluco pratincola, Strix pratincola.*

OTHER NAMES

AMERICAN BARN OWL   Frequently referred to by this name to separate it from other races elsewhere in the world.

CITRUS OWL   Primarily used in connection with the yellowish-orange color phase of the owl and not because it is especially fond of citrus groves, though it occasion-ally frequents such groves in the Far West and Deep South.

GHOST OWL   Because of the white, wraithlike appearance in flight, especially in the late twilight.

GOLDEN OWL   After the darker color phase.

LECHUZA MONO   Mexican-Indian name meaning "Monkey (Faced) Owl."

L'EFFRAIE   French-Canadian name meaning "The Frightener."

MONKEY-FACED OWL   For the distinctive, monkey-like configuration of the face, with the "monkey" aspect heightened by the smallish, dark, and somewhat beady-appearing eyes against the rather stark whiteness of the facial disks.

ORANGE OWL   For the yellowish-orange color phase of some.

QUEEN-OF-THE-NIGHT   Because of its grace in flight and its imperiality at roost.

SPIRIT OWL   Because it often inhabits deserted or abandoned buildings which the superstitious refer to as being "haunted" houses.

STONE OWL   For its habit in bygone years of nesting in cavities of the stone walls of barns, silos, and other farm outbuildings.

SWEETHEART OWL   Because of the heart-shaped configuration of its facial disks.

TAWNY OWL   For its general coloration.

WHITE OWL   For the distinctiveness of its light coloration in flight, especially at dusk. This local name, however, is also used for the Snowy Owl (*Nyctea scandiaca*) and, less often, for the Arctic Horned Owl (*Bubo virginianus subarcticus*).

DISTINGUISHING FEATURES

Medium-large in comparison with other North American owls, the Barn Owl has a large head without ear tufts and its facial configuration is distinctively long, somewhat triangular, and heart-shaped. Its legs are quite long and it often takes a rather knock-kneed stance when perched. Because of its expansive wingspan, it appears much larger in flight, especially at dusk or during the night, than when perched in the daytime. Its face is distinctly white and the generally tawny body coloration takes on a peculiar whitish appearance in dim light. This whiteness, especially of the underside, tends to frighten some people, who associate it with a ghost flying through the dusk or darkness. Because of the smooth density of the plumage, the bird has a more streamlined appearance than most other owls of this continent. The unusually long beak imparts an aquiline, somewhat long-nosed aspect, and its expression seems to the viewer to be a bit catlike and almost haughty.

Rank in over-all size among the eighteen species: Sixth.

SHAPE AT REST

Tends to stand well erect when perched, whether on the branch of a tree, a fence post, a barn rafter, or even on a flat surface. This erectness of posture tends to impart a generally slimmer contour for its size than is seen in other owls.

SHAPE IN FLIGHT

Most likely to be mistaken for the Short-eared Owl (*Asio flammeus flammeus*) in flight, especially since their ranges often overlap, but can be distinguished from that owl by not having quite so pronounced a short-necked, rather blunt appearance. In flight the wings appear rather long.

FLIGHT PATTERN

The Barn Owl flies with fairly rapid wingbeats (6.7 strokes per second on the average) in a strangely moth-like fluttering. Frequently the bird moves lightly from side to side during its flight rather than following a direct-line sort of flight pattern. This characteristic of reeling flight becomes even more noticeable at times when the bird is frightened from its perch during the daylight hours, when there is a very distinct aspect of bewilderment to the bird's flight. Despite the irregularity of its flying, it is quite swift on the wing when it wishes to be and flies lightly, gracefully, and noiselessly on long, broad wings. Often, for steering purposes, the wings will flap in an erratic manner, out of concert with one another.

Measurements have been based on 96 measured birds: 46 males and 50 females.

WEIGHT

Species average: 442.2 gr. (15.5 oz.).

	Male	Female
Average	383.9 gr. (13.4 oz.)	500.5 gr. (17.5 oz.)
Minimum	311.9 gr. (10.9 oz.)	383.0 gr. (13.4 oz.)
Maximum	507.5 gr. (17.8 oz.)	573.2 gr. (20.1 oz.)

Rank in weight among the eighteen species: Sixth.

TOTAL LENGTH

Species average: 441.8 mm. (17.4").

	Male	Female
Average	423.0 mm. (16.7")	460.5 mm. (18.1")
Minimum	360.7 mm. (14.2")	386.3 mm. (15.2")
Maximum	485.4 mm. (19.1")	534.7 mm. (21.1")

Rank in total length among the eighteen species: Sixth.

WINGSPAN

Species average: 1,084.4 mm. (42.7").

	Male	Female
Average	1,066.1 mm. (42.0")	1,102.6 mm. (43.4")
Minimum	1,029.0 mm. (40.5")	1,062.1 mm. (41.9")
Maximum	1,105.0 mm. (43.5")	1,143.0 mm. (45.0")

Rank in wingspan among the eighteen species: Fourth.

INDIVIDUAL WING LENGTH

Species average: 328.8 mm. (13.0").

	Male	Female
Average	324.9 mm. (12.8")	332.7 mm. (13.1")
Minimum	311.2 mm. (12.3")	317.0 mm. (12.5")
Maximum	341.9 mm. (13.5")	356.6 mm. (14.1")

Rank in wing length among the eighteen species: Fourth.

TAIL LENGTH

Species average: 156.6 mm. (6.2").

	Male	Female
Average	136.8 mm. (5.4")	176.4 mm. (7.0")
Minimum	124.8 mm. (4.9")	160.3 mm. (6.3")
Maximum	151.1 mm. (6.0")	192.6 mm. (7.6")

Rank in tail length among the eighteen species: Sixth.

BEAK LENGTH

Species average: 24.4 mm. (1.0").

	Male	Female
Average	23.4 mm. (0.9")	25.4 mm. (1.0")
Minimum	21.1 mm. (0.8")	22.9 mm. (0.9")
Maximum	25.4 mm. (1.0")	30.5 mm. (1.2")

Rank in beak length among the eighteen species: Third.

LEGS, FEET, TALONS

The unusually long tarsus of this owl, which averages 73.3 mm. (2.6") in the male and slightly longer in the female, is nearly twice as long as the middle toe, excluding the talon. The upper legs are coarsely but not densely feathered, and the lower legs are much more

---

LIFE STUDIES OF BARN OWL

A Barn Owl captured in a silo near Cedar Lake at Lake Villa, Illinois, showed little fear or hostility. Placed unharmed upon a fence, the bird sat quietly for a considerable while under the bright sunlight—allowing the artist time for a number of quick sketches—before casually taking wing and flying methodically off, close to the ground.

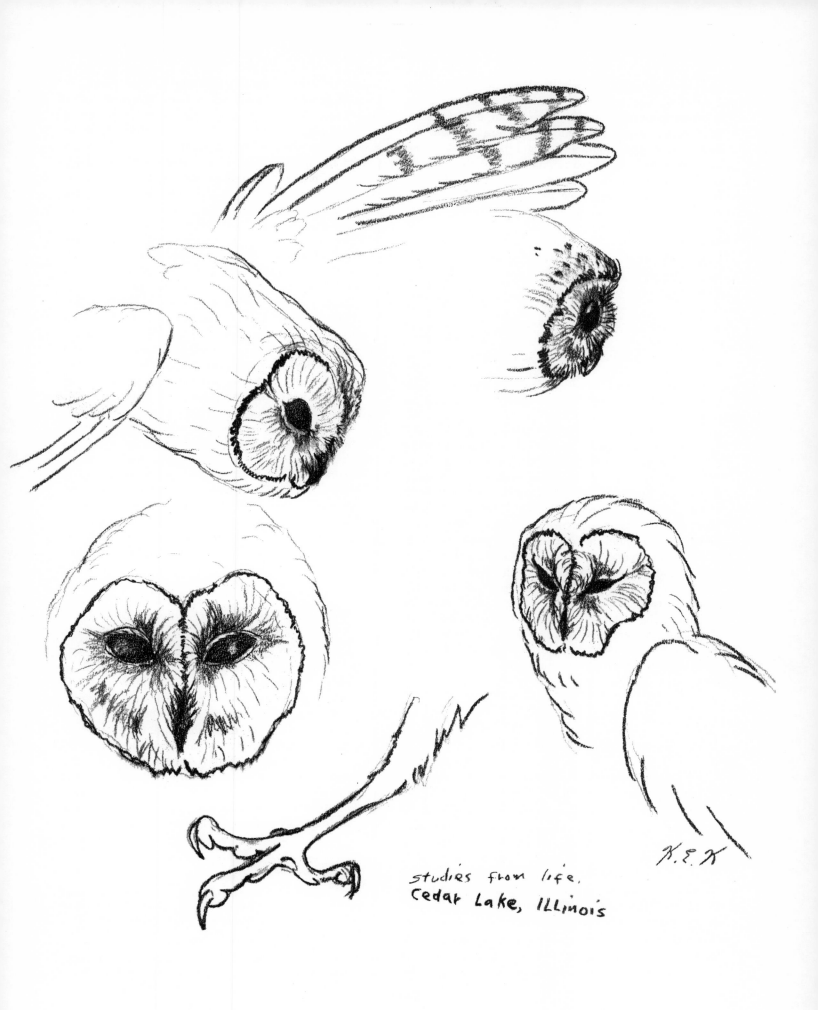

studies from life,
Cedar Lake, Illinois

K.E.K

scantily feathered and these feathers are shorter than those of the upper leg. The feathers of the tarsus along the backside point upward rather than downward as the frontside feathers do. All the toes are only sparsely covered with fine, almost indistinguishable bristles. The inner toe is as long as the middle toe and the talon of the middle toe has its inner edge pectinated with close, short, comblike teeth which evidently aid the bird in maintaining a grip on its prey. Legs and feet where scales are evident range from dusky yellowish green to dark gray and the talons are uniformly black. The Barn Owl has a very powerful grip and with simple muscle pressure alone can drive the talons their full length into their usual rodent prey.

EYES AND VISION

As with all North American species, the eye is protected against the struggles of its prey (as well as possibly against collision with brush and against extremely bright light) by a nictitating membrane. The eyes are unusually small for an owl of this size. Most often the eyes are described as being black, but this is an inaccuracy, albeit an understandable one. In actuality, the iris is a deep mahogany brown, with such depth of hue as often to appear as black as the pupil under poor lighting conditions. Although the Barn Owl's night vision is acute, the ears play a far more important role in hunting than do the eyes. (See Ears and Hearing.) Unlike the majority of North American owls, which can see quite well in the daytime, the Barn Owl shows a strong dislike for any bright light and has difficulty adjusting its vision to daytime conditions, even after long exposure to daylight. During nighttime hunting, the eyes are used more for locating and avoiding branches and other obstructions than for pinpointing the location of prey.

EARS AND HEARING

It is possible that the Barn Owl may have the most acutely developed sense of hearing of all our owl species. Unlike most North American owls, which tend to have asymmetrical ear cavities on opposing sides of the skull as an aid to accurate location of prey even on extremely dark nights, the Barn Owl's ear cavities are symmetrical. However, the lightly feathered flaps of skin in front of the widely separated ears are asymmetrically placed and muscularly controlled to such degree that they can work independently of each other, in concert or in opposition. Evidently this is a tremendous aid in pinpointing the location of prey through a process of triangulation. In a series of well-publicized experiments reported to the

American Ornithological Union Annual Convention, in 1957, Roger Payne and William Drury discovered that Barn Owls could locate prey very accurately by sound alone, wholly without use of the eyes. In a specially sealed room, from which all light was excluded, tests proved the Barn Owl could repeatedly and unerringly detect the presence of prey on the leaf-littered floor by hearing alone. As soon as the prey animal stopped moving, the Barn Owl would launch itself from its perch and soundlessly snatch the prey with incredible 100 per cent accuracy. The wide-set character of the ears and the asymmetrical placement and muscular ability of the ear flaps permit a differential reception of sound; thus, the noise made by the potential prey reaches one of the owl's ear chambers slightly before reaching the other. This permits not only accurate identification of the direction from whence the sound originates, but equally a remarkably flawless gauge of distance to the prey from where the owl is perched. The ears also showed a distinct adaptability to distortion as well. When one of the Barn Owl's ears was temporarily and harmlessly plugged with a piece of dampened tissue, the bird would miss its prey by ten or twelve inches on the first attack, but would always home in accurately on the second attempt. In hunting, the owl's ears and eyes work well in concert, but the primary function of the eyes is to avoid obstacles during the attack flight. Location of prey is chiefly by sound, and so keen is the owl's hearing that this species' auditory senses are said to be able to hear the patter of a running mouse's feet on a hard-packed earthen path at a distance of thirty yards or more.

EAR TUFTS, PLUMAGE, ANNUAL MOLT

The Barn Owl has no ear tufts. The bird's plumage is dense and tight to the body, but it is equally very soft, with the flight feathers having rather furry serrations called flutings on the leading edges which cushion the passing air in flight and diminish sound. Observers have had Barn Owls fly past their heads so closely that the slight breeze of their passage could be felt on the skin of cheek or neck, yet with no slightest whisper of sound to be heard. A complete molt of plumage occurs each year, usually in August, September, and October, although it has been recorded beginning as early as July

---

I BARN OWL

Tyto alba pratincola (Bonaparte). Male. White-breasted color phase, Peotone, Will County, Illinois, November 12, 1943. A.O.U. (American Ornithological Union) Number 365

II NORTHERN BARRED OWL

Strix varia varia Barton. Male. Poplar Creek near Elgin, Cook County, Illinois, April 1, 1968. A.O.U. Number 368

Barn Owl

Karl E. Karalus

and ending as late as November. Since only a few feathers are lost at a time, hunting ability of the bird is not noticeably affected.

VOICE

The Barn Owl makes a variety of sounds, including hissings, groaning noises, raspy screeches, beak snappings, and rather unearthly tonal fluctuations. When hatched, and before their eyes have opened, the baby owls are limited to a feeble and high-pitched, wavering, whining cry, which continues nearly all the while the hatchlings are awake. This is evidently a persistent appeal for food. The call deepens and becomes louder with each passing day. By the time they are a couple of weeks old, they've learned to hiss angrily when disturbed and also tend to make a throaty, raspy, hissing scream if allowed to become too hungry. This angry, rather wet sound has been termed the "snoring" call and is reminiscent of the sound which might be made if the hungry young bird continually kept sucking saliva from mouth into throat, although the bird's mouth is wide open as the cry is uttered. It is a call which can be simulated by clenching the teeth and inhaling sharply through one corner of the mouth. This call is not too unlike the cry of the adult bird, but usually higher in pitch and of shorter duration. Like all cries of the Barn Owl, it is devoid of musical quality. If ignored by the parent birds, the call tends to become louder and more dramatically insistent. The young birds continue to make this same call for some time after leaving the nest, usually uttering it while on the wing.

The adult Barn Owl seems to be limited to five vocal sounds, plus the beak snapping, which is common among most owls and usually made when angry. It can be heard for a considerable distance and is rather menacing in character. The five basic adult calls, however, are as follows:

1. A contact call, normally given in flight, which permits traveling birds to keep within audible range of one another. It is, considering the nature of the alarm cry, a much softer sound, though not much more melodious. It has been likened vaguely to the call of the nighthawk, but probably more because of the regular intervals at which it is repeated than because of tonal quality. It is best described as a prolonged clicking sound, as in the letters *cliaaackkk!*, repeated at about ten-second intervals at first, but becoming more closely spaced toward the end and with lessening volume. There may be as many as twenty of these sounds issued in succession or as few as eight.

2. An alarm cry which is a fearsome, shattering, discordant shriek or scream which, coming unexpectedly in the darkness, can easily cause even the most stalwart human a strong momentary apprehension. There is no adequate combination of letters in the alphabet through which to attempt duplication of this harsh and wholly unmelodious cry.

3. A heavy growling sound, not unlike a large dog which can't seem to make up its mind whether to whine or snarl and so combines both. This is a particularly frightening cry in the darkness, especially if the Barn Owl uttering the sound is flying toward the listener. The growl is prolonged for six or seven seconds and usually repeated from three to five times at intervals of several seconds between. It has not been definitely established what this sound means, but it may be a sort of recognition signal given by the male bird only to alert his mate of his approach to the nest. The nearest form in which it can be imitated in print is *ssschnnaair-rkk!*

4. A mating call, evidently given only by the male bird and uttered during the courtship flight. As the male hovers in one spot not far above where the female is perched, he raises his head until the beak is skyward, and makes this excited chanting cry in a distinctly breathless manner. It is the softest and least displeasing of all the Barn Owl utterances and most nearly sounds like a faintly raspy, monotonous *whee-tuh . . . whee-tuh . . . whee-tuh . . . whee-tuh* which may continue for many minutes and with intervals of no more than two seconds between each cry.

5. Finally, there is a peculiar rattling call for which no explanation is known. This call, given in flight, has a sound not unlike a pea-sized pebble vigorously shaken from end to end in a short plastic cylinder. Some listeners have suggested that this is merely a different caliber of beak snapping, but because of the rapidity with which it is issued and the fact that it has never been heard coming from a perched bird snapping its beak, it is more likely that the call is vocal. The sound cannot well be reproduced in print.

III FLORIDA BARRED OWL

Strix varia georgica Latham. Female. Three miles southeast of Englewood, Charlotte County, Florida, June 20, 1969. A.O.U. Number 368-A

IV TEXAS BARRED OWL

Strix varia helveola (Bangs). Female. Vicinity of Corpus Christi, Nueces County, Texas, January 20, 1910. A.O.U. Number 368-B

SEXUAL DIFFERENCES

As in most birds of prey, the female Barn Owl is larger than the male, although not so markedly larger as in many species of North American owls. There are two distinct color phases and some degree of gradation between these phases (see Coloration and Markings:

Adult), but studies have indicated there is no correlation of color phase to sex. Vocally, the male bird is reported to issue a deeper cry than the female and not so harshly grating. His repertoire of calls also seems to be greater than the female's.

MORTALITY AND LONGEVITY

The Barn Owl has been studied in this respect more closely than any other owl species, but more conclusive results even for this species are needed. As nearly as can be determined from bird-banding data, out of every 100 birds hatched, 60 will die before reaching the age of one year. Available evidence seems to indicate that a sizable percentage of this mortality occurs from consumption of mice and rats which have themselves eaten rodent poisons shortly before being taken as prey. Of the remaining 40 birds of each 100, 14 more will die some time during their second year. Nine others will live to between three and four years of age, six more will die during their fifth year, and four each will die during the sixth and seventh years. Two birds may live to see their tenth year and only one of these 100 will live beyond that time. As far as longevity is concerned, the oldest banded wild bird recovered was just past its eleventh year and still in good condition when struck by a car and killed. However, there have been numerous cases of captive birds living well over fifteen years, and even one unconfirmed report of a captive Barn Owl which finally died of old age during its fifty-first year. Average lifespan in the wild seems to be between five and eleven years.

COLORATION AND MARKINGS:
ADULT

The Barn Owl is to some degree dichromatic within its race, though not so markedly so as in some species, as for example the Eastern Screech Owl (*Otus asio naevius*) in which the dichromatism is quite manifest in sharply defined red-phase and gray-phase birds. The Barn Owl color-phase difference is limited to a light tawny whitish coloration generally, which is referred to as the white-breasted phase (see Color Plate I), and a darker and somewhat more yellow-orange-brownish shade termed the orange-breasted phase. In the former color phase the upperparts are a distinctly yellowish orange which is mottled and dappled with generally small scattered spots of dark grayish brown, and more delicately dusted with very light spots ranging from a faint tawny to white. This spotting and a hint of white and blackish mottling is continuous across the entire

dorsal surface and onto the inner scapulars. The wings are usually well mottled with grayish black or, less frequently, distinctly barred. Breast, belly, and other underparts are essentially very light tawny to pure white and spotted or distinctly marked with small V-shapes of dark brown or orange brown. These V-shapes may be well scattered in some individuals and quite heavily peppered across the underside of others. The tail is sometimes dorsally white, but far more often a medium-orange, well mottled and crossed by about five distinct bars of dark grayish brown, terminating in white at the tips of the rectrices. The heart-shaped facial disk is pure white except for medium to heavy brownish encircling the upper half of the eye and much darker near the front of the eye than toward the rear. The facial disk is encircled by a narrow ruff of vaguely darker brown to sometimes almost wine-red feathering, with scattered blackish in the ruff across the throat. The primary wing coverts are a decided darker orange brown, tending to become mottled toward the tips, and usually a small spot of white on the top near the outer end of the feathers.

In the orange-breasted phase the plumage is considerably darker orange above and a somewhat deep, though not dark, yellowish orange beneath, and similarly V-marked or sometimes spotted with brown. The tail is a darker sienna tawny with bars of mottled dark brown. The facial disk is a medium-sienna tint rather than white.

Plumage coloration variations seem to have nothing whatever to do with sex, geographic locale, or age of the bird. The beak on both color phases is a pale yellow tan, but the scaled portion of legs and feet is somewhat darker in the orange-breasted than in the white-breasted phase.

COLORATION AND MARKINGS:
JUVENILE

Juvenile birds in their first-winter plumage are quite similar in coloration and markings to the adult birds, with but a few minor exceptions. The gray spottings on the back and other dorsal portions are less extensive and more interspersed with tints of tan. The crown and hindneck vary from a sandy-cinnamon to a sandy-cream color instead of being uniform with the back coloration and markings as in adults, and both crown

---

Field sketches of the Barn Owl (*Tyto alba pratincola*) standing and listening for prey in northern Illinois barn. Stance is reasonably erect until sound of prey is detected, whereupon head is lowered, location of prey accurately triangulated by the bird, followed by instant attack.

K.E.K.

and hindneck are sparingly spotted with salt-and-pepper spots of gray and black.

GENERAL HABITS AND CHARACTERISTICS

The Barn Owl is one of our most strictly nocturnal owls, disliking leaving its roost even on the cloudiest of days, when many other owls are abroad. An exception is during the nesting season when procurement of food for the young birds is a constantly increasing burden. At such times the Barn Owl will hunt late in the day when it is overcast. Normally it prefers to remain very inactive during daylight hours and is not easily aroused from its sleep.

At Lake Villa, Illinois, a pair of Barn Owls roosting in a silo permitted the author to scale the iron rungs to their perch, watching him sleepily as he ascended. Even when he stopped three feet from them, they were not unduly alarmed. One was a partial albino and permitted the author to reach out and touch it before taking wing rather sullenly through an opening in the silo roof. The second, a normal white-breasted-phase bird, allowed itself to be picked up across the back, wings closed, and made no sign of alarm other than a muted beak snapping until nearly to the bottom of the rungs, where it began struggling. The bird was checked thoroughly, found to be in good health and had no band on its leg. It was placed upon a fence post in the open barn lot and for fully five minutes it sat there squinting against the brightness of the day before finally fluffing its feathers and then taking wing. It flew rather lazily off low across a meadow and disappeared into a dense growth of tamarack. This exemplifies another facet of the bird's character—that it is normally a calm-natured owl, not easily excitable and slow to become angry. This is true even if its eggs are handled.

Not until about sunset does the Barn Owl leave its roost and begin its evening hunt. Though it may occasionally perch and sleep for a short interval or two during the night, it is normally active the night through, returning to its favorite roost about half an hour before sunrise.

Quite a heavy eater, it is not at all fastidious in its habits and the nest area or roost is usually rather messily cluttered with regurgitated pellets, bones, fur, feathers, and excrement. It is especially fond of roosting and nesting in old buildings, silos, different kinds of farm buildings, steeples, windmills, churches, beneath bridges, and other such normally undisturbed places.

Although it is relatively close in size to the Short-eared Owl (*Asio flammeus flammeus*) and is a hunter of the same terrain, distinguishing between the two is usually easy enough. The stubby-necked, bullet-headed aspect of the Short-eared Owl immediately identifies it. Further, the Short-eared Owl regularly hunts its territory in the daytime and is more apt to be seen, since the Barn Owl rarely ventures out before dusk and is normally already at roost before sunrise.

HABITAT AND ROOSTING

Tyto alba pratincola is distinctly a bird of open country rather than a woodland owl and much less inclined to avoid the proximity of man than other owls. Probably no other North American owl spends its lifetime so close to man and yet is observed less. Often pairs will take up residence in the very midst of a bustling town or city and yet remain undetected, primarily because they are so thoroughly nocturnal in their hunting habits and so exclusively retiring during the daylight hours. Their comings and goings are seldom observed by man, even in heavily settled communities. They have adapted extremely well to a close existence with man, taking advantage of the fact that the rodents upon which they feed, very nearly to the exclusion of all else, are more abundant near man than anywhere else.

Most highly favored roosts are usually high on the darkest ledges and crannies of old buildings of all sorts —residences, barns, churches, water towers, silos, belfries, attics, vine-covered porches, on wall projections inside open wells, tank houses, steeples, farm outbuildings of all kinds, windmills, institutional buildings, factories, granaries, and similar places in the midst of the community of man and yet where people themselves rarely come. Often large hollows in trees beside residences or in city parks will be used as roosts. On occasion it will dig a tunnel as a nesting site or roost, going inward horizontally for three or four feet in easily excavated stream banks. In areas where there are cliffs, such as along Pacific coastal areas, roosts are often in cliff crannies. Clefts in quarry walls are also favored, as are old mine shafts. In areas like southern California, roosting is frequently in areas of live oak trees and in the smaller canyons, barrancas, and the fringes of the lower slopes of foothills. In such areas they will very often roost beneath railroad or highway bridges and in culverts.

The presence of Barn Owls is more often detectable from the "whitewash" staining of their excrement at the roost than from actual sightings of the birds. When the daylight hours have passed and they begin their nightly foraging, they still remain close to human habitation, flying low through large-treed parks, over open fields, deserted lots, prairies, orchards, truck-farm plots, near corncribs and other grain storage areas, down alleys,

---

Miscellaneous field studies of the Barn Owl (*Tyto alba pratincola*) in northern Illinois.

Legs very
Long and
bare

Elgin Illinois
1959

bird looks almost
white in flight
From below

Fishers farm
Wood dale Illinois
DuPage Co.

K.E.K.

and especially along railroad tracks and other places where mice abound.

Very often in autumn and winter the Barn Owl becomes gregarious in its roosting and upward of ten or twelve birds may be found roosting together in the same tree or within the same ramshackle building. There have been cases reported occasionally where even as many as fifty Barn Owls had assembled and roosted together in the same small grove of trees, taking shelter in the thick foliage of living trees or neatly hiding themselves among dead leaves of more scattered open-land trees. In such community roosts, the owls have a habit of leaving the roost singly, beginning at sunset or shortly thereafter, with an interval of from less than a minute to several minutes or more between departures. The owl leaving the roost will frequently circle at first, making several passes around the tree it has just vacated, calling in its raspy voice to those remaining behind before setting off alone on its way.

Because of its proclivity for roosting and nesting in old abandoned houses, the Barn Owl is often responsible for the reputation such a house will get for supposedly being "haunted." The bird's weird and rather frightening calls, along with its ghostlike flight and whitish appearance in the dusk, inspire the "ghost" stories as it flies through darkened rooms of the old buildings and out of broken windows, fallen-door openings, and other such places of entry or exit.

ENEMIES AND DEFENSES

As with practically all owl species, the Barn Owl's greatest enemy is man. More are destroyed, undoubtedly, by man than by any other enemy, either directly or indirectly. Fortunately, destruction is not as great in recent years as it was in the past. Farmers, for example, who often shot the birds wherever they saw them, have learned that the Barn Owl is probably the most beneficial bird to have around and they now welcome its presence and actively protect it. Good conservation education has also aided in stopping the pointless destruction of the birds. Nevertheless, a great many are still shot or clubbed to death when they are encountered, simply because they are a large and rather fearsome-appearing bird. Many are still killed through indiscriminate use of rodent poisons spread by man.

Where natural enemies are concerned, there is only one of any consequence, and this is the Great Horned Owl (*Bubo virginianus virginianus*) or others of the *Bubo virginianus* subspecies. The larger and more ferocious owl will attack, kill, and devour a Barn Owl without hesitation. Strangely, if there is no building or natural hollow nearby into which the Barn Owl can quickly fly and hide itself at the appearance of the Great Horned Owl, it will often seem to give up and allow the

Great Horned Owl to pounce and kill it without any real effort to defend itself.

The Barn Owl that begins flying too early in the day runs the risk of encountering another natural enemy of some consequence—the Prairie Falcon. This bird will harass the Barn Owl at every opportunity and with a deadly savagery if given half a chance. From above, the falcon will "stoop" into its dive at the flying owl and crush its skull with the rock-hard blow of its fisted foot. Sometimes the owl is merely bowled over with the first blow, but it makes no effort at defense other than to seek the nearest cover to get away from the feathered enemy.

Though not really an enemy, the Burrowing Owl (*Speotyto cunicularia* sp.) will occasionally fight with a Barn Owl. This normally occurs as a territorial dispute and, though the Barn Owl is considerably the larger, usually it is the Burrowing Owl which succeeds in driving off the Barn Owl.

Many of the North American owl species are victims of harassment by small birds wherever encountered, but such is not the case with the Barn Owl. Songbirds such as wrens, warblers, catbirds, kingbirds, robins, and mockingbirds, along with crows, jays, and magpies, often take great delight in mobbing an owl they discover at roost, but they do not seem to recognize the Barn Owl as an enemy and generally pay no attention to it.

Though its principal defense is to seek sanctuary in some old building or natural hollow, this is not to say the Barn Owl has no fighting ability. To the contrary, it can put up a respectable fight on occasion and, in the manner of most owls, use its powerful feet well in defense. When threatened, the Barn Owl tends to crouch or lie flat on the ground with wings outspread, facing the enemy, glaring and hissing malevolently, while at the same time snapping the beak sharply as a warning. The head is often swung back and forth at this time, as if the owl is looking for an opening for attack. If the intruder continues to press in, the Barn Owl will launch itself feet first at the enemy and strike accurately with its talons toward the enemy's head, especially the eyes.

Even when still quite young, the Barn Owl can put up a good defense. Fledglings in the nest will snap their beaks and sway their heads much in the manner of adults. If the enemy comes too close, they will throw themselves upon their backs and strike out with the powerful talons. Even if the enemy does not attack but

---

RODENT FOOD OF THE BARN OWL

Although on occasion the Barn Owl will eat sparrows, or other small birds and, more often, frogs and snakes, its most important prey by far consists of small rodents, some of which are shown here. Normally, this owl confines itself to rodents up to a large rat in size, although cottontail rabbits and snowshoe hares are occasionally taken.

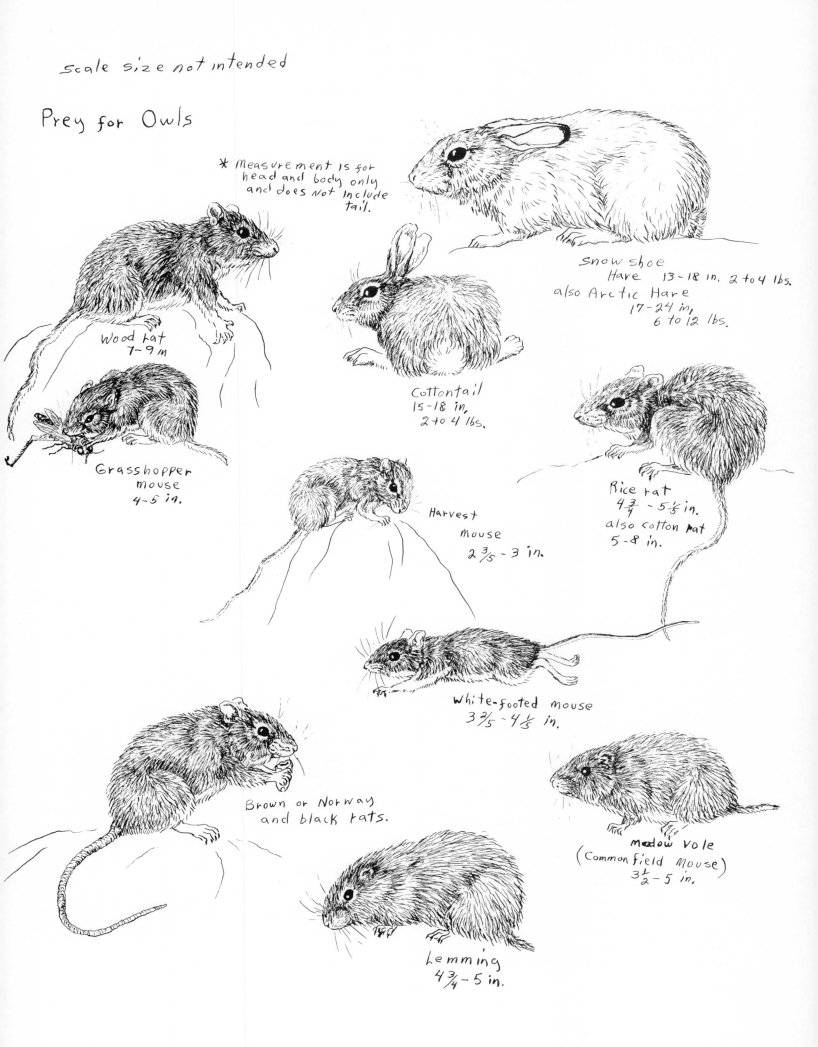

scale size not intended

Prey for Owls

* measurement is for head and body only and does not include tail.

Wood rat 7-9 in

Grasshopper mouse 4-5 in.

Snowshoe Hare 13-18 in, 2 to 4 lbs.
also Arctic Hare 17-24 in, 6 to 12 lbs.

Cottontail 15-18 in, 2 to 4 lbs.

Harvest mouse 2 3/5 - 3 in.

Rice rat 4 3/4 - 5 1/5 in. also cotton rat 5-8 in.

white-footed mouse 3 2/5 - 4 1/5 in.

Brown or Norway and black rats.

meadow Vole (Common field mouse) 3 1/2 - 5 in.

Lemming 4 3/4 - 5 in.

remains close, the young owls will often assume the offensive. With head upraised and beak snapping violently, while at the same time issuing the angry hissing croak, they will open their wings and run fiercely at the intruder.

The feet of the Barn Owl, even when it is quite young, are tremendously powerful and certainly weapons deserving of respect. They strike out with considerable accuracy and, upon encountering flesh, instantly curve inward with amazing pressure which drives the talons deeply inward. The author, carrying a Barn Owl he had captured for study, carelessly brought it too close to his own body and instantly one foot shot out and the talons gripped his thigh, puncturing the flesh deeply and painfully. There was no desire to harm the bird and so it was only with the greatest of difficulty and with the help of a friend that the talons were extricated from the flesh.

HUNTING METHODS AND CARRYING OF PREY

A prodigious eater and dedicated provider of food for its young, the Barn Owl hunts almost incessantly during its waking hours. A seemingly tireless hunter, it probably spends more time on the wing than any other owl. Although it will occasionally perch on rafters, eaves, or tree limbs and await the appearance of prey, more often it prefers to range silently back and forth, less than ten feet off the ground, over meadows, stubble fields, marshes, open woodlands, and orchards. During such times its eyes are used primarily for avoiding obstructions and its incredibly sensitive hearing is attuned to locating prey. This hunting-by-sound is aided by the utterly silent flight of the bird. When the prey—usually a mouse or rat—is heard moving, the Barn Owl swiftly angles toward it. When a few feet away, the bird will often snap its beak once, or issue a brief growling hiss. This evidently has the faculty of making the prey, unaware of danger until then, freeze in its tracks in an instinctive protective reaction. Without hesitation the owl arrows to the exact spot where the sound of movement ceased and strikes with wide-open talons on both feet. The instant that flesh is encountered, the foot making contact closes and the talons drive deeply into the prey, killing it at once. As is common among all owls, in that instant of contact the owl closes its eyes tightly until it has established a balance against the struggles of its prey, then opens the lids but still keeps the nictitating membranes closed until the struggles have terminated.

Rarely will the Barn Owl pounce on moving prey. If the mouse or rat does not instantly stop running at the sound of the hiss or beak snapping, the owl will pass low to the ground in front of the intended prey, then wheel back with remarkable agility as the rodent pauses and before it can collect its wits and begin running again. Even if it does manage to run before the owl can come back, it is almost certainly doomed. The owl continues to make close passes until the confused animal does stop, and then snatches it. But only rarely, if ever, will the prey be snatched while in the act of running.

So expert a hunter is the Barn Owl that a single owl will catch as much rodent prey in one night as a dozen or more well-experienced barnyard cats. More often than not the prey is carried off from where it is killed. During the nesting season the adult carries it directly back to the nest for its young, but at other times it flies to a convenient perch ten feet or more above the ground before feeding. Almost all prey carried away by the Barn Owl is carried in the beak. Only with the largest of rats or bigger prey are the talons used for carrying.

FOOD, FEEDING HABITS, WASTES

Although primarily a rodent eater—and mainly mice and rats among the rodents—the Barn Owl will also catch, kill, and eat a wide variety of other creatures. Large insects, for example, such as katydids, crickets, large moths, and grasshoppers, are often eaten. Equally, a certain number of frogs, snakes, lizards, and crayfish are consumed. Small birds are taken only rarely. The Barn Owl, in fact, is the least destructive of bird life of any North American owl that is not strictly insectivorous. More often than not when a bird is taken, it is a sparrow or starling. Birds make up less than 5 per cent of the annual diet of the Barn Owl. Although sparrows and starlings do make up the majority of the birds that are in fact taken, other species have been recorded through dissection and analysis of Barn Owl pellets. These include grackles, cowbirds, wrens, swallows, warblers, towhees, bobolinks, meadowlarks, and sometimes even birds as large as blue jays, sora rails, green herons, clapper rails, flickers, pigeons, and occasionally even a small duck. Seldom, if ever, does the Barn Owl attack domestic poultry. Now and then, though never on a regular basis, the Barn Owl will catch and eat fish. Usually this occurs when a fish has become trapped in a drying pool area of a stream, pond, or marsh, and therefore becomes easy prey. Among mammals, although various species of mice and rats are the principal prey, the Barn Owl has also been known to take gophers and ground squirrels of many kinds, shrews, moles, bats, young rabbits, and even mammals as large as full-grown jackrabbits, cottontails, muskrats, and spotted skunks.

In the pattern of most owls, the Barn Owl is definitely not a fastidious eater. All smaller prey—insects, mice, small birds, small mammals, reptiles, and amphibians—

are swallowed whole, usually in two or three convulsive gulps followed by a gaping of the mouth once or twice as if to clear it of any residue of the prey. The Barn Owl can very easily swallow whole prey up to the dimensions of a medium-sized house rat. Prey bigger than that is vigorously torn into swallowable chunks with the beak and devoured.

The Barn Owl, of course, as other owls do, regurgitates compact waste pellets containing the fur, bones, feathers, and other undigestible material of their prey. For the Barn Owl, each pellet averages about one inch to an inch and a half in length and about a half-inch to three-quarters of an inch in width. The shape of the pellet is roughly cylindrical with the ends rounded or, less often, tapered. Undigested material from three to six small mammals is usually contained within each pellet, and from two to three pellets are cast by the individual owl during each 24-hour period. Digestion in the Barn Owl is very rapid and the individual owl will almost always eat at least half its own weight in prey nightly and often much more. Young in the nest are even more voracious and require their own weight or more in food every day.

Pellets are regurgitated while the owl is perched and, more often than not, this occurs at the nest site or the most frequently used roost. As a result, roosts and nests are usually rather disreputable in appearance with the debris of new, old, and decomposed pellets virtually carpeting the area. Sometimes the owl retains its roost so long that the whole floor area becomes covered with a deep, ruglike covering of prey fuzz from the mouse hairs in the decomposed pellets. On the ground beneath the nest area, pellets ejected by the young owls may build up to a height of two or three feet before the birds leave. Even beneath a normal adult bird roost there may accumulate as much as two or three bushels of pellet material, with those on top very fresh and lower levels gradually settling and disintegrating.

In addition to pellet wastes, the normal excrement of the Barn Owl is frequently expelled and does much to heighten the sorry appearance of the nesting or roosting area. The excrement is normally a viscous mass mainly white in color from unassimilated bone matter of the prey. Drying of the excrement causes the whiteness to intensify and after a prolonged period, the roosting or nesting area tends to look as if it had been poorly whitewashed.

COURTSHIP AND MATING

Because of the nocturnal habits of so many owls, the courtship and mating habits are not easily observable, as they are in other avian species. Consequently, details of these activities are relatively sketchy. Among some North American owl species, virtually nothing is known about the courtship and mating activities; in others, enough bits and pieces of such activities have been witnessed over a period of years by trained observers to enable some fairly solid conclusions to be reached. In the case of *Tyto alba pratincola,* some gaps in our knowledge are gradually being filled. It is suspected, for example, though not yet proven, that the Barn Owl mates for life, since the same pairs have been observed together over a period of years.

Where courtship is concerned, it is known that the female is usually perched and is approached by the male on the wing. He makes a peculiar rattling cry as he nears her. Unlike some owl species, where the female feigns lack of interest in anything the courting male does, the perched female Barn Owl watches intently all actions of her suitor. If she does not wish to be courted by the approaching male, she will almost immediately fly off swiftly. If she remains in place, the male will circle her roost several times and then hover in place in front of and above her by about 10 or 15 feet. Though a soundless flier, at this time the male deliberately makes a muted fluttering sound with his wings. At least once and perhaps several times during this fluttering action, the male will rise 50 feet or more and then fall, while at the same time clapping the wing tips together beneath him with a crisp slapping sound, catching himself and resuming his fluttering as his fall takes him to within a dozen feet or so of where the object of his attentions is perched. At intervals between the falling and clapping, but while he is still hovering, the male will issue the unmusical courtship cry of a repeated *whee-tuh* sound. (See Voice.)

At length, evidently satisfied that the female has approved of his antics, the male will soar quickly away. Usually he returns in less than 10 minutes with a mouse or some other form of prey gripped in his beak. Again he issues the rattling cry as he nears her, but this time he flies directly to the perch and settles beside her. With surprising delicacy, the female accepts the prey from him and, after holding it quietly for as long as a minute, throws her head back and swallows it whole.

Following this, copulation usually occurs. The female goes into a sort of squat as the male edges toward her and as he places a foot low on her back with his wings partially outspread, she partially spreads her own and tilts her underside toward him. The male presses his cloacal opening close to hers and copulation commences, continuing for as short a time as 5 or 10 seconds to upward of 30 seconds.

The act of copulation is sometimes repeated within about five minutes but more often the two birds fly off immediately after the first, the female leading the way and the male close behind her. Copulation probably occurs numerous times over the next eight or ten nights.

ANNUAL BROODS, NEST, NESTING HABITS

Except in the more northerly portions of its breeding range, the Barn Owl is double-brooded, usually having its first brood in late winter or early spring and the second brood in late summer or early autumn. However, this is only a generalization, since the Barn Owl, unlike other owls, will evidently breed at any time of the year. Baby Barn Owls have been banded in the nests during every month of the year except December and February, but they are known to be in their nests during those months also.

Tyto alba pratincola is not at all choosy in regard to a nesting site. Nests have been found in a wide variety of settings. Natural tree hollows, especially in live oaks, with the hollows about 10 to 20 feet high, are a favored site, and even more so if the tree is near a marshy meadow. Occasionally, abandoned crow, hawk, or magpie nests are used. More often the eggs are laid on bare ledges in silos, barns, and abandoned houses, beneath bridges, and in old water towers. Church steeples and belfries are also selected for nesting sites and, on occasion, the owl will rather stupidly select a completely exposed location on a rooftop to lay her eggs. Such exposed nestings are rarely productive, since the heat of the sun tends to cook the eggs and destroy them. Protected ledges in cliff faces are often used and once in a while eggs will be laid on a convenient flat spot within some large abandoned piece of farm or railroad machinery, construction equipment, or dredge.

Very often the Barn Owl will nest underground in the abandoned burrow of a badger, woodchuck, or other such mammal and, when it does so, it tends to adopt the habit of sitting exposed at the mouth of the burrow much in the manner of the Burrowing Owl. Equally, it is fond of nesting in holes in the sides of stream banks and barrancas. Such holes are usually 8 or 10 feet above stream level and go inward on a horizontal plane for two or three feet before angling downward slightly to end in a more commodious chamber, perhaps two or three feet in diameter, where the eggs are laid. Although such holes are usually the abandoned holes of ground squirrels, the Barn Owls use their own talons to enlarge the tunnels and chambers for themselves. Not uncommonly, if the hole is too low in the bank of a stream, the nest will be destroyed by floodwaters.

No actual nesting material is collected. If the site is a building ledge, rafter, cliff ledge, rooftop, or other such area, the eggs are simply laid on the bare surface. In natural tree hollows they are laid on the wood chips or whatever other debris may have collected naturally or been brought in by the previous occupant. Underground, the eggs are usually laid on or near the bedding material collected by the ground squirrel, badger, or woodchuck that previously used the burrow. In all cases the whole nesting area is soon carpeted with the debris of pellets in various stages of decomposition, and the whole area badly stained by excrement. Barn Owls, if undisturbed on their nests, will return to the same nesting site year after year and, as a result, the pellet, bone, feather, hair, and excrement deposits become cumulative and sometimes build up to an enormous extent. The filth and stench are sometimes almost overpowering to humans.

Normally the nesting male and female roost close together during the daytime. Underground, the female will sleep on the nest while incubating the eggs and the male will sleep to one side of the nest near her.

EGGS

Number per nesting Usually there are a minimum of four and a maximum of seven eggs per nesting, but exceptions occur frequently. Sometimes as few as three eggs are laid, though rarely fewer than that. Eight, nine, ten, or eleven eggs in a single nesting is not terribly uncommon. Once in a while there may be twelve and rarely thirteen or fourteen. The largest single deposit of eggs on record was twenty-four. This was an unsuccessful nesting on a bare tin roof; although the female owl spent all the daylight hours shielding the clutch with her wings and body from the sun's rays, the radiant heat from the tin destroyed them.

Color Normally a pure, dead white, but occasionally having a vague yellowish or bluish cast. There is no gloss whatever to the eggs and they are usually badly stained with blood from prey and caked with dried excrement.

Shape Whereas the eggs of most North American owls are very nearly round, the eggs of the Barn Owl are considerably more ovate. On rare occasions they may even be an elongated ovate, but most often they are elliptically ovate with one end slightly smaller than the other.

Texture Very finely granulated but never entirely smooth.

Size The average egg size, based on the measurements of 97 eggs, is 42.4 mm. long by 32.4 mm. wide (1.7″ × 1.3″). The extreme measurements are as follows:

Maximum length:	48.3 mm. (1.9″)
Minimum length:	35.1 mm. (1.4″)
Maximum width:	39.8 mm. (1.6″)
Minimum width:	26.8 mm. (1.1″)

Interval of egg-laying The eggs may be laid singly at intervals of two or three days, or in pairs at intervals of about two days followed by a pause of about a week before the next two eggs are laid two days apart.

Egg-laying dates Western North America: earliest,

January 17; latest, June 7; normally between March 9 and April 16.

Northern North America: earliest, February 27; latest, July 18; normally between March 28 and May 3.

Eastern North America: earliest, February 22; latest, June 29; normally between April 9 and May 3.

Southern North America: earliest, December 24; latest, March 31; normally between March 2 and March 24.

Florida: earliest, December 12; latest, March 13; normally between January 26 and February 28.

INCUBATION AND BROODING CHARACTERISTICS

Incubation begins with the first egg laid and therefore hatching of the owls is staggered. Well-developed owlets about the size of a pigeon and with dark pin-feathers in the wings will be found in the same nest with eggs just ready to hatch. Normally the first egg hatches about 18 days before the last egg.

There is some divergence of opinion about the incubation period required for the hatching of an individual egg. Some authorities have stated as short a period as 21 to 24 days, while others say as much as 35 days. Evidently, much depends on how well incubated the eggs are and how often or for what length of time the eggs are exposed to the air. Probably the majority of eggs, under normal conditions, hatch in 30 to 34 days, with the most usual incubation term being 33 days.

Both male and female assist in brooding the eggs and often they will sit side by side, with each bird brooding a portion of the clutch. The female, though, normally does most of the brooding and the male keeps her well supplied with food during this period.

When disturbed while brooding, the female will fly a short distance away, alight, flutter, and prance about in a highly agitated manner, hissing and screaming. Rarely will either male or female attack a human intruder who approaches or handles the eggs.

YOUNG AND FAMILY LIFE CHARACTERISTICS

At hatching, the babies are sparsely feathered and very weak, barely able to lift their heads. By the end of the first day they are covered with a warm white fuzzy down and are somewhat stronger, able to raise their heads high for short periods, and even able to stand clumsily for brief moments. The elongated facial characteristic of the hatchling owls immediately identifies them beyond doubt as Barn Owls, even if the parent birds are not nearby. They are hatched with well-advanced appetites and the initial food brought to the nest is torn into tiny chunks and fed to them by the mother owl. At first they are fed only the actual meat free of bones, fur, or feathers.

The fuzzy white down covers the nestlings through the fifth day. On the sixth day a buffy second down begins appearing and the natal down is carried away on the tips of the new down. Movements of the nestlings against each other and the nest surface quickly wear off the vestiges of the natal down, and by the ninth day little trace of it remains. The babies are more attractive now and rather comical in actions and appearance.

By the ninth day the second down is dense and woolly and this covering is worn by the young bird until the beginning of the seventh week.

On the thirteenth day the young owl becomes much more alert to everything. At this stage it can stand and walk about on the nest surface without difficulty and is still relatively docile to handling, though it hisses sharply when disturbed.

By the twenty-second day the bird is very lively and extremely demanding of its parents. It eats upward of one and a half times its own weight in prey brought by the parents during each 24-hour period. At this age it often stands to its fullest height, craning its neck to see its surroundings better. When disturbed it hisses sharply, spreads its wings, lowers its head, and sways it from side to side menacingly; but it can still be handled without danger. However, if severely provoked, it will roll over onto its back and strike out angrily with grasping feet.

On the twenty-sixth day the primary feathers begin pushing through their sheaths, but the wing coverts are still downy. The young bird's hunger continues at a high peak. A nestling of this age, given all the mice it could eat, swallowed six in succession before refusing the seventh.

The defensive reaction of the fledgling becomes more apparent by the thirty-first day, and hunger remains at peak levels. The young bird strikes out at intruders without hesitation. Fed all the mice it wanted, a fledgling of this age swallowed nine, although the tail of the last one continued to hang out of its mouth for some time. By the end of three hours it showed signs of hunger again and rapidly swallowed four more mice.

Wings and tail are developing well by the thirty-sixth day, and by the forty-second day the young birds weigh more than their parents. The babies are very aggressive and, if food is scarce, cannibalism may occur in the nest. The youngest bird in the nest is usually trod upon and bedraggled, and should it become weak and fail, it is quickly torn apart and devoured by the others.

The primaries are becoming well advanced by the forty-fourth day and the residue of downy plumage is wearing off the tips. These primaries remain as part of

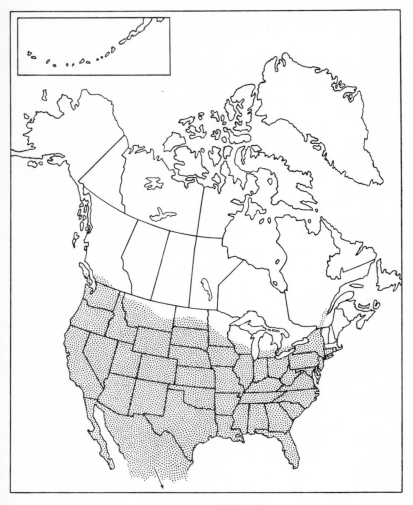

BARN OWL

Tyto alba pratincola (Bonaparte)

birds which, being so much smaller than the others, are often bowled over and stepped upon by their larger nestmates.

In the earliest stages of the care of the young, all feeding seems to be done by the female bird, but by the time the young are several days old and have begun to take whole food and swallow it, the male feeds them as well.

Throughout each night the young birds are fed almost continuously by the hard-pressed parents. When the babies are younger, the hunting of the parents sometimes results in an overabundance of food, which is nevertheless deposited in the nesting area. This food is always consumed by the young during the daylight hours which follow, while the parent birds are sleeping close by. In one well-observed case, a parent bird brought to the nest in less than half an hour a total of 21 mammals, including 1 squirrel, 3 gophers, 1 rat, and 16 mice.

DISTRIBUTION IN NORTH AMERICA

As a species, *Tyto alba* is the most widely distributed nocturnal bird in the world, populating most of the world's major land areas. Among all birds of prey, only the duck hawk has so extensive a range, although it is nowhere near the population level of the Barn Owl.

In North America the subspecies *Tyto alba pratincola* breeds from southwestern British Columbia (Ladner, Duncan, Vancouver Island), North Dakota (Grand Fork County), southern Minnesota (Hennepin County), southern Wisconsin (Dodge County), southern Michigan (Genesee County), extreme southern Ontario (Lambton County, Middlesex County), southern Quebec (Berthierville), and Massachusetts (Wenham), southward through all the contiguous United States to Baja California (Cape San Lucas), through Mexico to eastern Guatemala, probably to eastern Nicaragua, and from Texas through the Gulf States to southern Florida.

Casual Range: Northward to southern Saskatchewan (Aylesbury), southern Manitoba (St. Anne), northern Minnesota (Roseau County), southern Ontario (Sault Ste. Marie, Bruce County, Carleton County), northern Vermont (Lyndon), southern Maine (Portland), and Nova Scotia (Yarmouth County).

the first-winter plumage. The young Barn Owl, however, does not become clad in a long, soft, fluffy juvenal plumage, as is so characteristic of other North American owls.

From the forty-fifth to the fifty-eighth day the young birds begin losing some weight, as the parent birds are no longer able to provide as much for them as they demand. Wings and tail are developing well, and by the sixty-sixth day the young owl is fully feathered in the first-winter plumage and weighs about as much as the parent bird. It leaves the nest at this time but remains in the immediate area and is still fed by the parents for another two or three weeks, even after beginning to hunt for itself.

On the seventieth day at the earliest and by the eighty-sixth day at the latest, the young owls disperse in random directions. There is no further tendency to remain in the nesting area or to return to it any time in the future. The young owl merely begins wandering and adopts as its own territory whatever area it has happened to reach by the time winter sets in.

The deplorable condition of the nesting area increases daily and soon is a filthy mess; somewhat surprisingly, however, the baby owls are very clean except for their feet, and with the exception of the one or two youngest

MIGRATION

First-winter juveniles from more northerly portions of the Barn Owl's breeding range tend to move southward with the coming of winter in a movement that has some of the characteristics of a true migration, but this is not a general characteristic of the first-winter Barn Owl juveniles elsewhere. Generally speaking, *Tyto alba pratincola* is a permanent resident throughout its breeding range, but during especially severe winters there is a slight withdrawal southward, though not a true migration. All Barn Owls are more inclined to wander aimlessly and for greater distances during late autumn and early winter than at other times during the year, although such wandering is usually haphazard and not specifically in any one direction. Occasionally they have wandered far out on the sea and landed on ships to rest.

ECONOMIC INFLUENCE

The Barn Owl is among the most valuable birds not only in North America but throughout the world. It is a voracious predator throughout its life, and well over 90 per cent of its diet on an annual basis is made up of animals highly injurious to man and his crops. Extensive studies of Barn Owl pellets have been made in various areas of the world and the conclusions are markedly similar. In a study carried out in Poland, for example, pellets were analyzed which contained the remains of 15,587 vertebrate animals. Of this total, 95.5 per cent were small mammals, almost exclusively mice and rats. Of the remaining 4.5 per cent, birds—mainly house sparrows—made up 4.2 per cent and amphibians, primarily frogs, made up the remaining .3 per cent.

Studies in southern California have shown that an individual adult Barn Owl destroys pocket gophers to the value of $20 to $30 annually, and far more than that in meadow mice. Its value as a destroyer of cotton rats in the South is practically inestimable. The same holds true for its value as a destroyer of grain-eating mice throughout the prairie croplands of mid-America.

In a classic case where a pair of Barn Owls nested in an unused tower of the Smithsonian Institution in Washington, D.C., Dr. A. K. Fisher conducted an analysis of 200 pellets recovered close to the nest. They contained the skulls of 225 meadow mice, 179 house mice, 20 rats, 20 shrews, 6 jumping mice, 2 pine mice, 1 mole, and 1 sparrow.

Because of these highly beneficial feeding habits, the Barn Owl is a protected species throughout North America, as well it should be. In other countries throughout the world the value of this bird is becoming recognized, and steps are being taken to protect it. In Australia, for example, the Barn Owls were once killed indiscriminately. That ended after a study was made by the Australian Department of Agriculture. It was determined that the average Barn Owl regurgitates a total of 730 pellets each year. Therefore, that number of pellets was collected and carefully analyzed. They contained the identifiable remains of 2,239 animals, of which 2,162 were vertebrate animals and 77 were insects. The individual totals were important in pointing out the great value agriculturally of the Barn Owl. The 2,239 animal remains in the pellets, which approximate what one Barn Owl alone eats in the course of a single year, included:

1,407 mice	34 other birds
143 rats	4 lizards
7 bats	174 frogs
5 young rabbits	25 moths
375 house sparrows	52 crickets
23 starlings	

As a result of this study, legislation was enacted which makes it a crime in Australia to kill a Barn Owl, with an automatic fine of $25 for each Barn Owl killed.

SPECIES

ORDER: STRIGIFORMES

FAMILY: STRIGIDAE

GENUS: *Strix* Linnaeus

SPECIES: *varia* Barton

SUBSPECIES

varia Barton — NORTHERN BARRED OWL

georgica Latham — FLORIDA BARRED OWL

helveola (Bangs) — TEXAS BARRED OWL

NORTHERN BARRED OWL

(COLOR PLATE II)

SCIENTIFIC NAME AND ORIGINAL DESCRIPTION

Strix varia varia Barton. Original description: *Strix varius* Barton; *Fragments of the Natural History of Pennsylvania*, 1799, page 11, based on a specimen from Philadelphia, Pennsylvania. Former scientific names: *Syrnium nebulosum, Strix nebulosa, Strix varius.*

OTHER NAMES

HOOT OWL   Because of its distinctive hooting cry.

LA CHOUETTE RAYÉE   French-Canadian name meaning "The Striped (or Barred) Owl."

LE CHAT-HUANT DU NORD   French-Canadian name meaning "The Hooting Cat of the North."

RAIN OWL   Because of its habit of hooting before a rainstorm.

ROUND-HEADED OWL   For its distinctive, large, tuftless head.

SWAMP OWL   For the type of habitat it favors.

WOOD OWL   Similarly, for the woodland habitat it likes.

DISTINGUISHING FEATURES

One of our largest owls, the Northern Barred Owl (*Strix varia varia*), is easily recognizable because of its distinctly barred plumage, its large rounded and earless head, and the rather swollen appearance of its neck plumage. A heavily built and rather obese-appearing owl, it is surpassed in size among North American owls only by the Snowy Owl (*Nyctea scandiaca*), the Great Horned Owl (*Bubo virginianus virginianus*), and the Great Gray Owl (*Strix nebulosa nebulosa*). Because of the barred ruff encircling its throat it tends to have a peculiar double-chinned appearance. There is always an aspect of brooding thoughtfulness about the bird and an odd sense of innocence, rather than the fierce look of the Great Horned Owl. It is distinguishable from the latter owl by the fact that it is somewhat smaller, has no ear tufts, and is a much grayer owl in over-all coloration. The horizontal barrings on throat and upper breast and, below that, the heavy vertical stripings are further unmistakable identity markings.

Rank in over-all size among the eighteen species: Fourth.

SHAPE AT REST

Because of the manner in which it tends to couch its head in the plumage of neck and breast when perched, the Northern Barred Owl seems almost to be neckless and endowed with an especial chunkiness of body shape. It rarely stretches its body position into a slim, elongated form for concealment when perched, as does the Screech Owl (*Otus asio* sp.) and, to some extent, the Great Horned Owl.

SHAPE IN FLIGHT

The heaviness of form that is so apparent when the owl is at rest on a perch is carried over to its form in flight. It tends to have a thick, lumbering, easygoing aspect when flying, with a somewhat slower wingbeat than that of the Great Horned Owl. In flight, the wings tend to look stubby and broad because of the dense plumage of the body; actually the wings are quite in proportion to the body.

PATTERN OF FLIGHT

For such a large, bulky-appearing bird, it is a very light and graceful flier despite the fact that its wings beat rather slowly, heavily, and methodically. It rarely, if ever, soars on motionless wings, although it will occasionally make long direct glides through the woods while hunting. Such glides usually terminate in a graceful upward curve as the owl alights. It can and often does fly quite high and swiftly, especially when attempting to elude a mob of pursuing crows. The skill with which it can maneuver in extremely dense forest and swamp growth, intricately weaving its way through the interlaced branches, is little short of miraculous. Its flight is smooth and its body never undulates in flight as does that of the Snowy Owl. It is another extremely silent flier, rivaling the Barn Owl in this respect. On a bright moonlit night it may pass overhead within inches of a person and never betray its presence except by the passing shadow. When gliding, the flight pattern is a flat and level trajectory and the glides are usually made low to the ground, below the lowest limb levels of the surrounding trees.

Measurements have been based on 21 measured birds: 9 males and 12 females.

WEIGHT

Species average: 450.9 gr. (15.8 oz.).

	Male		Female	
Average	395.8 gr.	(13.9 oz.)	506.0 gr.	(17.7 oz.)
Minimum	330.0 gr.	(11.6 oz.)	388.4 gr.	(13.6 oz.)
Maximum	569.3 gr.	(20.0 oz.)	651.2 gr.	(22.8 oz.)

Rank in weight among the eighteen species: Fourth.

TOTAL LENGTH

Species average: 497.7 mm. (19.6").

	Male		Female	
Average	484.1 mm.	(19.1")	511.3 mm.	(20.2")
Minimum	407.9 mm.	(16.1")	452.1 mm.	(17.8")
Maximum	565.2 mm.	(22.3")	613.7 mm.	(24.2")

Rank in total length among the eighteen species: Fourth.

WINGSPAN

Species average: 1,092.2 mm. (43.0").

	Male		Female	
Average	1,073.1 mm.	(42.3")	1,111.3 mm.	(43.8")
Minimum	963.9 mm.	(38.0")	1,003.3 mm.	(39.5")
Maximum	1,098.6 mm.	(43.3")	1,139.2 mm.	(44.9")

Rank in wingspan among the eighteen species: Fifth.

INDIVIDUAL WING LENGTH

Species average: 324.3 mm. (12.8").

	Male		Female	
Average	320.1 mm.	(12.6")	328.5 mm.	(12.9")
Minimum	307.3 mm.	(12.1")	320.5 mm.	(12.6")
Maximum	330.0 mm.	(13.0")	355.6 mm.	(14.0)

Rank in wing length among the eighteen species: Fifth.

TAIL LENGTH

Species average: 235.2 mm. (9.3").

	Male		Female	
Average	216.7 mm.	(8.5")	253.7 mm.	(10.0")
Minimum	212.3 mm.	(8.4")	247.4 mm.	(9.7")
Maximum	228.6 mm.	(9.0")	260.4 mm.	(10.3")

Rank in tail length among the eighteen species: Third.

BEAK LENGTH

Species average: 23.5 mm. (0.9").

	Male		Female	
Average	23.3 mm.	(0.9")	23.7 mm.	(0.9")
Minimum	21.1 mm.	(0.8")	22.1 mm.	(0.9")
Maximum	23.9 mm.	(0.9")	24.6 mm.	(1.0")

Rank in beak length among the eighteen species: Fifth.

LEGS, FEET, TALONS

Feathered to or near the base of the talons, but very sparsely from the last joint to the talon. The naked or sparsely feathered portion of the toes is a dull yellowish gray, with the larger scales a slightly clearer yellow. The soles of the feet are a much deeper yellow and the talons are a dark horn color near the base but deepening to black at the tips. The denser leg plumage is a buff white and marked with numerous but faint transverse bars or spots of dun brown. The feet are rather small for an owl of this size and also not as strong as might be expected.

EYES AND VISION

Although not especially small for the size of the owl, the Northern Barred Owl's eyes seem small, because of the concentric rings of dark brown encircling them on the facial disks. The seeming solid darkness of the eyes, too, tends to impart a character of beadiness and small size. Actually, the iris is not black as sometimes described; it is a very deep brown with often very little demarcation between iris and pupil. In contrast, the pupil often seems to be bluish black. To the viewer there is, despite the slight beadiness of character about the eyes, a sense of soulfulness and softness in them which gives the owl an appealing expression. The vision of the Northern Barred Owl is extremely keen at night and quite good by day. Although like most owls it is bedazzled by a sudden bright light at night, it can see very well to hunt during the day and often ranges in the daytime, especially when skies are overcast. So keen is its vision in daylight that, although it may squint against the brightness of the sky, it can see flying birds passing overhead which the human eye, unaided by binoculars, cannot see. Its vision at night is not as good as the Barn Owl's and on heavily overcast nights when it is especially dark, it prefers not to fly.

EARS AND HEARING

As with North American owls in general, the hearing of the Northern Barred Owl is very keen. Not only are the ear cavities very large in order to pick up sounds of extremely low intensity, they are asymmetrical in size and shape, permitting highly accurate sound locating. This owl will come from a distance of over 50 yards to the faint squeaking of a mouse and can detect the running of a mouse on open hard-packed earth at half that distance, even farther when the rodent is rustling across dried leaves or grasses. As with the Barn Owl (*Tyto alba pratincola*), it can strike well by sound alone, and the combination of eyes and ears working together makes this owl a deadly accurate hunter. Though it may be sound asleep in its roosting tree and its location known in advance, the Northern Barred Owl's hearing is so acute that, even using great stealth, a human will find it practically impossible to approach it unheard.

EAR TUFTS, PLUMAGE, ANNUAL MOLT

The Northern Barred Owl has no ear tufts. The plumage of head and body is dense and heavy and not tight to the body, as is that of the Barn Owl. The leading edges of the flight feathers are very well fluted for fully silent flight. The adult birds have one complete molt of their feathers during the summer and early autumn. This molt generally begins around mid-July or early August and is finished by late October or early November. Flight ability is not noticeably hampered by the molting.

VOICE

Without doubt this is the most vocal of all the owls of North America and the owl with the widest range of

calls. To attempt to imitate all these calls in print would be an impossible undertaking, since so many of them are weird shrieks, screams, cries, trillings, grumbles, squeaks, and hootings. Yet there are a number of basic calling patterns that lend themselves reasonably well to written description.

The most common and often heard utterance is the resonant and far-carrying hoot for which this bird is nicknamed "Hoot Owl." This cry can be heard at a distance of several miles or more on a still night and is an impressive and rather enjoyable sound. It is comprised of two groups of four or five notes each, virtually belched outward in the night air, very strongly accented and with a definite rhythm and imparting a sense of wildness. Transposed to print, it can be written as *HOO-hoo-to-HOO-oooo, hoo-hoo-hoo-to-HOO-ooooo,* with the first two notes in the first group and the first three in the second being very clearly enunciated, deliberately given, and relatively low in tone. The last two in each group are closely melded, but with the hardest accent of the entire call on the next-to-last note and this sliding downward in tonal quality to the final note, which slowly dwindles away.

The second most frequently given call, equally familiar and wild, is a very loud and strenuously uttered four-syllable call of *hoo-hoooo hoo-WAAAHHHHhhhh,* gradually fading away.

Often the Northern Barred Owl will give voice to a long tremulous call which is much in quality like that of the Eastern Screech Owl (*Otus asio naevius*) but delivered with greater force and a more pronounced degree of harshness: *WHOOOO-O-O-O-O-o-o-o-o-o-o-o-o.*

Another call frequently given resembles the distant baying of a hound so very closely that experienced raccoon hunters have often been fooled by it.

An apparent recognition call given back and forth between roosting owls is a loud but relatively uninflected series of eight notes, these being crisply issued and sounding like *HOO-HOO-HOO-HOO-HOO-HOO-HOO-HOO.* Often there is a throaty whistling call which rises sharply at the end, not unlike a boy giving a sharp whistle through his fingers. Sometimes this is heard in conjunction with a low whining note, also relatively uninflected, which might be written as *whee-ooo-wheeeee-ooo-we-oooooo.*

These are only the basic and most commonly heard calls. There are many others uttered by the Northern

---

V CALIFORNIA SPOTTED OWL

Strix occidentalis occidentalis (Xantus). Male. Piru Creek, Ventura County, California, February 5, 1971. A.O.U. Number 369

VI NORTHERN SPOTTED OWL

Strix occidentalis caurina (Merriam). Female. Six miles southwest of Prospect, Jackson County, Oregon, March 25, 1930. A.O.U. Number 369-A

Karl E. Karalus

Karl E. Karalus
1971

Karl E. Karolus

Barred Owl, as well as numerous variations to each of the calls. There are, in addition, specialized calls made with relative infrequency which virtually defy written description. Some are coarse, guttural, and, to human ears, almost uncouth in character. Others are much like the fierce, hair-raising shrieks of mating alley cats. There are deep chucklings, harsh laughing sounds, maniacal gibberings and gabblings, disconsolate mutterings, howls, and yells. Occasionally there will even be a decidedly disconcerting humanlike scream of pure agony.

Although the call of the Great Horned Owl (*Bubo virginianus virginianus*) is a hooting somewhat similar to the basic call of the Northern Barred Owl, the latter's cry is never quite so deep and booming and it always ends in a descending, prolonged trailing note, which the Great Horned Owl does not utter.

There is a marked difference between the voices of the male and female Northern Barred Owl—his being considerably deeper and somewhat mellower than hers. The voices of the young birds differ also, being much higher in tone than the female's. Young birds will also make a peculiar ratlike squealing cry when first on the wing.

As with other owls, this species also snaps its beak loudly and hisses in a penetrating manner when alarmed or angry. Young birds still in the nest often make the hissing cry in lieu of a tonal call, but the hiss is eerie in quality and can be heard at a distance of 100 yards.

Almost all the wide variety of sounds made by the Northern Barred Owl are appalling and decidedly frightening to the superstitious. When calling from a perch, the owl swells visibly as it inflates its lungs, then thrusts its head forward and slightly downward to expel the call. Any of the calls are just as apt to be uttered during daytime as they are at night, and there are very often actual concerts of calls between perched owls of this species in the daytime before the onslaught of a thunderstorm.

SEXUAL DIFFERENCES:
SIZE, COLORATION, VOICE

As noted in the previous section, there is a distinct difference in the voices of male and female birds. Fur-

---

VII   MEXICAN SPOTTED OWL

Strix occidentalis lucida (Nelson). Female. Bear Canyon near Fairview, Sierra County, New Mexico, October 31, 1970. A.O.U. Number 369-B

VIII   GREAT GRAY OWL

Strix nebulosa nebulosa Forster. Female. Hay Creek near Salol, Roseau County, Minnesota, April 7, 1963. A.O.U. Number 370

ther, the female is invariably the larger of a pair—sometimes quite noticeably larger and at other times only slightly so. In coloration and markings, however, the sexes are identical.

MORTALITY AND LONGEVITY

Not a great deal is known of this aspect of the Northern Barred Owl's life cycle. Infant mortality at the nest or shortly after leaving it is not as great as with the Barn Owl (*Tyto alba pratincola*), but then the Northern Barred Owl does not lay as many eggs as does the Barn Owl. No thorough study has been made of the Northern Barred Owl's expected lifespan in the wild, but in various zoos it has been known to live well over twenty years.

COLORATION AND MARKINGS:
ADULT

The crown, back of head, sides of head, hindneck, throat, and upper breast are broadly and regularly crossed with heavy rufous-brown to grayish-brown bars separated by somewhat narrower pale buffy-white bars. Feathers of the belly, sides and flanks are buffy white, each with a broad central vertical stripe of dark, warm, gray brown, these stripes often overlaying one another to form a pattern of broken and unbroken stripes longitudinally down the front of the perched bird. The undertail coverts have similar but rather narrower stripes which tend to be more of a reddish brown. The area of the vent, called the crissum, is usually a very pale buff in color, but may be immaculate white on some birds. The middle and greater coverts have roundish white spots on the outer webs of each feather, but the lesser coverts are a plain deep brown. The secondaries are plainly crossed by five, six, or seven bands of pale grayish brown which becomes grayer near the edges, and the terminal band on each feather becomes white on the margin. The primary coverts have four bands of brown, which may range in shade from deep gray brown to a decided orange brown. The primaries are transversed by a series of rather square spottings of pale brownish on the outer webs of each feather, this brown becoming deeper in hue on the inner quills. The longest primary usually has eight spots. The tail has six or seven sharply defined bands of pale brown, with the outermost band continuing to the tips of the feathers. Facial disks range from grayish white to a pale buffy gray and have four or five concentric semicircular rings of darker brown. Feathers of the eyebrows and lores are a grayish white, each feather having a thin black shaft. There is a narrow

Karalus

Barred Owl
Cook Co., Illinois

crescent of very dark brown or black against the inner angle of the eye. The over-all impression is of cool grayish brown rather than the warm buffy brown over-all impression of the Great Horned Owl, and the placement of stripes and bars on breast and belly is just opposite that of the Great Horned Owl.

COLORATION AND MARKINGS: JUVENILE

Basically similar to adult plumage on wings and tail, but the neck, head, and all underparts are regularly and broadly barred with buff white, buff, and brown. The wing coverts, back, and scapulars are even more broadly barred, with the brown barrings of a deeper shade and each of the feathers tipped with white.

GENERAL HABITS AND CHARACTERISTICS

Although most often nocturnal in its habits, *Strix varia varia* is not so disinclined as the Barn Owl to hunt by day. When it does so, it tends to sleep throughout the following night. Next to the Screech Owl (*Otus asio* sp.) it is the most commonly seen owl. An accurate judge of speed and distance, it seems to enjoy flitting swiftly through the headlight beams of cars passing along woodland roads at night, yet is rarely struck by a vehicle. A relatively non-aggressive owl, it tames quite readily if taken when young. Aggressiveness becomes apparent, however, if the bird is hungry.

The Northern Barred Owl has the habit of drinking water frequently and bathing often, usually with seeming delight, even in the midst of winter. Its sense of smell is well developed and it will often follow a scent trail from considerable distances to where a trap has been baited with a commercial trapping scent.

Not infrequently this owl will visit campsites, take a low perch not very far from the fire and glare with rather comical sternness at the humans lounging about. Sometimes it will even alight on the ground only a few feet from the flames, evidently in the hope of catching insects attracted by the glow. The authors on numerous occasions have had Northern Barred Owls fly in and perch within the glow of a gas lantern by which they

were fishing at night in a woodland stream. At such times the owl shows remarkably little fear of the human voice or movement.

Equally, the owl evinces little apprehension over entering towns or even rather large cities at night to hunt for house mice and rats. More so than most other owl species, it remains rather closely attached to the area it selects in which to nest, often remaining there long after the nesting season has passed. It is an incredibly agile flier and will often be seen winging at top speed through cover so dense and interlaced that it seems the bird must surely collide with the branches.

The Northern Barred Owl has earned the enmity of many a trapper by stealing the meat used to bait the traps. On occasion it will also bully a Goshawk away from a kill and claim the carcass as its own.

HABITAT AND ROOSTING

The Northern Barred Owl is essentially a forest-loving bird and rarely strays too far from deep swamp tangles or woodlands. The deeper and darker the woods, the more they seem to attract this owl. Thick stands of dense tall pines and hemlock are especially favored, particularly for roosting, although well-established hardwood forests are also well frequented. Even isolated woodlots will attract and hold them if the trees are mature and numerous. Woodlands which border lakes, streams, swamps, marshes, and low meadows are ideal habitats for *Strix varia varia,* especially if the woods are a mixture of conifers and hardwoods.

The habitat of this owl coincides very closely with that of the Red-shouldered Hawk, and the owl appears to be reasonably compatible with that bird, often using its nests and hunting by night the same areas that the hawk hunts by day.

Occasionally the Northern Barred Owl will roost exposed in an isolated tree, but more often than not it prefers the quiet seclusion of a dense, tall pine or hemlock, perching on a large limb very close to the bole of the tree and quite well camouflaged against the bark.

ENEMIES AND DEFENSES

For a bird of prey, the Northern Barred Owl is an uncommonly gentle bird and not easy to goad to anger. Unlike so many other owls, even the very smallest, it will rarely make any attempt to attack a human being, even when that human is molesting its nest, eggs, or young. More often than not when such occurs, it will simply fly off and return later when the human has gone away. Occasionally a more aggressive bird of the species will fly to a nearby tree and give voice to a series of hair-raising cries, hissings, and beak snappings, but

Detail of the upperside surface of the outstretched left wing of a Northern Barred Owl (*Strix varia varia*). Note how wing coverts overlay the feathers behind and beneath them, and also the flutings on the leading edge of the flight feathers, which permit soundless flight.

without following through with an attack on the intruder. Yet, despite this, it is a bird of great courage if a fight is unavoidable. A terrible opponent, it strikes with flailing wings, savage bites, and deadly clutchings of its sharp talons. Once in a while an individual bird becomes extremely combative and will readily attack an intruding human, swooping down from above and attempting to bite and tear with beak and talons as it passes, and often with marked success. It does not as often turn over onto its back on the ground and strike out with its claws, as so many North American owls do.

As usual, man is the worst enemy. Though well protected by law in many areas, the Northern Barred Owl still falls in great numbers to the guns of hunters and farmers. Hunters (squirrel hunters in particular, who encounter the bird most often) see in this owl a fine trophy to have mounted and hung from their wall; farmers who should know better see the bird as a threat to their poultry. In both cases it's a tragedy, since *Strix varia varia* is no longer anywhere nearly as abundant as it once was, and as more and more of its habitat is destroyed in the name of progress, fewer and fewer of the impressive birds survive.

Where natural enemies are concerned, the crow causes the most strife for the Northern Barred Owl. Though crows rarely inflict injury on the owl, much less kill it, they torment the big bird of prey unmercifully. As soon as one crow discovers such an owl at roost it sends out vocal notice of the fact in strident calls, and within minutes all crows within hearing have hastened to the scene to join the attack. Time after time they dive in at the big owl, causing it to duck and flinch in order to avoid being struck by the strong sharp beaks of the passing crows. It glares and snaps its beak in anger, but to no avail. Eventually it flies, followed closely by the noisy throng and often routed three or four times before finally eluding the pursuers by arrowing swiftly into the heaviest of woodland cover or by flying very high and with great speed away from the area.

The Goshawk is also an enemy, and with some justification, since the Northern Barred Owl will not infrequently take its prey. Usually the Goshawk will simply flee in silent anger, but occasionally it may defend its kill with vigor. Usually neither bird is badly hurt in such an altercation, but there have been times when one or the other of the two birds has been killed —though more often the Goshawk than the Northern Barred Owl.

Next in line as enemies come the multitude of smaller woodland birds which gang up on the roosting owl with almost as much effectiveness as do the crows. Flickers and other woodpeckers, blue jays, chickadees, red-eyed vireos, kingbirds, shrikes, warblers, wrens, and many others join in the affray with great enthusiasm and make life generally unpleasant for the big owl until at last it is forced to rouse itself sufficiently to wing swiftly away into the deeper recesses of the forest.

The one truly dangerous natural enemy is the Great Horned Owl. Just as *Bubo virginianus virginianus* will attack, kill, and devour the Barn Owl, so also will it destroy the Northern Barred Owl, which is not very much smaller than the attacker. *Strix varia varia* is simply no match at any time for the considerably more fierce *Bubo*. Almost invariably in such encounter, the Northern Barred Owl is killed and eaten. Its only hope of escape, and a slim one at that, is flight with the greatest speed and agility possible through the densest of forest cover. Only in this respect does the Northern Barred Owl have a very slight edge over the Great Horned Owl.

HUNTING METHODS AND CARRYING OF PREY

Although certainly not the versatile hunter that the Great Horned Owl is, the Northern Barred Owl is nevertheless highly skilled as a predator. Because of the weaker nature and smaller size of its feet, it prefers much smaller prey than does *Bubo,* confining itself largely to rodents up to the size of a squirrel and occasional birds up to the size of a quail.

Two principal hunting methods are employed and both are effective. The first is merely to perch in the woods or in isolated trees overlooking marshlands or meadows and wait. Sooner or later the incredibly sharp hearing detects the movements of prey and it arrows to the attack with uncanny accuracy. The second method is to wing through the heaviest tangles of woodland or swamp and frighten potential prey into movement. As soon as the quarry is flushed, the owl pounces. Not infrequently it will nail squirrels against limbs or trunks as they try to flee, and while it is not swift enough to catch small birds on the wing, it does take a certain toll on them as they stir on their roosts during the night. And, though it is not a customary method of hunting, the Northern Barred Owl has been witnessed hovering over a covey of quail in broad daylight and eventually pouncing successfully upon one of the birds.

Now and again somewhat larger prey than normally will be attacked, but even though the owl might be successful, it is usually not without some sort of difficulty. One was witnessed as it pounced upon the back of a fleeing adult cottontail rabbit. Balancing itself with its wings, as the rabbit continued trying to escape, the

---

Detail of the underside surface of the outstretched wing of a Northern Barred Owl (*Strix varia varia*). Note overlay of underwing coverts on feathers above and behind them; also flutings on leading edges of flight feathers, and emargination of the outermost primaries.

Barred Owl

owl strove to drive its talons inward deeply enough to kill the mammal. For 84 yards—running, falling, scrambling up, and running again—the rabbit carried the big owl on its back until at last it could run no more. The owl then used its strong beak to break the rabbit's neck. Unable to lift the heavy prey, the owl tore it apart and devoured it in place, all but one hind foot, and then flew ponderously away to perch and digest the large meal.

Though it favors hunting in woodlands, swamps, and the margins of marshes and meadows, the Northern Barred Owl also frequently hunts in quite open country as well as in close proximity to farm buildings. Now and again it comes well into cities seeking prey and is a not uncommon visitor to town dumps and railroad yards where mice and rats proliferate.

Like the Great Horned Owl, the Northern Barred Owl will often catch fish in shallow waters, wading in knee-deep after them in sluggish streams and ponds, snatching them with the talons and dragging them ashore. Usually these fish are of a size which can be swallowed whole, and they are most often horned pout, suckers, chubs, and small carp.

Strix varia varia rarely carries prey in its talons. If the prey is small enough, it is carried in the beak. If too large for that, it is normally devoured on the spot where killed. However, during the nesting season when there are young birds at home to feed, some prey animals are carried in the talons to the nest. This always seems to be done with difficulty, though, and so the owl often will tear the larger prey into chunks of manageable size and make two or three trips to the nest, carrying the dismembered pieces in its beak.

FOOD, FEEDING HABITS, WASTES

Almost without exception, prey that can be swallowed whole is juggled about in the beak until properly in position to be swallowed head foremost. This holds true even with small mice, which the owl could swallow sideways with ease if it choose to.

Somewhat more detrimental to bird life than the Barn Owl, Northern Barred Owls have been observed to kill and eat a rather wide selection of birds of woodland, meadow, swamp and marsh, including mourning doves, bobwhite quail, purple gallinules, flickers and other woodpeckers, kingfishers, blue jays, towhees, juncos and other sparrows, blackbirds, warblers, cardinals, brown thrashers, robins and other thrushes, catbirds, swallows, and—not as often—birds as large as crows, pigeons, ruffed grouse, spruce grouse, and some other species of owls, particularly Screech Owls (*Otus asio* sp.). Even Long-eared Owls (*Asio otus* sp.) have been killed as prey.

Among fish, horned pout, perch, bluegills, suckers, bullheads, chubs, eels, carp, and other relatively slow-water fish are taken.

Strix varia varia is one of the few North American owl subspecies that will bother catching and eating turtles and tortoises. Box tortoises often fall prey, providing the owl can get its talons well embedded in flesh before the tortoise has a chance to withdraw into the safety of its shell. Terrapins are taken by this owl without hesitation, though not without peril, as some owls have lost chunks of their toes to turtles before being able to kill them. Where reptiles other than turtles are concerned, some lizards and snakes are consumed, though these make up a small part of the entire diet. Frogs are freqently taken and, less often, other such amphibians as salamanders.

Among invertebrate animals, the Northern Barred Owl will eat crayfish, scorpions, snails, slugs, large spiders, and many large insects such as beetles, katydids, grasshoppers, and crickets.

The bulk of this owl's diet, however, is comprised of mice and rats, along with other small mammals such as chipmunks, ground squirrels, gray squirrels, red squirrels, flying squirrels, and sometimes fox squirrels, young hares and rabbits, bats, shrews, and moles. Now and again this owl will successfully take even some larger mammals such as opossums, mink, and smaller weasels.

Its habit of preying occasionally upon young chickens, ducks, pigeons, and other barnyard poultry accounts for the enmity harbored by many a farmer for this owl, but such prey is taken so rarely that the species can hardly be considered a major threat in this respect.

Pellets of compacted undigestibles are regurgitated at the rate of about one to three per night. More often than not these pellets are not expelled near the nest site, but rather from the first perch the owl takes after leaving the nest. There is not the difficulty in pellet regurgitation that seems to plague some owl species. Usually one convulsive belching action sends the mucus-slickened pellet shooting several feet out of the widely opened mouth. This action is often followed by a ruffling of the feathers and a haphazard and brief preening of the plumage.

Excrement is generally of a darkish nature, rather viscous in texture, and seldom expelled near the nest. As much as two or three ounces may be expelled in a swift, powerful evacuation as the owl leans forward on its perch and briefly raises its tail. The feces may be squirted with such force that they travel a dozen feet or more on a horizontal trajectory before dropping to the ground.

COURTSHIP AND MATING

Courtship normally begins in late winter or very early spring and involves a wide variety of antics and callings, especially on the part of the male bird, but

Barred Owl

copied to some extent by the female. As with most of the cries made by this owl, duplication of its courtship calls in print is very difficult and less than satisfactory at best.

As the male flies to the female and takes up a perch in an adjoining tree or in the same tree some distance from her, he engages in a complex series of bobbings, weavings, wing flappings, and vocal presentations. Almost all the cries given at this time are emphatically uttered and rather thrilling to hear. Some are little short of spectacular, while others border on being sounds that can best be described as uncouth. While most are issued with the full power of the lungs and carry great distances, now and again a series of shorter, softer, and more rhythmical calls are uttered which are far more in keeping with the love cooings that one might expect. The mood instilled by them, however, is almost always broken when they conclude in a strange chuckling which quickly degenerates into what sounds like a weird, rather insane cackling. These, in turn, often give way to calls not unlike the squalling of an angry bobcat. Interjection of the female's voice is infrequent but always noticeable because of the higher pitch of her voice, as much unlike his as the broken and squeaky cawing of a fledgling rooster is unlike the strong crowing of a full-grown rooster.

During the display, the male will often crouch low on his branch, half open his wings, and lean so far forward that it seems he cannot possibly maintain his grip or recover his balance, yet he seldom fails to do either.

Since the two owls eventually fly off together following the male's courtship antics, the actual copulation has been infrequently observed and poorly described, but it is evidently similar to the copulation of other owl species.

Courtship and mating almost always occur in late February or early March, but on occasion may be delayed until as late as early April.

The eggs are merely laid on the rotting wood chips or other debris on the bottom of the cavity. A hole about thirty feet above the ground is preferred.

Failing to find a suitable cavity, *Strix varia varia* will almost certainly adopt as its own the abandoned nest of a hawk or crow and sometimes even the leafy nest of a fox squirrel. When the latter is used, the owl tears off the top and hollows out the chamber to accommodate itself better. If an old bird nest is used, very little is done to improve it beyond possibly enlarging the hollow and, far more rarely, vaguely lining it with a few bunches of grasses or clusters of pine needles. Now and again the rim will be rebuilt slightly, with some fresh twigs or sticks.

A peculiar situation sometimes develops in the nest-selection of the Northern Barred Owl. It will find a nest being used by a Red-shouldered Hawk and move in to share it with that bird of prey, even to the point of laying its own eggs alongside those of the hawk's. The owl broods the eggs by day and the hawk by night. The outcome of such an arrangement is not definitely known, although it is highly unlikely to be successful for either bird.

Failing to find an abandoned nest to take over as its own, the Northern Barred Owl will occasionally build its own nest—one of the exceptions among North American owls. However, such a nest is so slovenly and inexpertly constructed that quite often the eggs will fall out and be smashed, or the hatchlings will fall to their death through holes in the bottom.

Nesting is sometimes on the ground, but most often in pines or other dense conifers, but a large-limbed, heavily leafed oak tree near a river or lake is often used. The nest may be located as low as 20 feet in the first major crotch of the tree, or as high as 60 feet in the uppermost sturdy branches. If successful in its nesting, the Northern Barred Owl is inclined to use the same nest in successive years.

ANNUAL BROODS, NEST, NESTING HABITS

There is only one brood per year, although if the first set of eggs is destroyed, the pair will mate again and a second set is laid in about three weeks. On rare occasions even a third set will be laid if the second is similarly destroyed. As long as the first laying is successful, however, there will be no other.

Although the nest is most often the abandoned nest of a Red-shouldered Hawk or Crow, the Northern Barred Owl shows a preference for nesting in a natural tree hollow if one can be found which is suitable. In such cases the cavity must normally be roomy and quite deep. No nesting materials are brought in from outside.

EGGS

Number per nesting Two eggs are the most common number, although three are by no means uncommon. On rare occasions four are laid, and very rarely there is only one.

Color Pure, unmarked white.

Shape From vaguely round-ovate to very nearly round.

Texture Somewhat more granulated than those of the Barn Owl; enough so that there is a faint sense of roughness to the touch. Oddly, some Northern Barred Owl eggs have been observed which had a definite glossiness to them, but normally they are dull and not at all glossy.

Size Average egg size, based on the measurements of 86 eggs, is 50.0 mm. long by 41.9 mm. wide (2.0″ × 1.7″). Extreme measurements are as follows:

Maximum length:	55.5 mm. (2.2″)
Minimum length:	42.5 mm. (1.7″)
Maximum width:	45.0 mm. (1.8″)
Minimum width:	37.1 mm. (1.5″)

Interval of egg-laying Eggs seldom, if ever, follow one another by an interval shorter than 48 hours; sometimes as much as a week separating them.

Egg-laying dates Midwest: earliest, February 25; latest, April 30; normally between March 6 and April 13.

Northern: earliest, March 13; latest, May 18; normally between April 2 and April 21.

Eastern: earliest, February 28; latest, April 25; normally between March 17 and March 29.

Southern: earliest, February 17; latest, June 4; normally between February 27 and March 25.

INCUBATION AND BROODING CHARACTERISTICS

Although incubation is generally considered to begin with the laying of the first egg, there is some reason to believe that incubation begins even before laying, since relatively well-developed embryos have been found in eggs removed from the female's oviduct. Incubation on the nest, however, is stated to be a minimum of 21 days to a maximum of 30 days, with the most normal duration evidently being close to 28 days.

Almost all the incubation is done by the female, with the male bringing her food during this period. Occasionally, however, especially when the female wishes to drink or bathe, the male will assume the incubating or brooding position.

Strix varia subspecies, along with the very closely related Spotted Owl subspecies (*Strix occidentalis* sp.) are among the least aggressive of North American owls where protection of nest is concerned. Often a human can approach to within 10 feet without the brooding bird taking alarm and flying off. In some cases the birds will pay very little attention to an intruding human, coming and going at the nest as if the person were not there at all, though he may have climbed to within a few feet of the nest.

Now and then the Northern Barred Owl will nest in a tree right next to another where a Red-shouldered Hawk is nesting, but the two raptors seem to get along well enough, without one or the other attempting to cause problems to either the adults or young birds. In fact, the adult birds tend to watch the activities of the other species with some degree of fascination.

YOUNG AND FAMILY LIFE CHARACTERISTICS

As with other owls, hatching is at intervals, with the first hatchling emerging as much as fourteen to eighteen days before the final one emerges. The newly hatched owlets have their eyes closed and are clad in a fairly thick covering of fluffy white down, which is particularly soft and silky down the length of the back. They are very weak at first and parents must tear the food into tiny bits for them. This food-rending process continues for the first three weeks of their lives.

By the end of the fourth day, they begin to utter a whining, peeping sound which increases in volume with each passing day, but at this time their eyes are still sealed. It is not until near the end of the first week that the eyes become partially opened. As soon as this occurs they begin to show a marked activity within the confines of the nest. It is mostly a poorly controlled activity and somewhat disruptive to the nest, with occasional dire results. Holes are torn in the bottom of the structure and baby birds fall through and are killed when they strike lower limbs or the ground or, if surviving the fall, finally succumb to exposure.

From the second to the third week, the woolly white down begins being pushed out by the secondary down, which is called the first downy plumage. On both back and wings these distinctive downy feathers are broadly white at their tips, sooty-brown banded across the center and buff colored closer to the bird's body. The new breast feathers are quite similar, though considerably paler in over-all coloration. The belly and flanks now have long fluffy down feathers, and even longer down feathers yet are on the thighs. These ventral down feathers are yellowish white to pure white at the tips, but a light buffy color at the base. It is at this time that the wing feathers begin to sprout, but the rectrices—tail feathers—are not yet evident.

By the end of the second week after the final egg has hatched, all brooding of the baby birds ceases and full attention of both parents is devoted toward bringing home enough food to satisfy the demands of their offspring. By the end of the third week the babies are very active, but more sure of themselves now and capable of keeping themselves from falling should they inadvertently step into a hole. It is at this time, as well, that they give first evidence of aggressive and defensive characteristics.

Between the beginning of the fourth week and the ending of the sixth week, the young birds leave the nest for the first time and take up positions on branches nearby. Although they rarely fall at this stage, sometimes it happens. If so, the young bird flutters downward and usually lands unharmed. It will then remain on the ground beneath the nest tree and be fed there by the parents.

By the seventh week the downy plumage has become

quite well developed. The white tips of the feathers of the upperparts are much more conspicuous now. Those of the underparts have become irregularly spotted or barred with a medium brown over a general coloration of gray white. Little of the base color of buff on these feathers shows now. It is at this time that the molt into the first-winter plumage begins and the first firm feathers to appear are those on the scapulars and back. Next to appear are the long feathers of flanks and belly, each having a broad brown stripe down the center. All these feathers are fully developed before the horizontally encircling of the upper breast—the true "bars"—are well developed.

Flight is attempted between the twelfth and fifteenth week, though usually with poor results at first and, for a few days at least, the entire family of owls finds itself on the ground near the nest tree. However, as the wings quickly strengthen and flying skills improve, they move back up into the branches, though not to the nest, and continue to be attended by the parents. During their brief flights at this time they tend to squeak like a family of rats. Plumage of body, wings, and tail is well developed, but that of head and thighs is still the soft downy juvenal plumage.

Although the flights of the young birds become progressively longer and more dextrous, they continue to be fed and attended by the parents throughout the remainder of the summer and possibly even longer. By late September the young birds have their full dress of first winter plumage and equal the parent bird in size. Their coloration at this stage is much like that of the parents except that they are a somewhat more red brown in general tone than the more gray brown of the adults, and with buff-colored instead of white bars on the hindneck. Also, there is slightly more pale buff on the underparts and in the light bars of wing and tail.

As the end of the first year is reached, the young birds are wholly indistinguishable from the adults.

DISTRIBUTION IN NORTH AMERICA

Northern and central British Columbia (rare, Hazeltine Creek, Liard Crossing), southeastwardly through north and central Saskatchewan, Alberta, (Fort McMurray), south-central Manitoba (Chemawawin), central and southern Ontario (Ingolf, Port Arthur, Amyot, Moose Factory), Quebec (Montreal, Godbout, Anticosti Island), Nova Scotia (Pictou), Prince Edward Island, and south through northwestern Minnesota, southeastern North Dakota, all but northwestern South Dakota, eastern Wyoming (Bear Lodge), and eastern Colorado (Holyoke), to western Oklahoma (Kenton), northern Arkansas (Mountain Home), northern and eastern Tennessee (Knoxville), down the Blue Ridge of

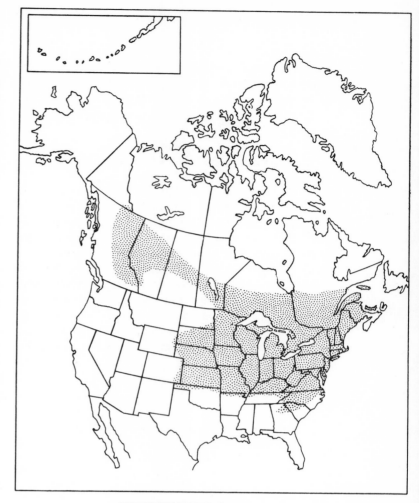

NORTHERN BARRED OWL
Strix varia varia Barton

North Carolina, through northwestern South Carolina and northeastern Georgia, angling northward again from this point to southeastern Virginia, but not in coastal areas until about the mouth of Chesapeake Bay.

More casual in the southeastern tip of Yukon and District of Mackenzie, northern Saskatchewan, Alberta, and Manitoba, and sometimes southern Keewatin, to the area of Churchill Bay, Manitoba, and southward along coastal Hudson Bay and James Bay, to southwestern Labrador and, more often, much of Newfoundland and islands of the Gulf of St. Lawrence. Occasionally to northern Texas panhandle, central Oklahoma and Arkansas, southern Tennessee, northern Alabama and Georgia.

MIGRATION

No distinct migration, although more northerly birds have a slight tendency for somewhat southerly movement during late autumn. Normally, this owl is a permanent resident within its range. There have been several authenticated sightings in Louisiana during the winter months.

ECONOMIC INFLUENCE

The Northern Barred Owl (*Strix varia varia*) is reputedly destructive to half-grown poultry but, as is so often the case, individual instances of poultry destruction are often enlarged all out of proportion to the actual damage done, and a blanket defamation of the species results. Certainly in this age, where poultry methods have improved, loss of poultry to the Barred Owl is virtually negligible. On the whole, because of its extensive preying upon rodents—especially mice, rats, and ground squirrels—the species must be regarded as far more beneficial than destructive and it should be protected.

FLORIDA BARRED OWL

(COLOR PLATE III)

SCIENTIFIC NAME AND ORIGINAL DESCRIPTION

Strix varia georgica Latham. Original description: *Strix georgica* Latham, *Index of Ornithology*, Supplement, 1801, page 15 (Georgia americana), based on a specimen from southern Georgia. Former scientific names: *Strix georgica, Strix varia alleni*.

OTHER NAMES

The Florida Barred Owl is called by most of the same names by which *Strix varia varia* is known, as well as one other—Allen's Barred Owl, a name rarely in use now and formerly used in connection with the previous subspecific name, *Strix varia alleni*.

DISTINGUISHING FEATURES

Considerably darker in over-all coloration than the Northern Barred Owl, but basically similar in most other respects. It tends to be a little more inclined toward regularly perching on very low branches than is the more northern race.

WINGSPAN

About five inches greater in the maximum figure than *Strix varia varia*. Maximum wingspan of the female has been recorded at 1,270.0 mm. (50.0″).

INDIVIDUAL WING LENGTH

About a half-inch longer in the maximum figure than that of the Northern Barred Owl.

LEGS, FEET, TALONS

Unlike those of *Strix varia varia,* the toes are nearly naked and with a somewhat grayer cast to the yellowish coloration of the scales. There is a narrow strip of short, bristly feathering on the outer side of the middle toe, but this is not apparent except upon close, in-hand examination.

VOICE

The voice is very much like that of the Northern Barred Owl, although possibly even more vociferous than in the northern race. Before intensive development of Florida began, sometimes upward of 100 of these owls could be heard calling back and forth to one another in the same general area. There was a peculiar pattern to the delivery of these calls. After a period of quiet, one bird—usually a female—would utter a loud call. Another—often (but not always) a male—would answer from some distance away in the same note but deeper in tone, and this would be followed by calls from three or four others in turn from different directions. Then another bird, which evidently had not called previously, would issue a very penetrating call with the sound of *UH-UH-UH-WHOOO-WAAA-aaahhhh,* or a different call sounding like *WHOOO-WAAAaahhh aah-aah-WHOOO-WAAAaaahhhh.* Instantly upon conclusion of this call the others would

A variety of field sketches of the Barred Owl (*Strix varia*). Upper left, adult male of subspecies *Strix varia georgica* from the vicinity of Fort Drum, Florida. Upper right, roosting posture of subspecies *Strix varia varia* in Schiller Park, Illinois. Middle right, month-old juvenile of subspecies *Strix varia varia* from near Chillicothe, Ross County, Ohio. Lower left, slouched posture of the Schiller Park bird immediately after awakening and, lower right, the same bird disturbed from below and preparing to take flight.

Barred Owl

Very dark specimen
from Florida

Schiller Park
Illinois
1965

Juvenile

K.E.K.

FLORIDA BARRED OWL

Strix varia georgica Latham

breast is horizontally barred with pure white and deep snuff brown, showing more contrast between the bars than in *Strix varia varia*. Belly plumage ranges from pure white to pale buffy cinnamon, streaked longitudinally with deep snuff brown and here also showing more contrast between light and dark than in the Northern Barred Owl.

HABITAT AND ROOSTING

Favors mixed hammocks of cabbage palm and live oak in the grasslands or in tangled swamplands. In the more northerly parts of its range it shows a marked preference for densely wooded river valleys. Roosting is normally closer to the ground than with *Strix varia varia*, except in the cypress heads of the northwestern Everglades, where roosting is primarily near the uppermost branches of bald cypresses when those trees are in leaf, but not when bare of foliage.

FOOD

Much like that of *Strix varia varia* except for geographical variants such as marsh rabbits, cotton rats, occasional young armadillos, occasional baby alligators, and frequently fiddler crabs. Tends to prey upon Screech Owls (*Otus asio floridanus*) more often than the Northern Barred Owl.

join in, sometimes in concert and sometimes successively, with some birds giving utterance to the first succession of notes and others giving voice to the second. This cacophony would build as their voices came closer and closer together, overriding one another until it was a veritable bedlam of calls, and then very quickly all the calls would die away and there would be silence again. This phenomenon was most often heard immediately preceding a severe thunderstorm, although such was not always the case.

NEST AND NESTING HABITS

Earliest nesting occurs shortly before Christmas and the latest is during the first week of March. Favored nesting sites include the tops of broken-off cabbage palms, cavities in the trunks of large live oaks, in low crotches of longleaf pines in the midst of thick groves of these trees, and in the hollow limbs of hardwoods. The nest is normally lower than that of *Strix varia varia*, even in the case where the abandoned nest of hawk or crow is used. Usual nesting height is from 15 to 25 feet, but sometimes up to 65 feet high in abandoned nests. The female evidently makes a halfhearted effort, when adopting the abandoned nest of crow or hawk, to line it with bits of Spanish moss and sometimes with a few feathers from her own breast, though never as a rule in the latter measure.

COLORATION AND MARKINGS: ADULT

Similar to the Northern Barred Owl, but darker. The underparts tend to have a deep snuff-brown or sepia coloration, with the terminal edges of the feathers marked broadly in white or buffy white. The upper

EGGS

Egg size averages slightly larger in the Florida Barred Owl than in the Northern Barred Owl. Average length, based on the measurements of 37 eggs, is 51.1 mm. (2.0″) and average width is 43.5 mm. (1.7″). Extreme measurements included:

Maximum length: 55.6 mm. (2.2″)
Minimum length: 45.8 mm. (1.8″)
Maximum width: 46.6 mm. (1.8″)
Minimum width: 40.4 mm. (1.6″)

Egg-laying dates Earliest, December 23; latest, March 3; normally between January 6 and February 14.

DISTRIBUTION IN NORTH AMERICA

Central and western Arkansas (Hot Springs, Little Rock), southwestern Tennessee, northwestern to east-central Alabama, across central Georgia, coastal South Carolina, and coastal southeastern North Carolina (to Cape Hatteras), southward throughout all of Florida and the Gulf Coast to eastern Texas. Though somewhat limited on the Florida Keys, this owl has been reported on a fairly regular basis as far as Key West. Especially abundant in the northern Everglades where every suitable hammock seems to harbor at least one pair of them.

TEXAS BARRED OWL

(COLOR PLATE IV)

SCIENTIFIC NAME AND ORIGINAL DESCRIPTION

Strix varia helveola (Bangs). Original description: *Syrnium nebulosum helveolum* Bangs, *Proceedings of the New England Zoological Club,* Volume 1, March 31, 1899, page 31, based on a specimen from Corpus Christi, Texas. Former scientific names: *Strix varia albogilva, Syrnium nebulosum helveolum.*

DISTINGUISHING FEATURES

Slightly smaller than the Northern Barred Owl (*Strix varia varia*) and a considerably more pallidly yellowish-colored race than either the Northern Barred Owl or the Florida Barred Owl (*Strix varia georgica*).

LEGS, FEET, TALONS

The toes are naked, as in *Strix varia georgica,* but without the side bristles down the length of the middle toe.

COLORATION AND MARKINGS: ADULT

The Texas Barred Owl is much paler in its coloration than the Northern Barred Owl. All the lighter markings are much more conspicuous than in the more northern race, and the underlying coloration on the upperparts ranges from pale yellow to yellowish cinnamon. The wings and tail are especially pale.

HABITAT AND ROOSTING

Confined almost entirely to well-wooded river valleys and lowland forests.

EGGS

In color, texture, and shape the eggs are similar to those of both *Strix varia varia* and *Strix varia georgica,* but they are smaller than either. A measurement of 43 eggs determined the average length of 49.2 mm. (1.9″) and average width of 42.3 mm. (1.7″). The extremes of those measured were:

Maximum length: 53.6 mm. (2.1″)
Minimum length: 45.0 mm. (1.8″)
Maximum width: 46.5 mm. (1.8″)
Minimum width: 39.1 mm. (1.5″)

Egg-laying dates Earliest, January 2; latest, March 11; normally between January 12 and February 17.

TEXAS BARRED OWL

Strix varia helveola (Bangs)

DISTRIBUTION IN NORTH AMERICA

Most limited in range of the three subspecies of barred owls, it is found from south-central Texas to the adjacent Gulf Coast. Primarily found in Bexar and Lee counties to Nueces and Brazoria counties, and probably northwestward as far as Tom Green county, but in more limited numbers in this more northwestwardly portion of its range. There is some evidence that this subspecies has been extending its range in a limited degree over recent years and casual specimens are being recorded in counties outside the limits of the above-described range.

ECONOMIC INFLUENCE

The Texas Barred Owl is generally considered to be the most destructive to poultry of the three Barred Owl subspecies, primarily because of abundant and less protected poultry raising within its very limited range. Nevertheless, despite the fact that it will prey upon poultry to some extent, the damage it does to the individual poultry raiser is more than offset by the savings it provides that same poultry raiser through destruction of rodents which make extensive inroads into chicken-feed storage areas.

Barred Owl

WOOD OWL   Because of its preferred habitat.

XANTUS'S OWL   After the original describer of the species and this particular subspecies.

SPECIES

ORDER: STRIGIFORMES

FAMILY: STRIGIDAE

GENUS: *Strix* Linnaeus

SPECIES: *occidentalis* (Xantus)

SUBSPECIES

occidentalis (Xantus)   CALIFORNIA SPOTTED OWL

caurina (Merriam)   NORTHERN SPOTTED OWL

lucida (Nelson)   MEXICAN SPOTTED OWL

CALIFORNIA SPOTTED OWL

(COLOR PLATE V)

SCIENTIFIC NAME AND ORIGINAL DESCRIPTION

Strix occidentalis occidentalis (Xantus). Original description: *Syrnium occidentale* Xantus, *Proceedings of the Academy of Natural Sciences of Philadelphia,* Volume 11, signatures 15–19, August–September, 1859 (January 10, 1860), page 193, based on a specimen from Fort Tejon, California.

OTHER NAMES

HOOT OWL   Because of its distinctive call.

WESTERN BARRED OWL   Because of the close relationship to *Strix varia* sp., the Barred Owls.

DISTINGUISHING FEATURES

This Spotted Owl and the other two subspecies, *Strix occidentalis caurina* and *Strix occidentalis lucida* are the western representatives of the Barred Owls (*Strix varia* sp.) of the East and South, to which they are closely related and which they resemble to some degree in general configuration, size, and habits.

The California Spotted Owl is a rather large, round-headed owl with large, dark, rather soft eyes, and a generally appealing facial character. Its most distinguishing characteristic is the liberal and conspicuous spotting of white on both the upperparts and underparts. The species is just slightly smaller than the Barred Owl species.

Rank in over-all size among the eighteen species: Fifth.

SHAPE AT REST

When perched it is a bulky owl, tending to crouch somewhat more than do the Barred Owls. It is also decidedly more restless on a perch and often engages in a peculiar and distinctly parrotlike movement. When determined to sit still and stare, it does so with great stubbornness, and it becomes difficult to force it into flight.

SHAPE IN FLIGHT

A heavy, short-necked, large-winged bird much like the Northern Barred Owl in appearance when flying.

FLIGHT PATTERN

Basically similar to that of the Northern Barred Owl, although seemingly not as inclined to make long flat glides to its perch. The California Spotted Owl flies with methodical, rather heavy wingbeats, yet it is surprisingly buoyant in the air for its size. There is no undulation of the body during normal flight.

Measurements have been based on 24 measured birds: 11 males and 13 females.

WEIGHT

Species average: 446.9 gr. (15.6 oz.).

	Male	Female
Average	391.0 gr. (13.7 oz.)	501.7 gr. (17.6 oz.)
Minimum	312.1 gr. (10.9 oz.)	383.6 gr. (13.4 oz.)
Maximum	513.5 gr. (18.0 oz.)	591.1 gr. (20.7 oz.)

Rank in weight among the eighteen species: Fifth.

TOTAL LENGTH

Species average: 472.1 mm. (18.6″).

	Male	Female
Average	461.6 mm. (18.2″)	482.6 mm. (19.0″)
Minimum	389.3 mm. (15.3″)	456.5 mm. (18.0″)
Maximum	552.5 mm. (21.8″)	606.3 mm. (23.9″)

Rank in total length among the eighteen species: Fifth.

WINGSPAN

Species average: 1,078.1 mm. (42.5″).

	Male	Female
Average	1,063.9 mm. (41.9″)	1,092.2 mm. (43.0″)
Minimum	942.0 mm. (37.1″)	993.4 mm. (39.1″)
Maximum	1,092.8 mm. (43.1″)	1,130.5 mm. (44.5″)

Rank in wingspan among the eighteen species: Sixth.

INDIVIDUAL WING LENGTH

Species average: 327.8 mm. (12.9″).

	Male	Female
Average	324.1 mm. (12.8″)	331.5 mm. (13.1″)
Minimum	322.8 mm. (12.7″)	325.1 mm. (12.8″)
Maximum	326.4 mm. (12.9″)	355.5 mm. (14.0″)

Rank in wing length among the eighteen species: Sixth.

TAIL LENGTH

Species average: 231.4 mm. (9.1″).

	Male	Female
Average	215.1 mm. (8.5″)	247.0 mm. (9.7″)
Minimum	210.1 mm. (8.3″)	232.2 mm. (9.2″)
Maximum	220.0 mm. (8.7″)	254.5 mm. (10.0″)

Rank in tail length among the eighteen species: Fourth.

BEAK LENGTH

Species average: 22.1 mm. (0.9″).

	Male	Female
Average	21.5 mm. (0.9″)	22.6 mm. (0.9″)
Minimum	20.3 mm. (0.8″)	21.2 mm. (0.8″)
Maximum	22.0 mm. (0.9″)	23.5 mm. (0.9″)

Rank in beak length among the eighteen species: Sixth.

LEGS, FEET, TALONS

Much like those of the Barred Owl species of the East and South, the feet of the California Spotted Owl are somewhat smaller than might be expected for a bird of its size, and they are not as powerful in gripping and carrying as those of some smaller species of owls on this continent. The legs are well feathered, but the toes are bare for the final half of their length. The toe scales, where visible, are a dusky orange yellow on top, and the larger scales are more clearly colored. The soles of the feet are a slightly brighter orange yellow. The talons are jet black for their entire length.

EYES AND VISION

As in the *Strix varia* species, concentric rings around the eyes on the facial disks of the *Strix occidentalis* species make the eyes seem somewhat smaller than they actually are, although this is not quite as pronounced in the California Spotted Owl and the other Spotted Owls as it is in the Barred Owls because of a lesser contrast between the lightness and darkness of the rings. The irides are a warm, deep gray brown in color but with slightly more demarcation between iris and pupil than in the Barred Owls. Vision is excellent, day or night. Full sunlight seems to have no particularly disturbing effect on vision, and the pupils are capable of contracting to such pinpoint size tnat they may at times seem almost to be absent.

EARS AND HEARING

Auditory cavities that are asymmetrical in both size and placement on the head are of great aid to the California Spotted Owl in locating prey through a triangulation process similar to that used by the Barn Owl (*Tyto alba*) and the Barred Owls (*Strix varia*). From a perch about 50 feet high and at least fifty yards distant, the California Spotted Owl will unerringly locate the source of the sound made by a pine mouse running across an expanse of solid rock. As in the case of the Barred Owls, it is most difficult—if not impossible—to creep up unheard on a sleeping California Spotted Owl.

IX   SAW-WHET OWL

Aegolius acadicus acadicus (Gmelin). Female. Lac Etchemin, Sainte Germaine, Quebec, Canada. A.O.U. Number 372

X   QUEEN CHARLOTTE OWL

Aegolius acadicus brooksi (Fleming). Male. Vicinity of Masset, Queen Charlotte Island, British Columbia, Canada, January 28, 1938. A.O.U. Number 372-A

Spotted Owl

Karl E. Karalus
1971

Karl E. Karalus
1972

Karl E. Karalus

Karl E. Karalus
1969

EAR TUFTS, PLUMAGE, ANNUAL MOLT

Strix occidentalis occidentalis is decidedly round-headed, with no vestige of ear tufts. Its plumage is dense and fluffy, though not quite as much so as that of the Northern Barred Owl. All flight feathers have the flutings of soft, comblike serrations on their leading edges for soundless flight. Adult birds begin their annual molting in early August, replacing all their feathers by late October or early November. Loss of the feathers is so staggered and widespread throughout the bird, however, that no flight facility appears to be hampered during this process.

VOICE

As with the Barred Owls, the California Spotted Owl is gifted with a wide repertoire of calls and with a surprising number of variations to each call. In essence, however, there are six basic calls which differ enough for some attempt at written description. The most ordinary call, uttered by both male and female—though evidently more often by the female—is an explicit enunciation of three equally loud and identically toned notes, with the first two of them voiced rather rapidly and then a three-second to five-second pause before the third. This calling has the distinctive sound of: *HOO-HOO . . . HOOOO.*

Another group of notes comprising one call may be uttered by the male only, whose voice is vaguely deeper and more resonant than the female's. This call has a decidedly canine quality and from a distance sounds remarkably like the baying of a hound. The four notes of this call are strung together in a rapid delivery, but sliding upward in the scale and becoming quite emphatic with the final note. It sounds like: *oh-ooh-oou-ooOOWWW!*

The female, and possibly the male as well, sometimes utters a sort of warning whistle to her young as she approaches or leaves the nest. It has the quality of a soft whistling a human might make by pursing his lips and whistling with indrawn air rather than with exhaled air. The whole call has a steadily rising inflection and lasts for about four seconds, sounding similar to: *wheee-e-e-e-E-E-E.*

A fourth call, which may be given by the male only, is a melodious yet somewhat guttural and rather far-carrying cry of: *whooo-whooo-WHOO-WHOO.*

The fifth basic call, given by the female, has been likened to a turkeylike chuckle or low, pleasant, dovelike call which sounds like: *COOO-COOO-coo-coo.*

Finally, both male and female birds utter a call of two variants which has much of the quality of the calling of the Great Horned Owl (*Bubo virginianus virginianus*), though not as resonantly given. At times it will sound something like: *hoo-ah HOO-ah.* At other times an extra note will be added and more emphasis placed on the final note: *hoo-ah-HOO-HOO-AHHH!*

There are, of course, numerous variations as well as other calls which do not lend themselves to emulation in print—strange whinnies, squeals, rattlings, and grating whines. A study of the calls turns up an odd factor: with but few exceptions, almost all of the calls are given in a series of four notes, usually in couplets of two and two. What significance this may have is not yet known.

Generally speaking, the calls of the Spotted Owls are slightly more muted and therefore not quite as frightening to humans as those of the Barred Owls.

SEXUAL DIFFERENCES: SIZE, COLORATION, VOICE

As noted, there is a slight difference in tonal quality between the voices of male and female birds. The female is slightly larger as a rule, though this size differential is not as visually evident in *Strix occidentalis* as in many other owl species. There is no sexual difference in their coloration or markings.

MORTALITY AND LONGEVITY

Few studies have been made concerning the mortality and longevity of the California Spotted Owl or the other two subspecies, but it is not unreasonable in view of parallel development to consider that they would approximate those of the Barred Owls. It is known that captive Spotted Owls have lived for as long as twenty-one years and they may possibly live half again that long.

COLORATION AND MARKINGS: ADULT

Unlike the Barred Owls, the California Spotted Owl is finely and regularly spotted down the length of breast and belly, with the spots on the upper breast smaller

---

XI   RICHARDSON'S OWL

Aegolius funereus richardsoni (Bonaparte). Male. One mile from west shore of Mud Lake, Aroostook County, Maine, January 12, 1970. A.O.U. Number 371

XII   LONG-EARED OWL

Asio otus wilsonianus (Lesson). Male. Vicinity of Meredosia, Brown County, Illinois, October 23, 1899. A.O.U. Number 366

and gradually enlarging as the pattern continues downward. The ground color is a rich, warm cinnamon brown, each feather having a narrow central line of the brown separating the pure white into two spots on opposing webs of the same feather. Often, but not always, there is a horizontally elongated white patch on the throat which is about twice as long as it is wide. Almost always, but with occasional exceptions (especially among female birds), there is a narrow but fluffy stripe of pure-white feathering running from mid-breast to belly and widening toward the bottom. The tail is basically brown, crossed by a regular series of thinner white lines and terminating in a thin white margin. Dark buff spots on the primaries alternate regularly with similar-width spots of deep brown. Eyebrows and lores are white near the top and shade into buff near the bottom, enclosing the beak in a clearly evident back-to-back-crescent formation. Facial disks are a warm cinnamon buff overlaid by (usually) three narrow semicircles of deep red brown emanating outward from the eyes in concentric fashion. The facial rim is a very deep brown black. The center line of the head from between the brows and above the beak to the midpoint of the head is normally a deep and unspotted brown.

COLORATION AND MARKINGS: JUVENILE

Very similar in first-winter plumage to adults, but with the white spots more buffy or ivoried, and with not as much contrast to the brown. Gular and breast patches of white are absent. The facial disks are a trifle darker, with not as much contrast between the concentric rings.

GENERAL HABITS AND CHARACTERISTICS

Although the California Spotted Owl can see and fly well during the day, it is more retiring diurnally than are the Barred Owls. Except on the cloudiest of days, it will seldom fly in daytime unless forced to do so, and even then only reluctantly.

When startled, its facial expression can undergo a marked alteration—from what seems to a human viewer to be a suspicious, catlike expression at first to a softening and somewhat quizzical look. Even when it is alarmed its expression has the appearance of being more friendly than ferocious, and some of its habits seem to border on the ludicrous. There is no clear explanation, for example, for the peculiar parrotlike movements it so often makes when perched—and these movements appear all the more comical as the bird

gravely winks one eye, then the other, opens each in turn, closes both together and then blinks both open simultaneously. Occasionally it will perch for long moments with one eye shut and the other widely open.

More than any other North American owl species, it seems to take tremendous delight in preening itself, rarely sitting on a perch for long without doing so. First it shakes its feathers very carefully into place and then one by one begins to preen away every frayed feather tip with its beak, contorting itself into the most unusual positions as it works. Very often it falls asleep in the midst of such preening, then awakens with a start and continues the job. Because of its uncommon placidity and reluctance to take flight, it is an interesting owl to observe, once located. Unfortunately, it is a relatively rare experience to observe one in the wild at any time. Its evident fearlessness, mild curiosity, and general tameness when approached have given it a reputation for stupidity which is largely undeserved.

HABITAT AND ROOSTING

The habitat that it prefers causes the California Spotted Owl to be rarely seen in the wild. It is inclined to stay within the confines of the deepest portions of very dense fir forests, on sheer but heavily wooded cliffsides, in narrow canyons with equally sheer walls and, much less regularly, in wide, flat, parklike forest pastures. Occasionally it will frequent stream valleys well grown with oak, sycamore, willow, cottonwood, and alder tangles. At no time is it an easy bird to locate. Roosting is normally done about two-thirds of the way up in a dense fir tree, close to the bole, and with the bird well camouflaged against the dappled background of bark. If disturbed it will fly only a short distance and then promptly go to roost again.

ENEMIES AND DEFENSES

Strangely limited in offensive qualities, this owl has been known to perch close at hand and watch an intruder destroy its nest, eggs, or young, with never a move on the adult bird's part to attack or even attempt

---

Perched hunting postures of the California Spotted Owl (*Strix occidentalis occidentalis*) in northeastern Los Angeles County, California. Difference of breast-plumage markings shown on magnified individual feathers to left of middle bird. Amazing turning radius of head is depicted by light head sketch behind darker head sketch of middle bird. Turning its head on its own right, the owl accomplishes a turn of about 270°, but can return its gaze forward in so swift a time that the blink of a human eye will miss the movement.

Spotted Owl

spotted

REK

to drive off the intruder. On occasion it has been bodily lifted by unprotected human hands off its clutch of eggs with never a protest. Its greatest defense seems to be a natural camouflage in its speckled plumage, which makes it virtually invisible when roosting in a sun-dappled shady spot against bark or foliage, even when the observer is very close.

Where natural enemies are concerned, it is believed to fall prey on occasion to the Pacific Horned Owl (*Bubo virginianus pacificus*). Otherwise, its only natural enemies seem to be the hordes of smaller birds which delight in harassing it, though rarely if ever with actual injury to the owl. These smaller bird antagonists include vireos, flycatchers, California woodpeckers, blue-fronted jays, California jays, Sierra creepers, and a variety of warblers.

HUNTING METHODS AND
CARRYING OF PREY

More often than not its preference is to perch quietly in a tree near a small grassy forest glade, watching and listening intently until some manner of prey comes along, at which time it launches itself with thunderbolt speed and great accuracy to the attack. The prey it normally takes is small enough so that it has no difficulty carrying it back to nest or perch in its beak. Occasionally, however, when a somewhat larger animal is killed, the feet are used for carrying. Sometimes the owl will range through the woods or along small watercourses much in the manner of the Barred Owls, but this is more the exception than the rule.

FOOD, FEEDING HABITS, WASTES

This is one of the few owls that are known to be fond of various forms of offal and garbage. If it is seen at all, chances are that the California Spotted Owl will be seen at some woodland picnic disposal area. There it will walk about nonchalantly, picking up a morsel of meat here, a bit of muskmelon there, a piece of hard-boiled egg elsewhere. Even the heads of camp-fire-fried trout will be eaten if discovered. Where living prey is concerned, the California Spotted Owl concentrates mainly on rats and mice of various species, such as wood rats, white-footed mice, red tree mice, pine rats, brush rats, and also chipmunks and small squirrels. Though not noted as a feeder on other birds, it will occasionally kill and eat warblers, crested jays, Screech Owls, and the Coast Pygmy Owl (*Glaucidium gnoma grinnelli*). Pellet ejection and defecation are much as in the Barred Owls.

COURTSHIP AND MATING

Not a great deal is positively known about the courtship of this owl species, mainly because of the difficulty of observation. It is known that courtship generally begins anywhere from late February to very early April, with mating following immediately. Much information still needs to be gathered in this regard, however.

ANNUAL BROODS, NEST,
NESTING HABITS

Strix occidentalis occidentalis is always singlebrooded. It is doubtful that it will lay a second clutch of eggs if the first is destroyed. Unlike the Barred Owls, it will seldom take occupancy of an abandoned hawk or raven nest, but when it does do so, such a nest will usually be from 30 to 50 feet in height, in an oak or pine growing on the edge of a canyon, at an elevation of about 6,000 feet.

Far more often the California Spotted Owl prefers to nest in a natural tree hollow or sheltered in highly inaccessible cliff crannies, usually with a sheer drop of 100 to 400 feet directly beneath the nesting cranny. Occasionally, almost as if throwing caution to the winds, it will nest in surprisingly exposed areas, such as a hollow log lying on the ground, or in a declivity of a stream bank no more than a few feet above the lower ground level of the creekside.

No effort is made to build a nest and the eggs are laid directly on whatever surface is available in the chosen site. Very soon, however, the nest is surrounded by a motley collection of such debris as feathers, bones, fur, pellets in various stages of decomposition, and other rubbish. This species is not as fastidious about the condition of its nesting area as are the Barred Owls.

EGGS

Number per nesting Two or three eggs are laid, but most often only two. On rare occasions there will be four.

Color Pure, unblemished white.

Shape Round-ovate to very nearly globular. Virtually indistinguishable from those of the Barred Owls.

Texture As in the Barred Owls, slightly granulated. Never, however (as may occur with Barred Owls), with the eggshell being in any degree glossy.

Size Based on a total of 23 eggs measured, the average size was 50.0 mm. (2.0″) in length and 41.3 mm. (1.6″) in width. The extreme measurements were:

Spotted Owl

Maximum length: 54.0 mm. (2.1″)
Minimum length: 42.3 mm. (1.7″)
Maximum width: 43.2 mm. (1.7″)
Minimum width: 33.5 mm. (1.3″)

Interval of egg-laying Not incontrovertibly established but probably very similar to that of the Barred Owls.

Egg-laying dates Earliest, March 1; latest, May 10; normally between March 27 and April 17.

INCUBATION AND BROODING CHARACTERISTICS

Incubation begins with the first egg laid and is probably from 25 to 28 days in duration. As nearly as can be determined, all incubation is done by the female bird, while the male supplies her with food. Occasionally she will leave the nest for brief periods, possibly to drink or bathe, but there is no evidence to show that the male will take over incubation duties even then, though he evidently does stay close by.

So unaggressive is the female that, although she will sit tightly on her eggs in the face of disturbance, she will allow herself to be lifted off the eggs without protest and even with an odd sense of disinterest or detachment over what is occurring.

YOUNG AND FAMILY LIFE CHARACTERISTICS

Little solid information has been gathered on the nest life and juvenal life of the California Spotted Owl. It has been noted, though, that late each afternoon—usually around 4 P.M.—there is a period of marked increase of activity within the nest, although what connotation this may have remains a mystery. Fledgling birds have been seen at this time moving about in the nest and flapping their wings vigorously. There is some unusually interesting but inclusive evidence that the parent birds may, if young birds are endangered, physically move them to a safer location—perhaps a protected ledge on a nearby cliff face. Reportedly, the baby birds are carried in the beak of the parent by one foot and make no effort to flap or struggle while being so transported. It should be borne in mind, however, that the report may be at best somewhat embellished, and at worst entirely fanciful.

At about twelve or fifteen days of age, the young birds are clad in soft, grayish-white down on the upperparts and buffy-white on the underparts. At this age they tend to shrink slightly from an extended hand, but do not hiss or threaten.

CALIFORNIA SPOTTED OWL
Strix occidentalis occidentalis (Xantus)

DISTRIBUTION IN NORTH AMERICA

On the west slope of the Sierra Nevada in California from Tehama County to Tulare County, and the mountains of southern California from Santa Barbara County to San Diego County.

MIGRATION

None.

ECONOMIC INFLUENCE

Undoubtedly of some benefit in forest-rodent control, but to what extent is not known.

NORTHERN SPOTTED OWL
(COLOR PLATE VI)

NORTHERN SPOTTED OWL

Strix occidentalis caurina (Merriam)

SCIENTIFIC NAME AND ORIGINAL DESCRIPTION

Strix occidentalis caurina (Merriam). Original description: *Syrnium occidentale caurinum* Merriam, *The Auk,* Volume 15, Number 1, January 1898, pages 39–40, based on a specimen from Mount Vernon in the Skagit Valley of Washington.

OTHER NAMES

LE CHAT-HUANT TACHETÉ DU NORD French-Canadian name meaning "The Speckled Hooting Cat of the North."

DISTINGUISHING FEATURES

Similar in size and markings to the California Spotted Owl (*Strix occidentalis occidentalis*), but considerably darker. Also darker, and with a richer brown than that on the plumage of the Mexican Spotted Owl (*Strix occidentalis lucida*).

TAIL LENGTH

Slightly shorter than that of *Strix occidentalis occidentalis,* averaging 204.7 mm. (8.1″).

EARS AND HEARING

Extremely keen, and this bird may be decoyed into close observation range from comparatively long distances by emulating the squeak of a mouse.

VOICE

Very much like *Strix occidentalis occidentalis,* with the addition of one cry best described as a prolonged, eerie and rather nerve-racking whining sound which gradually rises in tone and volume to a grating noise that can set the teeth on edge in the daytime and cause the hair at the nape to tingle at night. Once heard, this cry is never forgotten and, if properly identified, is never mistaken for anything else.

SEXUAL DIFFERENCES: SIZE, COLORATION, VOICE

Voices of males and females primarily indistinguishable. There is very little, if any, difference in size between the sexes, and both are marked and colored similarly.

COLORATION AND MARKINGS: ADULT

As noted, similar to *Strix occidentalis occidentalis,* but everywhere darker. Generally speaking, the white spots and markings are smaller than those of the California Spotted Owl, and this is especially apparent on both the head and back, where the white spotting is reduced to a minimum and in some cases practically absent. The dark markings on the sides, flanks, and feet are more extensive and considerably darker than in the California Spotted Owl. The most obvious difference between the two races, however, is on the wings. The primary feathers are a great deal darker and the broad whitish tips on *Strix occidentalis occidentalis* are absent in *Strix occidentalis caurina* and are represented instead by a vague, pale, buffy-gray band which becomes slightly whiter on the outer edge of the vane. On some of these feathers there is a faint whitish edging at the outermost tips. The three or four pale bars nearest the tips of the feathers in *Strix occidentalis occidentalis* are imperfectly developed in *Strix occidentalis caurina*.

HABITAT

Confined to the dense timberlands of the humid Pacific coastal forests.

FOOD

Primarily mice, rats, chipmunks, squirrels, and rabbits.

EGGS

Two or three, but usually two. Four eggs in a nesting have not been recorded, as they have been in the California Spotted Owl.

DISTRIBUTION IN NORTH AMERICA

From southwestern British Columbia (north to Alta Lake and east to Hope), through western Washington (east to Lake Wenatchee, Chelan County; Cle Elum, Kittias County), western Oregon, and coast ranges of California southward from the Oregon border to San Francisco Bay, Marin County.

MEXICAN SPOTTED OWL

(COLOR PLATE VII)

SCIENTIFIC NAME AND ORIGINAL DESCRIPTION

Strix occidentalis lucida (Nelson). Original description: *Syrnium occidentale lucidum* Nelson, *Proceedings of the Biological Society of Washington*, Volume 16, Number 40, November 30, 1903, page 152, based on a specimen from Mount Tancitero, Michoacán, Mexico.

OTHER NAMES

ARIZONA SPOTTED OWL Because of geographical location.

CANYON SPOTTED OWL Because of preferred habitat.

TECOLOTE MANCHADO DE NELSON Mexican-Indian name meaning "Nelson's Spotted Owl."

DISTINGUISHING FEATURES

Slightly smaller than either the California Spotted Owl (*Strix occidentalis occidentalis*) or the Northern Spotted Owl (*Strix occidentalis caurina*), but darker than the former and lighter than the latter. The beak is a brighter yellowish ivory than that of either of the other two subspecies, and it is also a thicker beak, though the significance of this is unknown.

TOTAL LENGTH

Average length is slightly less than the other two Spotted Owl subspecies, being 427.5 mm. (16.8″) for the male and 458.5 mm. (18.1″) for the female.

BEAK LENGTH

Slightly greater than that of either the California Spotted Owl or the Northern Spotted Owl, averaging 23.0 mm. (0.9″).

VOICE

Generally higher in pitch than that of the other Spotted Owls, but with specialized calls of its own. One common call not shared by either of the other two races is a simple, medium-pitched *whoo-whoo-WHOOO*, with a strong inflection on the last note, but each note about two seconds long, with a one-second pause between them.

On brightly moonlit nights these owls tend to call back and forth across canyons for long periods. The usual call made at this time is a pleasing and rather conversational *who-who-who-who-who-who-who*, delivered in an evenly spaced musical monotone. This call is almost invariably answered immediately by a rather grating and particularly unmusical cry of *wheck-*

MEXICAN SPOTTED OWL

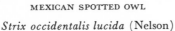

Strix occidentalis lucida (Nelson)

wheck-wheck-wheck-wheck, similar to but much harsher than the distant quacking of a duck.

The voice of the female is recognizably higher in pitch than that of the male.

COLORATION AND MARKINGS: ADULT

The Mexican Spotted Owl is darker (though on rare occasions lighter) and has much less buffy-yellowish suffusion of general coloration than the California Spotted Owl. In almost all cases it has a vaguely grayer general coloration than the Northern Spotted Owl, even though its browns more nearly approach those of the California race than they do those of the Northern race. Its white spottings, like those of *Strix occidentalis occidentalis,* are much larger than the very small white spots on *Strix occidentalis caurina.* In a very general way, the California Spotted Owl could be called a cinnamon-brown owl with large white spots; the Northern Spotted Owl could be called a chestnut-brown owl with small white spots; and the Mexican Spotted Owl could be called an ashy chestnut-brown owl with large white spots.

HABITAT

Forested mountain tablelands and canyons between the elevations of 5,500 and 9,000 feet are favored, especially those with dense aspen clumps and creek-fringe maples. Deep, narrow, well-wooded canyons dotted with caves and craggy clefts seem definitely to be a requirement for residency.

ENEMIES

The Mexican Spotted Owl's greatest natural enemy is the Western Horned Owl (*Bubo virginianus pallescens*), and it strives to avoid those areas where the range of the two species might overlap.

FOOD

Consumes considerably more insect and other invertebrate life such as spiders, scorpions, and centipedes than do either of the other two subspecies. The Mexican Spotted Owl seems especially to favor feeding on large moths.

NEST

On rare occasions *Strix occidentalis lucida* will build its own poorly constructed nest in a crotch about 30 feet high, usually in a cottonwood or very dense Douglas fir, at an altitude of about 7,500 feet. However, it prefers a natural cavity in a large oak tree or on a ledge near the entrance to a rather spacious but relatively inaccessible cave.

EGGS

The eggs of the Mexican Spotted Owl are slightly larger than those of either the California Spotted Owl or the Northern Spotted Owl, averaging 50.8 mm. (2.0″) in length and 42.9 mm. (1.7″) in width. Two or three are the usual number laid, although three are more often laid than two. Rarely, four will be laid.

DISTRIBUTION IN NORTH AMERICA

Northern Arizona (Grand Canyon), central and western New Mexico, southeastern Utah (Navajo Mountain), central Colorado (Park County, Colorado Springs), and western Texas (Guadalupe Mountains), southward into Mexico, where it has been recorded in northern Sonora (Sierra de Oposura), Chihuahua (Pinos Altos, Vasagota), Michoacán, Guanajuato, and Nuevo León (Cerro Potosí).

MIGRATION

No true migration, but evidently a fair number of the Mexican Spotted Owls do come down to lower altitudes into the near-mountain lowlands during years when winter is especially severe. This is not, however, an annual occurrence.

SPECIES

ORDER: STRIGIFORMES

FAMILY: STRIGIDAE

GENUS: *Strix* Linnaeus

SPECIES: *nebulosa* Forster

SUBSPECIES

---

nebulosa Forster GREAT GRAY OWL

GREAT GRAY OWL
(COLOR PLATE VIII)

SCIENTIFIC NAME AND ORIGINAL DESCRIPTION

Strix nebulosa nebulosa Forster. Original description, *Strix nebulosa* J. R. Forster, *Philadelphia Transactions,* Volume 62, article 29, 1772, page 424, based on a specimen from the Severn River of northwestern Ontario. Former scientific names: *Strix cinera, Syrnium cinereum, Scotiaptex cinera, Scotiaptex nebulosa nebulosa, Strix nebulosa.*

OTHER NAMES

CINEREOUS OWL Because of its generally ashy coloration.

GREAT CINEREOUS OWL After size and ashy coloration.

GREAT GRAY GHOST Because of size, coloration, and ghostly appearance as it flies in the late twilight.

LA CHOUETTE CENDRÉE D'AMÉRIQUE French-Canadian name meaning "The Ashen-colored Owl of America."

NUHL-TUHL Northern Indian name meaning "The

Heavy Walker" because of its awkward movements on the ground.

SPECTRAL OWL Because of the fanciful notion that it is associated with being a phantom or other object of superstitious terror or dread.

DISTINGUISHING FEATURES

An unusually large-appearing, tuftless, roundheaded owl with remarkably large facial disks and having distinct concentric circles around the eyes. With its uncommonly dense and fluffy plumage and long, broad wings, this owl is generally gray in color because of the over-all intermingled pattern of black and white along with gray. The huge beak, which is almost lost in the deep facial plumage, is greenish, but becoming yellowish toward the tip. The expression of *Strix nebulosa nebulosa* seems not as fierce as that of the Great Horned Owl (*Bubo virginianus virginianus*) nor as benign as that of the Barred Owls (*Strix varia* sp.) or Spotted Owls (*Strix occidentalis* sp.). While the bird seems to be as large as a golden eagle, this is largely an illusion because of the huge head, the long tail, and the amazing denseness of the bird's plumage. The owl's actual body is not much larger than that of the Northern Barred Owl (*Strix varia varia*) and quite a good bit smaller than either the Great Horned Owl or the Snowy Owl (*Nyctea scandiaca*).

Rank in over-all size among the eighteen species: Third.

SHAPE AT REST

Always a very bulky-appearing owl, the Great Gray Owl perches in a relatively upright position, wears a rather scholarly expression, and has a medium piercing gaze. When walking it moves slowly, rather awkwardly, and with a decided heaviness of character, though it is not anywhere near as heavy in body weight as it appears. It seems to be almost without a neck because of the enormity of the great rounded head, which is usually about 20 inches in circumference and seems to emerge directly from the bird's shoulders without benefit of neck. It seems all out of proportion to the body.

SHAPE IN FLIGHT

The wingbeats of the Great Gray Owl are generally slow and ponderous and not quite so graceful or assured as are those of the Barred Owls, Horned Owls, or Snowy Owl. The illusion of necklessness is continued in flight, as the head is couched heavily on the shoulders, imparting a silhouette in flight of considerable stubbiness, despite the broad expanse of wings. The tail, unusually long for an owl, is quite apparent in flight and when perched. The Great Gray Owl always appears to be a much larger bird than it actually is.

FLIGHT PATTERN

This owl does not have the buoyancy and lightness in flight that is exhibited by most owls and it rarely flies more than 20 feet high, actually preferring to range across its hunting territory at heights of less than 10 feet and frequently only two or three feet off the ground. The wings beat ponderously and there is very little gliding. However, there is no fluctuation of the body to the wingbeats, as is the case with the Snowy Owl, which undulates markedly in flight. The Great Gray Owl is not especially graceful in flight and it seldom—except during migration—flies great distances before coming to perch. Normal flight is relatively short, from one low perch to another, almost always landing very close to the trunk of the tree selected as a perch.

Measurements have been based on 13 measured birds: 5 males and 8 females.

WEIGHT

Species average: 1,340.0 gr. (46.9 oz.).

	Male	Female
Average	1,288.8 gr. (45.1 oz.)	1,390.9 gr. (48.7 oz.)
Minimum	1,056.8 gr. (37.0 oz.)	1,077.5 gr. (37.7 oz.)
Maximum	1,384.6 gr. (48.5 oz.)	1,523.9 gr. (53.3 oz.)

Rank in weight among the eighteen species: Third.

TOTAL LENGTH

Species average: 704.9 mm. (27.8″).

	Male	Female
Average	692.2 mm. (27.3″)	717.6 mm. (28.3″)
Minimum	617.3 mm. (24.3″)	670.2 mm. (26.4″)
Maximum	755.7 mm. (29.8″)	845.3 mm. (33.3″)

Rank in total length among the eighteen species: First.

WINGSPAN

Species average: 1,409.7 mm. (55.5″).

	Male	Female
Average	1,397.0 mm. (55.0″)	1,422.4 mm. (56.0″)
Minimum	1,303.8 mm. (51.4″)	1,412.3 mm. (55.6″)
Maximum	1,447.3 mm. (57.0″)	1,524.8 mm. (60.1″)

Rank in wingspan among the eighteen species: Third.

INDIVIDUAL WING LENGTH

Species average: 388.2 mm. (15.3″).

	Male	Female
Average	379.3 mm. (14.9″)	397.0 mm. (15.6″)
Minimum	358.2 mm. (14.1″)	381.1 mm. (15.0″)
Maximum	386.8 mm. (15.2″)	426.2 mm. (16.8″)

Rank in wing length among the eighteen species: Third.

TAIL LENGTH

Species average: 311.6 mm. (12.4″).

	Male	Female
Average	299.2 mm. (11.9″)	323.9 mm. (12.8″)
Minimum	287.0 mm. (11.3″)	305.2 mm. (12.0″)
Maximum	335.7 mm. (13.2″)	344.8 mm. (13.6″)

Rank in tail length among the eighteen species: First.

BEAK LENGTH

Species average: 37.7 mm. (1.5″).

	Male	Female
Average	32.1 mm. (1.3″)	43.2 mm. (1.7″)
Minimum	28.0 mm. (1.1″)	35.6 mm. (1.4″)
Maximum	42.5 mm. (1.7″)	47.0 mm. (1.9″)

Rank in beak length among the eighteen species: First.

LEGS, FEET, TALONS

The legs and feet are completely and rather heavily feathered to the base of the talons, and this feathering is rather finely barred with gray white and slatish gray. The talons are a dull lead color, becoming more deeply black toward the tips. The feet of the Great Gray Owl are somewhat small for the size of the bird and this fact may be contributory toward its awkwardness when walking on the ground. Though small, the feet are by no means weak.

EYES AND VISION

The iris of the eye of *Strix nebulosa nebulosa* is a bright lemon yellow, and though the eyes are actually quite large, they appear to be small because of the enormous bulk of the head and the expansive facial disks enclosing five dark gray concentric circles around each eye. Vision is excellent both during the night and in the daytime. In the more northerly parts of its range, the Great Gray Owl hunts more by day than by night and sees well at all times. It has been known to observe a mouse moving through the grasses at distances of well over 100 yards. Vision plays a strong role in hunting, equaling the role played by hearing, instead of being subordinate to hearing as in many other North American owl species.

EARS AND HEARING

While the ear cavities are slightly asymmetrical, to aid in pinpointing the sound of prey, the asymmetry is not quite as marked as in some other owl species of this continent. Consequently, hearing is not as extremely important a factor in the Great Gray Owl's hunting as it is with those other owl species—such as the Saw-whet Owl (*Aegolius acadicus acadicus*)—where asymmetry extremes of the ear cavities are reached. This is not to say that the hearing of the Great Gray Owl is poor or not beneficial to the bird. Quite the contrary; but whereas many other owl species depend far more upon their ears than upon their eyes for locating prey, the Great Gray Owl depends equally upon eyes and ears in hunting and would be greatly hampered by the loss of either sense. Its ear openings are large and have conspicuous anterior flaps which can be outspread at will as an aid to sound locating.

EAR TUFTS, PLUMAGE, ANNUAL MOLT

The Great Gray Owl has no ear tufts, the top of the head being quite smoothly rounded. No other North American owl species has plumage so dense and fluffy. Even that of the Snowy Owl, which is remarkably dense, is more tightly compacted to the body form than is that of the Great Gray Owl. This density and fluffiness of plumage in *Strix nebulosa nebulosa* is as much as three inches thick, providing the big bird with an effectively insulating blanket against temperatures which often plunge to more than —50° F. Because of the density of the plumage, the Great Gray Owl appears to be larger in over-all size and body weight than either the Great Horned Owl or Snowy Owl, but such is not the case, since it is a good bit lighter than either bird. Adult Great Gray Owls undergo one complete annual molt which begins in mid-July. The wing feathers molt first, over a period of several weeks, then the body plumage. New and old primary feathers will be found in the wings at the same time. The molt is completed by the end of November normally, but occasionally not until as late as early December.

VOICE

There are three basic calls uttered by the Great Gray Owl, and very little tonal difference between the calls of male and female birds. The most common call is a very deep, booming, four-note utterance which is usually repeated at least three times at intervals of about 15 seconds. Often this call will be sounded as many as eight or ten times. It has the sound of *WHOOOO-OOO-OOO-OOO* and is not greatly dissimilar to that of the Great Horned Owl.

The second most common call uttered is a far-carrying but rather soft and lyrically musical whistle, repeated as often as twenty times in succession. This rather unusual call has the sound of: *OOOO-EEE-HHHH*.

Finally, there is a low, occasionally uttered cry of a decidedly tremulous nature not unlike that of the Eastern Screech Owl (*Otus asio naevius*) in structure, but considerably louder and farther-carrying.

SEXUAL DIFFERENCES: SIZE, COLORATION, VOICE

The female bird is distinctly larger than the male and almost always exceeds his body weight by about half a pound and his body length and wingspan by at least an inch each. However, there is no appreciable difference between the sexes in vocal qualities or in coloration and pattern of markings.

MORTALITY AND LONGEVITY

Few studies have been completed in these aspects of the Great Gray Owl's natural history but, in view of its nesting habits and lack of natural enemies, early mortality is probably not as high as in many other owl species. No information is available on the lifespan of wild birds, but captive Great Gray Owls have lived for upward of forty years.

The Great Gray Owl (*Strix nebulosa nebulosa*) appears to be a much larger bird than it actually is, because of the great density of the plumage. The rendition at upper right depicts how this heavy plumage covers the actual body of the bird. Also, because of the dense feathering and the concentric rings encircling the eyes, the eyes themselves seem to be rather small.

dark area will
illustrate heavily feathered
body

Great Gray Owl

KE.K

COLORATION AND MARKINGS: ADULT

The general coloration of the bird is a mottled gray without any distinctive brownish cast. More specifically, the upperparts are a dusky slate gray to sooty brown gray, and this is broken by deeper mottlings of very dark gray black interspersed with grayish-white mottlings, mostly on the edges of the feathers. The center of each feather is uniformly sooty in coloration and produces an over-all effect of irregular dark stripes which are most conspicuous on the shoulders and across the back. The same central sooty gray of each feather continues on the plumage of breast, neck, belly, sides, and flanks, but on these feathers the whitish edges are more uniformly barred. There is a more profuse mottling of grayish and black on the rump and uppertail coverts, which contributes to the general gray aspect of the bird.

The outer webs of the feathers on the wing coverts have distinctive whitish mottlings and the primary coverts have relatively indistinct bands of pale ash brown. Nine bands of grayish brown mark the outer webs of the secondaries, with the final band continuing to the tip and the innermost three being concealed by the greater coverts. The primaries themselves are crossed by nine rather square patterns of brownish gray on the outer webs, with those nearest the tips of the feathers being less distinct than those closer to the flesh. Rather coarse mottlings or even marblings of sooty brown and sooty grayish white tend to make a pattern of irregular broken bars across the inner secondaries and the middle tail feathers. The remainder of the tail is generally dusky in color and crossed by about nine somewhat smaller and paler grayish bands.

The lores and superciliaries are usually distinctly grayish white and form two opposing crescents between the eyes. There is a very dark area on the chin directly beneath the beak, and a deeply dusky-colored space between eye and lores. The facial disks are a clear light gray with (usually) five concentric, narrow, semicircular bands of deep brown gray. The narrow facial rim is dark brown, passing into ash white on the foreneck and broken by a spot of brownish black on the throat. Iris coloration, which is usually a clear lemon yellow, may sometimes be a deeper straw color.

COLORATION AND MARKINGS: JUVENILE

Juveniles in first-winter plumage are very little different in coloration and markings from adults. Downy young, however, are a buffy white in general coloration, with the down feathers on the hindneck, shoulders, wings, and back being a dark sooty brown at the base and pale, dull, brownish buff at the tips.

GENERAL HABITS AND CHARACTERISTICS

A reasonably fearless bird—whose fearlessness is mistakenly interpreted by some as being stupidity—the Great Gray Owl is not easily put to flight. It is, however, scarcely as aggressive and antagonistic an owl as the Great Horned Owl.

Never at any time a gregarious species, *Strix nebulosa* prefers a relative solitude, even during the late autumn migrational period.

Although virtually diurnal in the northerly portions of its range, it becomes far more crepuscular and nocturnal in the southern portions.

HABITAT AND ROOSTING

Although a bird of the far north, the Great Gray Owl has a decided preference for timbered areas and rarely strays far out into the tundra barrens and muskeg marshes, as does the Snowy Owl and, to a lesser extent, the Arctic Horned Owl (*Bubo virginianus subarcticus*). Dense forests of pine and fir are most favored, although this bird will often be found during migrational periods in the brackish tidal meadows near costal river mouths and in more lush meadows farther inland, especially if they are traversed by streams and have a scattering of small spruce trees.

More often than not the roosting choice is a well-hidden location within the mid or low recesses of an especially dense evergreen, with the bird perched very close to the trunk of the tree and frequently even leaning against it as it sleeps.

ENEMIES AND DEFENSES

Although *Strix nebulosa nebulosa* will sometimes arouse to anger enough to snap its beak irritably, spread its wings threateningly, and give voice to a peculiar growling sound, it is essentially very non-aggressive and has often been caught by hand during daylight hours.

Young birds in the nest are sometimes taken by Horned Owls (*Bubo virginianus* sp.), martens, and wolverines, but the adults have no really deadly natural enemy. Man, of course, constitutes its greatest threat, particularly during the southward migrations. At such times, hunters will often shoot the bird to have it mounted as a trophy. Some of the northern Indian tribes still kill the bird as food, but more as an emergency measure than as a staple item. Far more regularly, the eggs are gathered by Indian women as a food source.

Surprisingly, in view of its large size, the Great Gray Owl is rarely bothered by harassing jays, warblers, kingbirds, shrikes, or other smaller birds. Oddly, this owl evinces the greatest agitation when it spies a prowling cat or dog; it remains very nervous until that particular animal has moved out of range.

HUNTING METHODS AND CARRYING OF PREY

Although as a general rule the Great Gray Owl most actively hunts during the early morning and late afternoon and evening hours, there is no time of day or night when it cannot be seen engaged in hunting. Unlike the Snowy Owl, however, it does not often care to range back and forth close to the ground in search of prey. Rather, it prefers to move frequently from one low perch to another. It will sit low in a tree for anywhere from a couple of minutes to a quarter-hour, then wing ponderously—and usually no more than a few feet off the ground—to another tree not very far distant. From such perches it watches and listens for prey which, when detected, it attacks with great accuracy.

Prey is killed by the clutching feet driving the huge talons deeply into the prey animal's body and most often piercing the heart. Smaller prey is normally carried in the beak. Larger prey is most often torn apart on the spot where killed and is eaten there but, if carried whole to the nest, is transported in the feet.

FOOD, FEEDING HABITS, WASTES

All prey up to and including the size of a red squirrel, and occasionally even larger, is swallowed whole without difficulty. Larger creatures are quickly torn apart by the powerful beak into huge chunks just within the limits of being swallowed and are devoured with no attempt to first dispose of bones, feathers, or fur.

Pellets are ejected regularly and are relatively large, averaging about three to four inches in length and one to two inches in width. They are ejected at random wherever the bird happens to be perched, and usually this occurs just prior to the bird taking wing.

Fecal material is somewhat more dense and less viscous than in many other owls, and is of a marbled coloration when fresh—greenish, grayish, brownish, and black. Feces normally drop beneath where the bird is perched. Evacuation of such wastes rarely, if ever, occurs during flight.

There are few small animals that are not considered as prey by *Strix nebulosa nebulosa,* although it tends to seek, most specifically, rats, mice, shrews, squirrels,

rabbits, and hares, along with occasional birds up to the size of grouse and ptarmigan. Not infrequently it feeds upon crows; these being taken by the owl as they roost. During migration into more populated areas to the south, poultry is readily taken.

COURTSHIP AND MATING

Although the male will engage in a certain amount of peculiar flight maneuvers before the perched female, and just as often alight on the ground before her and march about in a rather ridiculous, pompous manner, there is little actual courtship demonstration beyond this. Now and again, though not as a general rule, the male will present the female with a freshly killed prey animal, usually a mouse or rat. Little vocal ceremony is involved. Actual copulation seems more apt to occur on the ground than on a perch. Though male and female remain together throughout the nesting season and perhaps remain mated for years, there is little demonstration of affection between them other than that which immediately precedes copulation.

ANNUAL BROODS, NEST, NESTING HABITS

The Great Gray Owl has only one brood per year, though there is some indication that a second laying will occur if the first nest is destroyed. There is no evidence that a third clutch of eggs will be laid if the second is lost. In by far the greater majority of cases, the nest choice of the Great Gray Owl is an abandoned nest of a Goshawk, Red-tailed Hawk, or Broad-winged Hawk. Some attempt is made to refurbish the nest, but this effort is haphazard at best. Some new twigs may be added, along with fragments of mosses and somewhat more feathers than most owls will use. Often green pine needles will be added, as well as tufts of deer hair, sphagnum, shredded bark, and rootlets.

Though the nest may be in either a hardwood or conifer, *Strix nebulosa nebulosa* shows a preference for those which are relatively high—50 to 100 feet—in a dense spruce or fir. However, sometimes nests will be used in rather unprotected cottonwoods or other deciduous trees and as close to the ground as 12 or 15 feet.

Once established in its nest, the Great Gray Owl will stick determinedly with it, despite the efforts of any intruder to make it leave. Even the pounding of a club on the tree trunk will have little effect other than to make the owl glare downward at the disturbance. If, as occurs on rare occasions, it does decide to leave the nest, it will usually fly to an adjacent tree, remain there briefly as it moves about on its perch nervously, then return to the nest.

EGGS

Number per nesting From two to five eggs are laid, but most commonly three.

Color Dull white and often with a peculiarly spoiled look about them, even though they are not spoiled.

Shape Not quite so globular as in many other North American owl species; ranging between oval and elliptically oval, and normally more pointed at one end than the other.

Texture Quite roughly granulated, with no gloss.

Size For the size of the owl, it lays relatively small eggs. Based on the measurements of 65 eggs, the average egg size for the species is 55.3 mm. (2.2″) in length and 43.9 mm. (1.7″) in width. Extreme measurements were:

Maximum length: 58.8 mm. (2.3″)
Minimum length: 48.3 mm. (1.9″)
Maximum width: 49.0 mm. (1.9″)
Minimum width: 41.9 mm. (1.7″)

Interval of egg-laying No less than 48 hours between eggs and more often closer to a week apart.

Egg-laying dates Earliest, March 23; latest, July 19; normally between April 9 and May 1.

INCUBATION AND BROODING CHARACTERISTICS

The incubating female has bare thighs and lower abdomen and the flesh in these areas is well layered with fat. Whether the loss of feathers here is a natural breeding loss, or the feathers have been deliberately plucked away by the female, is not known. The incubation begins with the first egg laid and continues for from 28 to 30 days before hatching. All, or almost all, incubation is performed by the female.

YOUNG AND FAMILY LIFE CHARACTERISTICS

Extensive observation of nestling life has not yet been recorded, but certain spaced observations have been made which provide some illumination in regard to the young birds. Newly hatched birds are covered with a somewhat woollier and denser down than that of most other owls on this continent. The down is al-most pure white at hatching, but within a day or so begins assuming an ashy-bluff coloration.

By the time the nestling is two weeks old, the down is being forced out by a downy plumage which is essentially olive brownish in general coloration.

Fledglings almost ready to leave the nest exhibit nearly fully developed wings and tail which are indistinguishable from those of adult birds. The underparts, however, are still clad in soft juvenal plumage, each feather a dusky white and having three or four sooty-gray bands, and these feathers broadly tipped with white. Long, fluffy down remains on flanks and thighs and is a grayish white with pale sooty-olive bands. The downy plumage still around the neck is similarly banded with olive brownish and pale buff. Adult plumage is nearly fully developed on the back, scapulars, and wing coverts. Facial disks are not yet fully developed, nor has the head yet taken its enormous globular shape.

By the end of the first week in September, the young birds are flying well. They are at this time equal to the size of their parents and have assumed most of the distinguishing physical characteristics of the adult bird, the only significant difference being that the head and facial disks are still somewhat small, and some vestige of downy plumage remains on the throat and underparts, giving the young bird a slightly unkempt look.

DISTRIBUTION IN NORTH AMERICA

Strix nebulosa nebulosa breeds in the boreal forests from central Alaska (Nulato, Fort Yukon), northern Yukon (La Pierre House), northern Mackenzie (Anderson River), central Keewatin, northern Manitoba and northern Ontario (Severn River), south to the central Sierra Nevada in California (Madera County, Yosemite), northern Idaho (Fort Sherman), western Montana (Lincoln County), Wyoming (Moose), northern Minnesota (near Roseau), and in the Nipissing District of Ontario. It is found in summer in Gaspé County, Quebec.

Although it usually winters within its breeding range, irregularly over the years it does move southward and

XIV SHORT-EARED OWL
Asio flammeus flammeus (Pontoppidan). Female. Vicinity of Glen Ellyn, Du Page County, Illinois, November 10, 1969. A.O.U. Number 367

XV EASTERN SCREECH OWL
Otus asio naevius (Gmelin). 3 young, female, male. Young: Northlake, Cook County, Illinois, May 19, 1962. Gray-phase female: Vicinity of Forest Park, Cook County, Illinois, January 10, 1968. Red-phase male: two miles south of Bensenville, Cook County, Illinois, February 6, 1948. A.O.U. Number 373-M

Karl E. Karalus

Karl E. Karalus
1972

eastward to northern California (at lower elevations to Butte County), southern Montana (Billings), southern Minnesota (Goodhue County), Wisconsin (Racine), Michigan, New York (Painted Post, Fulton County), and Massachusetts (Springfield).

Casual to southern Idaho (St. Anthony), Nebraska (Omaha), Iowa (Hillsboro), northernmost Illinois (Rock River, Zion), Indiana (Posey County), Ohio (Clark County), and New Jersey (Mendham).

MIGRATION

The migrations of the Great Gray Owl are essentially sporadic and dependent upon cyclic levels of small mammal life in the North. In some years there is scarcely any southward movement at all; in others, a rather heavy general movement of the species to the South. The winter movement, when it occurs, seems to move as much in an eastward direction as a southward one. Nearly all the records for eastern North America occur between October and March.

ECONOMIC INFLUENCE

Decidedly detrimental to populations of grouse and ptarmigan, and undoubtedly the root of certain economic losses to poultry raisers during those years when southward migration becomes more extensive. Yet, these detrimental factors are largely offset by the highly beneficial and much more extensive predation at all times upon mice, rats, and other destructive rodents.

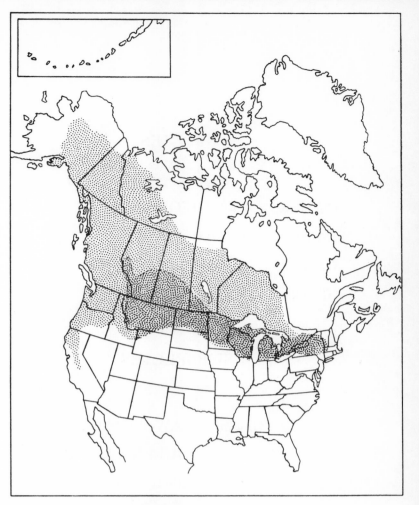

GREAT GRAY OWL

Strix nebulosa nebulosa Forster

XVI AIKEN'S SCREECH OWL

Otus asio aikeni (Brewster). Male. South slope of Eagle Mountain, El Paso County, Colorado, June 3, 1933. A.O.U. Number 373-G

SPECIES

ORDER: STRIGIFORMES

FAMILY: STRIGIDAE

GENUS: *Aegolius* Kaup

SPECIES: *acadicus* (Gmelin)

SUBSPECIES

acadicus (Gmelin) SAW-WHET OWL

brooksi (Fleming) QUEEN CHARLOTTE
OWL

SAW-WHET OWL
(COLOR PLATE IX)

SCIENTIFIC NAME AND ORIGINAL DESCRIPTION

Aegolius acadicus acadicus (Gmelin). Original description: *Strix acadica* Gmelin, *Systematica Natura*, Volume 1, Part 1, 1788, page 296, based on the Acadian Owl of Latham (*Gen. Syn.*, Vol. 1, p. 149); in America *Septentrionali*, from Nova Scotia. Former scientific names: *Nyctale albifrons, Nyctale acadica, Strix frontalis, Strix passerina, Cryptoglaux acadica acadica, Strix acadica.*

OTHER NAMES

ACADIAN OWL Because of the geographical location of a part of this owl's range.

ACADIAN SAW-WHET OWL For geographical location in part, and for the tonal quality of one of its calls.

KIRTLAND'S OWL Honorary name.

LA CHOUETTE DES GRANGES DE L'EST French-Canadian name meaning "The Barn Owl of the East."

LA PETITE NYCTALE French-Canadian name meaning "The Little Night Owl."

TECOLOTITO CABEZÓN DE GMELIN Mexican-Indian name meaning "Gmelin's Little Big-headed Owl."

SPARROW OWL Because of its diminutive size, as well as for its predeliction for preying upon sparrows.

WHITE-FRONTED OWL After the generally light coloration of breast and belly plumage.

DISTINGUISHING FEATURES

The Saw-whet Owl is the smallest of the eastern owls and easily distinguishable from the Screech Owl (*Otus asio* sp.) in that it is not only a bit smaller but has a well-rounded head without ear tufts. Its face is rather shallow and the facial disks are small, thus making the eyes appear quite disproportionately large and imparting an appealing, somewhat sorrowful expression to the bird. Not much larger than a fat sparrow when perched, this little owl is rarely seen by the casual woodland visitor because of its small size, nocturnal habits, and the difficulty of the visitor in moving about in the type of terrain the owl prefers.

Aegolius acadicus acadicus is not likely to be mistaken within its range for any other owl, with the possible exception of Richardson's Owl (*Aegolius funereus richardsoni*), but it is noticeably smaller than Richardson's, its beak is black instead of yellow, and it is lighter in general coloration. It also lacks the prominent black rim around the facial disk which is so evident in Richardson's Owl. Further, the Saw-whet Owl's crown is streaked rather than spotted.

One of the most peculiar and appealing characteristics of the Saw-whet Owl is the seemingly impossible positions into which it moves its head—sometimes with its chin virtually resting on its feet, sometimes with the face looking straight backward, as if the head had been put on a full 180° off kilter, and even more startlingly, turning its head so amazingly that the eyes are below the beak as it stares balefully at an intruder. In this latter position it seems that the head has somehow been taken off and then reattached upside down. The tail is short and blunt, and the head seems not only oversized but badly misshapen because of the grossly asymmetrical ear construction.

Rank in over-all size among the eighteen species: Thirteenth.

SHAPE AT REST

Although like all the North American owls it has a reversible toe and is capable of perching with three toes forward and one behind, as well as with two forward and two behind, it nevertheless invariably perches with two toes forward. When perched it appears to be much smaller than when in flight, largely because of the oversized wing expanse for a bird of this length. Its coloration blends extremely well with a sunlight-dappled background, and it is often overlooked as it sits motionlessly on its roost. This is not always easy for the bird, for when awake it seems to have a difficult time sitting still; the head seems to want to bob constantly, and the bird is continually swiveling its head to look in various directions with what appears to be unlimited curiosity. It also tends to shuffle about considerably on its perch. The tail is held downward when the bird is perched.

SHAPE IN FLIGHT

In flight, the body of this owl seems abnormally short for the expanse and breadth of wings, imparting a vague batlike quality to it, especially when observed at dusk. In flight, the tail is rarely spread and is so short that it may even seem to be absent.

FLIGHT PATTERN

The flight pattern of *Aegolius acadicus acadicus* is very rapid and distinctive, usually suggestive of the flight of a woodcock, though with slightly more of an undulative character, like a woodpecker. Hunters have often mistaken it for a woodcock when it flushes. When emerging from its hole in a tree, the Saw-whet Owl drops swiftly to near the forest floor, wings rapidly to where it wishes to go, and then rises sharply to take its perch at about the height from which it originally dropped.

On occasion, the wings of this little owl will beat alternatively, especially when it is maneuvering through tangled thickets. At such times the flight becomes particularly jerky in character.

Measurements have been based on 68 measured birds: 37 males and 31 females.

WEIGHT

Species average: 104.4 gr. (3.7 oz.).

	Male	Female
Average	101.5 gr. (3.6 oz.)	107.2 gr. (3.8 oz.)
Minimum	84.3 gr. (3.0 oz.)	87.9 gr. (3.1 oz.)
Maximum	119.2 gr. (4.2 oz.)	124.1 gr. (4.3 oz.)

Rank in weight among the eighteen species: Fifteenth.

TOTAL LENGTH

Species average: 196.4 gr. (7.7″).

	Male	Female
Average	194.3 mm. (7.7″)	198.6 mm. (7.8″)
Minimum	179.1 mm. (7.1″)	183.5 mm. (7.2″)
Maximum	203.2 mm. (8.0″)	217.2 mm. (8.6″)

Rank in total length among the eighteen species: Thirteenth.

WINGSPAN

Species average: 504.8 mm. (19.9″).

	Male	Female
Average	494.0 mm. (19.5″)	515.6 mm. (20.3″)
Minimum	458.5 mm. (18.1″)	478.8 mm. (18.9″)
Maximum	516.9 mm. (20.4″)	562.6 mm. (22.2″)

Rank in wingspan among the eighteen species: Thirteenth.

INDIVIDUAL WING LENGTH

Species average: 136.8 mm. (5.4″).

	Male	Female
Average	133.2 mm. (5.3″)	140.3 mm. (5.5″)
Minimum	127.0 mm. (5.0″)	131.6 mm. (5.2″)
Maximum	139.2 mm. (5.5″)	144.9 mm. (5.7″)

Rank in wing length among the eighteen species: Fifteenth.

TAIL LENGTH

Species average: 71.8 mm. (2.8″).

	Male	Female
Average	70.3 mm. (2.8″)	73.3 mm. (2.9″)
Minimum	66.9 mm. (2.6″)	69.9 mm. (2.8″)
Maximum	72.4 mm. (2.9″)	74.0 mm. (2.9″)

Rank in tail length among the eighteen species: Fifteenth.

BEAK LENGTH

Species average: 12.0 mm. (0.5″).

	Male	Female
Average	11.7 mm. (0.5″)	12.3 mm. (0.5″)
Minimum	11.5 mm. (0.5″)	11.7 mm. (0.5″)
Maximum	11.8 mm. (0.5″)	13.0 mm. (0.5″)

Rank in beak length among the eighteen species: Fourteenth.

LEGS, FEET, TALONS

The feet of the Saw-whet Owl are quite small, although not disproportionately so for the size of the bird. The toes are trim and rather gracefully formed, terminating in very long, well-curved, sharply tapering talons which are jet black. The legs and feet are thickly feathered to the last ball of the toe, and the scales of this final naked portion are a pale dull yellowish.

EYES AND VISION

The eyes of *Aegolius acadicus acadicus* are quite large, with brilliant yellow irides. The bird's night vision is excellent, but it tends to exhibit some difficulty seeing well in bright sunshine. Despite this fact, the Saw-whet Owl will occasionally be witnessed hunting on heavily overcast days. Evidently its sight, whether it is hunting by day or night, is not as important in location of prey as is its hearing.

EARS AND HEARING

This little owl has extremely acute hearing. It has been attracted from quite phenomenal distances by emulation of the squeak of a mouse. One observer, squeaking faintly to watch the reaction of an Eastern Screech Owl (*Otus asio naevius*) in a tree, watched a Saw-whet Owl streak with unerring accuracy directly toward the sound he was making, the bird coming from a wooded area over half a mile distant across a meadow. So intent was the owl on the sound that the observer had to throw up his hands to ward it off. Even then the owl circled him twice at very close range before arrowing back toward the distant woods from which it had emerged.

The ear cavities of this little owl are so huge and so asymmetrical in size, shape, and placement that the skull is oddly misshapen and the head of the living bird often appears to be badly distorted. Quite frequently when perched it will lean forward and raise one or the other of the ear flaps located at the back curve of the facial rim and listen intently. More often than not, after a moment or so, it will drop from its perch, skim along over the ground, and with uncanny accuracy suddenly plunge to fasten its talons in a mouse, shrew, grasshopper, or other creature which made the faint sound that the owl detected.

EAR TUFTS, PLUMAGE, ANNUAL MOLT

The Saw-whet Owl has no ear tufts. Its plumage is exquisitely soft and delicate, neatly overlaid and with all flight feathers well fluted for perfectly soundless

flight. There is one annual complete molt which begins about early August and is completed by mid-November.

VOICE

The somewhat metallic string of notes this owl utters, which have been rather grossly likened to the filing of a saw—and the call for which the bird has been named—is really not the unpleasant sound one might expect. Nor is it the most common call that the Saw-whet Owl utters. This supposed saw-filing call, uttered primarily during courtship—mainly from mid-March to late April—is rarely very harsh in nature and, though it has a decided metallic ring to it, the sound is pleasantly muted. It has a sound like *SWEEE-awwww SWEEE-awwww SWEEE-awwww SWEEE-awwww* and once the owl has begun voicing it, he may continue the call most of the night without appreciable pause.

Another relatively common metallic-sounding note this owl makes has a decidedly anvil-like ringing quality. It is usually uttered in groups of four notes, each of the four following one another rapidly, then a pause of about five seconds before the next set of four is begun. The entire calling session of this song may last for as long as ten minutes. As closely transliterated as possible, the song sounds like: *TAAAaannggg-TAAA-aannggg-TAAAaannggg-TAAAaannggg.*

Again during courtship, the male often voices a series of three notes every two seconds, and this call may also last throughout much of the night. It is rather melodious and quite a pleasantly soft little call, sounded in a rather breathless manner, but never imperatively given. It sounds like: *WHOOOOOK-WHO-OOOOK-WHOOOOOK.*

Probably the most common utterance made by this bird—a call which may be heard at practically any time of the year—is a questioning, rather raspy sound of low timbre, sounding like: *SSSsss-haaayyyyyyyyy-y—y-y-y.* It is not far-carrying and is seldom audible beyond a distance of 100 feet.

As with many owls, especially the smaller species, the Saw-whet Owl is capable of producing remarkably ventriloquistic effects. The authors have actually watched one of these interesting little owls calling from a branch about 20 feet in front of us and yet both of us were utterly convinced for a time that another owl was calling, first from behind us, then off to the left, and finally from far ahead of us past the owl we were watching. It was only through associating the sounds we were hearing with the movements of the bird's beak as it sang that we were able to convince ourselves that the bird we were watching was the one who was doing all the singing.

One of the more pleasant calls for which the Saw-whet Owl is noted is a very melodious, tinkling sound that just cannot be reproduced in print but which has the remarkable quality of sounding almost exactly like a tricklet of water falling into a quiet little pool.

Next to the Barred Owls (*Strix varia* sp.) and the Spotted Owls (*Strix occidentalis* sp.), the Saw-whet Owl probably has the widest variety of calls among North American owls. As with those larger species, many of the calls have numerous variations given at different times. No attempt will be made to enumerate or emulate them here, but one other call is quite worthy of noting. This is a very gentle and very pleasing little mouselike squeaking that is both harmonious and surprisingly far-carrying. Not infrequently, tamed Saw-whet Owls will respond to a gentle stroking of their backs by uttering this delightful sound.

SEXUAL DIFFERENCES:
SIZE, COLORATION, VOICE

While there is no difference in coloration, markings, or voice between the sexes, the female is slightly the larger.

MORTALITY AND LONGEVITY

Aegolius acadicus acadicus seems to be particularly susceptible to sudden, unexpected snowstorms accompanied by severe temperature drops during which time prey virtually disappears and the high metabolic rate of the owl cannot be adequately refueled. Numerous times in the past, large numbers of these little owls have been found dead following such inclemencies. No reliable information seems to be available regarding expected lifespan in the wild, although several zoos have reported that specimens in their collections have lived for over eight years.

COLORATION AND MARKINGS:
ADULT

The general color of the crown, back, and other upperparts is a rich Vandyke brown. The crown itself is narrowly streaked with short, irregular white lines; these streaks often are restricted to just the forehead and sides of the crown. On the lower hindneck there are large spots of white, mostly triangular in shape, but largely concealed by overlying plumage. The shoulder feathers are margined terminally in brown, but with the outer webs mostly white. A few white spots speckle the outer wing coverts, mainly on the larger

feathers. The outer edges of the outermost primaries are spotted with white along their lengths. Two or three narrow and usually interrupted bands of white cross the tail. The tail tip has a white margin. The "eyebrows" (superciliaries), lores, and chin are a dull white, as is the ground color of the facial disks. A dusky coloration surrounds the eyes, especially off the outside corners, and extends downward along the facial rim. A band of chestnut-brown to dark-brown spots outlines the bottom of the facial rim at the throat and extends on each side to the ear ruff; sometimes, but not always, forming a patch of the same speckling on the upper throat. Sides of the head are streaked with brown and white.

The entire underparts are basically white or buff-tinged white and broadly but irregularly striped (except for the median line) with chestnut brown. The undertail coverts are usually pure white, but sometimes may have indistinct little spottings of brown, these spottings sometimes becoming elongated into short streaks. Leg plumage varies from cinnamon buff to a very pale buff, and the foot plumage is a pale buffy white. The inner webs of the primaries and secondaries on the underside have large spots of white on grayish brown.

COLORATION AND MARKINGS:
JUVENILE

Only the wing and tail feathers are identical to those of the adult birds. The superciliaries and the forward portion of the forehead are white, in strong contrast to the uniformly blackish brown to lighter brown of the ear region. The rest of the crown, along with all the upperparts except on tail and wings, is plain deep brown. The chin and sides of the throat are dull white. The entire breast is an unblemished brown that is lighter than the brown of the upperparts. All the remaining underparts are unmarked tawny buff to cinnamon buff. The facial disks are blackish brown except between and over the eyes, where they are whitish. Such marked difference between juvenal and adult plumage is practically unique among North American owls, and for some time juvenal birds of this subspecies were thought to be a different species of owl entirely. However, the full juvenal plumage is worn for only a few weeks after the young bird has left the nest.

GENERAL HABITS AND
CHARACTERISTICS

The Saw-whet Owl has inordinate patience. If some manner of prey should happen to elude it under a log or rock or in a hole, the owl will take a perch as closely overhead as possible and wait for hours, if necessary, for the reappearance of the animal. Usually the patience reaps its expected reward.

Relatively fearless, the Saw-whet Owl does not take alarm too easily and may be approached rather closely if spotted at roost. It is reasonably sociable where humans are concerned and not infrequently will come quite close to a campfire and join the campers grouped around it, even to the point of perching on a convenient shoulder. Nor is it hesitant about entering a camper's tent. Occasionally this bird will be found deep within the confines of a major city. The author observed one for a considerable while as it perched and preened itself on a window ledge of the Wrigley Building in downtown Chicago. However, though relatively tame, it is far more often heard than seen. This is probably because of its remarkably well-developed ventriloquistic abilities, as well as its small size, protective coloring, and retiring habits.

Despite its small size, *Aegolius acadicus acadicus* is extremely fierce with prey and has been known to kill a mammal as large as a cottontail rabbit, although it rarely attacks any creature larger than a full-grown rat.

The greatest likelihood of seeing one of these owls in the woods comes very early in the morning when it seems to delight in perching temporarily in full view atop the uppermost spire of a fir tree.

HABITAT AND ROOSTING

The Saw-whet Owl mainly prefers to keep to the deepest recesses of dense woods, strictly coniferous or mixed hardwoods and coniferous. It especially likes tangled swampy areas within such woods. It tends to frequent tamarack bogs, alder thickets, and heavy groves of cedar. Occasionally it will take up temporary residence in or around a barn and will remain there until it is either frightened off or the food supply of mice and rats has been exhausted through its hunting efforts.

By far the most preferred roosting site is in a dense conifer, especially a cedar—sometimes close to the trunk, but just as often on the outer branches, well camouflaged in the foliage. Quite often such a roosting branch will be within a foot or so of the ground, and once it has used a roost it will come back to it time and again. Dense vine clusters are also a favorite roosting site when such vines are in foliage, but not during the winter.

ENEMIES AND DEFENSES

The Saw-whet Owl's greatest natural enemies are larger owls of almost any species. Even the Screech Owl will not hesitate to attack and kill a Saw-whet Owl if the opportunity arises. Because of the owl's secluded habitat and retiring nature, man is not a considerable enemy except during the woodcock-hunting season, when owls are frequently shot by mistake because of their initially similar flight pattern to that of the woodcock.

Basically unaggressive, the Saw-whet Owl's principal defense is one of protective coloration. Its speckled appearance and small size so well camouflage it that quite often an observer standing only a few feet away will miss seeing the perched bird unless it moves. If it is seen at all under such circumstances, it is usually because the owl's hiding place has been discovered by one or more of the many smaller songbirds which delight in tormenting it wherever they find it—birds such as bush-tits, chickadees, kinglets, sparrows, and warblers, to name only a few.

HUNTING METHODS AND CARRYING OF PREY

Utterly fearless with any manner of prey it attacks, the little owl often does not eat its entire kill, but dines only on the head—or sometimes only the brains. It hunts more in the evening and early morning hours than any other time and exhibits remarkable inventiveness and versatility in hunting. Should it manage somehow to come upon a number of mice at the same time, it will quickly descend and snatch one and then, while holding it with one foot, pursue another and catch it with the second set of talons. If there are still others about at this point, it will finish killing those it is holding by swiftly tearing off the heads with its beak and then go after the living ones still remaining. In this way it has been known to kill five or six mice in rapid succession.

When the attack is launched, the owl arrows directly to the prey—say a mouse—and slams a sharply taloned foot to the middle of the furry back. As soon as contact is made, the talons jerk convulsively inward, penetrating deeply into the prey's body and almost always killing it instantly as the heart and other vital organs are punctured. While in the process of killing its prey, it ruffles its feathers and snaps its beak in agitation.

A variety of field sketches of the *Aegolius acadicus* subspecies, the Queen Charlotte Owl (*Aegolius acadius brooksi*) and the Saw-whet Owl (*Aegolius acadicus acadicus*). The normal sleeping posture of bird at middle left is on a slightly more forward-inclined plane than is common among most other North American owls.

Saw-whet Owl

Queen charlotte Owl
A. acadicus brooksi
very dark subspecies
28 Jan. 1938

Saw-whet Owl

Elk Grove, ILL.

Anger, rare attitude

K.E.K.

Except with very small prey, such as insects, the majority of prey is carried in the talons, and very often with only one foot doing the carrying. Insects and other quite small prey creatures are normally carried in the beak.

FOOD, FEEDING HABITS, WASTES

Regardless of what sort of prey it has killed, the Saw-whet Owl will almost invariably eat the head first. If the prey is large enough so that only head or brains are eaten, it will abandon the rest of the carcass. Most mice, shrews, insects, frogs, and other prey of this size will be swallowed whole in a series of convulsive, seemingly difficult gulpings. Although the Saw-whet Owl has been known to swallow whole an animal as large as a young flying squirrel, normally such larger prey is torn apart. An exceedingly voracious eater, it will regularly eat double its own weight in prey each night. With such an appetite, its digestive processes are necessarily very rapid. As many as four or five pellets may be regurgitated in a single night, and feces may be expelled at the rate of once or twice every ninety minutes.

Prey includes a wide variety of small animals: red-backed mice, house mice, woodland mice of all kinds, meadow voles, rats of different varieties, red squirrels, flying squirrels, bats, shrews, moles, young rabbits, and occasionally prey as potentially dangerous to the owl itself as the least weasel. Birds are also eaten—such as juncos, vireos, and warblers—but rodents and frogs seem to make up the bulk of the diet. Because of its high rate of metabolism, the Saw-whet Owl must eat often during its active periods. If denied food for more than a couple of days—such as when severe weather strikes and food becomes unobtainable—it will very suddenly weaken and die.

Most of the pellets this owl ejects—and they are always ejected with what is evidently great difficulty—fall to the ground beneath the bird's daytime roost. And, much along the line of the habits of the Barn Owl (*Tyto alba pratincola*), the Saw-whet Owl tends to "whitewash" the area below its roost with its droppings.

As many as 100 pellets—each about three-quarters of an inch long and half an inch wide—have been discovered on the ground beneath a roosting area. At the time of pellet regurgitation, the owl stands high on its perch, then crouches while leaning forward and gapes several times, simultaneously shaking its head violently back and forth sideways. At last the pellet, covered with a slick coating of mucus, flies out of the mouth as much as a foot from the bird and drops to the ground. Once the pellet is out, the little owl evinces a relieved aspect that is most comical to witness.

COURTSHIP AND MATING

As the female sits in relative serenity upon her perch, the male bird will circle her as many as fifteen or twenty times before alighting a foot or so away, normally on another branch. During this circling and after he lands, he voices a variety of calls which she appears to listen to with great attentiveness. Once he has landed he engages in a complex series of bobbings, shufflings, and maneuverings on foot which gradually bring him closer to her. Occasionally he will be holding a gift of an insect or some other small prey in one set of talons while he moves about. Finally, when he is only inches from her, he will drop the food and then move away a short distance and watch closely to see whether or not she will accept what he has offered. No case has been witnessed where she has refused it. Once she has in fact taken it into her beak and then swallowed it, the male breaks into a series of tooting calls of a pleasingly whistled nature. The female normally flies off while he is whistling and he follows her, continuing his call, which gradually fades away as the pair move out of hearing.

Copulation generally occurs on a branch at mid-height in a tree and lasts for only a few seconds, but it is repeated several times each night for several nights.

ANNUAL BROODS, NEST, NESTING HABITS

Double-brooding is not unknown to the Saw-whet Owl, although it is primarily single-brooded, and on a few recorded occasions, triple-brooding has occurred, although the success of the third nesting is unlikely, especially at higher altitudes. The first brooding normally takes place in April or May.

Almost invariably the nest is an abandoned flicker hole in a tree stub, although sometimes the holes of hairy woodpeckers are used. The cavity within the hole is about a foot deep and normally the hole is from 18 to 50 feet above the ground.

Reluctant to leave the nest once eggs have been laid, the owl will poke its head from the hole if the tree is banged with a branch, but it will rarely be alarmed enough to fly off.

EGGS

Number per nesting Three to seven eggs are laid, but usually four, five, or six. Five is the most common number, and six oftener than four.

Color Pure white and rarely nest-stained.

Shape Oval to slightly ovate and sometimes very nearly globular.

Texture Very smooth and moderately glossy, although the glossiness is variable and there may be dull eggs as well as highly shiny ones, though never in the same clutch.

Size Based on the measurements of 164 eggs, the average length is 30.5 mm. (1.2″) by an average width of 25.1 mm. (1.0″), with extremes of:

Maximum length: 31.5 mm. (1.2″)
Minimum length: 27.0 mm. (1.1″)
Maximum width: 28.3 mm. (1.1″)
Minimum width: 23.6 mm. (0.9″)

Interval of egg-laying No less than 24 hours apart and usually closer to 72 hours separating them.

Egg-laying dates Earliest, March 19; latest, July 3; normally between April 6 and May 2.

INCUBATION AND BROODING CHARACTERISTICS

Incubation is set at not less than 21 nor more than 29 days, with from 26 to 28 days the most likely figures. Although both parents assist in incubation and brooding of the young, most of this activity is accomplished by the female. Incubation begins with the first egg laid.

YOUNG AND FAMILY LIFE CHARACTERISTICS

Because of the interval of egg-laying and the fact that incubation begins with the first egg laid, newly hatched babies may be found in the same nest with fully fledged young.

When first hatched, the babies are very tiny, helpless, blind, and virtually naked, with only the scantiest covering of sparse white down. However, this down grows quite rapidly and the birds appear woolly within three days. By the fourth day they utter almost continuous liquid peepings. The eyes begin partially opening on the eighth or ninth day, but at this time the irides are inky dark and without much luster.

The first down is worn from 10 to 14 days, and this is pushed out by the juvenal plumage. By the beginning of the third week they snap their beaks ferociously and make a rasping call to their parents. On the sixteenth or seventeeth day, the downy underparts have become a deep chocolate brown in color and now the irides begin to brighten, although they are still not fully colored, nor the eyes yet fully open. That does not occur until about the twenty-second day, at which time the iris is a brilliant lustrous yellow.

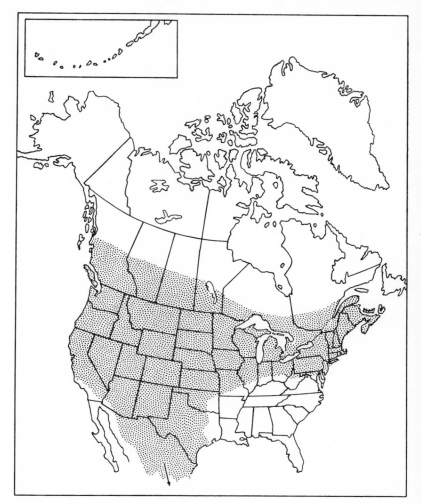

SAW-WHET OWL
Aegolius acadicus acadicus (Gmelin)

Feather development is fairly rapid, and by the end of the fourth week the young birds are able to flutter 15 or 20 feet through the air, but they are poorly skilled at landing and unable to launch themselves from level ground.

By the end of the thirty-fourth day the young birds fly quite well and the full juvenal plumage is evident. This is worn until late July and early August, when a complete molt occurs, producing the first winters plumage, exactly like that of the adults. At about this time, parental care ceases.

DISTRIBUTION IN NORTH AMERICA

Breeds from southern Alaska (Mitkof Island), central British Columbia (Nulki Lake, Indianpoint Lake) exclusive of Queen Charlotte Islands, central Alberta (Carvel), central Saskatchewan (Nipawin), southern Manitoba (Aweme), northern Ontario (probably from Moose Factory), central and eastern Quebec (Anticosti Island), and Nova Scotia (Sydney), southward to southern California (mountains of San Diego County), in the highlands of Mexico to Veracruz, and to Oklahoma (near Tulsa), central Missouri (Bluffton), central Ohio, West Virginia, and Maryland (Cumberland).

The Saw-whet Owl winters throughout its breeding range, but also moves sporadically to Queen Charlotte Islands, the southwestern deserts (Desert Center, California; La Osa, Pima County, Arizona), Louisiana (Madisonville), South Carolina (St. Helena Island), Georgia (Tybee Island), and Florida (Fort Myers).

Casual in Bermuda and Newfoundland.

MIGRATION

There is something of a migrational movement, though it is not truly a migration in the strictest sense of the word. Much depends upon the weather conditions. During more severe winters, the Saw-whet Owl moves much farther southward than at times of mild winters. Sometimes there is no migrational movement whatever. Even bad weather does not always make this owl move, as evidenced by the large numbers found dead after especially severe storms. Some which wait until such storms strike and then attempt to migrate do make it farther south, but these arrive at their destination in such emaciated condition that their chances for recovery are slim. Normally, if there is to be a migrational movement southward at all, it will begin in October and reach its peak in December. Such migration is always done at night and is rarely witnessed.

ECONOMIC INFLUENCE

Although it does kill a certain number of pigeons, barnyard chicks, and songbirds, *Aegolius acadicus acadicus* destroys such numbers of injurious rodents and insects that in the final result it must be considered a highly beneficial bird.

QUEEN CHARLOTTE OWL

(COLOR PLATE X)

SCIENTIFIC NAME AND ORIGINAL DESCRIPTION

Aegolius acadicus brooksi (Fleming). Original description: *Cryptoglaux acadica brooksi* Fleming, *The Auk,* Volume 33, Number 4, October 11, 1916, page 422, based on a specimen from Graham Island, Queen

Charlotte Islands, British Columbia, Canada. Former scientific names: *Nyctala acadica scotaea, Cryptoglaux acadica scotaea, Cryptoglaux acadica brooksi.*

OTHER NAMES

BROOKS'S OWL   Honorary name from the subspecific nomenclature which honors the ornithologist and bird artist, Major Allan Brooks.

LA CHOUETTE DE REINE-CHARLOTTE   French-Canadian name meaning "Queen Charlotte Owl."

NORTHWEST SAW-WHET OWL   Because of geographic location and relationship to the Saw-whet Owl.

PACIFIC SAW-WHET OWL   For the same reasons.

DISTINGUISHING FEATURES

A much darker bird than the Saw-whet Owl (*Aegolius acadicus acadicus*), though very closely related, of the same size and general physical construction. The principal differences are in coloration, and these are so striking that there is a good possibility it may not be merely an *A. acadicus* subspecies, but rather a species in its own right. This is particularly true in light of the fact that there is an absence of any known intergrades of race between this owl and *Aegolius acadicus acadicus*. At present, however, it is still recognized by the American Ornithological Union as a subspecies of *Aegolius acadicus*.

LEGS, FEET, TALONS

Thick feathering continues down legs and feet and on the toes to the base of the talons, instead of the last ball of the toe being bare of plumage, as in the Saw-whet Owl.

COLORATION AND MARKINGS: ADULT

The markings are practically identical to those of the Saw-whet Owl, but there is a very decided difference in coloration. Everywhere that the Saw-whet Owl is white, the Queen Charlotte Owl is a strong light rufescent in tone, and all the browns are much deeper and richer in the Queen Charlotte Owl than in the Saw-whet Owl.

COLORATION AND MARKINGS: JUVENILE

Much like the juvenal form of the Saw-whet Owl, but with all colors richer and darker.

GENERAL HABITS AND CHARACTERISTICS

If anything, even more reclusive than the Saw-whet Owl and therefore difficult to detect and observe. A close study of this handsome little owl is sorely needed. So far as is known at this time, the Queen Charlotte Owl is very much like the Saw-whet Owl in general habits and characteristics, with the possible exception that it is a much more wary bird and far more inclined to flee in the face of disturbances. Body shape at rest or in flight, the flight pattern and, as far as is known, choice of habitat, courtship, nesting, incubation, and family life characteristics are very similar to those of the Saw-whet Owl.

DISTRIBUTION

Although it was previously thought to have extended to the British Columbia mainland and as far coastally southward as the Puget Sound area of British Columbia and Washington, it has now been determined that this little owl is confined strictly to the Queen Charlotte Islands. As far as can be determined, it is completely non-migratory.

QUEEN CHARLOTTE OWL

Aegolius acadicus brooksi (Fleming)

SPECIES

ORDER: STRIGIFORMES

FAMILY: STRIGIDAE

GENUS: *Aegolius* Kaup

SPECIES: *funereus* (Linnaeus)

SUBSPECIES

---

richardsoni (Bonaparte) RICHARDSON'S OWL

RICHARDSON'S OWL

(*COLOR PLATE XI*)

SCIENTIFIC NAME AND ORIGINAL DESCRIPTION

Aegolius funereus richardsoni (Bonaparte). Original description: *Nyctale Richardsoni* Bonaparte, *Geographic and Comparison List,* 1838, page 7; new name for *Strix tengmalmi* Audubon, *Birds of America,* folio, Plate 380; based on a specimen from Bangor, Maine. Former scientific names: *Strix tengmalmi, Glaux funerea richardsoni, Cryptoglaux funerea richardsoni, Nyctale tengmalmi richardsoni, Nyctale Richardsoni.*

OTHER NAMES

AMERICAN SPARROW OWL Referring to geographic location and to the prey sparrows that this owl often seeks.

ARCTIC SAW-WHET OWL From geographic location in part, and superficial similarity to the Saw-whet Owl.

BOREAL OWL Meaning "Owl of the North," although this term is in more familiar use with the Old World race, Tengmalm's Owl.

LA CHOUETTE DE RICHARDSON French-Canadian name meaning "Richardson's Owl."

LA NYCTALE BORÉALE French-Canadian name meaning "Night Owl of the North."

PILLIP-PILE-TSCHISH Montagne Indian name meaning "Water-dripping Bird," due to liquid notes of one of its calls.

SPARROW OWL After the prey this owl frequently kills.

TENGMALM'S OWL Erroneously, after the Old World race of the species, *Aegolius funereus tengmalmi.*

TUCKWELINGUK Eskimo name meaning "The Blind One," because this owl can be easily approached in daytime.

DISTINGUISHING FEATURES

Richardson's Owl rather closely resembles the Saw-whet Owl (*Aegolius acadicus acadicus*) but is a good bit larger, though still by no means a very large owl. Unlike the Saw-whet Owl, with its black beak coloration, Richardson's Owl has a yellow beak, and there is a distinctive facial rim of black that is lacking in the Saw-whet Owl. In addition, where the Saw-whet Owl has white streaks on crown and forehead, Richardson's Owl has white spots. It is also about two inches longer than the Saw-whet Owl. A variable but rather distinctive feature, sometimes quite apparent and sometimes almost absent, depending upon the stance of the perched bird, is the unusual flat-topped appearance of the top of this owl's head. As with the Saw-whet Owl, it has no ear tufts.

Rank in over-all size among the eighteen species: Tenth.

SHAPE AT REST

Aegolius funereus richardsoni has the inclination quite frequently to stand high but lean its body well forward so that its underside is almost parallel with its perch. In this stance it tends to resemble vaguely an oversized sparrow. Despite its evident chunkiness of shape, the flat-topped aspect of the head and the tightness of the plumage impart a sort of stylized or streamlined look. Not only more or less flattened, the top of the head may at times appear to be slightly concave rather than convex as in other owls.

SHAPE IN FLIGHT

Not unlike the Saw-whet Owl, but with a longer and broader spread of wings and with the tail slightly more apparent in silhouette than is the case with the Saw-whet Owl. There is not as much of the batlike similarity as is evident in smaller owls; it is more streamlined.

FLIGHT PATTERN

Again, it differs only slightly from that of the Saw-whet Owl, the differences being that it gives the appearance of a bit more directness and determination in its flight. The wings beat rather rapidly, and this is especially noticeable when it approaches its nesting cavity in a tree and tends to hover momentarily before the entrance in a mothlike manner.

Measurements have been based on 49 measured birds: 26 males and 23 females.

WEIGHT

Species average: 217.5 gr. (7.6 oz.).

	Male	Female
Average	210.9 gr. (7.4 oz.)	224.1 gr. (7.8 oz.)
Minimum	192.7 gr. (6.8 oz.)	199.2 gr. (7.0 oz.)
Maximum	226.7 gr. (7.9 oz.)	235.2 gr. (8.2 oz.)

Rank in weight among the eighteen species: Tenth.

TOTAL LENGTH

Species average: 247.7 mm. (9.8").

	Male	Female
Average	240.0 mm. (9.5")	255.3 mm. (10.1")
Minimum	209.6 mm. (8.3")	232.5 mm. (9.2")
Maximum	263.0 mm. (10.4")	308.6 mm. (12.2")

Rank in total length among the eighteen species: Tenth.

WINGSPAN

Species average: 602.7 mm. (23.8").

	Male	Female
Average	594.4 mm. (23.4")	611.0 mm. (24.1")
Minimum	499.1 mm. (19.7")	567.7 mm. (22.4")
Maximum	626.4 mm. (24.7")	654.1 mm. (25.8")

Rank in wingspan among the eighteen species: Tenth.

INDIVIDUAL WING LENGTH

Species average: 169.4 mm. (6.7").

	Male	Female
Average	166.0 mm. (6.5")	172.7 mm. (6.8")
Minimum	158.9 mm. (6.3")	164.9 mm. (6.5")
Maximum	174.0 mm. (6.9")	190.9 mm. (7.5")

Rank in wing length among the eighteen species: Tenth.

TAIL LENGTH

Species average: 103.0 mm. (4.1").

	Male	Female
Average	95.5 mm. (3.8")	110.5 mm. (4.4")
Minimum	88.1 mm. (3.5")	95.3 mm. (3.8")
Maximum	102.5 mm. (4.0")	119.9 mm. (4.7")

Rank in tail length among the eighteen species: Tenth.

BEAK LENGTH

Species average: 14.4 mm. (0.6").

	Male	Female
Average	14.1 mm. (0.6")	14.6 mm. (0.6")
Minimum	13.3 mm. (0.5")	14.2 mm. (0.6")
Maximum	15.8 mm. (0.6")	16.6 mm. (0.7")

Rank in beak length among the eighteen species: Twelfth.

LEGS, FEET, TALONS

Dense plumage, reminiscent of heavy leggings, covers the lower legs of Richardson's Owl and continues to be relatively thick on the feet, extending out onto the toes to the base of the talons. Occasionally the plumage of the feet will have a random dark brown spot here and there on the upper surface, though this is sometimes absent. The talons are uniformly black.

EYES AND VISION

There is some slight variation in iris color among different specimens. Though in most cases the irides are a strong lemon yellow, they may sometimes have considerably more orange coloration to them, or have gradations of orangish-yellow color between the two extremes.

Vision is extremely good at night and reasonably good by day, providing the owl is not subjected to abrupt strong light, at which it tends to become bewildered. It does not seem to care much for bright sunlight at any time and prefers not to fly at all when the sun is shining, though it is often abroad on cloudy days.

EARS AND HEARING

As with all the North American owl species, hearing is excellent and certainly the most important sense in hunting. Though this auditory sense of Richardson's Owl is not quite as well developed as in some species, such as the Barn Owl (*Tyto alba*) or Barred Owls

(*Strix varia* sp.), it is nevertheless an acute sense in this owl. The ear cavities are asymmetrically placed and vary slightly in physical dimensions from one another, but not to the extremes that may be found in many other owls, and certainly they are nowhere nearly as markedly asymmetrical as in the similar but smaller Saw-whet Owl.

EAR TUFTS, PLUMAGE, ANNUAL MOLT

Richardson's Owl does not have ear tufts. Its plumage is dense but relatively compact and close to the body, imparting an over-all streamlining to the general outline of the bird.

There is a complete annual molt once each year, beginning about the middle of July or early August and not completed until early or middle November.

VOICE

Aegolius funereus richardsoni has a wide range of calls, but not as many as the Saw-whet Owl, nor with as great a variation of the individual calls as that smaller owl. Richardson's Owl calls much less frequently than the Saw-whet Owl and is mainly heard only in the early spring during courtship and nesting season. It is capable of a series of very peculiar gaspings and piercing whistles, the latter being most un-owl-like in character. Its most charming and distinctive call is a distinctly bell-like sound, muted and tinkling in character, which carries considerable distances, is highly ventriloquial, and has the amazing proclivity of sounding like water dripping from a little trickling waterfall into a small pool below—not too unlike this same sort of call issued by the Saw-whet Owl. It is a delightfully charming sound, which may be continued for more than half an hour at a time, day or night; reduced to writing, it sounds something like: *TINGG-TINGG-TINGG-TINGG-TINGG-TINGG-TINGG,* at the rate of about two notes per second. Sometimes it will fade to the point of being nearly inaudible, then rise quite strongly again. After a series of these calls has been completed, the bird will fall into silence for about five minutes, then begin the same calling again. As with the Saw-whet Owl, Richardson's Owl is quite ventriloquistic at times and most difficult to locate by sound.

There are times when the female bird, and possibly the male as well, will utter an odd grating call which lasts for about seven or eight seconds. This may or may not be followed within five or ten seconds by a call which sounds remarkably like a small child whimpering. This latter call may be issued without the preliminary grating cry and, if so, is usually repeated three or four times with intervals of as much as two minutes between cries.

On rare occasions, this owl will give voice to a contented chirping sound at regular intervals.

SEXUAL DIFFERENCES: SIZE, COLORATION, VOICE

There is no difference of coloration or markings between male and female birds. The female is slightly larger than the male, and the voice of the male is generally a shade deeper in tone and mellower than that of the female.

MORTALITY AND LONGEVITY

To some extent, though not in as pronounced a degree as with the Saw-whet Owl, there is evidence of susceptibility to severe weather onslaughts. Numerous Richardson's Owls have been found dead in the snow from no apparent cause, beginning about the third or fourth day after an unusually heavy snowstorm has blanketed the terrain. There are no reliable statistics available regarding the number of years of normal lifespan this owl may have, although it is reasonable to expect that it would live at least as long as the Saw-whet Owl and perhaps even longer.

COLORATION AND MARKINGS: ADULT

The upperparts of Richardson's Owl are generally a deep Vandyke brown, with forehead, crown, and rear sides of head liberally spotted with white. Larger white spots, roughly triangular, on the hindneck are largely hidden by overlying plumage. Some of the greater coverts and the wing coverts near the edge of the wings have a distinctive scattering of white spots that are fairly large and generally round. The outermost half of the secondaries show two rows of small white spots on the edge of the outer webbing of the primaries, with these spots becoming smaller on the innermost quills. Four or five rows of white spots which do not touch the central shaft on either web cross the tail. Facial disks are a grayish white, as are the superciliaries. In front of each eye and immediately above the upper eyelid is an unblemished area of pure dark brown or black. A thin, irregular, concentric black ring in the mid-point of the facial disk surrounds the eye. The sides of the head are intermixed with dusky, although above and behind the ears the plumage is a uniform dark brown delicately dotted with white on the rear portion behind the ears. Sides of the neck are mainly white, although some of the feathers are brown-tipped. A broken band of mixed brown and white extends across the throat, with the brown predominating.

The underparts are generally white in ground coloration, although often tinged in some areas with buffiness. There are large brown spots on the breast, except for the median line which is clear. Sides and flanks are quite broadly brown-striped, each crossed by one or two horizontal bars of brown which cross the quill but do not reach the outer edge on either side. Undertail coverts have narrow, buffy-brown stripes. Upper and lower legs are buff, normally streaked irregularly with brown. The underwings are a grayish brown spotted with white, and the spots become larger and rounder on the secondaries and inner primaries.

COLORATION AND MARKINGS: JUVENILE

Only the wings and tail are similar to those of the adult birds. The entire underparts are a uniform deep slaty brown. The region back of the eye and in the area of the ear are unmarked black. Superciliaries, lores, and mouth corners are gray white, each feather possessing a thin black shaft. Occasionally there are a few white spottings on the primaries and tail feathers.

GENERAL HABITS AND CHARACTERISTICS

Richardson's Owl does not easily become angry or excited. As a result, when discovered on a low branch it can usually be approached quite closely for observation—sometimes to the point of actually allowing itself to be picked up without showing undue alarm. Although it is most active in the early evening until nightfall and during the first gray light of dawn, it can be found actively hunting at almost any time of day or night, particularly on overcast days. If agitated, this bird tends to sway back and forth on its perch, shifting its weight from foot to foot and sometimes using its beak to grip branches and climb about in a manner similar to a parrot. It is not a gregarious bird and even during courtship and nesting season it likes a certain amount of solitude. When perched in the daytime it often presents an amusing sleepy appearance, with heavily lidded eyes.

It is a strong flier and will sometimes make unusually long flights. Some years ago one landed on the rail of an ocean liner in mid-Atlantic and rested there for nearly three hours. It accepted pieces of raw chicken from passengers, slept briefly after devouring about an ounce or so of meat, and then winged silently away.

HABITAT AND ROOSTING

While it shows a preference for extensive growths of somewhat stunted spruce in relative proximity to grasslands, more often than not it will be found in mixed coniferous and hardwood forests. Farther north it is confined primarily to evergreen woods and dense alder thickets. During winter, when it occasionally wanders into more developed areas, it will roost in isolated deciduous trees, usually low and close to the trunk. Now and again it will roost on the rafters of barns or under the eaves of outbuildings. Most often, wherever it happens to settle, roosting is done in relatively thick growth and within a dozen feet of the ground. During the summertime it tends to wander into slightly higher mountain elevations.

ENEMIES AND DEFENSES

Not infrequently *Aegolius funereus richardsoni* falls prey to larger owls and hawks. Long-eared Owls (*Asio otus* sp.), Barred Owls (*Strix varia* sp.), and Horned Owls (*Bubo virginianus* sp.) are especially prone to prey upon Richardson's Owl. Newly flying fledging birds have often fallen victim to ravens. Yet, Richardson's Owl can put up a spirited defense, meeting its attacker with savage bites and grippings of its strong talons. It is not bothered as much by harassment from smaller birds as are many other species of owls in North America.

HUNTING METHODS AND CARRYING OF PREY

Richardson's Owl tends to sit motionless and watchful high in a tree on the edge of a dense forest growth overlooking sedge, meadow, swamp, or marsh, and then dive swiftly to the attack when prey appears. The talons of both feet usually strike the prey animal simultaneously, driving deeply into the body cavity, while the wings flutter rapidly to keep the owl upright and the tail is spread widely to act as a balancing prop against the ground. For this reason the tail feathers are often frayed. Although it has been known to catch smaller birds in flight, especially sparrows and linnets, this is relatively rare. If and when birds are taken, they are usually attacked at night when they have unconsciously given away their location by shuffling or otherwise making a slight noise in their sleep. Almost without exception prey is carried in both feet; less often in one foot and only rarely in the beak.

FOOD, FEEDING HABITS, WASTES

Rodents make up the bulk of the diet, especially various species of mice. Lemmings are extremely important to *Aegolius funereus richardsoni*, as are red-backed voles and deer mice. Sparrows, linnets, and other small birds are frequently taken during the nesting season, but very rarely at other times of the year. Bats are taken often, mainly while hanging, but sometimes when on the wing. Insects, especially crickets, grasshoppers, roaches, beetles, and moths, are often eaten, along with some frogs and salamanders, and occasionally a small snake or lizard.

The pellets are ejected without much difficulty, but rarely in the vicinity of either nest or roost. Each measures approximately an inch and a half in length by about a half to three-quarters of an inch in width, and they are uniformly dark gray in color. Most often they are regurgitated from the first perch the bird takes after leaving the nest or roost. The feces are dark, sometimes with marblings of white or greenish white, and more viscous than solid.

COURTSHIP AND MATING

Normally the courted female sits high atop the lofty spire of a fir or spruce while the male performs a series of swift and expert aerial maneuverings close by, including dives, dips, an occasional mid-air tumbling, hovering, and tight circling around her. Almost without exception he makes a continuous series of calls—mostly whistlings and odd chirpings—while so engaged. Now and again his primary feathers on opposing wings will strike each other with a muted clapping sound. This activity continues for upward of a quarter hour. As it nears termination, the male breaks into the call that sounds like distant dripping water. After several moments of this, the female takes wing and arrows swiftly toward deeper areas in the woods, very closely followed by the male. Copulation may occur on the ground but more often is accomplished on a branch at about mid-height in a tree. The copulation is swiftly begun and ended, though often repeated for several successive days at varying intervals.

ANNUAL BROODS, NEST, NESTING HABITS

Normally only one brood per year, although rarely two. Almost invariably the laying of a second clutch of eggs occurs only if the first set is destroyed. Less often, there is the possibility that a third set may be laid if the second set is ruined.

Most nesting occurs in abandoned flicker or pileated woodpecker holes in both dead and living trees, usually at a height of from 10 to 25 feet. Some nesting occurs in natural cavities and, much less often, the abandoned nest of a rusty blackbird or gray-cheeked thrush is used, especially in the more northerly limits of the bird's range.

Although the preference is for nesting holes to be in conifers, *Aegolius funereus richardsoni* will also use those which are in hardwoods. Almost without exception this owl will retire to the seclusion of such a hole, whether in the nesting season or not, at the approach of stormy weather and remain inside the hole until the storm has passed.

EGGS

Number per nesting As few as two and as many as eight, but both two and eight are rare layings. More normally from three to seven, and usually four, five, or six.

Color Pure white, though in exceptional cases with a vague yellowish cast, which may possibly be a dietary manifestation.

Shape Rounded oval, though sometimes nearly globular.

Texture Very smooth-shelled, without glossiness.

Size Average egg size for the species, based on the measurements of 49 eggs is 32.2 mm. (1.3″) in length by 26.9 mm. (1.1″) in width. The extremes of the 49 eggs measured were:

Maximum length:	36.6 mm. (1.4″)
Minimum length:	29.0 mm. (1.1″)
Maximum width:	28.8 mm. (1.1″)
Minimum width:	25.4 mm. (1.0″)

Interval of egg-laying Eggs are laid not less than 24 hours apart at intervals longer than 72 hours. Usually all eggs are deposited in eight to twelve days.

Egg-laying dates Earliest, April 11; latest, June 9; normally between April 16 and May 20.

INCUBATION AND BROODING CHARACTERISTICS

Incubation may not begin until the second or third egg is laid, and lasts for at least 25 days but rarely over 27 days. The female does all or almost all of the incubating, and the male provides food for her while she is thus occupied.

XVII SOUTHERN SCREECH OWL

Otus asio asio (Linnaeus). Female, male. Female: Vicinity of Elkin, North Carolina, March 7, 1968. Male: Myrtle Beach, South Carolina, October 3, 1966. A.O.U. Number 373

XVIII CALIFORNIA SCREECH OWL

Otus asio bendirei (Brewster). Male. Three miles north of Zenia, Trinity County, California, November 10, 1965. A.O.U. Number 373-C

Karl E. Karalus
1971

YOUNG AND FAMILY LIFE CHARACTERISTICS

Because of staggered hatching, the young will vary considerably in size in the nest—a fact that becomes quite evident because of the number of birds in the individual brood. The smallest may be a baby newly out of its shell, the remainder being progressively larger in stair-step fashion to the eldest, which may already be well feathered in juvenal plumage.

The babies are clad in white down upon hatching but soon develop a distinct brownish hue of new feathers on the back, especially down the dorsal centerline. Most of the down is lost within two weeks, with the residue still adhering to the outermost tips of the new juvenal plumage.

There is virtually complete juvenal plumage by the mid-point of the third week, with the entire upperparts a clear brown, which may have either a muddy or somewhat reddish cast. All the colors are darker than in the adult birds. This juvenal plumage is worn until early autumn when a molt occurs which involves all but the tail and wings, producing the first-winter plumage.

DISTRIBUTION IN NORTH AMERICA

Breeds from northern Alaska (Nulato, Fairbanks), central-western Yukon (Fortymile), Mackenzie (Lake Hardisty region), central Saskatchewan (Nipawin), northern Manitoba (probably York Factory), northern Ontario (around the area of Kapuskasing), Quebec (Magdalen Islands), Labrador (Hopedale), and probably Newfoundland, southward to northern British Columbia (Flood Glacier, Laurier Lake), central Alberta (Athabaska Landing, Belvedere), southern Manitoba (probably Winnipeg), western Ontario (around Wabigoon), Nova Scotia, and New Brunswick (Grand Manan).

Winters in part throughout its breeding range but, in especially bad-weather years spreads southward to southern British Columbia (Sumas, Okanagan), northern Montana, North Dakota (Fargo), southern Minnesota (Fillmore County), southern Michigan (Freeland), Ontario (north shore of Lake Ontario; Ottawa area), southern Quebec, and Massachusetts.

Casually to southern Oregon (Fort Klamath), Idaho

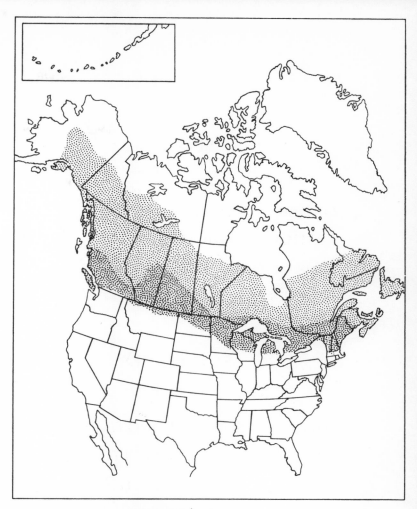

RICHARDSON'S OWL

Aegolius funereus richardsoni (Bonaparte)

(Fort Sherman), Colorado (Crested Butte), Nebraska (Lincoln), Illinois (Rockford, Sycamore, Cicero, Kenilworth), Pennsylvania (Allegheny County), New York (Fort Covington, Plattsburg), Connecticut (East Windsor Hill, Kent), and Rhode Island (vicinity of Providence).

MIGRATION

There is no regular annual migration, but during the more severe winters large numbers of Richardson's Owls do tend to move southward and appear in the northern tier of the United States.

ECONOMIC INFLUENCE

It cannot be denied that this owl does do some damage to songbird populations during its breeding season, but on the whole, considering its yearlong heavy diet of mice and other rodents, it is considerably more beneficial than otherwise.

XIX   BREWSTER'S SCREECH OWL

Otus asio brewsteri Ridgway. Female. Shinn's Peak, Lassen County, California, November 17, 1929. A.O.U. Number 373-J

XX   MEXICAN SCREECH OWL

Otus asio cineraceus (Ridgway). Female. Chiricahua Mountains, Cochise County, Arizona, June 20, 1968. A.O.U. Number 373-F

SPECIES

ORDER: STRIGIFORMES
FAMILY: STRIGIDAE
GENUS: *Asio* Brisson
SPECIES: *otus* (Linnaeus)

SUBSPECIES

---

wilsonianus (Lesson)   LONG-EARED OWL
tuftsi Godfrey   WESTERN LONG-
                          EARED OWL

LONG-EARED OWL
(COLOR PLATE XII)

SCIENTIFIC NAME AND ORIGINAL DESCRIPTION

Asio otus wilsonianus (Lesson). Original description: *Otus Wilsonianus* Lesson, *Traité Ornithologia, Livr. 2,* May 8, 1830, page 110 (*Etats-Unis et principalement dans l'automne Pennsylvanie*). Based on a specimen from Pennsylvania without locale signified. Former scientific names: *Strix otus, Otus americanus, Otus vulgaris, Otus vulgaris wilsonianus, Otus Wilsonianus.*

OTHER NAMES

AMERICAN LONG-EARED OWL To differentiate this race from others elsewhere in the world.
BRUSH OWL After the preferred type of habitat.
LE HIBOU À LONGUES AIGRETTES French-Canadian name meaning "Long-tufted Owl," referring to the ear tufts.
LE HIBOU À LONGUES OREILLES French-Canadian name meaning "Long-eared Owl."
LECHUZ BARRANQUERA DE WILSON Mexican-Indian name meaning "Wilson's Owl of the Barrancas."
LESSER HORNED OWL Rare term, distinguishing the Long-eared Owl from the larger Horned Owls (*Bubo virginianus* sp.).
WILSON'S OWL Honorary name.

DISTINGUISHING FEATURES

This is one of the more distinctive of all the North American Owl species, being quite heavily marked all over its plumage, having distinctly contrasting coloration, and exhibiting a set of ear tufts which tend to be more erect, narrower, and set somewhat closer together than those of the Horned Owls or Screech Owls (*Otus asio* sp.). These ear tufts, on occasion, tend to lean toward one another slightly and are faintly tapered toward the tips on their outer edges. The facial disks are in particular contrast to the general darkness of the head, being a strong medium orangish buff to reddish brown, which darkens considerably around the eyes. The disks are separated by distinctly gray white and unusually full superciliaries and lores. A medium-sized owl, *Asio otus wilsonianus* wears a constantly peeved expression.

Rank in over-all size among the eighteen species: Eighth.

SHAPE AT REST

Although the Long-eared Owl tends to slouch somewhat when relaxed on its perch, it can straighten and elongate its body to an amazing extent, becoming very long and slender in appearance—an action which effectively helps to camouflage the bird and make it appear to be the stub of a broken branch, a device especially effective under poor lighting conditions.

About midway in size between the Great Horned Owl (*Bubo virginianus virginianus*) and the Eastern Screech Owl (*Otus asio naevius*), it is easily distinguishable from both in that it lacks the white throat patch of the Great Horned Owl and is much larger, with facial disks much deeper red brown, than the Eastern Screech Owl.

The ear tufts are usually distinctive and held sharply erect when the bird is perched, but there are times when the sitting bird holds them almost flat against the head. The folded wings exceed the length of the tail and the owl is, on the whole, rather slenderly built.

Long-eared Owl

SHAPE IN FLIGHT

The wings are relatively longer and narrower for its body size than are those of the Great Horned Owl, and the ear tufts are virtually without exception held tightly to the head during flight. The tail is quite evident in flight silhouette.

FLIGHT PATTERN

The flight of the Long-eared Owl is somewhat wavering in quality and not as certain as is that of the Great Horned Owl. Even when the long wings are beating, there is the sense that the bird is doing a lot of gliding, probably because of the peculiar buoyancy of the flight, despite a somewhat erratic and bumpy flight pattern. Its silhouette from below is stubby-headed and somewhat long-tailed, resembling in size and manner the Short-eared Owl (*Asio flammeus flammeus*), but it should not be mistaken for that owl because the two do not normally range within the same type of habitat. Occasionally the Long-eared Owl will flutter and hover like an enormous butterfly or moth. When necessary, it is capable of quite swift flight.

Measurements have been based on 27 measured birds: 11 males and 16 females.

WEIGHT

Species average: 275.2 gr. (9.6 oz.).

	Male	Female
Average	258.5 gr. (9.1 oz.)	282.0 gr. (9.9 oz.)
Minimum	215.4 gr. (7.5 oz.)	227.0 gr. (8.0 oz.)
Maximum	299.4 gr. (10.5 oz.)	333.4 gr. (11.7 oz.)

Rank in weight among the eighteen species: Eighth.

TOTAL LENGTH

Species average: 354.4 mm. (14.0").

	Male	Female
Average	339.2 mm. (13.4")	369.6 mm. (14.6")
Minimum	328.9 mm. (13.0")	333.1 mm. (13.1")
Maximum	352.7 mm. (13.9")	407.7 mm. (16.1")

Rank in total length among the eighteen species: Ninth.

WINGSPAN

Species average: 978.1 mm. (38.5").

	Male	Female
Average	956.3 mm. (37.7")	1,000.0 mm. (39.4")
Minimum	920.9 mm. (36.3")	964.0 mm. (38.0")
Maximum	1,009.7 mm. (39.8")	1,098.7 mm. (43.3")

Rank in wingspan among the eighteen species: Eighth.

INDIVIDUAL WING LENGTH

Species average: 287.1 mm. (11.3").

	Male	Female
Average	285.8 mm. (11.3")	288.3 mm. (11.4")
Minimum	269.2 mm. (10.6")	274.3 mm. (10.8")
Maximum	295.9 mm. (11.7")	301.0 mm. (11.9")

Rank in wing length among the eighteen species: Eighth.

TAIL LENGTH

Species average: 151.5 mm. (6.0").

	Male	Female
Average	148.1 mm. (5.8")	154.9 mm. (6.1")
Minimum	143.1 mm. (5.6")	151.2 mm. (6.0")
Maximum	153.7 mm. (6.1")	168.9 mm. (6.7")

Rank in tail length among the eighteen species: Eighth.

BEAK LENGTH

Species average: 17.0 mm. (0.7").

	Male	Female
Average	16.6 mm. (0.7")	17.3 mm. (0.7")
Minimum	15.2 mm. (0.6")	16.0 mm. (0.6")
Maximum	17.8 mm. (0.7")	20.6 mm. (0.8")

Rank in beak length among the eighteen species: Seventh.

LEGS, FEET, TALONS

The tarsus of the Long-eared Owl is slightly longer than might be expected in relation to its body size, averaging between 38.1 mm. (1.5") and 46.0 mm. (1.8"). The legs and feet are very thickly feathered to the base of the talons, although the toe feathers, while thick, are quite short. The talons themselves are very black at the base but becoming a lighter slaty black at the tips. The feet have a powerful grip.

EYES AND VISION

Untroubled by the bright light of day, the Long-eared Owl is occasionally abroad during the daytime, though preferring cloudy days over clear if it is flying in daylight. Its bright golden-orange to yellow-orange irides are distinctive and its vision is best adapted to late evening and early morning hunting. The eyes of this owl have a considerably more staring aspect than do those of most other North American species, except possibly the Short-eared Owl (*Asio flammeus flammeus*).

EARS AND HEARING

Ear cavities are asymmetrical in shape and positioning, though not to as great a degree as in some species. Hearing is excellent and more an aid in hunting than is vision, though the two senses complement one another exceptionally well. It is practically impossible to creep up undetected on a roosting Long-eared Owl.

At times the head will appear greatly enlarged as the owl raises and extends the ear flaps, thus enlarging the facial disks and pushing them forward. This owl is said to be able to detect the squeak of a mouse from a distance of 100 yards and can sometimes be decoyed to within very close range by emulation of this sound.

EAR TUFTS, PLUMAGE, ANNUAL MOLT

The long and relatively narrow ear tufts are slightly closer together toward the center of the head than are those of the Great Horned Owl (*Bubo virginianus virginianus*) or the Screech Owls (*Otus asio* sp.) and much larger than those of the Short-eared Owl (*Asio flammeus flammeus*). They are always tipped with black and are a distinctive feature of the perched bird, although they are normally laid back flat against the head when the bird is flying. There is a complete annual molt of adult plumage beginning in mid-September and concluded by mid-December. This molt is progressive and has little, if any, effect upon flight.

VOICE

While its variety of calls is not as extensive as are those of the Barred Owls (*Strix varia* sp.), or some of the other species, it nevertheless has an interesting number of calls quite different from one another. However, it is certainly not as vociferous as many other North American owls can be and, except during courtship and nesting season, is rarely heard.

The most common call is a regularly intoned, mellow, and rather soft and musical *kwooo-kwooo-kwooo-kwooo*, with the emphasis, if any, on the first note. This call has a tendency at times to run together in a quavering manner not unlike that of the Eastern Screech Owl but louder and farther-carrying, sounding like: *KWOOOO-OOO-OOO-OO-OO-O-O*.

Now and again, for no known reason, this owl will produce a series of rapid, piercing shrieks. The first cry is loudest and each successive cry diminishes in volume and intensity until the sound eventually fades away entirely, the whole vocal utterance lasting for 30 to 40

seconds. It is most reminiscent of the screams of a bird caught in the talons of a hawk.

When danger threatens and the Long-eared Owl becomes irked, it tends to voice a three-syllable series of excited calls sounding like *wheck!-WHECK!-wheck!*, with emphasis on the middle syllable. This call is usually given while the bird is in flight, as it circles about the intruder, interspersing the calling with harsh snappings of the beak. As soon as the danger has subsided, however, the owl utters a long, low, seemingly satisfied squealing whistle.

Sometimes, after the male *Asio otus wilsonianus* has brought food to the brooding female, he will perch nearby and give a softer, encouraging three-note call sounding like *hoooof-HOOOOF-hooof,* often repeated five or six times. This is frequently accompanied by a rather pleased or self-satisfied low-pitched utterance of *woo-HUH-KK who-HUH-KK,* interspersed with a sound remarkably close to someone softly calling his cat in a high, musical tone: *kitty-kitty-kitty-kitty-kitty*.

Probably the most startling cry uttered by both sexes, though more by the female than the male, comes when eggs or young are in jeopardy. At such times the owl flutters wildly on the ground making sharply distressed cries, as if she were hurt. These cries sound like a series of overloud catlike mewings. (See Enemies and Defenses.)

In addition to these readily identifiable calls, the Long-eared Owl can make a variety of other sounds at infrequent intervals; some like the yappings of a puppy at a distance, along with prolonged, shrill squalls, some whistlings, deep chucklings, snorting sounds that are usually accompanied by a raspy hissing and the snapping of the beak. To many of these calls there is a marked ventriloquism.

SEXUAL DIFFERENCES: SIZE, COLORATION, VOICE

Male birds average generally paler in plumage coloration than female birds and, especially on the underparts, they are whiter. Females are a bit larger than males and in almost all cases the voice of the female is somewhat higher pitched and less melodious than that of the male.

Facial attitudes of the Long-eared Owl (*Asio otus wilsonianus*). Clockwise from upper left: roosting bird startled awake by intruder; perched bird assuming the elongated, erectile ear tuft, camouflage posture; newly awakened but not alarmed bird; defensive posturing when young are threatened; camouflage posturing.

Long-eared owl

K.E.K.

attitude studies

MORTALITY AND LONGEVITY

Not a great deal of study has been completed in this aspect of the Long-eared Owl's natural history, although it is known that they will survive for well over a decade in captivity. Mortality among the nestlings tends to be increased through cannibalism if there is a shortage of prey, or if one of the parent birds is killed and the remaining parent cannot bring an adequate supply of food to the nest. Cannibalism, if it occurs, is usually limited to the single smallest bird in the nest, though on rare occasions including the second smallest as well.

COLORATION AND MARKINGS: ADULT

The entire upperparts are strongly mottled with a slaty brown and grayish white, though the browns are in much greater dominance, particularly on the back. There are a few rather indistinct and irregular white spots on the outer webs of the shoulder feathers. The greater coverts are generally dusky but well peppered with buffy-gray spottings, usually of a transverse nature. The primaries, especially on the inner quills, are grayish toward the tips and more buffy toward the base, with fine dusky mottlings of a transverse nature and from five to nine (usually seven) transverse rows of rather square slate-brown spots. Nine to eleven (usually nine) bands of similar spots cross the secondaries and the tail. The general coloration of the wing coverts is like that of the back, but vaguely paler along the wing edges and with the feathers margined in white or buffy at their tips.

The uppermost feathers of the ear tufts are pure black, while those closer to the head are plain sooty in the center of each feather but with the edges buffy and with irregular mottlings of slate brown. Very tiny salt-and-pepper specklings of black and white are sprinkled on the forehead and sides of the head. Eyebrows (superciliaries) and lores are distinctly grayish white in strong contrast to the generally dark coloration of the head. The lores in particular are so distinctly contrasting that they appear to form something of a shortened walrus mustache on each side of and below the beak. Facial-disk feathers around the eyes are black, this black area being widest in a semicircle from the supraorbital area, passing around the inner side of the eye and then to the suborbital area. The rest of the facial disk is a rich orange-brown to reddish-brown coloration. The facial rim is narrowly black, becoming speckled with narrow white into a sort of vague collar across the throat.

General coloration of the underparts is buffy gray to gray white. The breast feathers have very distinctive cross-hatchings of a deep sooty brown, with these be-

coming broader and more distinct on sides, flanks, and belly. Lower leg and foot plumage is a deep buff, and the thighs are buffy white with cross-hatched brown. Undertail coverts have narrow center streaks of slaty brown which become Y-shaped toward the ends. The underwing lesser coverts are plain orangish buff, and the sooty-brown greater coverts form a conspicuous underwing mark.

COLORATION AND MARKINGS: JUVENILE

Facial disks of the juvenals are considerably darker than those of the adults. They are usually a deep cinnamon red brown. The ear tufts are smaller than they will be in adulthood, and the body feathers are mainly brown, tipped and barred with grayish white. Superciliaries and lores are black instead of gray white as in the adults, but wing and tail feathers are no different than those of the adults.

GENERAL HABITS AND CHARACTERISTICS

Primarily a nocturnal owl, *Asio otus wilsonianus* is nevertheless often on the wing in the morning and evening periods of twilight. Usually the daylight hours are spent well hidden in dense cover and for this reason the Long-eared Owl is rarely seen. This is a very difficult owl to locate when it is perched, because its protective coloration blends so very well with the type of cover in which it roosts for the day. It does not flush easily from such cover when discovered and seems more inclined to sit and stare at an intruder with a gaze which quickly goes from sleepy to indignant. Often it will stare at an intruder with slanted and slitted eyelids all but closed.

The Long-eared Owl tends to become rather gregarious in autumn and winter—a characteristic more noticeable in the West than in the East, though the reason for this may simply be a lack of more favored roosting areas and a good many owls taking advantage of those areas that are available. There is the possibility, too, that the family group is still together at this time.

HABITAT AND ROOSTING

For the most part, the Long-eared Owl keeps to well-timbered areas, especially in close conjunction with water—streams, river, and lakes. This is true even in the more remote regions of its habitat. Its preference is for dense groves of conifers or mixed hardwood and evergreen, but if no other cover is available it will use strictly hardwood or even low-growing scrub, especially when such growth is in the form of tangled thickets. Such areas that are well interlaced with vines are a particular favorite, with the roost site normally located in the midst of the heaviest cover.

Lacking satisfactory tree or brush cover, this owl will roost in caves or deep cracks in the walls of canyons or ravines. It may be found roosting in favorable locations at elevations up to 11,000 feet. The most preferred roost seems to be a low branch in very dense cover. In such type of habitat there may be six or seven Long-eared Owls roosting in a single tree.

ENEMIES AND DEFENSES

Other than man, the Long-eared Owl's greatest enemies seem to be ravens, crows, and jays, which harass it severely but rarely inflict physical injury, and the Horned Owls (*Bubo virginianus* sp.), which prey upon it wherever encountered. Pigeon Hawks, too, have been known to attack and kill them. In rare instances, the Northern Barred Owl (*Strix varia varia*) will kill and devour Long-eared Owls. There is also a certain amount of pestering from smaller birds such as wrens, blackbirds, cowbirds, kingbirds, and shrikes. Oddly, magpies seldom bother Long-eared Owls.

The defenses of *Asio otus wilsonianus* are impressive. With head lowered almost to the ground it will spread its wings so widely, with the upper surface of the wings facing the intruder, that the tips of the wings are nearly on the ground and the outermost margins of the primaries and secondaries are pointed nearly directly skyward, giving the impression of a much larger and fiercer bird than it actually is and, to some extent, looking like a tom turkey with its tail spread to fullest expanse. In this position it will glare with great ferocity at the intruder, sway its head back and forth menacingly, snap its beak, and hiss piercingly. This action is most often seen in connection with defense of its nest.

The Long-eared Owl uses with great skill two ruse-type defenses, especially where the safety of its young are concerned. One of the parent birds will make a show of exposing itself in flight and then suddenly plummet to the ground. Instantly there will rise the shrill cry of a different type of bird altogether. It sounds exactly as if the owl has plunged and caught some kind of bird as prey and as if that bird is voicing its frantic death cry. This is accompanied by a good bit of rustling and feather-rattling on the ground, as if the owl were struggling with some manner of prey. Once the intruder has been decoyed in that direction and away from the endangered young, the parent bird

begins moving away, still on the ground and still holding its wings partially open and acting as if it is carrying prey that is too large to be picked up and flown with. This will continue until the intruder has been lured some distance away, upon which the owl will rise and arrow off soundlessly away from the nest area, but making a wide, unseen circle back to the vicinity of the young birds.

Failing in that maneuver, the Long-eared Owl—possibly only the female—will emulate an injured bird, dragging one wing on the ground and hopping along in a stumbling, pained manner. Again the enemy will be led away in pursuit of her and when it is safe for her to do so, she will rise and fly swiftly away.

While normally this owl prefers such tactics to actual physical encounters, it is not terribly hesitant at actually launching itself at an intruder and attacking savagely with beak and talons, almost always aiming at face or throat where the most significant and discouraging damage can be inflicted. In this respect, and in its other defensive tactics, the Long-eared Owl is one of the most effectively demonstrative of North American owls in defense of its young.

A more subdued defense is its protective coloration, which so well camouflages the bird in heavy cover; a natural gift enhanced by the bird's ability to draw itself upward in its perched pose until it becomes almost impossibly thin—hardly more than three inches in diameter. In this pose, with ear tufts fully erected, the bird so closely resembles a broken branch that detection is extremely difficult. Often when going into this updrawn "beanpole" stance, the bird will hold one wing across breast and belly to hide the lighter plumage behind the more camouflaged plumage of primaries and secondaries.

HUNTING METHODS AND CARRYING OF PREY

While the Long-eared Owl favors timberlands as habitat, most of its hunting is done over open lands bordering woodlands. Only a small percentage of its hunting is done in dense woods, although its flying ability through tangled areas of brush and trees is little short of phenomenal. Tending to range back and forth more than many other owl species, it flies about six or seven feet off the ground in utter silence, its head usually canted slightly to one side, better to detect the sound of prey movements. When prey is detected, the bird darts to the exact spot and pounces with impressive skill on the exact spot where its ears have told it the prey is located, even though the prey may not be visible. Though it will eat birds, it seldom catches them on the wing. The birds that it does catch are normally taken as they roost on the ground or in low branches.

How prey is killed depends primarily upon its size. Up to the size of a small rat, most prey is carried in the beak; larger prey is normally carried in one or both sets of talons.

FOOD, FEEDING HABITS, WASTES

Rodents make up by far the greatest percentage of the Long-eared Owl's diet on an annual basis, but its prey can be widely varied. Among small mammals it often eats wood rats, deer mice, meadow voles, squirrels, house rats, chipmunks, bats, gophers, moles and shrews, and sometimes medium-grown cottontail rabbits. These creatures, along with a smaller number of frogs, small snakes, and some insects, make up virtually its entire diet during all but its nesting season. It is only when there are voracious young owls to feed that the Long-eared Owl attacks birds. At such times it will take as prey a wide variety of birds—quail, ruffed grouse, English sparrows, European starlings, doves, horned larks, red-winged blackbirds, towhees, finches, meadowlarks, juncos, cardinals, brown thrashers, bluebirds, kinglets, and even occasional Screech Owls.

Wherever possible, prey is swallowed whole but, if too large, will be torn into chunks just small enough to be swallowed. Digestion is very rapid and pellet regurgitation may occur as quickly as three or four hours after feeding. These pellets are normally gray, compact masses averaging an inch and a half to two inches in length and about three-fourths of an inch in width, being roughly oval in shape.

Defecation occurs regularly, with fecal matter in a largely liquid or semiliquid state and generally dropped straight down beneath the roosting bird.

COURTSHIP AND MATING

Since the Long-eared Owl is among the most nocturnal of our owls, few humans have ever witnessed the courtship machinations and, as a result, this aspect of the life history of *Asio otus wilsonianus* has not been well described. Some observers have claimed that the male will perform a series of dives and wing clappings over the perched female, but since this closely resembles the courtship action of the Short-eared Owl (*Asio flammeus flammeus*), misidentification is a possibility. The male is known to present the female occasionally with some sort of prey animal, which she deliberately but delicately takes from his beak with hers; however, this is not always done. Actual copulation, as it has been witnessed, occurs swiftly, sometimes on the ground but more often on a low limb in dense cover, and less often on the limb of a well-exposed tree.

ANNUAL BROODS, NEST, NESTING HABITS

Although there is some slight evidence of double-brooding in the more southerly portions of its range, the Long-eared Owl is essentially a single-brooded bird throughout its range. If, however, the first clutch of eggs is destroyed, a second laying will be made, beginning about twenty days later. Almost invariably its nest is the abandoned nest of a crow, magpie, raven, hawk, or heron, situated usually about 20 feet high near the main stem of a dense tree in the midst of heavy cover, especially in and around swampy areas. Unlike most other owls, there is evidently a certain amount of effort expended by *Asio otus wilsonianus* in rejuvenating the nest for its own use. Strips of bark are added, as well as some mosses or leaves and often breast plumage from the female owl. Although it will occasionally nest to heights of 40 or 50 feet in a tree and as low as three or four feet—and even on the ground in rare cases—most often the next will be between 15 and 30 feet in height. Nesting is sometimes done on protected cliff ledges or in a deep sheltered cleft in rocks, but this is commonly among those birds nesting at higher altitudes of up to about 10,000 feet.

In very unusual cases, the owl will actually build its own nest instead of taking over one that was previously used. In such cases the nest is flimsily built of poorly interlocked sticks and has little uniformity or strength. Nests like these are often blown apart by windstorms.

Once a nesting has begun and the female has settled in, it is very difficult to make her leave. Usually she will sit in it, watching and waiting while the male does all he can to decoy or drive the intruder away. Only if matters become extremely threatening will she actively join in and help her mate defend the nest, eggs, or young.

EGGS

Number per nesting Customarily the Long-eared Owl will lay four or five eggs and less often six or seven. As few as three and as many as eight have been recorded.

Color Pure white, sometimes slightly nest-stained with rusty spots, but mostly unblemished and with no tinge of any other color.

Shape Rounded oval, virtually without exception.

Texture Very smooth and glossy.

Size Based on a sampling of 112 eggs measured, the average size is 40.9 mm. (1.6") in length by 33.3 mm. (1.3") in width, with extremes of:

Maximum length:	43.4 mm. (1.7″)
Minimum length:	35.1 mm. (1.4″)
Maximum width:	37.6 mm. (1.5″)
Minimum width:	30.0 mm. (1.2″)

Interval of egg-laying Almost always about 48 hours apart.

Egg-laying dates Southern Canada: earliest, April 12; latest, June 5; normally between May 9 and May 19.

New England and New York: earliest, March 31; latest, May 31; normally between April 19 and May 15.

East: earliest, March 14; latest, May 30; normally between March 29 and April 11.

Midwest: earliest, March 15; latest, May 6; normally between March 20 and April 24.

West: earliest March 27; latest June 2; normally between April 17 and May 8.

INCUBATION AND BROODING CHARACTERISTICS

Data are not conclusive in this regard, but certainly no less than 21 days nor more than 28; probably most often 24–25 days. The male provides food while the female incubates and she will sit so tightly on her eggs that she can usually be approached and touched while on the nest.

YOUNG AND FAMILY LIFE CHARACTERISTICS

The birds are hatched at intervals of about two days apart, and in the larger broods the eldest fledgling is two weeks of age or older and fairly well fledged before the youngest has hatched. The result is that not infrequently the youngest one or two in the nest do not survive. Within the first three days—after being trod upon and shoved around by the older fledglings—the youngest become very weak. At this point it is not rare for them to be killed and devoured by their nestmates. Again, this occurs most often in overlarge broods, and in the normal brood of four or five young, it is uncommon.

At hatching, the eyes of the babies are closed; they do not begin opening until the third or fourth day. They are nearly naked, and only on the principal feather tracts is there a meager white down. The ex-

ception is the facial disk, which is quite well developed at hatching and covered with scraggly white down.

The egg tooth has disappeared by the seventh day but the young bird is still quite sluggish, though by now well covered in a more dense white down. This begins being replaced by juvenal plumage as early as the seventh day, but usually not until the eighth day. At this stage the babies still tend to cower in fear if disturbed.

By about the fifteenth to eighteenth day the young birds have undergone a noteworthy change of character. If danger threatens at the nest their first act will be to freeze in position; but if the danger does not go away immediately they become very aggressive in their actions, snapping their beaks, hissing loudly, and standing erect with their outstretched wings inverted and every feather upraised, in an accurate parody of the defensive posture of the parents.

During the third week it is not uncommon for at least one and sometimes several of the young birds to fall from the nest, but they flutter to the ground and are not usually hurt. Parental care continues on the ground for them. At this stage they are about half-grown, with their primaries and secondaries well emerging from their sheaths. Body plumage is now well-developed "soft plumage" which, on the upperparts, is dusky. These feathers have white tips which give the bird a sort of "frosted" appearance, especially on head and hindneck. The underparts are generally a pale buff, again with whitish tips, and with from two to four dusky narrow bands on each feather. The similar bands on the feathers of the back are somewhat more clearly defined. There is long grizzled down on the thighs, but the tail feathers are still unsheathed. At this stage the facial disks are becoming very dark.

Around the twenty-fourth or twenty-fifth day (but possibly not until the twenty-eighth day) the frosting on crown and hindneck starts to be replaced by short, soot-colored feathers with very bright white tips. Wings and tail feathers are growing rapidly and the first winter plumage is well on the way to replacing the downy plumage. This is completed first on the back and then on the underparts.

By this time the young are ready to leave the nest and venture out onto the nearby branches. They still cannot fly well and usually wind up on the ground and being cared for and well guarded there by the parents. However, by about the thirtieth to thirty-fifth day they can fly well, their wings and tail are identical to those of the adults, and all the downy contour plumage has been molted away except for perhaps a few traces remaining on the crown and lower belly.

The young birds continue to be fed by the parents, even after learning to fly, until about the end of the ninth week; even then the family tends to remain together through the remainder of summer and autumn and perhaps even through the winter.

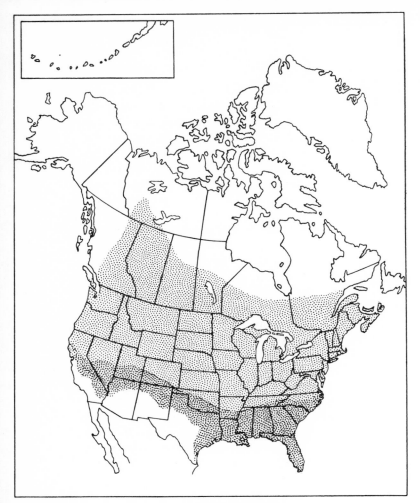

LONG-EARED OWL

Asio otus wilsonianus (Lesson)

DISTRIBUTION IN NORTH AMERICA

Breeds from southern Manitoba (Shoal Lake), western and southern Ontario, southern Quebec (Lake St. John), New Brunswick (Woodstock), and Nova Scotia (Kentville), southward to northern Oklahoma (Kenton, Gate), Arkansas, and Virginia.

Winters from eastern Canada southward to southern Texas (Brownsville), Louisiana, Alabama, Florida (Cape Sable), and the Bermudas, but is accidental in Cuba.

MIGRATION

A decided winterly southward movement is fairly regular with *Asio otus wilsonianus*, though far more pronounced in some years than in others. As mentioned, it is quite gregarious during these migrational periods, particularly in the western United States. Nor-

mally, all birds of the race that are going to migrate in any given year will have done so by the beginning of December, with the return northward well underway by March.

ECONOMIC INFLUENCE

Although a certain amount of damage is done to songbird populations during the Long-eared Owl's nesting period, this damage is not extensive. Its normal, year-round diet of large numbers of injurious rodents—which make up 80 per cent to 90 per cent of all prey devoured each year—clearly make this bird an economic asset.

WESTERN LONG-EARED OWL

(COLOR PLATE XIII—SEE ENDPAPERS)

SCIENTIFIC NAME AND ORIGINAL DESCRIPTION

Asio otus tuftsi Godfrey. Original description: *Asio otus tuftsi* Godfrey, *The Canadian Field-Naturalist*, Volume 61, Number 6, November–December, 1947 (February 13, 1948), page 196; based on a specimen from South Arm, Last Mountain Lake, Saskatchewan, Canada.

OTHER NAMES

CANADIAN LONG-EARED OWL After part of geographic range.

LONG-EARED OWL Erroneously, since it is the Western form and should always be listed with that descriptive term.

DISTINGUISHING FEATURES

The greatest and most immediately apparent difference between *Asio otus tuftsi* and *Asio otus wilsonianus* is one of coloration. The western race is generally much paler; a factor particularly noticeable on the facial disks, breast, and belly plumage. The markings on the underparts of the Western Long-eared Owl are much less distinct and the facial disks have an absence of the rufous coloration which so distinguishes the Long-eared Owl. The Western Long-eared Owl's facial disks are a pale tawny brown which may range from as light as an over-all pale buff to a distinct yellowish brown, but never with reddish traces.

TOTAL LENGTH

Asio otus tuftsi tends to average just slightly less in over-all length than *Asio otus wilsonianus*. Average total length for the western subspecies is 335.3 mm. (13.2″).

TAIL LENGTH

Surprisingly, though it is smaller than *Asio otus wilsonianus* in total length, the tail length of *Asio otus tuftsi* averages slightly longer at 154.6 mm. (6.1″).

VOICE

The Western Long-eared Owl is less vociferous than the Long-eared Owl and is normally quiet throughout most of the year except during the breeding season. Even then it does not call with as great frequency or with as wide a variety of calls as does *Asio otus wilsonianus*. The calls it does make are basically similar to those of the Long-eared Owl in tonal quality and pitch, except for a few muted, rather mournful moaning sounds it utters infrequently, which seem to be absent in the repertoire of the Long-eared Owl.

COLORATION AND MARKINGS: ADULT

Generally lighter, especially on the underparts, than *Asio otus wilsonianus*, although the ear tufts are as dark brown and conspicuous. The lighter facial disks, lacking in rusty tone, can sometimes be very pale buff, though they are normally a tan coloration. All underparts have a good bit of whitish and pale yellowish buff as the ground color and the streaks and bars, considerably less distinctly defined than in *Asio otus wilsonianus*, although by no means absent. The flanks are a soft, pale, yellowish sandy and are generally unspotted. The upperparts are similar to those of the Long-eared Owl, although essentially lighter, having less rufous undertone and generally a mottled tawny, gray and blackish, with wings and tail barred as in *Asio otus wilsonianus*.

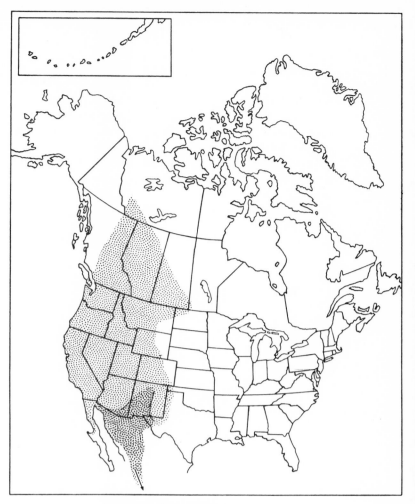

WESTERN LONG-EARED OWL
Asio otus tuftsi Godfrey

HABITAT AND ROOSTING

Even more reclusive than *Asio otus wilsonianus* and rarely seen by the casual observer, preferring to spend all daylight hours in the very deepest creek valley tangles or dense coniferous areas near streams, ponds, swamps, or lakes.

EGGS

Virtually identical in all respects to those of *Asio otus wilsonianus* except that earliest laying is March 13 and latest is June 10, with the height of the egg-laying season falling between March 26 and May 18.

DISTRIBUTION IN NORTH AMERICA

Breeds from southern Mackenzie (Fort Simpson, Fort Providence), central British Columbia (Nulki Lake), and extreme southwest Manitoba (Whitewater

Lake), central and southwestern (and narrowly to southeastern) Saskatchewan, then southward to southern California (including Catalina Island), northwestern Baja California (to Lat. 30° N.), southern Arizona (Bates Well, Pima County, Santa Rita Mountains), New Mexico (Sante Fe), and western Texas.

Winters from southern Canada south to northern Baja California, Sonora (Tiburón Island), and Durango.

Accidental in Alaska (Taku River).

MIGRATION

There is a slight migration of the Western Long-eared Owl, especially toward the coastal areas in Washington State, Oregon, and northern California during late autumn, but never a truly general movement of the subspecies.

SPECIES

ORDER: STRIGIFORMES

FAMILY: STRIGIDAE

GENUS: *Asio* Brisson

SPECIES: *flammeus* (Pontoppidan)

SUBSPECIES

---

flammeus (Pontoppidan)   SHORT-EARED OWL

SHORT-EARED OWL
(COLOR PLATE XIV)

SCIENTIFIC NAME AND ORIGINAL DESCRIPTION

Asio flammeus flammeus (Pontoppidan). Original description: *Strix flammea* Pontoppidan, *Danske Atlas*, Volume 1, 1763, page 617, plate 25; based on a specimen taken in Sweden. Former scientific names: *Brachyotus palustris, Brachyotus palustris americanus, Otus brachyotus, Strix brachyotus, Strix accipitrina, Asio accipitrina, Strix flammea.*

OTHER NAMES

GRASS OWL   Because of its preference for areas of deep meadow grasses or marsh grasses.

LE HIBOU À OREILLES COURTES   French-Canadian name meaning "Short-eared Owl."

LE HIBOU DES MARAIS   French-Canadian name meaning "Marsh Owl."

MARSH OWL   Because of one form of habitat this owl frequents.

MEADOW OWL   After another type of habitat the bird likes.

NORTHERN SHORT-EARED OWL   Especially applied to the more northerly specimens of the race within its range.

PALMETTO OWL   After the type of habitat preferred by the owl in Florida, especially during breeding season.

PRAIRIE OWL   Another name applied in respect to a form of habitat the bird prefers.

SWAMP OWL   Actually a misnomer, since the owl prefers treeless marsh areas rather than the tangled tree areas of true swamps.

TECOLOTE OREJAS CORTAS DE PONTOPPIDAN   Mexican-Indian name meaning "Pontoppidan's Small-eared Owl."

DISTINGUISHING FEATURES

Essentially about the size of a large crow, the Short-eared Owl is only very slightly larger than the Long-eared Owl (*Asio otus wilsonianus*), but with a much wider distribution and far more often seen because of its diurnal habits. The ear tufts, after which it has been named, are very small and widely separated and not a reliable factor for identification, since more often than not they are lying flat against the head and not perceptible. Even when raised they are not especially easy to discern but, when discernible, are a positive identity mark. These ear tufts are almost never raised in flight and only rarely when perched. There is a distinctive oblong patch of black on the underwing near the wrist, at the base of the primaries, similar to that on the Long-ear Owl and a good identifying mark. There are also large buffy wing patches which become visible in flight and provide good identity markings. The facial disks are somewhat small for the size of the owl, with the superciliaries extending into the facial disk on each side instead of running parallel with the supraorbital facial rim as in other owls.

Rank in over-all size among the eighteen species: Seventh.

SHAPE AT REST

The body shape of this owl is rather bulky when perched, although at times it can and does elongate itself as a camouflaging measure. In normal perching it tends to lean forward more than most other North American owls, and therefore takes on the general aspect in silhouette of a hawk, though with the head far less distinctly outlined and seemingly neckless.

SHAPE IN FLIGHT

Especially as it ranges back and forth low over marsh grasses and meadows, this owl appears very similar to the Marsh Hawk but can be distinguished from that bird by its much shorter tail, blunt-headed and bull-necked appearance in flight, and the absence of the highly distinctive white rump patch which the Marsh Hawk wears. The underparts are distinctly light in coloration, making the black underwing patches all the more distinctive. When wheeling low over marshes and meadows, these patches become very evident, even from considerable distances.

FLIGHT PATTERN

Normally, flight is low to the ground and rather sloppy in character as the bird ranges back and forth in quest of prey, although the wingbeat is buoyant and easy, interspersed with long glides. The flight from perch to perch is usually relatively short, covering a direct-line distance of from 200 to 300 yards, but in a rather zigzagging manner, not too unlike that of the Nighthawk, but not as markedly agile.

The wingbeats are normally silent except during the courtship maneuverings. (See Courtship and Mating.) During its ranging flight while hunting, there are frequent times when the forward, zigzagging flight is interrupted by brief mothlike hoverings as it pauses to listen or watch for prey. In taking off from the ground or a low perch, it rises in a rather hurried manner, usually into the wind and often going quickly into its first glide. When prey is detected it raises its wings over its back, spills out the air and drops with unexpected suddenness out of sight in the tall grasses. The wingbeat is normally slightly faster and with less gliding than that performed by the Marsh Hawk.

The Short-eared Owl shares a flight characteristic with the Snowy Owl (*Nyctea scandiaca*) which is very distinctive: the body has the appearance of rising and lowering with each wingbeat, while the wing tips themselves do not seem to vary much from the horizontal plane upon which they are held. It is almost as if the owl were holding its wings steady and flapping its body instead. There is a notable lack of the full sweep of wingbeat so common among most birds of prey. The downstroke is usually slow and steady when the bird is actively ranging close to the ground, while the upstroke is swiftly accomplished and the wing tips are brought up high over the back.

One of the unusual flight characteristics of *Asio flammeus flammeus* is its proclivity for high flight—often 200 to 300 feet high, but sometimes so high that it is almost out of sight of unaided human vision. This is more common during the breeding season than at other times of the year, and such high flight is occa-sionally punctuated by very steep, swift dives toward the ground.

Measurements have been based on 9 measured birds: 3 males and 6 females.

WEIGHT

Species average: 311.7 gr. (10.9 oz.).

	Male	Female
Average	286.9 gr. (10.0 oz.)	336.5 gr. (11.8 oz.)
Minimum	261.3 gr. (9.2 oz.)	276.0 gr. (9.7 oz.)
Maximum	345.9 gr. (12.1 oz.)	429.4 gr. (15.0 oz.)

Rank in weight among the eighteen species: Seventh.

TOTAL LENGTH

Species average: 394.5 mm. (15.5″).

	Male	Female
Average	385.8 mm. (15.2″)	403.2 mm. (15.9″)
Minimum	336.3 mm. (13.3″)	363.4 mm. (14.3″)
Maximum	429.2 mm. (16.9″)	434.7 mm. (17.1″)

Rank in total length among the eighteen species: Eighth.

WINGSPAN

Species average: 1,055.1 mm. (41.6″).

	Male	Female
Average	1,042.8 mm. (41.1″)	1,067.4 mm. (42.1″)
Minimum	970.2 mm. (38.2″)	1,009.8 mm. (39.8″)
Maximum	1,088.9 mm. (42.9″)	1,120.3 mm. (44.1″)

Rank in wingspan among the eighteen species: Seventh.

INDIVIDUAL WING LENGTH

Species average: 309.0 mm. (12.2″).

	Male	Female
Average	299.1 mm. (11.8″)	318.9 mm. (12.6″)
Minimum	284.9 mm. (11.2″)	290.8 mm. (11.5″)
Maximum	321.3 mm. (12.7″)	336.7 mm. (13.3″)

Rank in wing length among the eighteen species: Seventh.

TAIL LENGTH

Species average: 150.2 mm. (5.9″).

	Male	Female
Average	146.1 mm. (5.8″)	154.3 mm. (6.1″)
Minimum	135.9 mm. (5.4″)	139.4 mm. (5.5″)
Maximum	149.9 mm. (5.9″)	158.8 mm. (6.3″)

Rank in tail length among the eighteen species: Ninth.

A variety of field sketches done mostly in northern Illinois of the Short-eared Owl (*Asio flammeus flammeus*). Note the seemingly neckless shape of the bird in flight, which is characteristic of the species.

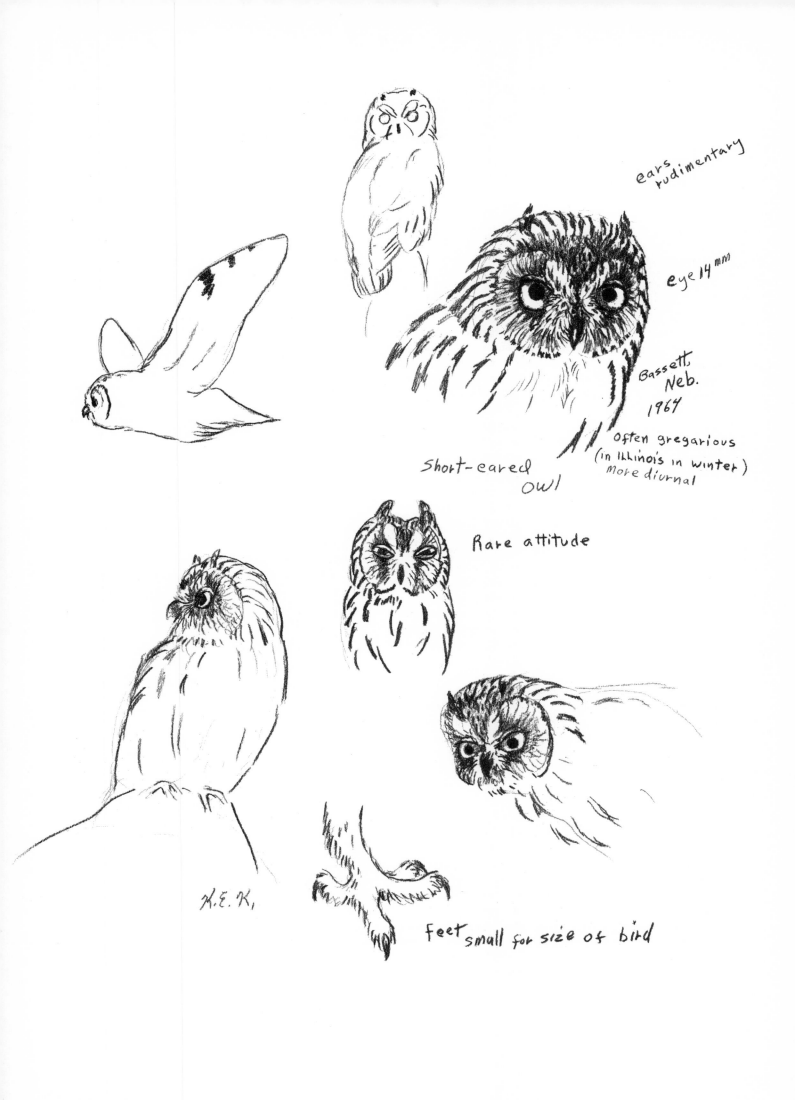

ears
rudimentary

eye 14mm

Bassett,
Neb.
1964

often gregarious
(in Illinois in winter)
more diurnal

Short-eared
Owl

Rare attitude

Feet small for size of bird

K.E.K.

BEAK LENGTH

Species average: 17.3 mm. (0.7″).

	Male	Female
Average	16.9 mm. (0.7″)	17.7 mm. (0.7″)
Minimum	15.8 mm. (0.6″)	16.8 mm. (0.7″)
Maximum	18.7 mm. (0.7″)	19.9 mm. (0.8″)

Rank in beak length among the eighteen species: Ninth.

LEGS, FEET, TALONS

The legs and feet of *Asio flammeus flammeus* are densely feathered to the base of the entirely black talons. The legs are somewhat longer than might be expected for an owl of this size—the tarsus measuring 44.5 mm. (1.8″) on the average—but because of the usual squatty posture of the perched bird, this is not apparent in casual observation. Leg plumage on the brown-phase bird is a warm buffy coloration, while on the gray-phase bird the coloration is a pure white or slightly dusky white. The bird's gripping strength with the feet is fairly strong and the talons are very sharply pointed.

EYES AND VISION

The Short-eared Owl has excellent vision any time of day or night and may be seen ranging for food on a bright, sunny afternoon as well as during the midst of night, although cloudy days are preferred and late evening is the peak hunting period. The irides are startlingly bright lemon yellow, much in contrast to the darkness of the surrounding facial-disk plumage. Because of the unusual darkness of the plumage close around both eyes, the eyes seem abnormally deep-set and the general aspect of the bird is one of dissipation. As with so many owls, quite often this bird will wear a very distinctly cross-eyed expression. The Short-eared Owl probably makes greater use of vision in hunting than the more strictly nocturnal owls, but hearing is still the more important sense in this respect.

EARS AND HEARING

The auditory sense, as in the other North American owls, is most acute and well performs its vital function in the predatory habits of the Short-eared Owl. But because of its more diurnal habits, the eyes and ears are more often used in concert for the location of prey than are those of the strictly nocturnal owls. The ear cavities are asymmetrical in placement, though not so markedly as in many species. There is, however, an enormous development of the actual ear parts, with the ear cavity fully two inches long—and that is as long as the skull is high—and proportionately broad. It has been stated that the hearing of *Asio flammeus flammeus* is so acute that it can hear the footfalls of a beetle at upward of 100 yards, the running of a mouse at 250 yards, and the squeaking of a mouse at an eighth of a mile. This owl, incidentally, decoys well to the simulated squeaking of a rodent.

EAR TUFTS, PLUMAGE, ANNUAL MOLT

Tending to lean or curve toward one another, the ear tufts are very small and inconspicuous, more often than not held flat to the head and projecting from slightly closer to the center of the head than do those of the Horned Owls (*Bubo virginianus* sp.), the Screech Owls (*Otus asio* sp.), or the Long-eared Owls (*Asio otus* sp.).

The plumage is reasonably tight to the body contour, though perhaps not quite as much so as in the Long-eared Owl. Because of the squat posturings of the bird, there is the impression that the plumage is much bulkier; an illusion which is dispelled when the perched bird elongates itself on its perch for purposes of camouflage.

There are two molts each year. The first is a molting of the body plumage only, which begins in January and is completed by mid-March. The second molt, begun in late July or early August and finished by mid-November, is a complete progressive molt of all plumage.

VOICE

The Short-eared Owl is not entirely silent during the non-breeding periods as is sometimes stated, but it is much less vociferous then as compared to the courtship and nesting time. One of its more common calls is a penetrating barking sound, much like the yapping of a very small dog. This call is repeated over and over for long periods, but almost always the delivery is in a series of three notes, sounding much like: *ANK-ANK-ANK ANK-ANK-ANK ANK-ANK-ANK ANK-ANK-ANK.* After a series of eight of these triplet yappings there is usually a slight pause before another series begins. Not

---

XXI FLORIDA SCREECH OWL

Otus asio floridanus (Ridgway). Male, female. Gray-phase male: Amelia Island, Nassau County, Florida, December 2, 1950. Red-phase female: Indian River County, Florida, September 11, 1939. A.O.U. Number 373-A

XXII SAGUARO SCREECH OWL

Otus asio gilmani Swarth. Female. Ten miles east of Sentinel, Maricopa County, Arizona, November 16, 1929. Not included in the 1957 A.O.U. Check-list

Short-eared Owl

Karl E. Karalus

infrequently there will be a prolonged single sound like: *A-A-A-A-A-A-A-N-N-N-K* after the eighth series has been uttered.

When solitarily hunting, the bird tends to issue a soft, persistent cooing note that has a pleasing musical quality. The same call is sometimes uttered during the courtship rituals (see Courtship and Mating) as a more distinct sort of *TOOT-TOOT-TOOT-TOOT*.

As is the case with the Long-eared Owl, the Short-eared Owl utters high, shrill distress cries while emulating an injured bird on the ground to decoy an intruder away from the nest area or young birds.

Once in a while this owl, while perched, utters a muted but shrill series of squeaking sounds similar to those made by a rodent. This could possibly be a call made in anticipation of hearing a reply from a nearby rodent, although this is entirely speculative as of this time. A weak, whistling cry, it is usually given only two or three times before the bird lapses into silence.

When approaching the nesting area where there are young birds waiting, the adults tend to issue a raspy note that sounds much as if a piece of metal were being cut with a hacksaw. This may or may not be followed by a clear, whistling squeal, degenerating into a muffled, sneezy, half-barking cry. The young birds in the nest respond at once with a sound much like that of steam escaping from a broken pipe—the sound lasts for about three seconds and is repeated two or three times.

When danger threatens, the adults give voice to a wide variety of strange cries, usually beginning with a low sound like *KUK!*, which evidently warns the young to be silent. The adult then breaks into a scolding note similar to that of a disturbed sea gull, and this cry is directed at the intruder. (The same note, in a more subdued manner, is given when one Short-eared Owl inadvertently invades the hunting territory of another.) It may then be followed by a variety of squeals, shrieks, raspy cries, chucklings, and weird groanings.

Young and adult birds alike snap their beaks and hiss at intruders. This sound is further varied by the adults with a "poofing" sound, like a short exhalation, followed by a sort of purring growl.

At times, while flying at great height, the male (and possibly the female) gives voice to a steady, monotonous, four-per-second tooting call which lasts for as few as 14 notes or as many as 30, but usually around 20. This call, strangely enough, is extremely ventriloquial and quite difficult to locate, even though the bird issuing it may be clearly in view high above.

XXIII HASBROUCK'S SCREECH OWL

Otus asio hasbroucki Ridgway. Male. Vicinity of Kerrville, Kerr County, Texas, February 8, 1915. A.O.U. Number 373-I

XXIV SOUTHERN CALIFORNIA SCREECH OWL

Otus asio inyoensis Grinnell. Male. Ten miles south of Independence, Inyo County, California, February 7, 1940. A.O.U. Number 373-O

SEXUAL DIFFERENCES: SIZE, COLORATION, VOICE

There is a surprising difference in coloration between male and female birds, with the female almost always a good bit darker in general. Some males will have a ground color of almost pure white on the undertail coverts, flanks, and belly, shading into a faint creaminess on the breast and sides, while the adult females are a distinct orangish buff on these parts. There is some speculation that such color differences may be due to color phase or seasonal changes, but they occur so generally on a year-round basis that there seems greater reason to believe that the difference is distinctly sexual. Not unexpectedly, the female is slightly larger than the male, and her voice is more shrill and squeaky, though with less of the hoarse quality of the male bird.

MORTALITY AND LONGEVITY

Nesting cannibalism has been noted on several occasions, but this is evidently far more the exception than the rule and is of little consequence in the general picture of infant mortality. Extensive tabulations on the mortality rates, in the nest or out of it, are lacking; though it is generally believed that mortality is somewhat less than that among owls inclined to nest in abandoned nests of hawks or crows. Several captive Short-eared Owls have been known to reach fifteen years of age, though no data are available on longevity in the wild state.

COLORATION AND MARKINGS: ADULT

Asio flammeus flammeus is to some degree dichromatic, although not as pronouncedly so as is the Eastern Screech Owl (*Otus asio naevius*). There is a brown phase and a gray phase.

In the brown color phase of the Short-eared Owl, the features of breast, belly, undertail coverts, and legs are generally a light warm buff to deep sandy coloration. Similar plumage in the gray-color-phase bird is white or only faintly creamy white, and the gray is a cold gray without any of the warm brownish tinge.

In general, coloration of the underparts is highly variable, not only because of dichromatism, but varying widely among birds of the same color phase, ranging from buffy white to warm orangish tan. Each feather, excluding those of the rump, has a blackish-brown center stripe. This striping is heaviest on the feathers of the shoulders, nape, back, and breast. Stripes on the belly and sides are considerably narrower and gradually disappear until, on flanks, legs, lower belly, and under-tail coverts, they are entirely absent. The rump plumage is more of a reddish buff, each feather with indistinct brown crescent markings.

The wing coverts are well mottled with irregular slaty brown and orangish buff. Normally, five bands of buff or orange buff cross the dusky-brown secondaries. The inner primaries may range from markedly orangish brown to light buff, becoming darker near the ends, but tipped in a broad buffy termination. This buff tipping becomes vague or may even be absent on the outermost primaries, and the quills here have three to five rather square, irregular splashings of dusky brown on the outer webs. The primary coverts have one (sometimes two) vague series of orangish-brown spots on a background of plain dusky brown. The tail may range from orange brown to light buff and is usually crossed by five equally wide slate-brown bands on the middle feathers, but narrower bands on the outer feathers. All rectrices terminate in an equally broad band of orange brown or dusky buff.

Throat, chin, and superciliaries are a dull white. The lores are similarly colored, but with each bristle shafted in black. Facial-disk coloration is widely variable and may range from a dingy buff white to a much deeper orange brown, but always with those feathers encircling the eyes very distinctly dark brown to black. The mottling of the facial rims is irregularly orange brown, grayish, dull buff and blackish, except at the ear coverts, where they become uniformly slaty black. The beak and talons are black.

The underwing coverts range from pale buff to pure, unblemished white except for the conspicuous blackish-brown spot—usually of oval or crescent shape—which appears on the terminal half of the greater underwing coverts. The underside of the primaries is normally buffy white, marked with one or two (usually two) broad grayish or dusky-buff bands.

It is interesting to note that the plumage of birds inhabiting sandy coastal regions tends to be considerably lighter than that of birds residing in more inland areas.

COLORATION AND MARKINGS: JUVENILE

The upperparts are generally a rather dark brown or slaty brown, with each feather tipped quite broadly with orangish buff. The facial disks are invariably a uniform brownish black. Underparts are generally dull in color, ranging from orange buff to smoky gray. Wings and tail are similar to those of adult birds.

GENERAL HABITS AND CHARACTERISTICS

Because of its frequent day-hunting activities, the Short-eared Owl is one of the most commonly seen owls in North America, although it is very often mistaken for a Marsh Hawk because it favors the same sort of habitat and tends to range back and forth low to the ground while hunting, much in the manner of the Marsh Hawk. It is most apt to be seen in the hours from mid-afternoon to early dusk, especially on overcast or partially cloudy days.

Next to the Barn Owl (*Tyto alba pratincola*), this species is among the most cosmopolitan of owls. It is found on all continents except Australia, and ranges from the Arctic Circle to the Antarctic Circle. It is not particularly bothered by cold weather, and there is little migrational inclination; though during the worst of winter's inclemencies, the owl may take a temporary refuge under a sheltered creek-bank overhang or on the leeward side of fence rows which have become heavily bedecked with tumbleweed.

Asio flammeus flammeus is not as gregarious as *Asio otus wilsonianus,* although it is often witnessed hunting in pairs, even during the non-breeding seasons, leading to the supposition that it mates for life. In most cases, however, the birds are rarely found closer together than 200 yards, even when mates. Some observers have noted that the Short-eared Owl will associate to some extent with Burrowing Owls (*Speotyto cunicularius* sp.) and, even more surprisingly, with Marsh Hawks. There seems to be something of a mutual territorial agreement, as well, among Burrowing Owls, Long-eared Owls, and Short-eared Owls in those areas where their ranges tend to overlap. In such areas, each bird seems to enjoy the uncontested privilege of hunting in a particular area of terrain—the Short-eared Owl in the meadows, marshes, and cereal grainfield edges; the Burrowing Owl in the pastures and open sagelands; the Long-eared Owl in the woodland groves and thickets.

When flushed from cover in marsh or deep grasslands, the Short-eared Owl will take to wing easily the first time and fly 200 or 300 yards before settling, but it tends to sit rather tightly after that and rarely will flush again unless nearly trod upon.

A rather unusual characteristic of *Asio flammeus flammeus* is the fact that it seems to take considerable sport in the harassment of large birds in flight, not with any intent to kill or even inflict injury, but evidently for something akin to amusement. This action has been observed many times as the Short-eared Owl has swooped and struck at such flying birds as Great Blue Herons, egrets, cranes, vultures, and occasionally even at waterfowl resting on pond surfaces. It is a remarkably agile flier, sometimes performing rather astonishing aerial maneuvers.

Short-eared Owl

HABITAT AND ROOSTING

In preference of habitat, the Short-eared Owl is one of the most varied species. While primarily a bird of marshland and deep grass fields, it is often found in open woodlands, desert areas, sagelands, open fields, pastures, villages, city park areas, prairielands, lower mountain slopes, canyons, arroyos, woodland ravines, scrub-oak cover, fresh- and salt-water bogs, swamps, tundra, stubble fields, dunelands, croplands, orchards, and other such areas.

More often than not a ground-roosting bird, it prefers a dense grass tussock for its roost, although it will often merely alight and sleep at an indistinguishable spot in the midst of a rye field or overgrown meadowland. Occasionally it will roost in low brush, especially along the fringes of marshes and streams. Less often, roosting will take place in low conifers, but this is a characteristic more evident in bad weather during winter than at other times. Rarely, if ever, will it roost in hardwoods. It is most often seen when inadvertently flushed by an individual progressing through deep grasses, particularly on the fringe of a marshland or low, wet meadow.

ENEMIES AND DEFENSES

As is common among the more cosmopolitan of owls, man is the greatest enemy, but where natural enemies are concerned there are few which bother the Short-eared Owl. Occasionally one will be struck at by a Prairie Falcon or Red-shouldered Hawk or harassed by a crow, magpie, raven, or jay. On the whole, however, smaller birds do not seem to recognize *Asio flammeus flammeus* as an enemy and tend not to pester it, despite the fact that during the nesting season this owl will prey upon a certain number of smaller birds. More often than not, if there is an incident of harassment, it is the Short-eared Owl itself that is harassing a heron, crow, hawk, or vulture.

In the matter of defenses, protective coloration plays a major role. The mottled orangish-buff-brown plumage is amazingly effective in camouflaging the bird as it sits amid dried cattail reeds, meadow grasses, weed-field growth, and the like. In addition, this owl has an amazing facility for alighting on a short, projecting branch close to the ground or water and so effectively molding its body to the configuration of the wood that even at close range it may readily be mistaken for a continuation of the broken stub.

A secondary defensive measure is an inclination to feign death. If discovered and attack, it may flop over onto its side and lie completely still on the ground with its eyes closed, even to the point of allowing itself to be picked up and handled. This, it should be noted, is not as common an attribute among the adult birds as it is among nestlings and yearling flying birds. If, however, the danger continues to threaten, the owl can become aggressive indeed. It will throw itself onto its back and hiss menacingly, snap its beak in great agitation, and lash out effectively with its sharply taloned feet. Though it will threaten with its beak, it rarely used the beak in an actual attack.

Among its most interesting defensive measures are those performed when its offspring are endangered. At the approach of an intruder, when it seems that detection of nest and young birds is imminent, one or both parent birds will feign injury in an effort to lead the intruder away. Usually one adult bird will flush much earlier than the other. Probably it is the male who always flushes first. He will usually take to wing and fly in a peculiarly injured manner at a height of about 20 to 30 feet, then in full view of the intruder he will cry sharply, execute a fluttering tumble to the ground, and lie there with wings outstretched, crying in a piteous way. A whole variety of calls may be uttered in an effort to bring the intruder closer to the supposedly injured bird, with the owl struggling along the ground and somehow just managing to stay out of reach and consistently leading the intruder away. If this ruse fails, however, and the intruder continues toward the nest, the bird will take to wing and circle above him. At this time the second bird, the female, will similarly take wing and both birds will circle and cry close overhead while the young birds scatter from the nest into the deeper surrounding grasses a short distance and then freeze in place. If the danger to the young persists or worsens, the flying adults may then even launch an attack of sorts. Flying at a height of about 50 feet, they will plunge almost straight downward very close to the intruder, causing him to flinch in an effort to ward off the expected assault. Rarely is contact made, however. The birds will deliberately miss very closely, and at a height of only a foot or two off the grasses they will sail away for about 100 feet before landing and voicing the same anguished cries again. The wings are left open and flapping weakly as a further enticement to the intruder. If the intruder approaches the grounded bird, the act continues until only about 20 feet separate them, at which time the adult will fold first one wing, then the other, take off in low flight to the ground for about another 100 feet, and repeat the act. Sometimes when the adult drops toward the intruder from its 50-foot height, it will clap its wings together with startling loudness as it falls. If it does not feel it is attracting enough attention on the ground with its thrashing and cries, it will smack its wings harshly against its own sides or breast, again causing a loud clapping. For all its defensive antics where its own offspring are concerned, however, actual attacks of the owl against an intruder are extremely rare.

HUNTING METHODS AND
CARRYING OF PREY

The most commonly observed hunting method favored by the Short-eared Owl is a low, ranging pattern interspersed with glidings over marsh fringes and deep weedy or meadow areas, much in the manner of the Marsh Hawk. Its flight is usually level as it hunts, even in the glides, but broken often with pauses to hover in one spot with wings treading air silently as it listens and watches for prey. This hovering in a wobbly, mothlike fluttering may last for a few seconds or upward of half a minute before it suddenly swoops neatly onto its prey, raising its wings high to spill out the air and stretching its feet well forward and downward, poised to grasp. Most commonly this form of hunting is done in late afternoon and early evening.

The level of hunting flight is usually somewhat higher in winter than in summer. When snow covers the ground, this owl tends to range at a height of about 15 to 20 feet, but zigzagging, pausing, hovering, whirling, and diving much as it does in summer. Expert at utilizing the wind, it takes advantage of the air currents over dunes, sagelands, and grasslands, gliding into the wind with consummate skill at heights of from five to thirty feet, turning its head from side to side as it listens and watches for prey. Often it will alight on an open-ground branch stub, fence post, hummock, or even bare ground and sit quietly, listening for prey, only to rise again in a hurried manner and zigzag once more back and forth as it resumes hunting in a more active manner.

While the hunting ranges of the Short-eared Owl, Great Horned Owl and Marsh Hawk overlap, and all three will patrol the marsh fringes, meadows, stubble fields, and cut cornfields in search of mice, there is little in the way of encounters between them, since the Marsh Hawk hunts mainly by day, especially in the mornings, the Short-eared Owl in the late afternoons and early evenings, and the Great Horned Owl in late evening and nighttime.

Although normally it prefers the more open areas for its hunting, *Asio flammeus flammeus* will frequently hunt through dense thickets, heavily overgrown willow clumps, and areas of small but densely overgrown evergreens. On occasion it will alight on the ground where it has seen a rat or mouse pop into a hole and will stand there quietly, straddling the hole for long periods, waiting for the rodent to reappear—with a patience that is often quite successful. Most often, however, it snatches up its smaller prey—mice in particular—without even alighting, carrying the small animal to some convenient perch nearby that is close to the ground and devouring it there. Almost all prey is carried in the talons rather than the beak.

FOOD, FEEDING HABITS, WASTES

The favorite food of the Short-eared Owl is, of course, mice—primarily meadow voles. Mice constitute almost the entire bulk of the bird's diet during all times of the year except for the period when there are young owls in the nest. At that time the quest for prey expands and takes in practically anything of a size which can be handled. It is during this period that *Asio flammeus flammeus* will kill fair numbers of songbirds and some game birds. Quail, rails, occasional pheasants, snipe, and other such birds will fall prey. If taken to the nest for the young, they are torn into bits to be fed to the baby owls; if devoured by the adult, they are torn into large chunks and swallowed on the spot.

A Short-eared Owl having caught a black rail, for example, will generally rip the bird in half, holding it down with its talons and jerking savagely with the beak. Then the two halves are swallowed whole in turn. Among the smaller birds also taken at this time are robins and other thrushes, pipits, buntings, juncos, various sparrows, grackles, red-winged blackbirds, cowbirds, kinglets, sapsuckers, flickers, and other woodpeckers, meadowlarks, and terns. Bats are frequently caught, both hanging and in flight, and larger insects such as crickets, beetles, roaches, grasshoppers, katydids, and large caterpillars are avidly taken. Mice and numerous other small mammals are included in the diet: pocket gophers, ground squirrels, shrews, moles, rats, rabbits, and young muskrats.

Pellet regurgitation by the Short-eared Owl is seemingly accomplished without undue effort; with one or two convulsive open-mouth flexings, the mucus-coated dark-gray pellet, about two inches long and an inch in diameter, pops from the mouth and is lost among the deep grasses wherever the bird is perched. Fecal wates are vicous in texture, mainly grayish with some mottling of white or greenish. These latter wastes are often ejected at the moment the bird takes to flight but before it rises clear of the surrounding grasses.

HARVEST MOUSE AS OWL FOOD

Probably no other creature in North America is more frequently and consistently taken as prey by almost all owl species on this continent than the harvest mouse, along with other mouse species. The Short-eared Owl in particular preys very heavily upon this species on a year-round basis. Without the control factor that owls exert on harvest-mouse populations, as well as those of other mice, great economic losses would result.

COURTSHIP AND MATING

The courtship flight of the male *Asio flammeus flammeus*, usually occurring in late April or early May, is one of the most spectacular among all North American owls. The individual, who is fortunate enough to witness it, is invariably held rooted to the spot in wonderment as the aerial display unfolds. The authors have watched this on three separate occasions and, while there were minor variations each time, a description of one of the sequences will be well representative of what occurs. This courtship flight occurred in McHenry County, Illinois, about a half mile from the west shore of Wonder Lake. It was a breath-taking exhibition. It began with the male Short-eared Owl rising high above a ground-perched female, all the while repeating a low-toned series of *whooot-whooot-whooot* cries at the rate of about four notes per second and repeated about 20 times. The male continued to climb in a steady spiral until he had reached an altitude of a thousand to fifteen hundred feet. Here he leveled off and, as we watched through binoculars, began circling with slow, even wingbeats, his body seeming to fluctuate from the horizontal more than his wings. This was interspersed with some gliding and occasional sideslipping maneuvers, and all the while the monotoned calling came faintly to us. Gradually the flight pattern became more erratic and excited and the owl introduced an irregular series of short dives and recoveries, dipping swiftly downward for perhaps a hundred feet and then recovering the former altitude with a steep upward curve and rapidly beating wings. During both the diving and the climbing, the wing tips smacked together rapidly under the bird's body, with a sharp clapping sound quite clearly audible to us. The sound was, in fact, suggestive of a large flag rippling and popping in a very stiff breeze. To make this sound occur, the male's wings not only are brought down smartly to meet far beneath the bird, but are also extended rearward so that the four or five outermost primaries of each wing are the only ones that meet.

This action continued for about ten minutes but was suddenly interrupted by a whole series of wild maneuverings on jerky wingbeats that seemingly were almost out of control, during which the male bird fell, recovered, tumbled in an amazing series of somersaults and roll-overs, and finally dropped in a flaccid and formless fall as if the bird had been struck dead in mid-flight. Recovering itself after a drop of at least two hundred feet, the bird returned to its former peak altitude, circled once very widely, and then dropped in a long swooping dive punctuated all the way down with wing clapping and a most peculiar chattering cry—a quavering, questioning sort of cry with an eerie and yet appealing quality to it.

The closer the plummeting bird came to the ground the more certain we became that it could never recover in time to prevent smashing into the ground with devastating force. But the dive stopped just in time and the male leveled off at great speed just above the reed-tops, made a wide circle only inches over them, and then slowed and settled gently to earth close to the female, who had been watching closely all this while.

For perhaps two full minutes after coming to a stop, the male merely stood quietly, as if regaining his breath. The female began moving gradually closer to him, but she was still three or four feet distant from him when he very gravely dipped his head and walked to her in a deliberate manner, stood beside her where she had stopped, and pressed his shoulder against hers. In a moment he turned his head to her and gently began preening her nape with his beak.

The female shivered rather strongly after a moment of this and suddenly dropped onto her side on the ground. At once the male partially straddled her, placing one foot low on her side and bringing his vent accurately into contact with hers. Copulation evidently took place immediately and accurately and lasted for no more than twenty seconds. As soon as it was completed, the female regained her feet, shook herself, made a low cooing sound, and took off, flying low over the grasses in a swift, direct line. The male followed close behind.

Observations of others indicate that such copulation will recur at intervals over the next few days, sometimes with more aerial acrobatics by the male, but usually without them or, more likely, with an abbreviated and lower-altitude modification of them. There is good reason to believe that once a pair have mated, they remain mated for life and stay reasonably close to one another the year around.

ANNUAL BROODS, NEST, NESTING HABITS

Although occasionally double-brooded in the more southerly portions of its North American breeding range, the Short-eared Owl is essentially single-brooded and almost invariably nests upon the ground. Most often the nest is no more than a slight depression in a little rise of ground, well hidden by heavy surrounding reeds or grasses, and the depression itself is carelessly lined with some dried grasses, weed stalks, and occasional feathers from the female's breast. At other times it may be no more than a shallow dip hollowed out of bare sand and strangely exposed. Only rarely, however, will the nesting occur in a low bush, and evidently never higher up in a tree.

Underground nesting in an abandoned mammal burrow is not too uncommon, and occasionally this owl will even dig its own burrow. This goes down at a slant for perhaps two feet, then moves horizontally for another two or three feet, ending in a small chamber which is usually a bit more elevated than the tunnel.

Short-eared Owl

The nest here will usually be a sparse padding of some grasses and a few feathers, from about 9 to 12 inches in diameter, and up to two inches thick. Most commonly, though, preference is for a nest in dry grasses on ground level, though often immediately adjacent to wet ground.

Often the nest will be hidden by a covering arch of reeds or saw grass; less often, the owl will actually make a tunnel of sorts through the grasses for 10 or 12 feet, through which it must walk after alighting in order to get to the nest.

If available, sometimes small sticks are used in the nest construction; more commonly, bits of decomposing vegetation; but the nest is always quite sloppily built. It does have the virtue, however, of being extremely difficult to detect. By the same token, such ground nesting does allow for certain hazards which do not normally affect other nesting owl species. Fire, for example, will often destroy the nest of the Short-eared Owl, and sometimes those that are constructed in meadow areas will inadvertently be plowed under by farmers. In coastal areas the nests built in salt bogs are sometimes too close to the sea, and when the highest tides of the month move in, these nests are inundated and the eggs destroyed.

Whenever a nest is destroyed in those or other ways, a second nesting is begun within about two weeks, but usually with fewer eggs deposited than were in the initial nesting. It has also been reported, though not substantiated, that if the nest is disturbed, the adults will move their eggs to a new location a short distance away and continue incubation there.

Quite often the nesting adults will sit on a raised tussock or branch stub fairly close to the nest and will doze there during the early and middle hours of the day. If disturbed while on the nest, the adult may hop off and run a short distance away, then stop and return part of the distance and stand to face the intruder with angry defiance.

EGGS

Number per nesting As few as four and as many as fourteen eggs may be laid, but the most usual nestings contain from five to seven eggs.

Color There is some color variation in the eggs, but only of a vague nature. At times they may be dull white; sometimes they will have a creamy cast to them, and on rare occasions they may be faintly yellow. Most often, however, they are white, with a faint suggestion of a bluish tinge.

Shape The eggs of the Short-eared Owl are only slightly more ovate than those of the majority of other owl species in North America. Rarely do they give the impression of being practically globular, as do those of some species.

Texture The shell surface is quite smooth, with only the faintest suggestion of granulation and little, if any, trace of glossiness.

Size Average egg size for the species, based on the measurements of 172 eggs, is 39.6 mm. (1.6") in length and 31.9 mm. (1.3") in width. The extremes among those measured were:

Maximum length: 44.5 mm. (1.8")
Minimum length: 33.0 mm. (1.3")
Maximum width: 37.6 mm. (1.5")
Minimum width: 29.0 mm. (1.1")

Interval of egg-laying The eggs are rarely ever laid at shorter intervals of time than 48 hours, and often upward of a week apart, especially in the smaller clutches of eggs.

Egg-laying dates Alaska and arctic Canada: earliest, June 5; latest, July 2; normally between June 10 and June 25.

Southern Canada: earliest, April 30; latest, June 22; normally between May 4 and June 17.

Northern United States: earliest, April 14; latest, June 15; normally between April 23 and June 10.

Midwest: earliest, April 4; latest, June 8; normally between April 16 and May 25.

Southern California: earliest, March 20; latest, May 18; normally between March 26 and April 26.

INCUBATION AND BROODING CHARACTERISTICS

The male will sometimes aid in the brooding, but mostly this is a job handled strictly by the female, with her mate supplying food to her at the nest for as long as brooding continues. Because of the staggering of the egg-laying, accurate establishment of incubation time is in question, especially since it is possible that incubation does not begin in some of the larger clutches until the second or third egg is laid. (In smaller clutches, it is probable that incubation begins with the first egg laid.) In most cases, it is believed, the full incubation period is never less than 21 days nor more than 28.

The brooding female is loath to leave her nest except under conditions of extreme danger from natural hazards such as fire or flood, or at the direct-line approach of an enemy such as man, and even then not until the enemy is only a few feet away and cannot help but encounter the nest.

YOUNG AND FAMILY LIFE CHARACTERISTICS

The interval between hatchings of the eggs is usually about three days, although it may be as little as

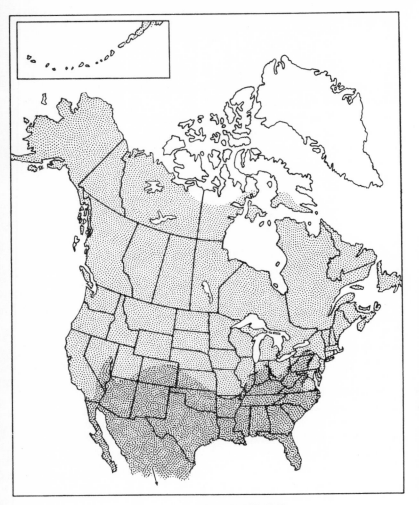

SHORT-EARED OWL

Asio flammeus flammeus (Pontoppidan)

inches in length and its back is well feathered with brown plumage, each feather broadly tipped with rusty buff. The wing feathers have begun growing, but the tail has not yet appeared. The down of the underparts is still a long, soft, cinnamon buff, and by this time the facial disks have become a variegated blackish brown.

Within the next two or three days the young bird begins to stray from the nest, but the parent birds keep close tabs on its whereabouts and continue to tend it wherever it stops to rest, though this is rarely far from the nest itself. This away-from-the-nest care continues until the young bird is six weeks old.

By the twenty-fourth day the first-winter plumage has begun to appear through the downy plumage and the body down is gradually molted as wings and tail continue developing. At the end of the fourth week the young bird is capable of short flight but continues to stay mainly on the ground, although it now tends to stray considerably farther from the nest area.

At six weeks of age the fledglings are straying as much as 150 yards from the nest, keeping to the dense grasses and causing the parent birds considerable difficulty in keeping up with them and supplying them with food. It is at this point that the fledglings begin catching some of their own food—principally insects and small amphibians.

By the eighth week the young birds fly very well but remain under the care of their parents. Not until late September or early October has all trace of down vanished, and then the young birds are fully bedecked in their first-winter plumage.

two days or as much, in rare instances, as fourteen days. The newly hatched young are quite weak for the first 18 to 24 hours. During this period they are covered with a short, grayish-white natal down which is inclined to have a buffy tinge on the upperparts, shading into grayish on the sides and to almost pure white on median line of breast and belly. The base of this natal down on wings and sides is darker and tends to form dark narrow patches or dark lines.

By the end of the fourth day (sometimes as early as the third day) the natal down starts being replaced by a secondary down and, almost simultaneously, with the first downy plumage, which is very soft and loose in structure. The secondary down appears all over the bird and is generally long, soft, and cinnamon buff in color; but the first downy plumage appears initially on the back. At this time the baby bird is about six inches in length.

By the tenth day the young are quite active and have learned to freeze if danger nears, and even to feign death if the hazard grows worse. By the twelfth or thirteenth day the nestling has reached about ten

DISTRIBUTION IN NORTH AMERICA

Breeds from northern Alaska (Cape Prince of Wales, Point Barrow), northern Mackenzie (Franklin Bay), District of Keewatin (Cape Eskimo), southeastern Baffin Island (Greater Kingwah, Kingnait Fiord), Labrador and Newfoundland, south to southern California (San Diego County), northern Nevada (Lee), Utah, northeastern Colorado (Sterling), Kansas (Manhattan, Neosho Falls), Missouri, southern Illinois (Odin), northern Indiana, southern Ohio (Circleville), northwestern New York (Brockport, Buffalo), New Jersey (Cape May), and the tidewater areas of Virginia.

Winters almost throughout breeding range and occasionally from southern British Columbia, east-central Washington, Montana, South Dakota, Minnesota, Wisconsin, southern Michigan, southern Ontario, and Massachusetts, southward to Baja California (Cape San Lucas), Mexico, Texas, the Gulf Coast, and Florida (Cape Sable).

Casual in Greenland (north to Upernavik District), Bermuda, Cuba, and Guatemala (Volcán de Agua). Accidental on St. Bartholemew.

Short-eared Owl

MIGRATION

Only slightly migrational in its habits, the Short-eared Owl often prefers to remain throughout the year in one area, tending to move southward to escape the more snowy areas in only the harshest of winters. It does not like to remain in areas where the snow completely covers the grass and weeds. Although not normally a gregarious bird, it may occasionally be seen in groups of 20 or 30 birds during those irregular migrational periods. It is not uncommon, for example, to see a score or more of these birds of prey simultaneously hunting the same California marshland. Long years ago, concentrations of more than 200 birds were recorded in some years, but no such extensive gatherings have been recorded during the past half century. The bird is certainly a powerful enough flier to make long migrations if it so desires, as is evidenced by its casual appearance on Bermuda, Cuba, and other islands. In one recorded case, a Short-eared Owl, which did not seem particularly fatigued and which rested only a short while before taking wing again, alighted on the foredeck of a passenger steamer in the Atlantic fully 800 miles from the nearest land.

ECONOMIC INFLUENCE

There can be no doubt whatever, despite its tendency to kill some game birds and songbirds during its nesting season, that *Asio flammeus flammeus* is of inestimable economic benefit to man in its reduction of injurious rodents, which comprise as much as 94 per cent of its total diet on an annual basis. There have been a number of cases in years past when there was suddenly a superabundance of rodents which wreaked considerable havoc until Short-eared Owls moved into the areas in large numbers and decimated the rat and mouse populations.

SPECIES

ORDER: STRIGIFORMES

FAMILY: STRIGIDAE

GENUS: *Otus* Pennant

SPECIES: *asio* (Linnaeus)

SUBSPECIES

---

naevius (Gmelin)	EASTERN SCREECH OWL
aikeni (Brewster)	AIKEN'S SCREECH OWL
asio (Linnaeus)	SOUTHERN SCREECH OWL
bendirei (Brewster)	CALIFORNIA SCREECH OWL
brewsteri Ridgway	BREWSTER'S SCREECH OWL
cineraceus (Ridgway)	MEXICAN SCREECH OWL
floridanus (Ridgway)	FLORIDA SCREECH OWL
gilmani Swarth	SAGUARO SCREECH OWL
hasbroucki Ridgway	HASBROUCK'S SCREECH OWL
inyoensis Grinnell	SOUTHERN CALIFORNIA SCREECH OWL
kennicottii (Elliot)	KENNICOTT'S SCREECH OWL
macfarlanei (Brewster)	MACFARLANE'S SCREECH OWL
maxwelliae (Ridgway)	ROCKY MOUNTAIN SCREECH OWL
mccallii (Cassin)	TEXAS SCREECH OWL
quercinus Grinnell	PASADENA SCREECH OWL
suttoni Moore	GUADALUPE SCREECH OWL
swenki Oberholser	NEBRASKA SCREECH OWL
yumanensis Miller and Miller	YUMA SCREECH OWL

THE SCREECH OWLS
Otus asio (Linnaeus)

Because no other group of owls in the world has more subtle differences and more nuances of vocal quality and delivery, size and coloration than those falling under the genus and species *Otus asio*—the Screech Owls—and because probably no owl is more familiar to more people on this continent, it becomes necessary to discuss them in a generic way before moving into specifics.

Unfortunately there is still great contention among various ornithologists about exactly how many subspecies (or races) of Screech Owls there are on the North American continent. As always, there are factions which are sometimes disrespectfully called "the lumpers," who prefer to see minor physical, behavioral, and characteristical differences largely overlooked and quite similar birds all lumped together under one subspecific nomenclature. At the same time, there are those factions branded as "hairsplitters," who tend to seize upon any variation, irrespective of how slight, as justification for the establishment of a subspecies.

Neither group is really wrong—nor, for that matter, entirely right—but a closer meeting of minds and sensible determination of what actually constitutes valid subspecific difference is very much needed. A great deal of effort is still required in this respect, but until such time as new standards are established and adhered to by all factions of the ornithological fraternity, the guidelines established by the American Ornithological Union seem to be the best.

This is not to say that the extensive work of such eminent men in the taxonomical field as Joe T. Marshall, Jr., of the University of Arizona at Tucson, should be given short shrift. Marshall is greatly—and probably justifiably—concerned over the present classifications in respect to *Otus asio* and, in fact, the entire Genus *Otus*.

There are presently three *Otus* species recognized in North America north of Mexico. Most abundant, of course, are the *Otus asio* races—the Screech Owls. But there is also *Otus trichopsis,* the present Whiskered Owl, which was for so long referred to as the Spotted Screech Owl; as well as *Otus flammeolus,* now known as the Flammulated Owl, which was previously called the Flammulated Screech Owl.

All three of these species are essentially gray birds (some with subspecific dichromatic color phases) and, in many cases, might better be classified through difference in vocal characteristics than through physiognomy or coloration. There is quite a distinct vocal difference among the three species. *Otus asio* gives voice to an extended, muted trill which falls pleasantly on the ear and is highly distinctive. *Otus trichopsis,* on the other hand, utters a decidedly slower, more syncopated trill of only six or seven notes. Finally, *Otus flammeolus* issues only a single hoot. Of these three species, *flammeolus* is the smallest, *trichopsis* is slightly larger, and *asio* is the largest. The three differ as well in territory and habitat; *flammeolus* having the most limited, *asio* the most extensive. Relatively high-altitude coniferous forests are inhabited by *flammeolus,* while *trichopsis* requires thick mixed woods of conifers and hardwoods at middle elevations. *Asio* is generally at much lower altitudes and in a wide variety of habitat—from desert terrain in the West to forested creek bottoms in prairie lands, hardwood forests in the East, and hammock, live oak, or cabbage-palm habitat in the deepest South. Yet, in the West—Arizona, for example—there is a certain slight amount of territorial overlap among all three species, but no interbreeding. There are, of course, physiological differences as well; both *asio* and *trichopsis* have yellow irides and their feet are naked, while the iris of *flammeolus* is soft brown and the toes are well feathered. Other differences (which will be noted in the specific sections on these owls) well establish their identity as distinct species in their own right.

The problem of classification, however, grows much more difficult and open to question in regard to the eighteen subspecific races of *Otus asio,* one or more of which can be found in virtually every type of habitat in North America. Some taxonomical authorities—Joe Marshall, for instance—strongly believe that the Screech Owl races of East and West are so distinct in their differences that they should be revised into separate species.* At this time they are not. One of the prime considerations for possible reclassification into two distinct species is the fact that the voices of the Eastern races differ considerably from those of the Western races. Marshall describes the vocal characteristic of the Eastern races as being a sort of trilled whinnying sound, whereas he says the Screech Owls of the West have much more of a "bouncing-ball" quality to their calls and a distinctly doubled trill. Further, the Eastern races are dichromatic, with red (or brown) and gray color phases, while the Western races are essentially monochromatic in gray. There are other geographical differences of note as well, which are pointed out in the specific descriptions of the various Screech Owl races. But just as Marshall urges a reclassification of Eastern and Western races of Screech Owls, other authorities feel similarly about separating the Northern and Southern races, and still others feel strongly about separating those of arid and humid areas.

What causes difficulty in establishing separate species classifications between the most distinctly different Western and Eastern races of Screech Owls is the fact that the characteristics among the Western birds are, unfortunately, not entirely constant. The exceptions are so distinct that they seem to prohibit blanket reclassification effectively for the Western races. For example, *Otus asio kennicottii*—Kennicott's Screech Owl—of the coastal area of the Northwest has the lighter beak and red color phase of the Eastern races, but its voice and markings are typically Western. Similarly, *Otus asio mccallii*—the Texas Screech Owl—has the markings of the Western races and lacks a red color phase, but its voice and beak color are like those of the Eastern races.

To compound the problem further, some of the races tend to interbreed and there are considerable gradations in size, coloration, markings, and tonal qualities among the intergrades. To make any real effort to establish subspecific nomenclature for all these intergrades would indeed be a taxonomic nightmare.

Generally speaking, with but few exceptions, the subspecies of *Otus asio* exhibit the following geographical and climatic characteristics:

Northern Screech Owls	Coarser markings.
Southern Screech Owls	Finer markings.
Northern Screech Owls	Larger in size.
Southern Screech Owls	Smaller in size.
Eastern Screech Owls	Yellow or greenish-yellow beaks.
Western Screech Owls	Slate-gray or blackish beaks.

* Because of the importance of his findings in regard to Screech Owls in the matters of voice, coloration, geographic variation, and taxonomy, the authors highly recommend Joe T. Marshall's monograph for the Western Foundation of Vertebrate Zoology (Number 1, 1967), entitled: *Parallel Variation in North and Middle American Screech-owls.*

Eastern Screech Owls	Voice, a long, quavering single trill.
Western Screech Owls	Voice, a shorter, bouncy double trill.
Eastern Screech Owls	Increased rufous coloration generally and a distinct red-phase bird.
Western Screech Owls	Decreased rufous coloration and no red-phase bird.
Arid Region Screech Owls	Paler, more subtle coloration and markings.
Humid Region Screech Owls	Darker, richer coloration and markings.

Thus, for the purposes of this book, the authors prefer to be guided in *Otus asio* nomenclature by the eighteen races with the strongest and most definitive traits, as included (with but two exceptions) in the most recent (1957) A.O.U. Check-list by the American Ornithological Union Check-list Committee as distinct and valid subspecies.

Naturally, many of the characteristics of the Screech Owls are species-wide and it would be pointless to reiterate these same characteristics for each of the eighteen subspecies included here. Therefore, to express them most completely yet succinctly, all major characteristics will be discussed under the heading of the most familiar subspecies, *Otus asio naevius*—the Eastern Screech Owl. Other subspecies will be described in detail only insofar as they differ from *Otus asio naevius*.

AVERAGE WINGSPANS OF THE SCREECH OWLS
(*Otus asio*)

(Number of specimens measured in parentheses following names)

Subspecies	Millimeters	Inches
O. a. kennicottii (16)	601.1	23.7
O. a. brewsteri (16)	599.8	23.6
O. a. macfarlanei (24)	585.7	23.1
O. a. swenki (11)	574.3	22.6
O. a. quercinus (9)	573.1	22.6
O. a. bendirei (19)	572.8	22.6
O. a. maxwelliae (15)	558.8	22.0
O. a. yumanensis (6)	554.0	21.8
O. a. naevius (87)	551.3	21.7
O. a. cineraceus (12)	551.2	21.7
O. a. inyoensis (9)	538.7	21.2
O. a. hasbroucki (9)	536.5	21.1
O. a. aikeni (15)	533.4	21.0
O. a. asio (28)	531.9	21.0
O. a. mccallii (5)	531.4	20.9
O. a. floridanus (21)	509.7	20.1
O. a. gilmani (4)	486.1	19.2
O. a. suttoni (4)	480.7	18.9

AVERAGE WEIGHTS OF THE SCREECH OWLS
(*Otus asio*)

(Number of specimens weighed in parentheses following names)

Subspecies	Grams	Ounces
O. a. kennicottii (16)	235.6	8.3
O. a. macfarlanei (11)	227.4	8.0
O. a. swenki (6)	225.6	7.9
O. a. brewsteri (14)	222.5	7.8
O. a. maxwelliae (12)	219.7	7.7
O. a. quercinus (5)	216.3	7.6
O. a. bendirei (10)	215.5	7.5
O. a. naevius (55)	205.5	7.2
O. a. inyoensis (5)	204.1	7.1
O. a. hasbroucki (7)	199.3	7.0
O. a. suttoni (2)	191.2	6.7
O. a. asio (20)	185.7	6.5
O. a. mccallii (2)	181.7	6.4
O. a. aikeni (12)	180.3	6.3
O. a. floridanus (17)	167.4	5.9
O. a. cineraceus (5)	166.1	5.8
O. a. yumanensis (3)	164.7	5.8
O. a. gilmani (2)	158.5	5.6

EASTERN SCREECH OWL
(*COLOR PLATE XV*)

SCIENTIFIC NAME AND ORIGINAL DESCRIPTION

Otus asio naevius (Gmelin). Original description: *Strix naevia* Gmelin, *Systematica Natura*, Volume 1, Part 1, 1788, page 289; based on the Mottled Owl of Pennant, *Arctic Zoology*, Volume 2, 1785, page 231; based on a specimen from Noveboraco, New York. Former scientific names: *Scops asio, Megascops asio, Strix asio, Strix naevia.*

OTHER NAMES

No other North American owl has more common names, regional names, and very localized nicknames than the Screech Owl (*Otus asio*) in general and the Eastern Screech Owl (*Otus asio naevius*) in particular. Among the most frequently used are these:

DEMON OWL Since its call in a darkening woods has a somewhat unearthly or supernatural quality affecting the superstitious.

DUSK OWL For the time of day when it is most often seen.

GHOST OWL For its silent, wraithlike flight through the dusky woods, so expertly avoiding collision with intertwined branches that it appears to go through them.

GRAY OWL After the coloration of the gray-phase bird.

LE PETIT-DUC DE L'EST French-Canadian name meaning "The Little Duke of the East," (as opposed to "The Grand Duke of the East," as applied to the Great Horned Owl [*Bubo virginianus virginianus*]).

LITTLE DUKELET Transliteration of the French-Canadian terminology.

LITTLE-EARED OWL As a contrast to the Long-eared Owl (*Asio otus wilsonianus*).

LITTLE HORNED OWL As a contrast, because of its superficial resemblance in miniature, to the Great Horned Owl.

LITTLE OWL For its diminutive size.

MOTTLED OWL After the impression it gives of having a sort of mottled and speckled plumage.

MOUSE OWL After the prey it most favors.

QUAVERING OWL For the quavering tonal quality of its call—a name which is actually far more appropriate than "screech" owl.

RED OWL After the coloration of the red-phase bird.

SCOPS OWL From the Old World scientific nomenclature.

SCRITCH OWL Dialectal pronunciation of "Screech Owl."

SHIVERING OWL For three reasons: 1, because of the shivering tonal quality of its call; 2, because of its ability to cause "shivers" among superstitious people; 3, because young nestling Screech Owls are subject to severe attacks of shivering.

SPIRIT OWL For a combination of the reasons it is called Demon Owl and Ghost Owl.

SQUINCH OWL For its habit of squinching its eyes to mere slits.

TRILLING OWL After the nature of its call.

WHISTLING OWL Inaccurately, after the nature of its call.

DISTINGUISHING FEATURES

All the Screech Owl subspecies are reasonably alike in their habits and characteristics. They are one of the more strictly nocturnal of North American owls and only on rare occasions will be abroad in daylight, much less hunt in the daytime, even though their vision is quite adaptable to the light of day. (See Eyes and Vision.) It is merely an ingrained characteristic of the bird to remain at roost until after the setting of the sun, with almost all hunting done during the first four hours of night.

It has been said that if the Great Horned Owl is the "feathered tiger," then the Screech Owl is the "feathered wildcat." This is a reasonable comparison because, despite its small size, it has great courage and

audacity. (See General Habits and Characteristics.) Though indeed small, it somehow gives the impression of being a larger bird than it is. Its wide-set ear tufts, which can be raised to a wholly erect position or laid almost flat against the head at will, are a very distinguishing characteristic. It is the smallest "eared" owl east of the Rocky Mountains. Facial disks, superciliaries, and lores are very well defined. This is one of the most amusing of our owls to observe.

Rank in over-all size among the eighteen species: Twelfth.

SHAPE AT REST

Next to the Saw-whet Owl (*Aegolius acadicus acadicus*), which has no ear tufts, the Screech Owl is the smallest of the Eastern owls. It is readily identifiable when perched, despite its ability to change its appearance considerably at times. In normal perching posture, this owl is short, thick, and well-fluffed, with the plumage hiding the feet and with the ear tufts usually raised or half-raised. If there is cause for apprehension, however (though sometimes for no apparent reason), the owl can elongate its perched body until it has stretched upward nearly half again its normal perched height, with the usual bulkiness of the body narrowing proportionately to a startling thinness. At such times the plumage is held tightly against the body and, with ear tufts erect, the bird becomes remarkably well camouflaged as a stub of branch—an aspect heightened by eyes squinted to mere slits on a slightly diagonal plane.

SHAPE IN FLIGHT

The wings appear oddly stubby when opened, even though they are long for the size of the bird. This is probably due to their unusual broadness. In flight it exhibits a decided batlike quality; with the head tucked in, no discernible neck, short tail, and broad wings, the flying bird has a roughly triangular shape.

FLIGHT PATTERN

Otus asio naevius has, as do most of the *Otus asio* subspecies, a fairly rapid and steady wingbeat of about five strokes per second. It rarely glides for more than a few seconds at a time and very seldom hovers. The normally steady wingbeat can become quite erratic when the owl flies through heavy forest cover and with uncanny ability, dodges through interlaced branches. When it is hunting insects on the wing, as it so frequently does, especially around the glow of isolated mercury-vapor lights which attract numerous insects, its flight becomes very jerky but extremely maneuverable, and in masterful fashion it plucks moths, flying beetles, and other insects out of mid-air.

Measurements have been based on 87 measured birds: 38 males and 49 males.

WEIGHT

Species average: 204.1 gr. (7.1 oz.).

	Male	Female
Average	199.8 gr. (7.0 oz.)	208.3 gr. (7.3 oz.)
Minimum	166.0 gr. (5.8 oz.)	174.5 gr. (6.1 oz.)
Maximum	212.5 gr. (7.4 oz.)	222.4 gr. (7.8 oz.)

Rank in weight among the eighteen species: Twelfth.

TOTAL LENGTH

Species average: 221.1 mm. (8.7").

	Male	Female
Average	209.2 mm. (8.2")	233.0 mm. (9.2")
Minimum	176.3 mm. (7.0")	195.2 mm. (7.7")
Maximum	233.2 mm. (9.2")	264.4 mm. (10.4")

Rank in total length among the eighteen species: Twelfth.

WINGSPAN

Species average: 551.3 mm. (21.7").

	Male	Female
Average	539.5 mm. (21.3")	563.0 mm. (22.2")
Minimum	479.7 mm. (18.9")	499.8 mm. (19.7")
Maximum	568.5 mm. (22.4")	617.2 mm. (24.3")

Rank in wingspan among the eighteen species: Eleventh.

INDIVIDUAL WING LENGTH

Species average: 165.1 mm. (6.5").

	Male	Female
Average	163.8 mm. (6.5")	166.4 mm. (6.6")
Minimum	154.9 mm. (6.1")	156.2 mm. (6.2")
Maximum	174.0 mm. (6.9")	177.8 mm. (7.0")

Rank in wing length among the eighteen species: Twelfth.

TAIL LENGTH

Species average: 84.7 mm. (3.3").

	Male	Female
Average	80.6 mm. (3.2")	88.8 mm. (3.5")
Minimum	75.1 mm. (3.0")	80.5 mm. (3.2")
Maximum	86.1 mm. (3.4")	95.5 mm. (3.8")

Rank in tail length among the eighteen species: Eleventh.

BEAK LENGTH

Species average: 15.3 mm. (0.6").

	Male	Female
Average	15.2 mm. (0.6")	15.4 mm. (0.6")
Minimum	14.0 mm. (0.6")	14.9 mm. (0.6")
Maximum	16.6 mm. (0.7")	18.8 mm. (0.7")

Rank in beak length among the eighteen species: Tenth.

LEGS, FEET, TALONS

The tarsi are short and partially feathered. Feet and talons are of average size for the size of the bird. The talons are a slaty black and well curved, though not quite as markedly curved as in some species. The tips of the talons are extremely sharp and the leg musculature is very powerful for driving the talons deep into prey. This owl is a very strong-footed species. It normally perches with two toes forward, two backward.

EYES AND VISION

Markedly convex in shape, the eyes of the Screech Owl are quite large and penetrating. They are set quite firmly in their sockets, allowing for virtually no rolling of the eyeballs themselves. As a result, the bird often tilts its head into highly ludicrous—and sometimes seemingly impossible—positions. The irides are a bright yellow and vision is extremely keen, especially during late twilight, but also very good at night and nearly as keen during the day. The pupils very swiftly adjust to existing light conditions, contracting to mere pinpoints on the brightest days, and expanding on the darkest nights until only a circular sliver of the brilliant lemon-yellow iris can be detected. Like nearly any creature—man included—it can be thrown into confusion and nearly blinded if, while the pupils are widely expanded in darkness, a bright light suddenly strikes the eyes. Sometimes when this occurs, the bird will deliberately swivel its head around 180° and wait for a moment for its vision to readjust before taking flight. The eyes and ears work well together for hunting.

RECONSTRUCTED EASTERN SCREECH OWL

In the autumn of 1949, the authors were on a field observation trip near Wooddale, Illinois, when they found the nearly complete skeletal remains of an Eastern Screech Owl. The authors positioned the bones on a bare, flat oak stump as nearly correctly as possible, under the existing conditions, and the artist made a few sketches. The carcass had been thoroughly devoured by ants even to the point where the ligature between bones was missing and virtually all the bones were separated. A few bones were missing and some were slightly gnawed-upon, evidently the work of mice.

Screech Owl

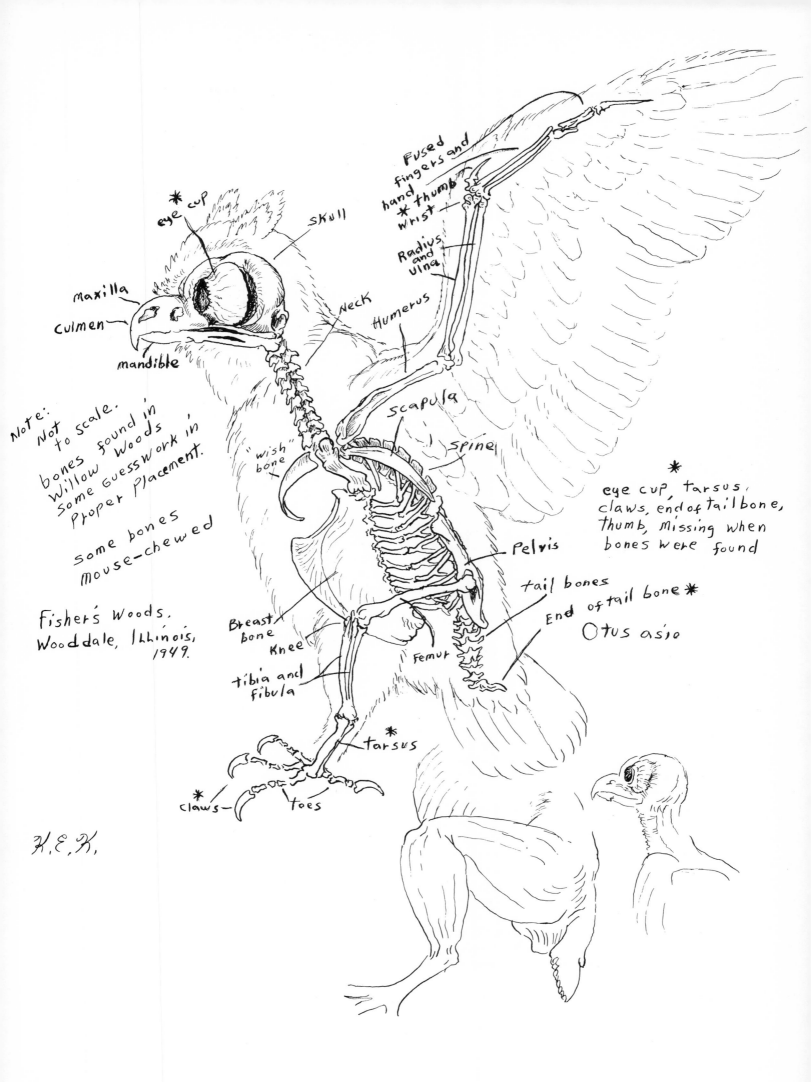

EARS AND HEARING

The ear cavities of the *Otus asio* subspecies are symmetrical in size and placement on the skull. Hearing is superb and a vital factor in pinpointing with extreme accuracy the location of prey. Because of its more strictly nocturnal habits, the auditory sense of the Screech Owl is probably very close to being on a par with the same sense in the Barn Owl (*Tyto alba pratincola*) and Great Horned Owl (*Bubo virginianus virginianus*). The ear cavities are of moderate size.

EAR TUFTS, PLUMAGE, ANNUAL MOLT

The ear tufts are wide apart and form a distinct characteristic of the bird. They are more often held erect than laid flat when the bird is perched, though in flight they are held rather close to the head. The plumage is normally of a fluffed and very soft appearance, though it can become tight to the body contour when the owl elongates itself for protective concealment. The softness of the plumage and the distinct fluting of the flight feathers permit remarkably soundless flight. There is a complete molt of all plumage beginning about late July. This molt is finished by no later than mid-November.

VOICE

A great injustice has been done to the Screech Owl by labeling it with such a name, for its call is by no stretch of the imagination a screech. Rather, it is a quite charming sound, imbued with a pleasantly poignant and plaintive quality. It is a mellow, muted trill which is quavering and lugubrious and which descends rapidly in tonal quality toward the end of the call. In the Western races of *Otus asio*, however, there is much less of a tendency for the call to descend toward the end. Even though there may, in the viewpoint of some listeners, be something of an eerie quality to the call of the Eastern Screech Owl, its voice remains one of the most delightful of North American bird calls. The cry of a heron or gull, rail or limpkin might well be considered a screech, but certainly not the call of the Screech Owl.

While older Screech Owls are normally silent when hunting, feeding, and engaged in other activities, there are times of the year when they become quite vocal.

Two of these are at the onset of the breeding season and for a period following the nesting season when the out-of-nest offspring are still being tended.

Not having quite the range of calls that the Northern Barred Owl (*Strix varia varia*) is capable of rendering, the Eastern Screech Owl nevertheless has an impressive variety of vocal utterances in its repertoire. The commonest call is the muted trill which has sometimes been described as a "wet whistling" sort of sound. Well within range of human hearing, it begins low and rises quickly in pitch and quaver, holds at this level for three to five seconds, then slides back down toward the starting point. The quaver becomes so pronounced at the end that the notes become practically individualized. It is a pensive, pleasantly mournful sound and easily identified. The sense of melancholy or sweet weirdness it imparts is more the effect of the muted, wavering tone than to the note structure of the call. This sound may be varied in several ways—sometimes beginning and ending on a higher or lower scale than the call that preceded it, and occasionally with barely discernible quaver. Sometimes the pitch will remain constant throughout the call; at other times it may rise two or three notes before falling at the end. The final notes may vary by as much as three or four tonal levels.

Another call, issued perhaps once for each ten of the common call utterances, is a soft, wheezing *ho-ho-ho*, most often given by itself but occasionally on the heels of the common cry. It is ordinarily four or five tones lower than the common cry (though on rare occasions higher) and so muted that it is often lost to human hearing at any appreciable distance. This call, which is now and then heard during the daytime, tends to remain on the same note, although occasionally the last note may be just a trifle higher in pitch.

The mating call is generally heard just at twilight in very early spring. It is a soft trilling with extraordinary ventriloquial delivery. One may be actually watching the bird doing the calling and yet still be almost convinced that the sound is coming from another owl some distance away and to one side or the other. It lasts for about three seconds and tends to end with a faint upward inflection. (See Courtship and Mating.) The call may be given in a number of ways, but usually consists of a succession of the three-second quavering notes, often beginning slowly but increasing in speed of

---

XXV KENNICOTT'S SCREECH OWL

Otus asio kennicottii (Elliot). Male. Northwestern corner of Ferry County, Washington, January 20, 1971. A.O.U. Number 373-D

XXVI MACFARLANE'S SCREECH OWL

Otus asio macfarlanei (Brewster). Male. Mouth of Soldier Creek, Priest Lake, Idaho. October 19, 1931. A.O.U. Number 373-H

Karl E. Karalus

Karl E. Karalus

delivery until the whole blends as a rapid trilling that lasts as long as ten seconds.

With extreme rarity there is another call which might, at the strain of the imagination, be considered a screech. It is not known why this call is given, but the cry itself is a peculiar sirenlike whistling which begins softly and, without the usual quavering, rises to a rather piercing cry.

The calls heard in late summer and autumn are most often family calls, presumably given so the birds can keep track of one another and remain comparatively close as a family unit while they range in search of food. At such times another fairly uncommon Screech Owl cry is heard—a rather sharp, demanding cry issued by one of the fledglings to signal its own whereabouts to the parent birds. It has the sound of *KEEEERR-R-R-R-R*, rolling slightly at the end. It continues as the young bird moves from one perch to another until its parents return.

Most often the Eastern Screech Owl restricts its calling to the period between sunset and an hour after full darkness has fallen. Occasionally it may call sparingly after that until around midnight. After that it is normally silent.

On a seasonal basis, calling is most pronounced during the initial stages of courtship in early spring and during the family hunting period very late in summer. In early summer and midsummer there is much less calling, and in late autumn and winter the birds are mainly silent.

Otus asio naevius does not normally make any vocal sound while flying, but occasionally an owl being chased by songbirds will utter an irritated little trilling cry. Too, juvenile flying birds will utter location calls as they fly in order to keep in touch with one another and the parent birds.

There are two other characteristic sounds made by the Screech Owl, though they are not actually vocal callings. The first is the sharp snapping of the beak, which most other owl species also make. This brittle, clicking sound can be heard at surprising distances and is usually made when the owl is irked or threatened. It is given as a warning to an intruder to keep his distance. The second sound, made by nestlings as well as adults, is a sort of hissing without any real tonal quality. Often this is given in conjunction with the snapping of the beak and generally signifies anger.

XXVII ROCKY MOUNTAIN SCREECH OWL

Otus asio maxwelliae (Ridgway). Female. Turkey Creek near Denver, Jefferson County, Colorado, November 10, 1971. Not included in the 1957 A.O.U. Check-list

XXVIII TEXAS SCREECH OWL

Otus asio mccallii (Cassin). Male. Two miles northwest of Brownsville, Cameron County, Texas, February 9, 1910. A.O.U. Number 373-B

Where the nestlings are concerned, there are four vocal utterances which differ from those issued by the adults. The first occurs almost as soon as the baby bird has emerged from its shell—a querulous peeping much like that of a little chick lost from the mother hen, though not quite as loud. This is a demand for shelter and food, since it ceases when the hatchling is fed and then warmly brooded by the mother owl. Such cries are heard only during the bird's first three weeks of life.

Just about the time that that call is ending, another begins; a peculiar mouselike squeaking which is issued as the baby bird scrambles about among the other nestlings in an effort to find the warmest spot. The third nestling cry is a sort of vibrant chatter, friendly enough in tone but evidently uttered to attract parental attention. It has been observed that if the baby owl does not give this cry, the parent returning with food ignores it and feeds the baby that chatters. Closely associated is the fourth cry, which is a strange humming sound given by the baby birds at night as long as they are hungry. This ceases, along with the chattering, when the nestling is fed.

SEXUAL DIFFERENCES: SIZE, COLORATION, VOICE

Although the Eastern Screech Owl is dichromatic, with two sharply defined color phases, these are in no way a sexual difference. Male and female birds occur haphazardly in both the red phase and gray phase. The female is a bit larger than the male and her voice is somewhat higher in pitch than his. On the average, the females of all *Otus asio* subspecies average about 15 per cent heavier than the males, and their individual wing is about 3 per cent longer than the male's.

MORTALITY AND LONGEVITY

Strangely, since this is one of the most easily located and observable of owls in North America, little research of a comprehensive nature has been done regarding mortality rates or longevity. Some incidence of cannibalism is known to occur, especially in larger nestings where the youngest bird is too small to compete successfully with its older and often much larger siblings. The incidence of cannibalism is not frequent, however, and cannot be considered a truly pertinent mortality factor. Diseases and parasites also cause a certain amount of death among the birds (see Enemies and Defenses) but little is known about such mortality on a large scale. On at least two occasions captive Eastern Screech Owls have lived for over twenty years.

COLORATION AND MARKINGS: ADULT

Markedly dichromatic, *Otus asio naevius* has two distinct color phases—gray and red. The latter color phase is the result of a dominant autosomal gene. The term "phase" is actually poor usage, even though commonly the accepted term, since it suggests a transitional coloration, when in actuality the so-called "phase" is genetically permanent. On rare occasions an intermediate color phase will also occur which is not quite gray, not quite red, and yet with some of the coloration and markings of both. This is evidently a rather recessive phase. When it does occur, the markings tend to favor those of the gray-phase bird, but in coloration it has more of the red-phase sienna orange on back and head and to a somewhat lesser degree on facial disks and underparts.

There was one relatively well-reported case where a gray-phase Eastern Screech Owl was captured, caged, and fed a strict diet of beef liver. It is reported that this owl's plumage subsequently changed from gray to red. This is doubtful but, even if true, it is the only such case on record and cannot be accepted as conclusive evidence that controlled diet can induce color change. Dichromatism is a phenomenon for which no really satisfactory scientific explanation has thus far been offered. It is important to note that in this dichromatism there is not only a change of coloration, but also a change in the pattern of markings.

Gray-phase Coloration and Markings Between the ear tufts on the crown, as well as on the nape, coloration is generally a brownish gray with small blotches and streaks of black or dark slate gray. Each feather has either a series of small dark gray or black spots along the shaft or an irregular streak of the same color similarly placed. The sides of the head are colored nearly the same, but include some narrow dusky-white barrings. Facial disks are dusky white with mottlings or streaks of dark brown in the supraorbital areas. The ear tufts are colored and marked on the outer sides like the head and nape, but the inner sides are coarsely mottled with grayish white or pale buffy brown. The beak always has a faint greenish cast but may range from a pale general coloration of dusky, slaty, bluish green to dull grayish yellow green. The cere is a dull gray, though occasionally with a distinct yellowness. The irides are always a brilliant lemon yellow surrounding the deep black pupil. The eyelids are sparsely feathered in jet black, often with the lighter gray flesh color showing through. There are narrow dusky-white barrings in the superciliaries and suborbital areas, and the lores are gray white and bristly, with each feather distinctly black-shafted. The facial rim is black or very dark brown in a narrow line from behind each ear tuft, encircling the facial disk to each side of the throat. The chin in generally dusky white tinged with reddish buff and narrowly barred from facial rim to facial rim with mottled streakings of dark gray or black. The upper nape is crossed by a vague band of lighter buff-colored spots or irregular dusky whiteness, while the lower nape occasionally has another band of similar coloration which is mostly concealed by overlying plumage. Small triangular spots of unmarked dull white are on the throat and these spots are often compressed or elongated by the stance of the perched bird. The breast is quite boldly cross-hatched with irregular stripes and unconnected bars of dark gray or black over dull gray white. The coloration of the back is the same as on the crown and nape, but with bolder black markings along the shafts and heavier dark gray blotchings. The secondaries are streaked with a few narrow bands of dull grayish buff, each enclosing a dusky-gray bar, but the mottlings are so broken by the general coloration that the bands are often indistinct. The webs of the outermost middle coverts and greater coverts have a large pale buff or gray spot on or near the tip. The outer webs of the inner primaries each have squarish spots of reddish buff, and these become larger and paler on the four largest quills.

The underwings are a general grayish buff with occasional random dark gray streakings. The sides are light to dull grayish white, with cross-hatching increasing toward the median line. Undertail coverts are an unblemished buffy gray, usually hidden when the bird is perched. Sporadically there will be some spottings or light barrings of black and light brown on these undertail coverts. The belly is buffy white, broken by bold but irregular narrow black bars and with the center feather-shaft streaks of the same, these often expanding into conspicuous rusty-edged spots at the sides. On the flanks, pairs of the same black bar tend to frame the buffy-brown area. Plumage on the upper parts of the legs is light rusty buff, fading into dull white on rear and lower tarsi. The thighs are usually unmarked, but the outer leg plumes are always heavily barred with dark brown on the upper portion and sometimes on the lower. Scales on the unfeathered portions of legs and feet are a dusky yellowish gray. Talons are sometimes jet black or slaty black for their entire length, but more often range from dusky tan or yellowish gray at the base to dusky dark gray at the tips.

Red-phase Coloration and Markings In this color phase, which is also referred to as the rufescent phase, the general pattern of barrings and streakings is basically similar to that of the gray-phase bird except that the gray or brown of the gray-phase bird is replaced by bright rust to chestnut red in the rufescent phase, and the underparts are without black. The streakings all tend to be less broad and more linear than in the gray-phase bird. Facial disks are usually plain rufous of varying shades, while lores and superciliaries are buffy white. The markings of the underparts in the red-phase bird are less intricate in cross-hatching, and the blackish to dull-gray barring of the gray-phase bird is here replaced by cinnamon-rufous spottings.

COLORATION AND MARKINGS: JUVENILE

Gray Phase Wings and tail are the same as in adults. The upperparts are brown with deep grayish overcast and are broadly but rather indistinctly barred with grayish buff. Many of the feathers are tipped with dull white. The underparts are barred with dusky buff gray over a dull-white ground color. At this age there is an absence of streakings on both upperparts and underparts. During the first winter the juvenile birds of both color phases have a more mottled appearance than the adults.

Red Phase Similar to the gray-phase juvenal except that the gray browns are replaced by rufescent coloration.

GENERAL HABITS AND CHARACTERISTICS

Otus asio naevius This and other *Otus asio* subspecies are audacious in the extreme. It will not hesitate to attack a bird, even another hawk or owl, or other creature larger than itself if motivated by hunger, brood protection, or self-defense. The Eastern Screech Owl has been known to attack and drive off the considerably larger Long-eared Owl (*Asio otus wilsonianus*), and it has attacked and killed birds as large as the ruffed grouse, barnyard hens, domestic ducks, and pigeons. There are many cases on record where human beings have been attacked by this little owl, usually in defense of its young. The renowned ornithologist-artist Alexander Sprunt, Jr., in a lifetime of observation of and contact with birds of all kinds, encountered only one that ever drew blood from him, and this was an angry Eastern Screech Owl that badly gouged his ear with its talons when he approached too near its babies.

Such savagery is not reserved for other creatures or humans. If two Screech Owls are caged together with insufficient food provided, there is the likelihood that, even though they be mates, one will ultimately attack the other, kill it, and eat it. Such cannibalism cannot, however, be considered a normal trait of the species.

Along with its savagery, the Eastern Screech Owl is very often incredibly audacious. In a case cited by Arthur Cleveland Bent in *Life Histories of North American Birds of Prey*, some years ago in Mendham, New Jersey, a Screech Owl came down the chimney of a

residence, entered the front room, flew directly to a canary's cage, and pulled the small yellow bird through the bars and swallowed it whole. In another case of unusual boldness on the part of an Eastern Screech Owl, the artist of this volume had a difficult time. At his suburban Chicago home he had been keeping a number of cocoons of *Telea polyphemus* and *Samia cecropia* moths in a screened box on his window ledge. When these large silk moths began to emerge one evening, he opened the lid and reached in to lift them out gently one by one. A gray-phase Eastern Screech Owl suddenly zoomed down and snatched one out of his hand and sped off with it. In a moment a second owl —this one in rufescent phase—did the same thing. To keep from losing more of his specimens to the birds, both of which had returned and were circling expectantly, it became necessary to unscrew the box from the ledge, bring it inside and close the window to get the rest of the emerged moths out safely. Even then one of the owls very nearly broke the window in its attempt to get inside.

Strangely, in the face of all this, the Eastern Screech Owl and its counterpart subspecies can be remarkably gentle. The Screech Owl is, in fact, more noted for its ordinarily placid disposition than for its ferocity. If startled by an intruder it may snap its beak in a most menacing manner, but will rarely follow through with an actual attack. Screech Owls are often kept as pets and they make very good ones, tending to be affectionate and companionable. They seem to delight in riding about on a human head or shoulder and very much enjoy having their own heads scratched or their plumage gently stroked from head to tail. Often at such times the owl will gravely and slowly wink first one eye and then the other, as if sharing some secret with its human companion.

Despite the squalid condition of their nests as a rule, Screech Owls are clean in their habits, often preening themselves and regularly taking baths. They are known to make frequent use of birdbaths and, in the days of the old rainbarrel under the downspout, tragedies sometimes resulted when Screech Owls attempting to bathe in them would instead get their plumage too wet for flight and thereupon drown in the deep water.

It comes as something of a surprise to learn that these owls will often live in reasonable harmony with unusual neighbors. On more than one occasion an Eastern Screech Owl has selected for its nest a compartment in a purple martin house. The martins continue to come and go and even raise their own families in the compartments right next door without any evident problems.

The instinct for protection of her young is pronounced in *Otus asio naevius*. In one case where a female's mate and eggs were destroyed, she simply moved farther up the tree to a hollow being used by flickers as a nest. Inside were four baby flickers not long out of the eggs. The owl transferred her affections to them and brooded them for five consecutive days. She made no objection and did not interfere when the flickers came to feed their young, simply moving back out of the way in the hollow until the feeding was finished, then gently settling over the young birds again. When at last she left the nest she was gone for only a short while before returning with a small dead bird in her beak. She deposited it in the nest beside the baby flickers and then flew away and did not return.

The fact that the owl's eyeballs are rather firmly fixed in their sockets and it must turn its whole head to see in different directions has given rise to a widespread superstition. It is believed that this and other owl species can turn their heads around in a complete circle if necessary to watch an observer circling around below. The erroneous belief is that if the person continues to walk around the owl, the head of the bird will continue to circle with him until it will eventually become unscrewed and fall off, whereupon the bird will fall dead off its perch. This, of course, is absurd. What actually occurs is that when someone does circle around below, the gaze of the owl will remain locked on the intruder until the head has turned an incredible 280° of the circle. Then, in the barest blink of an eye, the head will snap back in the other direction, returning to about the same spot where it was before but with the head having turned in the other direction. This action is so swiftly performed that it is easily missed, and so, if the observer does continue circling, it indeed appears that the head has followed completely around without pause. The ability of the owl to swivel or cock its head into what seem to be impossible angles adds greatly to its charm.

HABITAT AND ROOSTING

The Eastern Screech Owl favors an open-woodland type of terrain, especially when this is adjacent to grainfields, meadows, and marshes. Apple orchards are a particular favorite of this race, not only because the older apple trees often have ideal nesting and roosting hollows in them, but because they are also areas to which mice and insects are attracted.

Otus asio naevius is not at all loath to take up residence in or very near barns and outbuildings, in birdhouses where the holes are large enough, in fencerows along country lanes, and even in the hollows of shade trees in residential yards. It is quite common to see these owls in the suburbs and in small towns, and not at all rare to find them in large cities such as Chicago, where they often hunt into the late twilight hours along railroad tracks or in city parks. Such "city" owls will usually hide by day in hollow trees, water tanks, or in the dense scrub growth which is often growing near the tracks. Occasionally one will even take up lodging inside

a long-parked boxcar. As long as there are, within its range, hollows in which to nest and roost, an abundant supply of small prey to catch, and a reasonable lack of harassment by humans, the conditions are good for the Eastern Screech Owl.

Where roosting is concerned, more often than not *Otus asio naevius* prefers a natural hollow in a large tree. Abandoned flicker holes rank high as a second choice. If such sites are unavailable, however, it can be content in a hollow behind the loose siding of some farm building. Nevertheless, trees are definitely favored and it makes little real difference what kind of a tree it is; apples, oaks, elms, maples, pines, sycamores, willows, and many others provide cavities which this owl considers to be ideal.

During the daylight hours, the Eastern Screech Owl is mostly inactive within such a hollow or else well concealed on a perch in some dense evergreen or amid the heavy foliage of a hardwood tree. If an owl is roosting in a hollow of a tree and that tree is tapped with a stick, chances are good that the owl will poke its head out of the hole and look downward toward the disturbance. It will watch intently for a minute or so and then withdraw out of sight. Only rarely will it take wing from such a hollow. Not uncommonly it will sit inside the hollow with its head filling the opening, watching for hours what is going on outside. Even bright sunlight falling on its face does not seem to bother it as it watches the passage of small birds, squirrels, and other creatures with great care, often turning its head or sticking it out farther to watch their progress.

If the roost happens to be amid foliage rather than in a tree hollow, the Eastern Screech Owl prefers oak trees during the summer and conifers during the winter, almost invariably sitting very close to the trunk of the roost tree. When hollows are used, these are normally from 10 to 20 feet in height, but they may be from as low as 5 feet to as high as 50 feet. The same roosts are used over and again by the individual owl throughout its range, though one owl may have five or six different roosts or hollows that it regularly uses in summer. During winter it normally confines itself to one or two roosts.

On occasion, when the weather is fair and shows promise of continuing that way, the owl will roost in a large tree cavity which faces the sky—this is usually a tree that has been broken off by the wind 15 feet or more above the ground—and sleep while clinging to the side of the cavity. Generally, though, hollows exposed to bright sunlight or inclemencies are avoided, as are those which are regularly used by fox squirrels.

Roosts in areas of relatively sparsely scattered trees are favored over those located in the midst of heavier

---

Field sketch of an afterbath drying posture assumed by Kennicott's Screech Owl (*Otus asio kennicottii*).

Kennicott's
Screech owl

Karalee

forest growth, primarily because the latter is the more heavily frequented habitat of the Eastern Screech Owl's most deadly natural enemy, the Great Horned Owl.

An odd characteristic about roosting Screech Owls is that at times they appear to be perched in a mesmerized state and can be lifted off their perch simply by pushing a stick under their feet, upon which the feet seem to transfer their grip instinctively and unconsciously. This occurs most often when they are in a state of torpor while digesting a large meal.

ENEMIES AND DEFENSES

Many of the larger owls can and do prey upon the Eastern Screech Owl, as well as other *Otus asio* subspecies, but none so devastatingly and with such frequency as the Great Horned Owl. This is in part a result of the fact that *Bubo virginianus virginianus* and *Otus asio naevius* have a preference for essentially the same type of habitat and their territories overlap. The smaller size and faster wingbeat of the Screech Owl give it a greater maneuverability for escaping the Great Horned Owl in flight, and it also has the opportunity of hiding in hollows that are much too small for the large enemy to enter. Yet, the attack of the Great Horned Owl is so silent, so swiftly and unexpectedly launched, that once the bigger owl has located its target and moved to attack, there isn't much hope for the smaller owl.

Barred Owls (*Strix varia* sp.), Spotted Owls (*Strix occidentalis* sp.), Great Gray Owls (*Strix nebulosa nebulosa*), occasionally Snowy Owls (*Nyctea scandiaca*), Long-eared Owls (*Asio otus* sp.), and Short-eared Owls (*Asio flammeus flammeus*) will all take the Screech Owl as prey, and sometimes even the Barn Owl (*Tyto alba pratincola*) will kill and devour one. Equally, the Eastern Screech Owl is something of an enemy within its own race, since cannibalism can and does occur, not only among nestlings but now and again among adults as well. This occurs during especially bad-weather winters when small prey becomes very difficult to find. The individual owl is forced to range farther than normally and may inadvertently encroach upon the territory of another Screech Owl, which is itself having a difficult time finding enough food. With hunger strong upon them, and one of the birds additionally motivated by a territorial possessiveness, a fatal encounter between them is possible. If such occurs, it is not uncommon for cannibalism to follow.

Occasionally the Eastern Screech Owl will fall prey to some of the larger hawks, but this is far more the exception than the rule, since the owl is mainly nocturnal —active when the hawks have gone to roost and itself well hidden in its roost when the hawk is active. When a hawk does kill one of these owls, it is usually because the owl has been disturbed from its roost and is seeking another haven.

Prowling cats form a definite hazard, especially in circumstances where the owl has killed prey too heavy to be lifted and carried to a safer perch for eating. The owl at such times becomes engrossed in tearing apart and devouring its prey on the ground and is subsequently somewhat less attentive to its own dangers. This is the time when cats, and other carnivores as well, may kill it. Mink, weasels, otters, raccoons, skunks, bobcats, and even domestic dogs can all be counted as enemies. Tree-climbing carnivores in particular take a toll of roosting Screech Owls.

Now and again tree-climbing snakes will kill the owl as prey, but far more often they are a danger to the owl's eggs. If a Screech Owl is killed by a snake, it is more than likely the result of the owl's own audaciousness. Overestimating its own ability, the Eastern Screech Owl will sometimes attack a snake simply too large to be handled well. If the snake is of the type that constricts its prey—say a rat snake or corn snake—and in the ensuing struggle it manages to throw a coil or two around the owl's head or body, death is almost sure to follow for the owl.

Crows, blue jays, blackbirds, and numerous songbirds must also be considered as enemies, even though their intent is to harass rather than prey upon the owl. These birds, upon finding the roosting owl, pester it unmercifully until it is forced to take to wing in an effort to find solitude elsewhere. In this process of flying elsewhere as a result of an attack by a darting, shrieking mob of smaller birds, the Screech Owl becomes highly vulnerable to attack from hawks.

Parasites, though they rarely kill the owl, are certainly enemies of a sort. Most Screech Owls are subject to harboring fleas and bird lice beneath their feathers, and a variety of internal parasites as well. The danger of these creatures is their debilitating effect upon the owl, making the bird less able to elude its enemies and thus more subject to predation. Diseases do kill some, but studies along these lines have been less than definitive.

The single greatest threat to the Eastern Screech Owl, as it is to most other owl species, is man. This is not to say very many are deliberately slain with guns (although a certain number are killed this way) but rather that they become highway fatalities. Because of the openness of a highway and its shoulders, often running through areas of rather heavy woodland cover, the Eastern Screech Owl tends to perch and hunt near such a thoroughfare. A mouse, shrew, or large insect scampering across a road is an open invitation to any Screech Owl in the vicinity. But the owl, intent upon its intended prey, pays little heed to approaching vehicles and is quite often struck and killed.

In the state of Ohio, where for many years bird mortality counts have been made along highways, Eastern Screech Owls are the bird species second most frequently killed by vehicles, surpassed only by robins. The majority of Screech Owl deaths occur while the bird is in flight rather than while on the pavement with its prey. Often the owl flies into the side of the vehicle or collides with the windshield; evidently this is because it has been partially blinded by the bright lights and attempts to dart across the road the instant the headlights pass. Time of year obviously makes a difference, too, where highway mortality is concerned. The greatest number of Screech Owl casualties on the road occur in late fall and winter, when prey in field and forest becomes scarce. And, for whatever pertinence it may have, it is interesting to note that in Ohio highway casualty counts, 75 per cent of all Eastern Screech Owls killed by vehicles were gray-phase birds.

Where defense is concerned, the Eastern Screech Owl can be a savage opponent, utilizing its hooked beak, strong sharp talons, and flailing wings to ward off an attacker. More than one intruder—human as well as animal—has lost an eye in the process, and even more have backed away with painfully punctured nose, lip, or ear. *Otus asio naevius* prefers, however, not to have to fight for its life, and its greatest defense lies in its ability to camouflage itself incredibly well in order to escape detection from an enemy in the first place.

The gray-phase bird particularly, upon noting the approach of possible danger, will quickly straighten from its normal fluffed and somewhat slouchy perching pose. In an instant it has made itself closely resemble a stub of branch. Even the pattern and coloration of its plumage lend to the illusion, giving the appearance of coarse bark. In such a pose as this, the owl will often allow an intruder to come very close. Only when the bird becomes convinced that its disguise has been penetrated will it reopen its squinted eyes, resume normal shape, and quickly take flight.

The red-phase bird will sometimes do the same, although, unless it is perched near or amid reddish foliage of autumn-touched hardwood, it is more easily detectable. In both color phases, detection does not always predicate immediate flight. Now and then a strongly defensive posture will be assumed on the perch, wherein the bird turns one side or the other of its body toward the intruder, snaps its beak menacingly, glares fiercely, and lowers and outstretches the wing facing the intruder in order to cover and protect the vulnerable breast and abdomen.

Most often, though, *Otus asio naevius* spends its daylight hours safely in a hollow of a tree where, if danger threatens, it quickly drops out of sight inside. Should it be caught away from such a hollow and ultimately take flight in order to escape, almost invariably it flies directly to some other hollow it has used in the past and quickly vanishes within it.

HUNTING METHODS AND CARRYING OF PREY

Almost always after sunset, usually just at dusk but before the full fall of night, the Eastern Screech Owl leaves its roost or nest and begins its rounds, visiting a succession of places where it has had good luck hunting in the past—in woodlots, orchards, around farmhouses, barns, silos, corncribs, stock sheds and other outbuildings, in nurseries, stubbled grainfields and meadows, and in cornfields where the dried stalks have been allowed to fall over naturally or have been cut and shocked. At such times the owl is keenly alert for the slightest movement or sound in the darkness below which may indicate the presence of prey.

When it attacks, the little owl does so swiftly and unerringly, diving silently onto its prey with outstretched talons before the animal realizes the danger is present. The instant before contact is made, the owl's feet open widely and as they touch flesh the talons snap downward and inward, driving deeply with the full power of the leg muscles behind them.

If the prey is small enough, it will either be quickly swallowed whole on the spot or carried elsewhere in the bird's beak—to be swallowed whole or torn apart for the feeding of young birds. If the prey is too large for swallowing (and *otus asio naevius* can swallow astonishingly large prey), it may be carried to some safe place and there torn part and swallowed piecemeal. Rarely will this owl carry prey in its talons, and then normally only when it is simply too large to be carried in the beak.

FOOD, FEEDING HABITS, WASTES

What the Eastern Screech Owl eats depends largely upon where the bird happens to be and what kind of prey is available. Beyond any doubt, however, the most favored prey is small rodents—chiefly the meadow vole, but also such other species as white-footed mice, house mice, wood rats, and grasshopper mice. In addition, it consumes great quantities of insects and other invertebrate animals, as well as a certain number of fish, amphibians, reptiles, and small birds. In a survey conducted by John and Frank Craighead in Michigan, during the years 1942 and 1948, it was determined that the meadow vole and white-footed mouse alone comprised, respectively in those years, 95.3 per cent and 87.2 per cent of the Eastern Screech Owl's prey.

There are times, however—again, dependent upon what is available—when it feeds upon insects, birds, fish, or other prey forms almost to the exclusion of anything else. Quite frequently it catches insect prey in flight, swooping down and, without stopping, snagging them off twigs or walls with its talons and at other times catching them on the wing in its beak, maneuvering much in the manner of the nighthawk while doing so. One red-phase Screech Owl, discovering a large number of moths circling a barnyard light, was observed to catch 37 of them in flight and carry them each in turn to its nestlings waiting in the hollow of a nearby apple tree. It is theorized, though by no means proven, that the rictal bristles—hairlike feathers of the nasal portion of the owl's facial disks—perform the same insect-sensing function as do the enormously well-developed rictal bristles of the whippoorwill and other goatsuckers.

During a population explosion of locusts in Nebraska some years ago, the stomachs of eight Screech Owls were found to contain a total of 2,976 insects, two mice and one small bird. Oddly, just under 10 per cent of the insects were the extremely abundant locusts.

Fish do not play a major role in the Eastern Screech Owl's diet, but there are times when they are eaten avidly. Usually this occurs in winter when terrestrial prey becomes scarce and a nearby pond or stream has a pocket of open water surrounded by ice. At such a place the Screech Owl will stand intently on the edge of the ice or else circle the hole diligently until a fish rises, then take to wing and swoop across the surface, snatching the fish with its talons much as an osprey might. Arthur Cleveland Bent reported that in the winter of 1877 an observer checked the roosting hollow of an Eastern Screech Owl and found inside a total of 16 horned pout, four of which were still alive. It was subsequently discovered that all the ponds in the immediate area were frozen fast and under two feet of snow as well, but at a pond about a mile distant, a hole had been cut in the surface by some ice fishermen and then abandoned. It was from this hole that the Screech Owl was snatching the 5-inch-long horned pouts as they rose to the surface. For those 16 fish in its roosting hole, the little owl had already flown at least 32 miles!

Occasionally, during the breeding season in particular, Eastern Screech Owl depredations among smaller birds can become alarming. Fortunately this depredation is a temporary state of affairs. Dr. Arthur A. Allen, the famed Cornell University ornithologist, in 1924 listed the prey birds that a pair of Eastern Screech Owls brought to the trio of offspring in their nest. The prey birds comprised 24 species and totaled at least 98 individual birds. Dr. Allen wrote: "Since the feathers in the nest undoubtedly represent many more than one bird of each species, the grand total of birds required to feed the three young owls from time of hatching until left by the old birds was certainly over one hundred."

Amphibians make up a reasonable portion of the Eastern Screech Owl's diet, especially frogs and toads, although a fair number of salamanders are also taken. Some reptiles are caught and eaten, too, though fewer in number and these are normally limited to small nocturnal snakes and some lizards caught just after sunset. Once in a while a very small soft-shelled turtle will be devoured.

The appetite of this owl becomes prodigious indeed at times and it dauntlessly attacks creatures as large as itself or even much larger. As already mentioned, domestic hens, ruffed grouse, pigeons, and even ducks have been killed and at least partially eaten by the Eastern Screech Owl. Cases are also on record where domesticated ring-necked pheasants and golden pheasants have been lost to *Otus asio naevius*. In the wild, the little bird of prey has been known to kill woodcock and quail, and was even seen to kill a sparrow hawk. These, it should be noted, are isolated instances and certainly not indicative of the normal feeding habits of the species. There are also cases, more commonly, where the Eastern Screech Owl will gorge itself upon one form of prey that becomes suddenly abundant. In one owl stomach were found 13 large cutworms; in another there were 18 large May beetles; in a third there were a total of 50 medium-sized grasshoppers! As a matter of fact, with the exception of the Burrowing Owl (*Speotyto cunicularia* sp.), no other owl species consumes such a volume of insect life as *Otus asio*. This owl has been observed to walk about in the more heavily overgrown meadows, methodically harvesting night-dormant grasshoppers clinging to stems and grass-blades. Along those same lines, it has been reliably reported that now and again the little owl will deliberately wade into the shallows of streams, ponds, and marshes in search of frogs, tadpoles, minnows, crayfish, and aquatic insects.

While not normally herbivorous, *Otus asio naevius* will sometimes dine on vegetable matter. Certain small fruits and berries will be eaten, along with some whole green plants. One witness was nonplussed as he watched an Eastern Screech Owl alight in his garden just after sunset and begin nipping off the tender new growths from the ends of his nasturtiums and swallowing them.

The following list of animal life included in the Eastern Screech Owl's diet is not meant to be a complete listing of every type of creature this bird of prey will kill and eat. Rather, it is merely representative of the species that have been recorded from stomach analyses or pellet dissection. It does, however, provide a clear picture of the wide range of prey acceptable to this race of Screech Owl.

Mammals Wood rats, Norway rats, house rats, cotton rats, meadow voles, white-footed mice, chipmunks, gophers, flying squirrels, gray squirrels, red squirrels, spermophiles, shrews, bats, moles, etc.

Insects Beetles, katydids, grasshoppers, locusts, crickets, mantids, roaches, cicadas, noctuid moths, horseflies, hellgrammites, dragonflies, waterbugs, caterpillars, and other insect larvae of all kinds.

Birds Downy woodpeckers, kingbirds, pigeons, phoebes, grouse, wood pewees, snipe, blue jays, chickens, horned larks, starlings, juncos, blackbirds, cowbirds, orioles, canaries, catbirds, robins, grackles, English sparrows, and numerous native sparrow species, chickadees, wrens, warblers of various species, ducks, doves, woodcocks, cardinals, etc.

Fish Minnows of various species, small trout, chubs, fingerling carp, horned pouts, bluegills, suckers, bullheads, catfish, goldfish, small bass, dace, etc.

Reptile Small snakes, lizards, small soft-shelled turtles.

Amphibians Various frog species, including bull-frogs; toads, salamanders.

Invertebrates Crayfish, snails, spiders, scorpions, centipedes, earthworms, etc.

Almost without exception if the prey can be swallowed whole, this is how it will be eaten—and this includes animals as sizable as large mice, small rats, shrews, moles, birds up to English sparrow in size, insects, and fish. Larger prey is torn in half or into chunks and swallowed.

All digestible portions of the swallowed prey are either converted to use in the owl's body or else expelled as fecal waste. The undigestible materials—fur, feathers, claws, bones, teeth, chitin, etc.—become compacted into the tight, oval-shaped pellets. The pellets formed by *Otus asio naevius* average about an inch and a half in length and half that in diameter. As soon as the pellet is well-formed inside the owl and coated with a slippery mucus, it is regurgitated. Such pellets are generally dark gray in color and can easily be mistaken for animal droppings. Normally two to four pellets will be cast during each 24-hour period. A number of pellets found on the ground beneath a tree is a good indication that the tree is a regular roosting place, but the number of pellets found is not a reliable indicator as to the period of occupancy of the owl. Only a portion of the owl's pellets are regurgitated so that they fall directly beneath the roost. Some fall inside the hollow and a good many others are simply cast here and there as the owl makes its rounds while hunting.

Dissection of such collected pellets is highly important in this and other owl species in determining what the owls of any given area are eating. Numerous accurate statistical listings of prey animals comprising the food of wild owls have been compiled from close analysis and identification of the skulls and other undigestibles discovered within the pellets.

The fecal wastes are generally greenish black with white marblings. They are moistly viscous and are usually squirted well away from the perched owl. Feces are seldom expelled in flight.

COURTSHIP AND MATING

The pairing of unpaired Eastern Screech Owls begins late in the winter, usually in February at the earliest, although rarely as early as late January. The male bird sometimes finds the female of his choice by seeing her fly past while he is perched, but more often than not he actively seeks her out. He may stay silently in her vicinity, though at a respectful distance, for two or three days before making up his mind to woo her. When at last he reaches the decision to do so, he shows evidence of growing nervousness or excitement around sundown—fluffing his feathers, preening, stretching frequently while still on his perch. He may go in and out of his hollow a half dozen times or more.

Within a quarter-hour after the sun has set he takes to wing and flies to a perch more suitably near hers, where she has been stoically roosting during the day. Sometimes in flight, but more often immediately after he alights, the male begins trilling softly. The note is long and drawn out, pleasantly plaintive and lasting from three to six seconds. Toward the end of the call the tone rises slightly and there is almost the sense that with this rise in inflection he has asked a question. This call may be repeated several times, during which the male concentrates only on the female, and the female takes pains to act as if she is wholly unaware of his presence. As if to insure that she can't help but hear him, the male will move from perch to perch around her, stopping on a fence post, in a tree, on a barn eave or projecting rafter, on the roof peak of some outbuilding or on similar perches, making certain to issue the same call at least once from each place where he settles.

Most of these initial courtship maneuverings are rarely seen by humans, since by this time night has fallen. The preliminaries mentioned above may last for more than half an hour but, with each new perch he takes, the male has moved closer to her and soon he is hopping from branch to branch in the same tree where she is perched. He continues singing to her, but now begins swiveling his head back and forth in a ludicrous manner. Soon he starts nodding his head as well as swiveling it and then begins to bob his entire body up and down on the perch. Occasionally, in a rather hilarious way, he stops and stares at her and then quite deliberately winks at her, first with one eye, then with the other—long, slow winks. All this the female also ignores.

The more she refuses to heed his calls and actions, the more frantic become his bobbings and swayings and bowings. At this time his calling may cease. She continues to ignore him unless he tries to alight next to her, whereupon she will flail her wings savagely at him until he flits away. Sometimes he goes far off and the sound of his calling comes again from the distance, but soon he returns to renew his efforts to interest her. Not infrequently she will move to another perch, but he continues following and seemingly acting the part of the love-stricken swain.

At last, all else having failed, the male settles down on a perch not very far from her (often on the same branch but out of her reach). He fluffs his feathers, couches his head deeply in his upper-breast plumage until his beak is lost from sight, and sits there forlornly, all the while giving vent to a barely audible and deeply disconsolate groaning sound.

This becomes the crucial moment of acceptance or rejection. If the female intends to reject him, she will catapult herself away from the perch and disappear swiftly in the darkness, and this time he does not follow. If, however, she has decided to accept him—which is practically always the case—she turns her head and looks at him directly, then sidles over to sit as close to him as possible. Immediately he perks up and raises his head. Sometimes their beaks touch briefly, and not infrequently they will preen one another's nape or breast feathers.

Such courtship is extremely important, for the Eastern Screech Owl mates for life. Their relationship will continue from this point on until broken by death. This is not to imply, however, that if one mate is killed, the one remaining alive will not find another; but as long as both are alive and well they will remain together as mates. Even in fall and winter, when their association is most tenuous, the thread between them remains intact and they tend to stay in one another's vicinity.

Courtship is by no means predicated upon the color phase of the bird. Red-phase birds and gray-phase birds of this species mate without distinction and there is even a vague suggestion of gray-to-red preference. It seems to make no difference which sex is what color phase.

Caged Eastern Screech Owls have occasionally gone into courtship of sorts, and in such cases it is not uncommon for the male to bring bits of meat or an insect or some other item of food to the female, set it down before her and, with a series of bows and noddings, encourage her to accept it. This sort of activity has never been reliably witnessed between free birds in the wild, although there is no good reason for negating the possibility of it.

Actual copulation between Eastern Screech Owls is performed swiftly and in relative silence. While the female crouches on the ground or on the broad low limb of an oak or other hardwood, the male approaches boldly, grasps her nape feathers not too gently in his beak and usually places one foot on her rump or against her side. She then spreads her wings and tilts her body slightly to one side. His own lower body tilts toward hers and their vents are brought into close proximity, though not necessarily touching. Immediately the surprisingly elongated, sharply tapered penis emerges from the male and penetrates deeply into her cloaca. Introduction of the sperm follows immediately and the birds separate, fluffing their feathers. The whole act does not usually last for more than ten seconds at a maximum. Fertilization does not always occur with the first mating, and so copulation is repeated, perhaps a dozen times or more, over a period of two weeks.

ANNUAL BROODS, NEST, NESTING HABITS

Eastern Screech Owls have only one brood per year, but a second laying will probably be made if the first is destroyed. If the pair has mated and raised other families in the past, it is likely that they will return and reoccupy the same nest of the previous year. If this is a first pairing, nest selection does not occur until after mating has concluded. In by far the greater majority of cases, the Eastern Screech Owl chooses to nest in the hollow of a hardwood tree. The type of tree is not important (see Habitat and Roosting), but the cavity has to meet certain standards in most cases for the owl to consider using it as a nest. For example, it will usually not face into prevailing winds, although there are exceptions, nor will it be a hole directly facing the sky. Most preferred is an opening perpendicular to the ground, but there have been cases where it will be on the underside of a large upward-sloping branch or leaning tree trunk. The size of opening most preferred seems to be from three to five inches in diameter.

The highest recorded nesting hole of the Eastern Screech Owl was 50 feet above ground in a large sycamore, but this was unusual and it is rare to find a nesting cavity for this race that is over 35 feet high. (See Florida Screech Owl [*Otus asio floridanus*] for the highest Screech Owl nesting hole of record.) The preference seems to be for holes anywhere from as low as 5 feet off the ground to around 20 feet in height. Sometimes they will be even lower and in one case, where an Eastern Screech Owl nested in a cavity of a stump, the floor of the hollow was actually below ground level. Again, this is the exception.

When the nest is not in the natural cavity of a tree or in the abandoned nesting hole of a flicker, then it is in some other type of protected hollow. Sometimes birdhouses are used if the openings are large enough for the owl to enter. The owl tends to be more inclined to use a birdhouse or bird box as a nest if there is a scattering of sawdust or excelsior on the floor of it. In recent years the erection of numerous nesting boxes for wood ducks—boxes which well approximate a hollow in tree trunk or branch—has provided adequate nesting sites for Screech Owls as well, although the owls will usually avoid such boxes if they project from the water, as the majority of them do. Artificial cavities more commonly used than birdhouses or nest boxes are those to be found behind broken or loose siding boards of barns, old deserted buildings, and other such structures.

Whatever the hollow may be that is ultimately chosen as nesting site, it is used by the Eastern Screech Owl in exactly the condition in which it is found. No attempt is made to construct a nest in the bottom of the hollow or to improve, in any way, whatever sort of nest may already be there. The only contribution the owl makes to the chamber, other than the eggs deposited there, is the offal from prey, regurgitated pellets, and droppings.

Once the owl has taken possession of the hollow, it will not relinquish its claim voluntarily. Persistent pestering by birds, squirrels, or humans may possibly make the Eastern Screech Owl abandon the nest, but such cases are rare. Most often the owl stays, not only using the hollow for the rearing of its family the first year, but tending to return to it year after year for both roosting and nesting. Quite a number of tree cavities are known where the same pair of owls have nested for six or seven consecutive years, and other cases are on record where the same cavity has been used regularly each year for over twenty years by a succession of three or four owl families. It is quite evident that once the owl has taken possession of a nest hole it will return to it for as long as it lives, provided it is not repeatedly driven away or the nest disrupted or destroyed. And when that owl resident dies, it is usually not very long before another owl moves in, especially if the hollow is an exceptionally good one.

EGGS

Number per nesting Throughout the range of the various *Otus asio* subspecies there may be a slight variation in the number of eggs laid per nest. In some cases it will be as few as two or, rarely, as many as eight. Even nine was reported once. But where *Otus asio naevius* is concerned, there are normally four to six eggs per nest, with the usual number being five.

Color All Screech Owl eggs are pure white or occasionally a bit off-white with a faint creaminess. Usually, however, the eggs become blotched and stained from the wastes in the nest.

Shape Sometimes slightly ovoid, but more often nearly globular.

Texture Moderately glossy and, in the majority of cases, with the shell finely granulated but essentially smooth to the touch. On infrequent layings the granulation is more pronounced and the shell will feel faintly bumpy.

Size From a measurement of 286 eggs, the average length was 35.7 mm. (1.4″) and the average width was 29.9 mm. (1.2″). The extremes of the measured eggs were:

Maximum length: 39.3 mm. (1.6″)
Minimum length: 28.5 mm. (1.1″)
Maximum width: 32.0 mm. (1.3″)
Minimum width: 28.5 mm. (1.1″)

Interval of egg-laying Usually no less than 48 hours elapses between the laying of eggs, often as much as 72 hours, and occasionally even longer.

Egg-laying dates Earliest, March 3; latest, May 27; normally between March 26 and April 18.

INCUBATION AND BROODING CHARACTERISTICS

The exact term of incubation for the eggs of the Eastern Screech Owl is still open to question because of the problem of eggs being laid at irregular intervals and actual incubation possibly not commencing until the third or fourth egg has been laid. Some authorities have claimed that it doesn't begin until the fifth egg is laid. It would seem that incubation time, even under these circumstances, could be figured out very quickly, but it isn't all that easy. For example, in one nesting under close scrutiny, the first egg was laid the morning of March 27. The second egg did not appear until the afternoon of March 30. On April 1 the third egg was laid, and this was followed by the fourth egg on April 4. Both the first and second eggs hatched on April 27, the third on April 28 and the fourth on April 29. It therefore seems evident that the term of incubation is not constant; rather, it tends to fluctuate, depending upon conditions of weather, the time when incubation actually begins, and the hours of incubation daily, along with other related factors. The first egg, as we have seen, hatched in 31 days, the second in 28 days, the third in 27 days, and the fourth in only 25 days. The shortest term of incubation on record for *Otus asio naevius* was 21 days and the longest was 32 days. The generally accepted figure now for the average term of incubation is a rather nebulous "25 to 27 days."

While the savagery of the Eastern Screech Owl in hunting is well known, as is its ferocity at times in the protection of offspring against even the most powerful of adversaries, this bird is strangely docile when brooding eggs. An incubating female may snap her beak threateningly at a human who comes too close, yet more often than not there will be no attack; just a stolid determination not to leave the eggs. On many occasions incubating females have remained on their clutch of eggs so tenaciously that they had to be physically lifted for the eggs to be seen and counted. As soon as such birds were released they returned to the nest at once and resettled over the eggs.

The authors once took a gray-phase incubating female from her somewhat oversized natural hollow in a northern Illinois oak, made note of the measurements of the six eggs in the nest, and then carried the female bird about 50 yards away from the tree. Here she was tossed into the air and instantly she found her bearings and arrowed directly to the nesting hollow and disappeared within it. Evidently, once incubation has begun, little will discourage it.

Perhaps this is part of the reason why the male does

so little of the actual incubating, even though he is evidently quite willing to do so. It is simply a matter of the female refusing, in the face of practically any deterrent, to forsake her duty. On the rare occasions that she will leave—mainly for water to drink and briefly bathe in—the male settles over the eggs as soon as she leaves them. He is very nearly as tenacious in this responsibility as she, and even when she returns he is reluctant to leave the eggs until she virtually shoulders him aside. Of course, as has many times happened, should she be killed while away from the nesting hollow, the male bird will continue incubating until the eggs have hatched, then care for the young until they are able to fend for themselves.

It is this reluctance on the part of both parent birds to leave the job of incubating which causes the nest hollow to become so filthy. The processes of evacuation of wastes, whether these be fecal discharges or pellet regurgitations, continue unabated during incubation, and by the time the hatchlings appear the nest hollow has become a foul place indeed. It gets no better after hatching, since the young birds add their own wastes to those already accumulated.

YOUNG AND FAMILY LIFE CHARACTERISTICS

While the female is incubating and as long as she continues to brood the young after they have hatched, the male Eastern Screech Owl acts as purveyor of food. Until the eggs hatch, the female eats only sparingly of what food he brings, so there always appears to be an abundance of food during incubation. Though sometimes she will reach out and take the offered food from his beak, more often he simply drops it beside her. Rarely, if ever, will male and female eat together from the same prey.

The eggs are first pipped by their occupants a day or two (sometimes even three) before actual emergence, but as soon as they commence hatching in earnest, the male bird redoubles his hunting efforts and brings back to the nesting hollow what seems to be a superabundance of food. Dead prey tends to stockpile at first, but as the baby birds continue growing and eating and their demands increase, the stockpile quickly disappears and all that remains is a clutter of fur, feathers, and bones.

Newly hatched, the baby owls are remarkably attractive. They are covered with a fine coating of snow-white fuzz which looks more like hair than feathers. This delicate natal down covers all parts of the hatchling except talons, beak, and eyes (although the latter could be considered as being covered, too, since at this stage they are still sealed). Struggling feebly to crawl about in the hollow, they look strangely like minute human babies wearing fuzzy pajamas. Their heads are abnormally large at this stage, and if they are facing downward so the beak cannot be seen, they might easily be mistaken for tiny kittens. They are too small to swallow prey whole as yet, and so the mother bird selects a mouse or other animal from the food supply and rips it into small pieces, feeding the babies only the meat and, herself, swallowing the residue of undigestibles. There is some indication, though no conclusive proof, that at least a portion of the food the babies receive from the mother during the first few days is predigested to some extent. The food is pulled from the mother's beak by the young and then swallowed with evident difficulty and no indication of pleasure. The tiny beaks and natal down, especially on the facial disks, quickly become blood-stained.

By the end of the second day after hatching, the baby birds begin to shiver. The shivering increases in severity and frequency until, by the end of the fourth day, the baby bird is constantly trembling. It may be that the shivering (for which the Eastern Screech Owl is sometimes called the "Shivering Owl") is caused by the natal down being too fine to provide adequate protection against the outside temperature. This trembling condition gradually abates until the end of the second week, by which time a new coat of plumage is protecting the bird. Until the shivering passes, however, the nestling seeks warmth beneath the brooding mother. All the nestlings sleep a great deal during this period and huddle tightly together when the mother is away from the nest.

On the third or fourth day after hatching, the natal down turns to dirty gray as the dingy pinfeathers of a secondary downy plumage begin appearing. On the upperparts this downy plumage is a pale olive tan at the base, grayish white toward the tips and barred with sepia, while the underparts are basically gray white and not so broadly barred. Even at this young stage each passing day shows clear evidence of what color phase the young bird will be. The natal down remains as white tipping on the new secondary down, and now the baby birds begin to be quite unattractive.

By the fifth day the baby birds frequently peck at the mother's beak as if teasing for food. They still have bluish-gray eyelids covering the bulging eyes and are decidedly repulsive in appearance, not only because of their coloring and physical aspect, but because by now their new pinfeathers have become clotted with blood and excrement. Beginning now and continuing for about a week, the baby birds become subject to attacks of a peculiar sort of yawning at frequent intervals.

Nesting hollow scene sketched from life in densely wooded area of DuPage County, southwest of Bensenville, Illinois, of a family of Eastern Screech Owls (*Otus asio naevius*).

From life
Bensenville, Illinois
W.E. Hanolus

The young birds are at their ugliest by the tenth to twelfth day. The not-yet-fully-opened eyes are a milky bluish in color and quite bulbous. The prominent beak is a slightly deeper blue and looks considerably like a hooked nose. They are filthier than ever and demand food constantly. By this time it is taking the combined efforts of both parents to hunt down food enough for them, and this food is now merely brought to the hollow and dropped inside without the parent bird even entering. This procedure can have tragic ramifications. Most of the nestlings will snatch at the prey at the same time and begin struggling for possession, their little hooked beaks tearing the meat in a sort of tug-of-war melee. At such a time one of the young birds may be mistakenly bitten by one of the others, who tugs just as hard as before. A chunk of flesh torn from one of the babies signals his death knell, for the fresh wound continues to attract the attention of the others, even after the prey is gone. They will fall upon the wounded bird, pull it apart as they did the prey, and devour it. Fortunately, this sort of thing does not too often occur.

During the period when the female is still brooding the baby birds, the male will perch near the nest hollow or find another hollow for himself close by, there to rest during the daylight hours. Sometimes, though, if the nesting hollow is large enough, the male will enter, lock his talons in the spongy wall about halfway between nest and entry, and remain clinging there as he sleeps.

Nest observations have indicated that the first feeding of the day usually comes at about 8:45 P.M. to 9 P.M., though rarely any earlier than 8:30 P.M. nor later than about 9:15 P.M. Feeding tapers off sharply about midnight but continues sporadically until about 3 A.M. or, rarely, until as late as 4:15 A.M. During this period the parent birds may bring food to the nest as few as only 10 or 12 times, but there are also times when they may return with prey as many as 60 times in a single night. In one carefully recorded case the parent birds returned to the nest with food 75 times in one night, delivering to the young birds 73 fair-sized moths and two large beetles. The young birds at this age stretch their bodies rather amazingly, and so great is their elasticity that they seem to be made of rubber. It is at this time, too, that they begin swallowing whole prey and regurgitating their first pellets.

By the twentieth day after hatching, the young owl's eyes are completely open, the irides have become brilliantly lemon yellow, and the fledglings are quite alert, staring at each other and their surroundings with intense curiosity. They are now covered with a thick, generally grayish or rusty (depending upon color phase) downy plumage which almost hides their limbs and makes them look like soiled clumps of wool with eyes. The young are now becoming rather attractive again.

The third covering—flight feathers—begins coming in on the twenty-fifth day, and these develop rapidly. The color phase is undeniably apparent now, and a curious fact emerges: while the offspring of two different-color-phase parents, or two red-phase parents may be all red or all gray, or even mixed red-phase and gray-phase young, not a single case has ever been recorded of two gray-phase parents having in their nest an offspring with even the slightest trace of red.

It is during the fourth or fifth week that the juvenal birds leave the nest. This is the age at which the young birds are most often seen. Normally they align themselves on a branch and continue their same demands for food from their parents, who remain close at hand to protect them, since they are still quite vulnerable. Now is the time, too, as they perch in a row on a branch, that the different size levels of the interval hatching can be readily noted.

At the ninth week the fledglings are more than half adult size and a molting of the body plumage occurs, beginning with the back and followed in succession by the underparts and head. The first-winter plumage begins appearing rapidly, first in the scapulars, followed by wings and tail. This first-winter plumage is more like that of the adult bird (see Coloration and Markings: Juvenile) and is worn by the young bird until the first postnuptial molt, which occurs the next summer.

The matter of the brood leaving the nest tree does not end the family life for the Eastern Screech Owl. For a period of another five weeks beyond this, the young are closely tended by their parents. In the initial stages of this out-of-the-nest togetherness, the adults are vigorously protective of the young and feed them to some extent, but as the young observe the parents and begin to emulate their hunting methods, the care diminishes. By late August the family finally splits up. The parent birds remain in their established territories and close to one another; the young birds go their own way, striking out to establish their individual territories at some distance.

YOUNG OWLS OFTEN MISS THEIR PREY

Until they become well experienced in their hunting, young owls frequently miss the prey they dive after. On a night when the full moon quite brightly lighted a snowy woods near Elk Grove, Illinois, the authors watched with interest as a first-winter Eastern Screech Owl made three successive dives after a white-footed mouse and missed each time. The mouse, running and dodging erratically, successfully made it to a mouse tunnel leading beneath a pile of brush. Such misses rarely occur among any of the owls after the first year, although the first winter is apt to be a difficult time for young owls that have not yet very well developed their hunting techniques and are more eager than skilled.

cene observed
moonlit night. youngscreech
made three tries
white-footed mouse (missed)
lk Grove, Illinois,
1965

K.E.K.

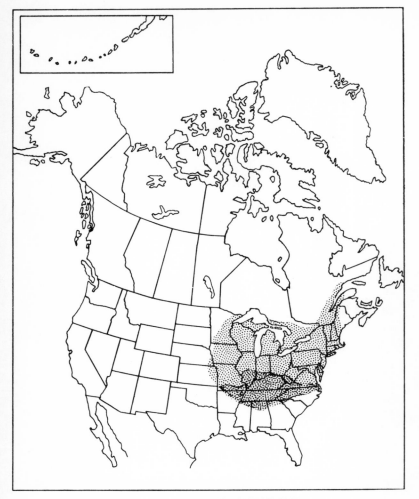

EASTERN SCREECH OWL

Otus asio naevius (Gmelin)

DISTRIBUTION IN NORTH AMERICA

Northeastern Minnesota, northern Michigan (Cheboygan County), southern Ontario (Lake Nipissing), southern Quebec (Montreal), and Maine (Franklin County), southward to eastern Kansas, Missouri, central Illinois, Ohio, and Virginia.

Winters somewhat southward, sometimes to Alabama (Ardell) and Georgia (Newton County.)

MIGRATION

Primarily resident within its range, the Eastern Screech Owl cannot rightly be termed a migratory bird. Yet there are times when some degree of seasonal movement can be noted—largely dependent upon the severity of the winter and the availability of prey. About the most extensive migrational movements of record, as determined from recovery of banded birds, has been less than 500 miles and usually no more than 200 miles.

ECONOMIC INFLUENCE

Otus asio naevius does destroy a certain number of songbirds, game birds, and some poultry each year, but the damage it may do is far more than offset by the enormous benefit it bestows in destruction of injurious rodents and insect pests. Much depends upon where the owl is located if one is to determine its ecological and economic value or detriment. In a bird sanctuary, for example, the Eastern Screech Owl is clearly detrimental, for it will kill large numbers of songbirds that are themselves economically valuable for their insect-eating habits. On the other hand, birds make up a relatively small percentage of the normal annual diet of *Otus asio naevius,* and the majority of its prey are creatures distinctly detrimental agriculturally.

Pellet analyses compiled from throughout its range indicate that at least 75 per cent of the Eastern Screech Owl's food on an annual basis consists of injurious mammals and insects, while only about 7 per cent is comprised of birds, including not only songbirds, game birds, and poultry, but equally many pest birds such as starlings, blackbirds, and English sparrows.

The comparative economic value of the Eastern Screech Owl can best be seen through projected statistical information. It has been determined that this owl consumes 25.3 per cent of its own body weight in prey daily during the autumn and winter months, and 10.3 per cent daily in the spring and summer months. Since the average weight of the adult male Eastern Screech Owl is 7.1 ounces, this means that in one year's time the average male bird consumes about 28.75 pounds of prey. Of this total, almost 22 pounds is comprised of injurious rodents and insects.

Therefore, from the standpoint of both ecology and economics, the Eastern Screech Owl must be rated as being of great benefit. Not only does it provide a real service in the destruction of agriculturally detrimental rodents and insects, it also acts as a check on population explosions of life forms which might otherwise increase to the point where the natural balance is upset. Like all other owls, *Otus asio naevius* is a vital link in the balance of nature.

XXIX PASADENA SCREECH OWL

Otus asio quercinus Grinnell. Female. Southeastern border of Kern County, California, February 17, 1969. A.O.U. Number 373-K

XXX GUADALUPE SCREECH OWL

Otus asio suttoni Moore. Male. Vicinity of Coahuila Noria de Gilberto, Mexico, April 2, 1945. Not included in the 1957 A.O.U. Check-list

Karl E. Karalus

AIKEN'S SCREECH OWL

(COLOR PLATE XVI)

SCIENTIFIC NAME AND ORIGINAL DESCRIPTION

Otus asio aikeni (Brewster). Original description: *Megascops asio aikeni* Brewster, *The Auk,* Volume 8, No. 2, April 1891, p. 139; based on a specimen from El Paso County, Colorado.

OTHER NAMES

GREAT PLAINS SCREECH OWL After its geographical distribution.

LE PETIT-DUC D'AIKEN French-Canadian name meaning "Aiken's Little Duke."

DISTINGUISHING FEATURES

Slightly smaller and somewhat darker in general coloration than the Eastern Screech Owl (*Otus asio naevius*) or the Rocky Mountain Screech Owl (*Otus asio maxwelliae*). It is larger than the Mexican Screech Owl (*Otus asio cineraceus*) but with the underparts more coarsely mottled or vermiculated and the blackish medial streaks broader and more strongly contrasted with the general coloration of the bird. The blackish pencilings of the underparts are also heavier but somewhat less numerous than in the Mexican Screech Owl. Aiken's Screech Owl is about the size of the California Screech Owl (*Otus asio bendirei*), but more generally ash-colored and with the dark markings considerably coarser and more numerous on both upperparts and underparts.

WEIGHT

Subspecies average: 180.3 gr. (6.3 oz.).

XXXI NEBRASKA SCREECH OWL

Otus asio swenki Oberholser. Female. Five miles north of Bassett, Brown Rock County, Nebraska, October 22, 1962. A.O.U. Number 373-N

XXXII YUMA SCREECH OWL

Otus asio yumanensis Miller and Miller. Male. Colorado River Basin, vicinity of Ripley, Riverside County, California, January 20, 1971. A.O.U. Number 373-L

TOTAL LENGTH

Subspecies average: 209.7 mm. (8.3″).

WINGSPAN

Subspecies average: 533.4 mm. (21.0″).

INDIVIDUAL WING LENGTH

Subspecies average: 163.9 mm. (6.5″).

TAIL LENGTH

Subspecies average: 88.9 mm. (3.5″).

BEAK LENGTH

Subspecies average: 15.0 mm. (0.6″).

HABITAT

Confined primarily to the cottonwood margins along streams.

FOOD

Almost entirely mice and grasshoppers.

NEST

Natural hollows or abandoned woodpecker holes from 8 to 35 feet high, especially in cottonwoods along streams.

EGGS

Two to five, but usually three or four. Based on the measurements of 28 eggs, average egg size was 35.9 mm. (1.4″) in length by 30.7 mm. (1.2″) in width, making them just a trifle larger than those of the Eastern Screech Owl.

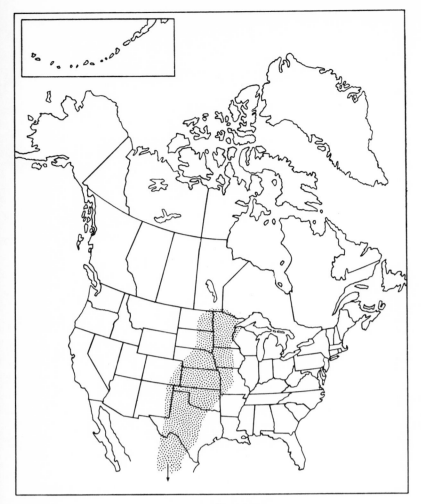

AIKEN'S SCREECH OWL

Otus asio aikeni (Brewster)

OTHER NAMES

BAYOU OWL From habitat in Louisiana bayou country.

SHOE OWL A superstitious application derived from the belief that in order to ward off evil spirits when the owl's call is heard, the individual must get out of bed and turn his left shoe upside down.

DISTINGUISHING FEATURES

The red-phase and gray-phase birds are both darker in tone than *Otus asio naevius,* but smaller and with the beak more arched.

The Southern Screech Owl is lighter in both color phases than the Florida Screech Owl (*Otus asio floridanus*), but larger.

Barrings and markings in the red phase are more abundant and blacker in tone, and the dark mottlings in the gray phase are in much greater contrast to the background color than in the Eastern Screech Owl. But in the red phase they are less numerous and not so dark as in the Florida Screech Owl, and the dark markings in the gray phase are not so clearly delineated.

DISTRIBUTION IN NORTH AMERICA

Northwestern North Dakota and northwestern Minnesota southward into extreme western Oklahoma (Kenton), extreme western Kansas, and eastern and central Colorado (El Paso County), into central New Mexico, central and western Texas, northeastern Arizona, and southward to northern Durango, Mexico.

SOUTHERN SCREECH OWL

(COLOR PLATE XVII)

SCIENTIFIC NAME AND ORIGINAL DESCRIPTION

Otus asio asio (Linnaeus). Original description: *Strix asio* Linnaeus, *Systematica Natura,* Edition 10, Volume 1, 1758, page 92; based on the Little Owl, *Noctua aurita minor* Catesby, *Carolina,* Volume 1, page 7; from a South Carolina specimen.

WEIGHT

Subspecies average: 185.7 gr. (6.5 oz.).

TOTAL LENGTH

Subspecies average: 216.0 mm. (8.5″).

WINGSPAN

Subspecies average: 531.9 mm. (21.0″).

INDIVIDUAL WING LENGTH

Subspecies average: 158.1 mm. (6.2″).

TAIL LENGTH

Subspecies average: 78.8 mm. (3.1″).

Screech Owl

BEAK LENGTH

Subspecies average: 15.2 mm. (0.6").

FEET

Very densely feathered.

VOICE

The principal call has occasionally been compared to the soft, far-distant whinnying of a horse.

COLORATION AND MARKINGS: ADULT

The beak coloration may vary from a dull blue gray to a rather bright pistachio greenish. There is a brownish intergrade between the red-phase and gray-phase birds which is not uncommon in some parts of the South, particularly in northern Louisiana. The markings of the brown intergrade are an intermediate blending of the markings of gray phase and red phase.

HABITAT

Primarily a lowland bird, preferring sparse woodlands and marshy meadows as well as open bayou country from coastal areas to the higher woodlands of the Appalachian slopes.

EGGS

Usually four to six eggs, but as few as two or as many as eight. These eggs are normally laid in late March or early April. From the measurements of 77 eggs, the average length was 35.0 mm. (1.4") and the average width was 30.0 mm. (1.2").

DISTRIBUTION IN NORTH AMERICA

Common in every state southward and eastward of a line from the northern Virginia coast westward to central Kansas, then southward to the eastern Texas coast. However, it is uncommon in northwestern Arkansas and absent in both central and southern Florida.

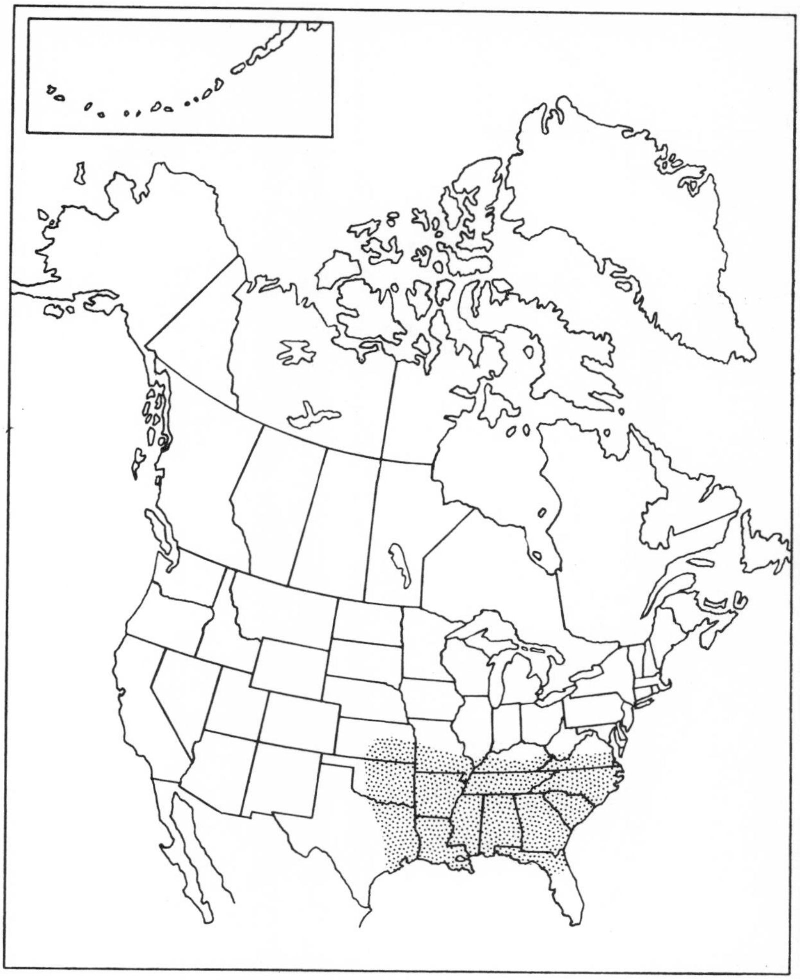

SOUTHERN SCREECH OWL

Otus asio asio (Linnaeus)

CALIFORNIA SCREECH OWL

(COLOR PLATE XVIII)

SCIENTIFIC NAME AND ORIGINAL DESCRIPTION

Otus asio bendirei (Brewster). Original description: *Scops asio bendirei* Brewster, *Bulletin of the Nuttall Ornithological Club,* Volume 7, Number 1, January 1882, page 31; based on a specimen from Nicasio, California.

OTHER NAMES

BENDIRE'S SCREECH OWL After the esteemed ornithologist Major C. E. Bendire.

CALIFORNIA SCREECH OWL

Otus asio bendirei (Brewster)

TOTAL LENGTH

Subspecies average: 226.1 mm. (8.9″).

WINGSPAN

Subspecies average: 572.8 mm. (22.6″).

INDIVIDUAL WING LENGTH

Subspecies average: 167.6 mm. (6.6″).

TAIL LENGTH

Subspecies average: 80.5 mm. (3.2″).

BEAK LENGTH

Subspecies average: 15.2 mm. (0.6″).

DISTINGUISHING FEATURES

This Screech Owl has no red color phase and is singularly uniform in its color tone. It is similar to the gray phase of the Southern Screech Owl (*Otus asio asio*) except that the Southern race has an unmarked median line down breast and belly, whereas the California Screech Owl is more notably ashy white and both barred and streaked thickly across the median line of breast and belly without break. These barrings and streakings are rather fine and tend to give a somewhat smoky appearance to the general coloration of the underparts.

The ear tufts are not quite as long as those of the Southern Screech Owl.

It is darker and vaguely browner than the Saguaro Screech Owl (*Otus asio gilmani*).

It is smaller than Brewster's Screech Owl (*Otus asio brewsteri*) and both smaller and a bit paler in general coloration than MacFarlane's Screech Owl (*Otus asio macfarlanei*).

COLORATION AND MARKINGS: ADULT

The shaft streaks of black on both belly and breast plumage are quite heavy, but the underparts are not as conspicuously crosslined as in the gray phase of the Eastern Screech Owl.

HABITAT AND ROOSTING

Prefers the timbered foothills of mountains at moderate elevations and normally roosts in woodpecker holes located from 20 to 60 feet high in conifers. When a hollow of a hardwood tree is used, the preference is for a natural hollow rather than an abandoned woodpecker hole.

FOOD

Preys heavily upon house sparrows and mice, but is less of an insect eater than most of the other Screech Owl races.

WEIGHT

Subspecies average: 215.5 gr. (7.5 oz.).

Screech Owl

NEST

Almost invariably in old woodpecker holes, but sometimes in natural cavities. On occasion it may make an indifferent effort to partially line the bottom of the nesting cavity with a few bits of pine-needle clusters, dried grasses, and a few feathers.

EGGS

As few as two, but not more than five; usually four. They average just slightly smaller than those of the Eastern Screech Owl. Based on measurements of 45 eggs, averages were 31.2 mm. (1.2") in length and 29.9 mm. (1.2") in width. Eggs are laid as early as late March and as late as mid-May, but most often during April.

DISTRIBUTION IN NORTH AMERICA

South-central Oregon (in Josephine, Jackson, Curry, and Klamath counties), and northwestern coastal region of California (exclusive of the narrow coastal strip in Del Norte and Humboldt counties), from Trinity County south to Monterey Bay, and inland to the edge of the Sacramento-San Joaquin Valley. In the Oregon-California border area it tends to intergrade with Brewster's Screech Owl, making it questionable as to whether specimens from the Eureka, California, area (where the intergrading is most distinct) should be referred to as *Otus asio bendirei* or *Otus asio brewsteri*. Extends northward to the Mount Shasta area on the western slope of the Sierras.

BREWSTER'S SCREECH OWL

(COLOR PLATE XIX)

SCIENTIFIC NAME AND ORIGINAL DESCRIPTION

Otus asio brewsteri Ridgway. Original description: *Otus asio brewsteri* Ridgway, *U. S. National Museum Bulletin,* Number 50, Part 6, 1914, page 700; based on a specimen from Salem, Oregon.

DISTINGUISHING FEATURES

This owl, named after the famed ornithologist, William Brewster, by Robert Ridgway, has no red phase, although occasionally there is a brownish-gray phase. Most often it is a warm gray and not considered as being dichromatic. Brewster's Screech Owl is similar to Kennicott's Screech Owl (*Otus asio kennicottii*) but it is smaller, grayer, paler, and with less brown. It is slightly larger than the Eastern Screech Owl (*Otus asio naevius*) and the shaft streaks on upperparts and underparts are more in contrast with the general coloration, although the crosslining on the underparts is less conspicuous than on the Eastern Screech Owl. It is a smaller and darker owl than MacFarlane's Screech Owl (*Otus asio macfarlanei*).

WEIGHT

Subspecies average: 222.5 gr. (7.8 oz.).

TOTAL LENGTH

Subspecies average: 229.8 mm. (9.1").

WINGSPAN

Subspecies average: 599.8 mm. (23.6").

INDIVIDUAL WING LENGTH

Subspecies average: 171.4 mm. (6.8").

VOICE

One of the most silent Screech Owl races; not particularly vociferous even during the courtship and nesting periods.

COLORATION AND MARKINGS: ADULT

Almost always with brownish or buffy markings on the underparts, and sometimes the entire ground color of the underparts suffused with a buff coloration.

GENERAL HABITS AND CHARACTERISTICS

Brewster's Screech Owl is the most common owl in the state of Oregon, but it is not very often seen be-

BREWSTER'S SCREECH OWL

Otus asio brewsteri Ridgway

EGGS

As few as two on rare occasions and, even more rarely, as many as ten. Normally three to six eggs are laid, and most often four. Measurements of 10 eggs averaged 37.3 mm. (1.5″) in length and 31.2 mm. (1.2″) in width.

DISTRIBUTION IN NORTH AMERICA

Brewster's Screech Owl normally resides at higher altitudes than does MacFarlane's Screech Owl. Found in Oregon (west of the Cascade Range and south of the lower Columbia River Valley), and a narrow coastal belt in northwestern California (Carlotta, Humboldt County). Continues northward to Chelan County, Washington, and westward from there to the Pacific coast.

MEXICAN SCREECH OWL

(COLOR PLATE XX)

cause of its highly nocturnal habits. If seen at all in daytime, it will almost certainly be in the midst of the nesting period and even then only on a heavily overcast day.

SCIENTIFIC NAME AND ORIGINAL DESCRIPTION

Otus asio cineraceus (Ridgway). Original description: *Megascops asio cineraceus* Ridgway, *The Auk*, Volume 12, Number 4, October 1895, page 390; based on a specimen from Fort Huachuca, Arizona.

HABITAT

Prefers the somewhat lower slopes and creek valleys well grown in oaks and cottonwoods.

OTHER NAME

ARIZONA SCREECH OWL   After its geographic distribution in the United States.

FOOD

Primarily mice and insects, but including a certain number of small birds during the nesting season.

DISTINGUISHING FEATURES

Closely related to the Saguaro Screech Owl (*Otus asio gilmani*) and still claimed by some authorities to be the same race; there are nevertheless some significant differences. Though their breeding ranges closely intermingle, the ear tufts of the Mexican Screech Owl are somewhat more conspicuous at all times, the wings are a little longer, and the tail a trifle shorter. Too, whereas the Saguaro Screech Owl tends to inhabit the slopes and hilltops, the Mexican Screech Owl shows a

NEST

Usually in old woodpecker holes, but occasionally in suitable natural tree hollows. The nesting cavity is rarely less than 20 feet high or more than 35 feet high.

Screech Owl

preference for valleys. One of the smallest of the Screech Owl races, the Mexican Screech Owl is somewhat smaller than the Eastern Screech Owl (*Otus asio naevius*) and is generally an undistinguished gray brown in over-all coloration.

WEIGHT

Subspecies average: 166.1 gr. (5.8 oz.).

TOTAL LENGTH

Subspecies average: 184.4 mm. (7.3″).

WINGSPAN

Subspecies average: 551.2 mm. (21.7″).

INDIVIDUAL WING LENGTH

Subspecies average: 163.2 mm. (6.4″).

TAIL LENGTH

Subspecies average: 87.7 mm. (3.5″).

BEAK

Varies from greenish yellow to deep slate green; most often is a dull shade of dusky yellow green.

EAR TUFTS, PLUMAGE

The ear tufts tend to be a shade wider at their base than those of other *Otus asio* subspecies, and perhaps just slightly longer on the average. The plumage of the eyelids is a bit heavier than in other races and quite distinctly black. When the eyes are closed there is the odd impression that very black eyes without irides are still watching.

COLORATION AND MARKINGS: ADULT

Strictly monochromatic in the gray phase only. The upperparts are a distinct ashy gray, sometimes with just a vague brownish cast, and with numerous black shaft streaks on the back. The shaft streaks on the underparts are narrower but are also very black, and there are no clear white interspaces in the delicate crossbars and vermiculation. The vermiculation on both upperparts and underparts is considerably more delicate than those of Aiken's Screech Owl (*Otus asio aikeni*). Though this bird often tends to give the impression of being somewhat brownish in general coloration, close examination invariably indicates that this is, instead, an illusion created by the shading of warm grays. There is little trace of real brown anywhere in the plumage and no brown-phase or red-phase bird has ever been found.

COLORATION AND MARKINGS: JUVENILE

Ordinarily much more narrowly crossbarred than the juveniles of other *Otus asio* subspecies.

GENERAL HABITS AND CHARACTERISTICS

The Mexican Screech Owl is more openly sociable in its habits than most other Screech Owl races. It is inclined to begin calling just after sundown, and soon upward of from four to ten birds will be calling back and forth. They begin moving gradually closer together and gather in loose groups for a short while before moving off generally together in the deepening twilight.

HABITAT

Most fond of moderately heavy scrub-growth areas of the desert, especially near moist creek valleys where foliage tends to remain greener and thicker than in surrounding areas.

ENEMIES AND DEFENSES

Superbly bark-camouflaged and well able to mimic equally a knob on the limb of the giant saguaro cactus or a stub of branch on an oak or willow. The Mexican

MEXICAN SCREECH OWL

Otus asio cineraceus (Ridgway)

EGGS

Normally there are three or four to an individual nesting, but very occasionally only two. Once in a great while five eggs will be laid. Though these eggs are pure white, they often seem to be reddish-brown speckled like the eggs of a sparrow hawk, but the speckles are merely stains resulting from the parasitic activities of the fleas which infest the parent birds. On the basis of measurements of 37 eggs, the average length was 34.3 mm. (1.4″) by 28.7 mm. (1.1″) in width.

DISTRIBUTION IN NORTH AMERICA

Southern Nevada (Grapevine Mountains, exclusive of the Colorado River Valley), and central and southern Utah, southward through central and eastern Arizona, southwestern and southern New Mexico to central Sonora, Mexico, southern California, Baja California, and mountainous west-central Texas.

FLORIDA SCREECH OWL

(COLOR PLATE XXI)

SCIENTIFIC NAME AND ORIGINAL DESCRIPTION

Otus asio floridanus (Ridgway). Original description: *Scops asio* var. *Floridanus* Ridgway, *Bulletin of the Essex Institute*, Volume 5, Number 12, December 1873, page 200; based on a specimen from Indian River, Florida.

Screech Owl seems to be one of the most susceptible of *Otus asio* races to infestations of fleas.

FOOD

Primarily mice, rats, and insects, but the diet varies widely according to season and availability of prey. Quite readily feeds upon lizards, frogs, small birds, kangaroo rats, ground squirrels, crayfish, scorpions, grasshoppers, locusts, and beetles.

NEST

Hollows from 10 to 30 feet high in oaks and willows along creek margins are especially favored, with no detectable preference between natural cavities and old woodpecker holes. Quite frequently takes up residence in the abandoned hole of a Gila woodpecker or gilded flicker located relatively high in a saguaro cactus.

OTHER NAMES

BEACH OWL   Because it is not uncommonly seen at dusk hunting along the fringe of beach grasses, especially on the Florida Gulf coast.

CAT OWL   For its superficial catlike appearance as it perches with its ear tufts upraised and eyes slitted.

DEATH OWL   For the superstitious belief that when its call is heard, someone of the hearer's acquaintance will soon die.

HAMMOCK OWL   For the hammocks it inhabits, especially in the Florida Everglades area.

OAK OWL   Because it often nests and roosts in hollows of the live oak tree.

PALM OWL   After its use of abandoned woodpecker and flicker holes in palm trees as nesting sites.

SAND OWL   For the same reason that it is referred to as the Beach Owl.

DISTINGUISHING FEATURES

This is the smallest of the Florida owls, including even the Florida Burrowing Owl (*Speotyto cunicularia floridana*); it is also the smallest eastern form of *Otus asio*. It is very markedly dichromatic with deeply and richly colored red and gray phases, although the red-phase bird is considerably less common than the gray. It is smaller and more deeply colored in both phases than either the Eastern Screech Owl (*Otus asio naevius*) or the Southern Screech Owl (*Otus asio asio*).

WEIGHT

Subspecies average: 167.4 gr. (5.9 oz.).

TOTAL LENGTH

Subspecies average: 211.0 mm. (8.3″).

WINGSPAN

Subspecies average: 509.7 mm. (20.1″).

INDIVIDUAL WING LENGTH

Subspecies average: 151.1 mm. (6.0″).

BEAK

Rather horn-colored, but with a pale greenish cast and becoming whitish at the tip.

FEET

The toes of the Florida Screech Owl are covered with sparse, bristly plumage.

EAR TUFTS

Slightly longer for the size of the bird than are those of the Eastern Screech Owl.

VOICE

Most calls are virtually identical with those of the Eastern Screech Owl, the difference being that those of the Florida Screech Owl tend to be slightly more tremulous and not quite as far-carrying. In addition, this bird has been known to utter a peculiar low-pitched drumming note unlike anything uttered by other *Otus asio* subspecies.

COLORATION AND MARKINGS: ADULT

Although it is classed as dichromatic, there are actually three color phases, with the gray phase predominating, the red phase occurring much less often and, even more rarely, a brown-phase bird. In the red phase the underparts are white, but quite heavily mottled with tawny and streaked with very dark brownish gray, and the same streaking is on the upperparts, which are generally a distinct russet in general coloration. In the gray-phase bird, the upperparts are a rather dark drab coloration somewhat indistinctly marked with brown-black streakings, and the underparts have narrow streaks of the same over a general coloration of gray brown. The rare brown phase replaces all ground-color reds or grays with a fairly deep brown on the upperparts and buffy brown to medium brown on the underparts.

GENERAL HABITS AND CHARACTERISTICS

As with the other Screech Owl subspecies, the Florida Screech Owl is primarily nocturnal, spending practically all daylight hours perched in a well-camouflaged position close to the trunk of heavily foliaged orange trees or mango trees, or else hidden in the hollow of a live oak or palm.

HABITAT

May be found equally well in various types of Florida terrain and cover, from oak hammocks and citrus groves to relatively open pine and cypress forests, palmetto scrublands, and tree-scattered grasslands along beaches.

FOOD

In addition to the mice and insects which make up the bulk of its diet, the Florida Screech Owl consumes

EGGS

Otus asio floridanus lays fewer eggs than do most other Screech Owl subspecies. Normally there are only two to four eggs, with three the most common number, but two eggs much more often than four. From the measurements of 57 eggs, the average egg size came to 33.7 mm. (1.3″) in length and 28.8 mm. (1.1″) in width.

DISTRIBUTION IN NORTH AMERICA

The range of this interesting little owl has increased considerably over recent decades. Although still primarily confined to the Florida peninsula from Key West northward to the Gainesville area, it is also found along the Gulf coast to eastern Texas, along the Atlantic coast to east-central South Carolina, and northward in the Mississippi River Valley as far as the mouth of the Ohio River. It has not been clearly determined whether this has been an actual increase in the *Otus asio floridanus* population with resultant expansion of range, or whether the form was over a larger region than realized when Robert Ridgway originally described the race in 1873.

FLORIDA SCREECH OWL

Otus asio floridanus (Ridgway)

SAGUARO SCREECH OWL

(*COLOR PLATE XXII*)

SCIENTIFIC NAME AND ORIGINAL DESCRIPTION

Otus asio gilmani Swarth. Original description: *Otus asio gilmani* Swarth, *University of California Publications Zoological*, Volume 7, 1910, page 1, and *The Condor*, Volume 18, 1916, page 163; based on a specimen from Blackwater, Pinal County, Arizona.

numerous salt-water crustaceans, lizards (mainly skinks and anoles), frogs, toads, fresh- and salt-water fish, spiders, and scorpions. Much prey is taken crossing little-traveled roads at night.

COURTSHIP

May begin as early as late November or December, but more commonly in January and February; occasionally not until March.

NEST

Quite often in the natural cavities of live oak, pine, and cypress, but more commonly in abandoned flicker or pileated woodpecker holes 8 to 30 feet high in the trunks of sabal (cabbage) palms. The Florida Screech Owl holds the record among the species for nest height, with a well-documented nesting having occurred in a palm hollow fully 80 feet above the ground.

FLORIDA SCREECH OWL FIELD SKETCHES

A Florida Screech Owl in the gray phase of coloration was captured by the authors in the hollow of a live oak near Englewood, Florida, in the summer of 1971. The bird at first struggled vigorously against being held firmly about the body but then settled down, at one point seeming almost to fall asleep, while portrait sketches were made. Finally, placed on the top wire of a fence, it remained there for about thirty seconds before winging off swiftly into some dense sabal palm growth.

otus asio floridanus.
head studies.

K E. K.

SAGUARO SCREECH OWL
Otus asio gilmani Swarth

OTHER NAMES

ARIZONA SCREECH OWL   Because of geographical location.

MEXICAN SCREECH OWL   For the same reason, though infringing on the common name of *Otus asio cineraceus.*

TECOLOTITO CHILLÓN DE LOS SAGUAROS   Mexican-Indian name meaning "Little Screech Owl of the Saguaro."

DISTINGUISHING FEATURES

Although it is included in many older listings as being identical with the Mexican Screech Owl, more recent descriptions substantiate the findings in the original description by Swarth that the differences are significant and constant and that it should be listed as a separate race. The Saguaro Screech Owl, which occurs only in the gray phase, is slightly smaller than the Mexican Screech Owl, though with tail a bit longer. In its darker markings it is more restricted than the Mexican Screech Owl, and the ground color is a paler gray. Underparts and upperparts tend to be very nearly the

same basic tone of gray, though sometimes faintly darker above than below. Plumage on legs and toes is white with a faint grayish touch and sparsely patterned with dusky. Recent accounts list this race as being the extreme in a line of divergence from the Eastern Screech Owl (*Otus asio naevius*).

WEIGHT

Subspecies average: 158.5 gr. (5.6 oz.).

TOTAL LENGTH

Subspecies average: 180.6 mm. (7.1″).

WINGSPAN

Subspecies average: 486.1 mm. (19.2″).

INDIVIDUAL WING LENGTH

Subspecies average: 155.5 mm. (6.1″).

TAIL LENGTH

Subspecies average: 92.5 mm. (3.7″).

BEAK LENGTH

Subspecies average: 13.3 mm. (0.5″).

VOICE

Differs considerably from the voice of the Eastern Screech Owl, having the distinct bouncing-ball double trill with less of a melodious quality and with the individual notes more clearly separated. The whole tone of the call is duller than is that of *Otus asio naevius.* In this subspecies, considerable calling occurs among family groups as the fledgling owls begin flying.

HABITAT

Almost strictly keeps to very arid desert terrain.

ENEMIES

Rarely, if ever, harassed by smaller birds, as so often occurs with the Eastern races.

HUNTING METHODS

Adults consistently catch enough food during the night to lay aside a small store of it to be fed to the nestling birds at intervals during the day, even when the nestlings are at an advanced age.

FOOD

Mice in abundance, but even more insects than mice and considerably more lizards than are caught and eaten by other races, including even the Florida Screech Owl (*Otus asio floridanus*). Scorpions also make up a substantial part of the diet.

NEST

Hardly without exception the nest is in a woodpecker hole in saguaro cactus, from as low as 4 feet high to about 35 feet. Sometimes in similar holes or (less often) natural cavities in creek valley live oaks, sycamores, and cottonwoods. On extremely rare occasions it may nest in an old magpie nest.

EGGS

As few as three, but usually four or five. Eight eggs have been recorded. Based on a sampling of 11 eggs, the average size is 34.1 mm. (1.3″) in length and 29.0 mm. (1.1″) in width.

FAMILY LIFE CHARACTERISTICS

No case has been recorded where the male has shared the nesting hole with the brooding female, as sometimes occurs with other Screech Owl subspecies. He roosts instead on a nearby branch or in another hollow not far distant.

DISTRIBUTION IN NORTH AMERICA

Southwestern California (especially the lower Colorado River Valley and the Imperial Valley) and east-ward through southern Arizona, northward in the Colorado River Valley to extreme southern Nevada, southward to northeastern Baja California and extreme northern Sonora, Mexico. It is plentiful in the lower plains from Santa Rita and Santa Catalina Mountains westward. The distribution on the whole is quite a bit like that of the Mexican Screech Owl except that the Saguaro Screech Owl is more inclined to inhabit the hotter valleys and desert flatlands, while the Mexican Screech Owl prefers the foothill slopes and oak-grown canyon areas.

HASBROUCK'S SCREECH OWL

(*COLOR PLATE XXIII*)

SCIENTIFIC NAME AND ORIGINAL DESCRIPTION

Otus asio hasbroucki Ridgway. Original description: *Otus asio hasbroucki* Ridgway, *U. S. National Museum Bulletin,* Number 50, Part 6, 1914, page 694; based on a specimen from Palo Pinto County, Texas.

DISTINGUISHING FEATURES

This generally gray Screech Owl was named by Robert Ridgway after E. M. Hasbrouck. It is similar in its markings to the Texas Screech Owl (*Otus asio mccallii*) but is a considerably larger bird, rather darker in general coloration and not as buffy gray on the upperparts. In addition, the underparts have broader and more numerous barrings and the leg plumage has mottlings that are considerably darker brown than those of the Texas Screech Owl. A rare red phase occurs about 5 per cent of the time and is a dark red like the Eastern Screech Owl (*Otus asio naevius*) but with a heavier pattern of markings.

WEIGHT

Subspecies average: 199.3 gr. (7.0 oz.).

TOTAL LENGTH

Subspecies average: 211.2 mm. (8.3″).

HASBROUCK'S SCREECH OWL

Otus asio hasbroucki Ridgway

WINGSPAN

Subspecies average: 536.5 mm. (21.1").

INDIVIDUAL WING LENGTH

Subspecies average: 157.8 mm. (6.2").

BEAK

Usually somewhat lighter greenish to dull greenish yellow.

GENERAL HABITS AND CHARACTERISTICS

Hasbrouck's Screech Owl has a very pugnacious nature and it is noted for its unusual belligerence toward humans when it has eggs or young, even when these may be in no particular jeopardy.

NEST

Mostly in natural tree hollows and woodpecker holes, but on occasion in martin houses.

EGGS

Sometimes three, usually four, occasionally five, rarely six. Based on the measurements of 27 eggs, the average size of the egg is 34.8 mm. (1.4") in length and 30.0 mm. (1.2") in width.

DISTRIBUTION IN NORTH AMERICA

Confined to an area from southeastern Kansas (Greenwood County, Cedar Vale) and northwestern Arkansas, through central and eastern Oklahoma to central Texas. In Texas it is well distributed from Travis and Kerr counties to Palo Pinto and Dallas counties, but less abundant in the counties of Lampasas, Cooke, Eastland, and McLenna.

SOUTHERN CALIFORNIA SCREECH OWL

(COLOR PLATE XXIV)

SCIENTIFIC NAME AND ORIGINAL DESCRIPTION

Otus asio inyoensis Grinnell. Original description: *Otus asio inyoensis* Grinnell, *The Auk,* Volume 45, Number 2, April 1928, page 213; based on a specimen from Independence, Inyo County, California.

DISTINGUISHING FEATURES

Named by the noted California ornithologist, Dr. Joseph Grinnell, after the Inyo Mountains of Cali-

---

Two common posturings of the Southern California Screech Owl (*Otus asio inyoensis*) including (left) normal relaxed perching pose and (right) elongated camouflaging posture assumed when disturbed. The individual shafting of each feather is black, the feet and legs are barred with dark brown, and the underside of the wing is somewhat darker than customary among Screech Owls.

Southern California
screech owl
O. a. inyoensis

spine black
barring med-brown
To very dark brown

facial disc
and facial rim
very dark

Bird Large

under-wing
dark

K.E.K.

feet and legs
barred with dark
brown

Inyo Co., California
Feb 7-1940

SOUTHERN CALIFORNIA SCREECH OWL

Otus asio inyoensis Grinnell

WINGSPAN

Subspecies average: 538.7 mm. (21.2″).

INDIVIDUAL WING LENGTH

Subspecies average: 162.3 mm. (6.4″).

TAIL LENGTH

Subspecies average: 81.3 mm. (3.2″).

BEAK LENGTH

Subspecies average: 15.2 mm. (0.6″).

HABITAT

Primarily oak-grown slopes and minor low-elevation canyons, especially where there is standing or running water.

FOOD

Mainly mice, insects, and lizards.

EGGS

From three to six, with four being the most common clutch and five not unusual. Average egg size, based on measurements of 17 eggs, is 36.0 mm. (1.4″) in length and 30.1 mm. (1.2″) in width.

fornia, this Screech Owl subspecies, which is fairly large as compared to most other southwestern *Otus asio* subspecies, is a somewhat paler ashy gray in general coloration than the Rocky Mountain Screech Owl (*Otus asio maxwelliae*) and has less of a brownish cast. The pattern of markings is similar to those markings on the Rocky Mountain Screech Owl except that the white spots on the closed-wing outer primaries are a good bit smaller and the vermiculations of belly, breast, and legs are almost black rather than a medium dark brown.

WEIGHT

Subspecies average: 204.1 gr. (7.1 oz.).

TOTAL LENGTH

Subspecies average: 218.5 mm. (8.6″).

XXXIII   WHISKERED OWL

Otus trichopsis trichopsis (Wagler). Female. West slope of Huachuca Peak, Cochise County, Arizona, May 8, 1969. Not included in the 1957 A.O.U. Check-list

XXXIV   ARIZONA WHISKERED OWL

Otus trichopsis asperus (Brewster). Male. South slope of Chiricahua Mountains, Cochise County, Arizona, May 10, 1930. A.O.U. Number 373-I

Karl E. Karalus
1971

Karl E. Karalus
1971

DISTRIBUTION IN NORTH AMERICA

Central Nevada (Fallon) and northwestern Utah to the Inyo region of California between the Sierra Nevada and Death Valley, onto the western slope of the Inyo Mountains, southwestwardly to the southern San Joaquin Valley, and southwardly west of the deserts to northwestern Baja California.

KENNICOTT'S SCREECH OWL

(COLOR PLATE XXV)

SCIENTIFIC NAME AND ORIGINAL DESCRIPTION

Otus asio kennicottii (Elliot). Original description: *Scops kennicottii* Elliot, *Proceedings of the Academy of Natural Sciences of Philadelphia,* Volume 19, Number 3, 1867, June–September (November 1, 1867); based on a specimen from Sitka, Alaska.

OTHER NAMES

COASTAL SCREECH OWL   For its habitat along the Pacific coast.

LE PETIT-DUC DE KENNICOTTII   French-Canadian name meaning "Kennicott's Little Duke."

LITTLE HORNED OWL   For its small-size similarity to the Northwestern Horned Owl (*Bubo virginianus lagophonus*), which is sometimes called "The Grand Duke."

PUGET SOUND SCREECH OWL   After part of its geographical location.

WASHINGTON SCREECH OWL   After part of its range.

A study is currently in progress toward the possibility of revising the nomenclature and status of this bird. An effort is being made to establish it as a separate species entirely, apart from *Otus asio,* with the new species to be called *Otus kennicottii,* and with the numerous Screech Owl subspecies of the West falling under this new classification. At this writing, however, Kennicott's Screech Owl and its near relatives are still considered as *Otus asio* subspecies.

DISTINGUISHING FEATURES

Named by Daniel G. Elliot after Robert Kennicott, this is the largest and most northerly of all the Screech Owl subspecies. It is slightly larger than MacFarlane's Screech Owl (*Otus asio macfarlanei*) and considerably larger than the Eastern Screech Owl (*Otus asio naevius*) or California Screech Owl (*Otus asio bendirei*). Although a western owl, Kennicott's Screech Owl has a distinct rufous phase which occurs occasionally, but most often it is a very dark bird, with a general coloration of deep brown. It is among the darkest of all North American Screech Owls, being considerably darker brown than either MacFarlane's Screech Owl or the California Screech Owl and much more heavily marked and spotted than the Eastern Screech Owl, with the spottings more buff than white.

WEIGHT

Subspecies average: 235.6 gr. (8.3 oz.).

TOTAL LENGTH

Subspecies average: 234.3 mm. (9.2″).

WINGSPAN

Subspecies average: 601.1 mm. (23.7″).

INDIVIDUAL WING LENGTH

Subspecies average: 181.4 mm. (7.2″).

TAIL LENGTH

Subspecies average: 99.3 mm. (3.9″).

BEAK LENGTH

Subspecies average: 18.5 mm. (0.7″).

XXXV   FLAMMULATED OWL

Otus flammeolus flammeolus (Kaup). Male. Vicinity of Mimbres, Grant County, New Mexico, April 11, 1887. A.O.U. Number 374

XXXVI   WESTERN BURROWING OWL

Speotyto cunicularia hypugaea (Bonaparte). Male. Four miles southwest of Oshkosh, Garden County, Nebraska, February 2, 1914. A.O.U. Number 378

KENNICOTT'S SCREECH OWL

Otus asio kennicottii (Elliot)

dark cinnamon buff. The sooty-brown upperparts are mottled and streaked with deep Vandyke brown to black and the scapular streaks and spottings on the wing edges range from pale buff to deep buff. The underparts are quite heavily streaked, barred, and somewhat mottled with a brown so very deep in tone it is virtually black. The plumage of legs and feet has fine buff mottlings over a richer buff-brown ground color. Individuals from the more southerly portions of its range tend to be somewhat lighter in coloration, with the gray tones more apparent. The red phase is a distinct and attractive subdued cinnamon buff.

GENERAL HABITS AND CHARACTERISTICS

A relatively unaggressive Screech Owl, *Otus asio kennicottii* will on occasion take up residence near farm buildings and become surprisingly tame.

HABITAT AND ROOSTING

Seldom found in the more densely forested areas or at higher altitudes, Kennicott's Screech Owl shows a marked preference for prairie ground with scattered large oaks, especially when these trees are relatively close to streams, lakes, or the ocean. Though it favors densely leaved maples and oaks for its roost, it will occasionally rest for the day in thick young firs.

VISION

Kennicott's Screech Owl has highly developed daytime vision and unlike most other Screech Owl races, which are almost entirely nocturnal, this bird is frequently seen actively on the hunt on cloudy days.

VOICE

Unexpectedly, considering its large size as compared to the other races of Screech Owls, the voice of Kennicott's Screech Owl is considerably more high-pitched and tremulous than is common among the other western races. Its calls are much more commonly heard during autumn than in spring and summer.

COLORATION AND MARKINGS: ADULT

Ground coloration of upperparts is a rather deep tawny brown and that of the underparts tends to be a

FOOD

Primarily an eater of rodents (especially mice) and insects, Kennicott's Screech Owl also shows a peculiar taste for ants, beetles, and caterpillars. It frequently eats crayfish and earthworms and, especially in spring when there are young to feed, it will attack and kill many varieties of birds, including even ducks now and then. Some poultry, too, is killed during this season, but in such cases the owl normally eats only the head of the prey. In one case a Kennicott's Screech Owl killed six full-grown bantam hens and a golden pheasant over a two-day period, eating only the heads of each and part of the breast of one of the bantams. Bird-killing activity is, however, almost nonexistent when the owl has no nestlings to feed.

Screech Owl

NEST AND NESTING HABITS

Otus asio kennicottii likes a natural hollow in a relatively isolated oak tree or dead fir stub, with the hole being from 10 to 15 feet in height and the hollow itself being at least six or eight inches deep. Unlike most other Screech Owl races, it makes a concerted effort to keep its nesting hollow neat and clean.

EGGS

From two to five eggs are laid; usually four, often three, infrequently two, and only very rarely five. The egg are most often laid between April 7 and May 15 and, based on the measurements of 33 eggs, average 37.8 mm. (1.5″) in length by 32.0 mm (1.3″) in width.

INCUBATION AND BROODING CHARACTERISTICS

The incubating female seems always to wear a markedly sleepy expression, and her reaction to disturbance on the nest is lethargic at best. She will usually allow herself to be freely handled, and her greatest reaction seems to be merely to close her eyes tightly.

DISTRIBUTION IN NORTH AMERICA

From southeastern Alaska (Situk River, Juneau), southward through coastal British Columbia and western Washington to the Columbia River Valley (Seaside, Clatsop County, Oregon, and Kalama, Cowlitz County, Washington). Occasionally strays as far northwestward as Sitka, Alaska.

MACFARLANE'S SCREECH OWL

(*COLOR PLATE XXVI*)

SCIENTIFIC NAME AND ORIGINAL DESCRIPTION

Otus asio macfarlanei (Brewster). Original description: *Megascops asio macfarlanei* Brewster, *The Auk,* Volume 8, Number 2, April 1891, page 140; based on a specimen from Fort Walla Walla, Washington.

OTHER NAME

LE PETIT-DUC DE MACFARLANE French-Canadian name meaning "MacFarlane's Little Duke."

DISTINGUISHING FEATURES

This quite large Screech Owl—only slightly smaller than Kennicott's Screech Owl (*Otus asio kennicottii*)— was named by William Brewster after R. R. MacFarlane. Its general coloration ranges from a normal dark brown to a dark, slaty gray brown, though never quite as dark as Kennicott's Screech Owl. Some researchers still contend, as a matter of fact, that MacFarlane's Screech Owl is merely an intergrade form between Kennicott's Screech Owl and the California Screech Owl (*Otus asio bendirei*). It is indeed similar in color to the latter, but much larger, as it is also larger and darker than the Eastern Screech Owl (*Otus asio naevius*). Its beak, surprisingly, is much smaller than Kennicott's Screech Owl and even smaller than that of the Eastern Screech Owl.

WEIGHT

Subspecies average: 227.4 gr. (8.0 oz.).

TOTAL LENGTH

Subspecies average: 228.4 mm. (9.0″).

WINGSPAN

Subspecies average: 585.7 mm. (23.1″).

INDIVIDUAL WING LENGTH

Subspecies average: 177.8 mm. (7.0″).

TAIL LENGTH

Subspecies average: 97.6 mm. (3.9″).

BEAK LENGTH

Subspecies average: 14.1 mm. (0.6″).

MACFARLANE'S SCREECH OWL

Otus asio macfarlanei (Brewster)

VOICE

Not uncommonly, this owl tends to mutter in what seems to human ears a rather petulant way prior to leaving its roost in the evening and at intervals as it rests while hunting. This muttering is sometimes interspersed with rather distinct calls, the notes clearly separated at first but becoming more rapid and closer together toward the end until they merge into a sort of trill deeper in tone than that of the Eastern Screech Owl and even more mournful. MacFarlane's Screech Owl voices a long series of quite doleful notes each evening immediately after sunset for about a month prior to and during the mating season, but generally becomes silent when incubation begins.

COLORATION AND MARKINGS: ADULT

Upperparts are generally brownish gray to dark sooty brown, with black shaft streaks and edges of wing and scapulars having creamy to buff-colored stripes. Underparts are numerously crosslined with black, and these lines are bisected by rather heavy dark-brown shaft streaks. There is usually a slight mottling of duskiness on the generally buff-colored plumage of legs and feet.

HABITAT

Tends to keep pretty much to the arid lower river plains and seldom moves very far up the mountain slopes. It has never been recorded above an elevation of 4,000 feet. Shows a preference for timber fringe areas, especially where these wooded borderlines are adjacent to densely brush-covered lower slopes or grassy valleys.

FOOD

Although it is known to kill domestic pigeons and other birds up to the size of a flicker, this is normally only a springtime manifestation and its food is primarily rodents and insects. This subspecies shows more of a preference for frogs—particularly tree frogs—and both trout and whitefish up to about eight inches in length than do most Screech Owl races.

COURTSHIP

MacFarlane's Screech Owl normally begins courting in very late February or early March.

NEST

Since it is too large an owl for most woodpecker and flicker holes, its preference is for natural hollows, especially in willows or cottonwoods along a watercourse. It does not care for a cavity located lower than 10 feet above the ground, and the nest is quite often as high as 60 feet.

EGGS

Three to six eggs are laid, but usually four or five, with an interval of 48 to 72 hours between layings. Eggs are normally laid between March 26 and May 7. Based on the measurements of 39 eggs, the average egg size is 37.6 mm. (1.5″) in length by 31.9 mm. (1.3″) in width.

DISTRIBUTION IN NORTH AMERICA

From the interior of southern British Columbia (Sicamous), through eastern Washington, eastern Oregon, and western Montana, west of the Continental Divide, to northeastern California (Shasta County), northern Nevada (northern Washoe County) and southern Idaho (Cassia County).

ROCKY MOUNTAIN SCREECH OWL

(COLOR PLATE XXVII)

SCIENTIFIC NAME AND ORIGINAL DESCRIPTION

Otus asio maxwelliae (Ridgway). Original description: *Scops asio maxwelliae* Ridgway, *Proceedings of the U. S. National Museum,* Volume 3, 1880, page 191, Number 402-c; based on a specimen from the vicinity of Denver, Colorado.

DISTINGUISHING FEATURES

This rather large Screech Owl, named by Robert Ridgway after Mrs. M. A. Maxwell, the noted taxidermist and hunter of Boulder, Colorado, is lighter in coloration than other more northerly Screech Owl races. Especially light specimens are among the lightest and most faintly marked of all races of *Otus asio.* The browns are generally paler, the whites purer, and in some specimens the underparts greatly predominate in white or very pale buff, especially on the lower breast and belly. It is somewhat larger than the Eastern Screech Owl (*Otus asio naevius*), though smaller than MacFarlane's Screech Owl (*Otus asio macfarlanei*).

WEIGHT

Subspecies average: 219.7 gr. (7.7 oz.).

TOTAL LENGTH

Subspecies average: 223.5 mm. (8.8″).

WINGSPAN

Subspecies average: 558.8 mm. (22.0″).

INDIVIDUAL WING LENGTH

Subspecies average: 173.3 mm. (6.8″).

TAIL LENGTH

Subspecies average: 89.0 mm. (3.5″).

BEAK LENGTH

Subspecies average: 16.8 mm. (0.7″).

COLORATION AND MARKINGS: ADULT

Although one extremely light-colored red-phase bird was once taken, this has been deemed an aberration and the Rocky Mountain Screech Owl is rated as a monochromatic form in the gray phase. The upperparts range from buffy brown gray to decidedly ash gray, with narrow streaks and vague mottlings of blackish brown. The underparts are almost unmarked white or buff white on lower breast and belly and narrowly barred in dark-brown crosslines on upper breast, sides, and flanks. The white streaks on the scapulars and wing edges are large and may show a faint trace of buffiness.

HABITAT AND ROOSTING

Prefers well-wooded creek bottoms, foothills, and plains along the easterly foot of the Rocky Mountains and, unlike the majority of Screech Owl forms, enjoys roosting on branches in heavy tree foliage during the warmer months, although it generally roosts in natural tree hollows during the winter.

FOOD

Primarily frogs, mice, crayfish, and some fish.

NEST

Most often in a natural cavity of a large tree, but on occasion will nest in an abandoned magpie nest in dense willows bordering slow-moving or stationary water.

ROCKY MOUNTAIN SCREECH OWL
Otus asio maxwelliae (Ridgway)

TEXAS SCREECH OWL
(*COLOR PLATE XXVIII*)

SCIENTIFIC NAME AND ORIGINAL DESCRIPTION

Otus asio mccallii (Cassin). Original description: *Scops McCallii* Cassin, *Illustrated Birds of California, Texas*, etc., Part 6 (September 12), 1854, page 180; based on a specimen from the Lower Rio Grande Valley, Texas. Former scientific names: *Scops McCallii*, *Megascops asio mccallii*.

OTHER NAMES

MCCALLY'S OWL   After Colonel George A. McCally, ornithologist, for whom it was named by John Cassin.

WESTERN MOTTLED OWL   For its geographic location and the pattern of markings on its plumage.

TECOLOTITO CHILLÓN DE TEJAS   Mexican-Indian name meaning "Texas Screech Owl."

EGGS

From a minimum of three to a maximum of seven. Usually there are three or four eggs, but not uncommonly five. Occasionally there will be six eggs, but only very rarely are there seven. The eggs tend to be somewhat more elongated in shape than those of other Screech Owl subspecies. Based on the measurements of 54 eggs, the average size is 36.3 mm. (1.4") in length by 30.2 mm. (1.2") in width.

DISTINGUISHING FEATURES

Larger than the Southern Screech Owl (*Otus asio asio*) but slightly smaller and paler than the Eastern Screech Owl (*Otus asio naevius*). It is listed as a monochromatic subspecies in the gray phase, but unauthenticated reports of red-phase birds have been recorded and are currently under investigation. This owl is very coarsely mottled and the lighter markings are most conspicuous. The ground coloration is a buffy dark gray.

WEIGHT

Subspecies average: 181.7 gr. (6.4 oz.).

TOTAL LENGTH

Subspecies average: 189.6 mm. (7.5").

DISTRIBUTION IN NORTH AMERICA

Southeastern Montana and western South Dakota to central Colorado along the east slope of the Rocky Mountains; may range as far northward as central or even northern Montana and adjacent plains (probably extending into much of the northern portion of Montana east of the mountains); also extending from southern Saskatchewan (Eastend, Regina) southward to Douglas County, Colorado, and probably westward through southern Wyoming to northeastern Utah.

Study of the flight maneuverability of the Rocky Mountain Screech Owl (*Otus asio maxwelliae*) in pursuit of an Io moth (*Automeris io*). Note widely spread rectrices and cupped wings to promote braking action as prey is neared and owl approaches point of snatching moth with talons.

Screech Owl

TEXAS SCREECH OWL

Otus asio mccallii (Cassin)

WINGSPAN

Subspecies average: 531.4 mm. (20.9″).

INDIVIDUAL WING LENGTH

Subspecies average: 150.1 mm. (5.9″).

TAIL LENGTH

Subspecies average: 84.5 mm. (3.3″).

BEAK LENGTH

Subspecies average: 15.2 mm. (0.6″). The beak on the Texas Screech Owl is usually a pale green, but sometimes shading into a very distinct turquoise.

COLORATION AND MARKINGS: ADULT

On the upperparts the shaft streakings are quite dark and in distinct contrast to the underlying light gray-buff ground color. The shaft streaks and cross-barrings on the underparts are sharply in contrast with the pale-gray to gray-buff ground coloration.

COLORATION AND MARKINGS: JUVENILE

All plumage with the exception of primaries and rectrices is barred or banded with grayish or whitish and the black streaks are absent.

HABITAT

Otus asio mccallii most prefers willow creek bottoms and somewhat more open mesquite plains.

NEST

The nesting holes (abandoned) of golden-fronted woodpeckers are very often used, as are natural cavities in hardwood trees. Holes in cactus are rarely, if ever, used as nesting sites.

EGGS

There are normally four eggs, but on occasion there will be as few as two or as many as five. Measurements of 43 eggs give an average egg size of 33.5 mm. (1.3″) long by 29.0 mm. (1.1″) wide.

DISTRIBUTION IN NORTH AMERICA

From southern Texas in Kinney, Bexar, Comal, and Refugio counties, and the area of the lower Rio Grande River upstream to the vicinity of Del Rio, Texas, and eastward from there to Comal County, then southward to the Gulf. Southward from the Texas range to central Nuevo León and south-central Tamaulipas (Forlón), Mexico, to the Gulf of Mexico.

PASADENA SCREECH OWL

(COLOR PLATE XXIX)

SCIENTIFIC NAME AND ORIGINAL DESCRIPTION

Otus asio quercinus Grinnell. Original description: *Otus asio quercinus* Grinnell, *The Auk,* Volume 32,

Number 1, January 1915, page 60; based on a specimen from Pasadena, Los Angeles County, California.

OTHER NAMES

OAK OWL After the live oak trees this owl favors and for which it was given its subspecific name of *quercinus* by Dr. Joseph Grinnell.

TECOLOTITO CHILLÓN ENCINERO Mexican-Indian name meaning "Live-Oak Screech Owl."

DISTINGUISHING FEATURES

The Pasadena Screech Owl, much lighter gray than the gray phase of the Eastern Screech Owl (*Otus asio naevius*), is probably most in appearance like the California Screech Owl (*Otus asio bendirei*) but its general coloration is slightly lighter. Instead of the more brownish coloration of the upperparts, it is a lighter ashydrab. On the underparts the dark markings are quite clearly outlined, but the ruddy margins on the markings are either entirely absent or only barely suggested. There is a distinctive though slight amount of rufous coloration in the plumage around the facial rim and on the ear tufts. There is some speculation that this race intergrades with the Saguaro Screech Owl (*Otus asio gilmani*).

PASADENA SCREECH OWL

Otus asio quercinus Grinnell

WEIGHT

Subspecies average: 216.3 gr. (7.6 oz.).

TOTAL LENGTH

Subspecies average: 227.3 mm. (9.0").

WINGSPAN

Subspecies average: 573.1 mm. (22.6").

INDIVIDUAL WING LENGTH

Subspecies average: 167.6 mm. (6.6").

TAIL LENGTH

Subspecies average: 80.8 mm. (3.2").

BEAK LENGTH

Subspecies average: 15.0 mm. (0.6").

EGGS

Rarely, if ever, fewer than three eggs are laid. Now and again there will be as many as six, but the most common clutch is four or five. Measurements of 46 eggs gave an average egg size of 35.8 mm. (1.4") in length by 30.2 mm. (1.2") in width.

DISTRIBUTION IN NORTH AMERICA

California west of the Sierra Nevada and west of the deserts, but excluding the northern coastal districts, from the Sacramento Valley (vicinity of Redding) and Monterey Bay south to about Latitude 30°30′ North in coastal Baja California; and from Mount Shasta in northernmost California southward along the west slope of the Sierra Nevada to southern California west of the desert regions and then coastally to Baja California.

GUADALUPE SCREECH OWL
Otus asio suttoni Moore

GUADALUPE SCREECH OWL
(COLOR PLATE XXX)

SCIENTIFIC NAME AND
ORIGINAL DESCRIPTION

Otus asio suttoni Moore. Original description: *Otus asio suttoni* Moore, *Proceedings of the Biological Society of Washington*, 1941, page 154; based on a specimen from Portezuelo, Hidalgo, Mexico.

OTHER NAME

SUTTON'S SCREECH OWL   Honorary name after bird artist and ornithologist, George Miksch Sutton.

DISTINGUISHING FEATURES

This is the darkest of all *Otus asio* races, with the ground coloration of the underparts a heavy gray and the upperparts a deep blackish gray. It is both boldly and densely marked with black on upperparts and underparts, though individual specimens tend to become slightly paler in the more southerly reaches of its range. The Guadalupe Screech Owl is fairly small, being not quite as large as Aiken's Screech Owl (*Otus asio aikeni*).

WEIGHT

Subspecies average: 191.2 gr. (6.7 oz.).

TOTAL LENGTH

Subspecies average: 152.7 mm. (6.0″).

WINGSPAN

Subspecies average: 480.7 mm. (18.9″).

INDIVIDUAL WING LENGTH

Subspecies average: 152.0 mm. (6.0″).

TAIL LENGTH

Subspecies average: 73.6 mm. (2.9″).

BEAK LENGTH

Subspecies average: 13.4 mm. (0.5″). The beak is black.

COLORATION AND MARKINGS:
ADULT

As noted, birds in the more southerly parts of the range, in the Chiricahua and Durango areas of Mexico, are much paler in color, almost approaching the coloration of the Mexican Screech Owl (*Otus asio cineraceus*), and there is only a small region where a color overlap tends to occur—this being at Chiricahua Mountain in southeastern Arizona.

HABITAT

High-altitude piñon and oak; low-altitude mesquite, willow, and greasewood.

EGGS

No data are available on egg sizes for this race, but they would probably be relatively similar, though slightly smaller, than those of the Mexican Screech Owl.

DISTRIBUTION IN NORTH AMERICA

Chiefly in the central portion of the Central Plateau of Mexico from Hidalgo northwest through Querétaro to Durango, the Big Bend area of Texas, southeast corner of Arizona at Guadalupe Canyon, and Las Cruces, New Mexico.

NEBRASKA SCREECH OWL

(COLOR PLATE XXXI)

SCIENTIFIC NAME AND ORIGINAL DESCRIPTION

Otus asio swenki Oberholser. Original description: *Otus asio swenki* Oberholser, *Journal of the Washington Academy of Sciences,* Volume 27, Number 8, August 15, 1937, page 354; based on a specimen taken at Chadron, Dawes County, Nebraska, at an elevation of 3,450 feet.

DISTINGUISHING FEATURES

The Nebraska Screech Owl, named by H. C. Oberholser in honor of ornithologist M. H. Swenk, is a dichromatic race but considerably more subdued in both color phases than is the Eastern Screech Owl (*Otus asio naevius*). A fairly large Screech Owl, it surpasses the Eastern Screech Owl in size but is not quite as large as MacFarlane's Screech Owl (*Otus asio macfarlanei*).

WEIGHT

Subspecies average: 225.6 gr. (7.9 oz.).

TOTAL LENGTH

Subspecies average: 225.1 mm. (8.9″).

WINGSPAN

Subspecies average: 574.3 mm. (22.6″).

INDIVIDUAL WING LENGTH

Subspecies average: 183.9 mm. (7.3″).

TAIL LENGTH

Subspecies average: 96.8 mm. (3.8″).

BEAK LENGTH

Subspecies average: 17.9 mm. (0.7″).

FOOD

Grasshoppers, along with some other insects, comprise about half this owl's diet, with mice and frogs making up most of the remainder. A few birds are taken during the nesting season.

NEST

It is not uncommon to find the Nebraska Screech Owl nesting behind the loose siding of an old barn, outbuilding, or derelict home, but more often the nest and roost will be in old flicker holes in cottonwoods and willows along creek valleys.

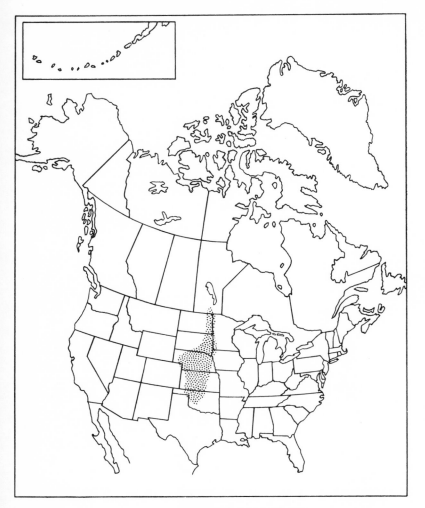

NEBRASKA SCREECH OWL

Otus asio swenki Oberholser

YUMA SCREECH OWL

(*COLOR PLATE XXXII*)

SCIENTIFIC NAME AND ORIGINAL DESCRIPTION

Otus asio yumanensis Miller and Miller. Original description: *Otus asio yumanensis* A. H. Miller and L. Miller, *The Condor*, Volume 53, Number 4, July 26, 1951, page 172; from a specimen taken 10 miles west of Pilot Knob, one mile south of the United States border in Baja California.

OTHER NAME

GILA SCREECH OWL   After part of its range along the Gila River of Arizona.

DISTINGUISHING FEATURES

A generally pale ashy-colored Screech Owl with a pinkish-sandy cast, but with individual specimens from the more northerly portion of its range (in and near the area where Nevada, Arizona, and California meet) having much less of the pinkish coloration or an absence of it. Normally it is a clear cool gray on the upperparts with a sort of pinkish "blush." The Yuma Screech Owl is very nearly identical in size to the Mexican Screech Owl (*Otus asio cineraceus*) but with its markings much narrower. The barrings across the underparts are very thin, medium brownish, and not well contrasted against the ventral surface. Although they are numerous, they are quite diffuse into the ground color of the underparts and therefore less conspicuous than in any other *Otus asio* subspecies.

WEIGHT

Subspecies average: 164.7 gr. (5.8 oz.).

EGGS

No cases have been reported of fewer than three eggs being laid at an individual nesting. On rare occasions there will be as many as seven, and only a little less rarely six. Most often there are four or five. From the measurements of 31 eggs, the average egg size is 37.0 mm. (1.5″) in length by 32.5 mm. (1.3″) in width.

DISTRIBUTION IN NORTH AMERICA

From southern Manitoba (Winnipeg), eastern North Dakota (Grafton, Hankinson), and western Minnesota (Roseau County), south to western and central Nebraska, western Kansas, and western Oklahoma (Arnett).

A variety of field study sketches of the Yuma Screech Owl (*Otus asio yumanensis*) near the mouth of the Gila River, southwestern Arizona. Barrings on the wings are very fine, as they are also on breast plumage and rectrices, the latter so numerous as to make the tail appear a solid ashy gray.

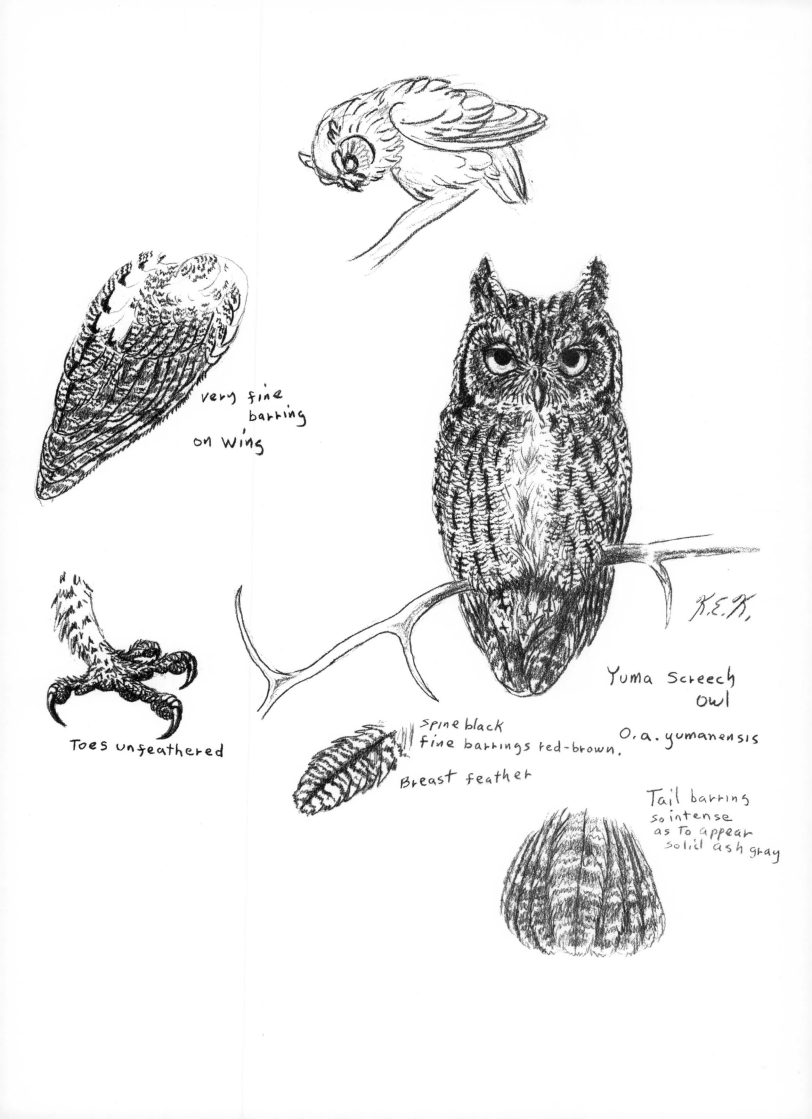

very fine
barring
on wing

Toes unfeathered

K.E.K.

Yuma Screech
Owl

O. a. yumanensis

Spine black
fine barrings red-brown.

Breast feather

Tail barring
so intense
as to appear
solid ash gray

YUMA SCREECH OWL

Otus asio yumanensis Miller and Miller

TOTAL LENGTH

Subspecies average: 184.6 mm. (7.3″).

WINGSPAN

Subspecies average: 554.0 mm. (21.8″).

INDIVIDUAL WING LENGTH

Subspecies average: 165.1 mm. (6.5″).

TAIL LENGTH

Subspecies average: 88.9 mm. (3.5″).

BEAK LENGTH

Subspecies average: 17.1 mm. (0.7″). The beak is black.

FOOD

Almost exclusively mice, lizards, insects, and scorpions.

NEST

Normally an abandoned flicker hole in a saguaro cactus.

DISTRIBUTION IN NORTH AMERICA

Lower Colorado River Valley and Gila River Valley, along with adjoining deserts in extreme southern Nevada, southeastern California (west to Coachella Valley), southwestern Arizona, northwestern Baja California, and northwestern Sonora, Mexico.

Screech Owl (Yuma)

SPECIES

ORDER: STRIGIFORMES

FAMILY: STRIGIDAE

GENUS: *Otus* Pennant

SPECIES: *trichopsis* (Wagler)

SUBSPECIES

trichopsis (Wagler)   WHISKERED OWL

asperus (Brewster)   ARIZONA

                      WHISKERED OWL

WHISKERED OWL
(COLOR PLATE XXXIII)

SCIENTIFIC NAME AND ORIGINAL DESCRIPTION

Otus trichopsis trichopsis (Wagler). Original description: *Scops trichopsis* Wagler, *Isis von Oken*, Heft 3 (March), 1832, Column 276; based on a specimen taken at an unspecified location in northern Mexico. Former names: *Scops trichopsis*, *Megascops trichopsis*.

OTHER NAMES

SPOTTED SCREECH OWL Former common name before revision.

TECOLOTITO MANCHADO LLANERO Mexican-Indian name meaning "Little Spotted Owl of the Grassy Plains."

WHISKERED SCREECH OWL Former common name before revision.

DISTINGUISHING FEATURES

The Whiskered Owl, formerly classed as a Screech Owl, is similar in many aspects of general physical characteristics and size to the *Otus asio* races, but there are differences of note. (See the preliminary section on *Otus asio* [Linnaeus], The Screech Owls.) Decidedly dichromatic in red phase and gray phase, it is somewhat like the Texas Screech Owl (*Otus asio mccallii*) and Mexican Screech Owl (*Otus asio cineraceus*), but smaller and quite a good bit darker, and with a heavier and longer beak. The upperparts are much more coarsely mottled, and there are large whitish spots on the scapulars, greater wing coverts, and hindneck. These spots, in fact, practically form a collar across the lower hindneck. Most distinctively, the facial feathers are a variegated brown and white with greatly developed bristly tips, especially in the malar region, giving the suggestion of whiskers, from which its name is derived. These "whiskers" are longer and more numerous than in the *Otus asio* races.

Rank in over-all size among the eighteen species: Fourteenth.

SHAPE AT REST

When perched, the Whiskered Owl tends to tilt its ear tufts backward considerably, not quite putting them flat against the head, but rarely holding them as distinctly erect as is common among the Screech Owl subspecies. It has an inclination to assume a more crouched and forward-leaning position on a perch, not unlike a modified version of the perching pose of one of the goatsuckers.

SHAPE IN FLIGHT

Otus trichopsis trichopsis, in flight, has a slightly greater sense of heaviness than the Screech Owls, with wings a shade narrower and shorter and the tail not quite as proportionately long.

FLIGHT PATTERN

Ordinarily a fairly direct flight line is taken, rather low to the ground, with wings seeming to beat more rapidly and with a somewhat greater effort than one might expect. Its flight is almost always terminated with a short glide, angling smoothly upward to the perch it has selected. There is, however, little gliding done in normal level flight, and rarely any hovering.

Measurements have been based on 11 measured birds: 4 males and 7 females.

WEIGHT

Species average: 165.2 gr. (5.8 oz.).

	Male	Female
Average	160.6 gr. (5.6 oz.)	169.7 gr. (5.9 oz.)
Minimum	145.6 gr. (5.1 oz.)	155.8 gr. (5.5 oz.)
Maximum	173.7 gr. (6.1 oz.)	186.7 gr. (6.5 oz.)

Rank in weight among the eighteen species: Thirteenth.

TOTAL LENGTH

Species average: 178.2 mm. (7.0″).

	Male	Female
Average	176.8 mm. (7.0″)	179.6 mm. (7.1″)
Minimum	166.4 mm. (6.6″)	174.1 mm. (6.9″)
Maximum	180.5 mm. (7.1″)	190.6 mm. (7.5″)

Rank in total length among the eighteen species: Thirteenth.

WINGSPAN

Species average: 464.7 mm. (18.3″).

	Male	Female
Average	453.3 mm. (17.9″)	476.0 mm. (18.8″)
Minimum	375.3 mm. (14.8″)	476.0 mm. (18.8″)
Maximum	478.3 mm. (18.8″)	509.0 mm. (20.1″)

Rank in wingspan among the eighteen species: Fourteenth.

INDIVIDUAL WING LENGTH

Species average: 138.8 mm. (5.5″).

	Male	Female
Average	133.7 mm. (5.3″)	143.8 mm. (5.7″)
Minimum	124.3 mm. (4.9″)	136.2 mm. (5.4″)
Maximum	137.8 mm. (5.4″)	148.8 mm. (5.9″)

Rank in wing length among the eighteen species: Thirteenth.

TAIL LENGTH

Species average: 66.0 mm. (2.6″).

	Male	Female
Average	58.5 mm. (2.3″)	73.5 mm. (3.0″)
Minimum	57.2 mm. (2.3″)	67.4 mm. (2.7″)
Maximum	65.3 mm. (2.6″)	76.3 mm. (3.0″)

Rank in tail length among the eighteen species: Fourteenth.

BEAK LENGTH

Species average: 15.0 mm. (0.6″). The beak ranges from a very light yellowish-green to a very dark yellowish green-gray drab coloration.

	Male	Female
Average	14.7 mm. (0.6″)	15.2 mm. (0.6″)
Minimum	13.4 mm. (0.5″)	13.8 mm. (0.5″)
Maximum	16.2 mm. (0.6″)	18.1 mm. (0.7″)

Rank in beak length among the eighteen species: Eleventh.

LEGS, FEET, TALONS

Though distinctly bristled, the toes are not heavily covered with plumage, and the scales of the feet, which are a dingy sand color, can be clearly seen. The tarsus is fairly long for the size of the bird, averaging 29.7 mm. (1.8″), but the feet are much smaller and weaker in comparison to the smallest races of *Otus asio*, though still powerful enough to handle any prey the Whiskered Owl normally takes. The talons are a deep slate gray at the base, darkening to jet black at the tips.

EYES AND VISION

The irides are a bright yellow, with sometimes a vague tinge of yellow-orange coloration. Daylight vision is quite as good as night vision, and *Otus trichopsis trichopsis,* unlike the Screech Owls, is frequently seen hunting in late afternoons, even on very clear days. A perched owl has been seen to watch intently the flight of a locust 50 or 60 yards distant in the daytime and arrow to the attack as soon as the insect lands.

EARS AND HEARING

While the Whiskered Owl's hearing is excellent, it may not be quite as superbly developed as in the more highly nocturnal species. Nevertheless, hearing is still the primary means of prey location. The ears are not

---

XXXVII FLORIDA BURROWING OWL

Speotyto cunicularia floridana Ridgway. Male. Five miles north of La Belle, Hendry County, Florida, June 9, 1971. A.O.U. Number 378-A

XXXVIII WHITNEY'S ELF OWL

Micrathene whitneyi whitneyi (Cooper). Female with young. South Bank of Rincon Creek, Pima County, Arizona, October 22, 1955. A.O.U. Number 381

abnormally asymmetrical in size and placement as in so many other owl species.

EAR TUFTS, PLUMAGE, ANNUAL MOLT

The ear tufts are slightly narrower than those of the *Otus asio* subspecies and not as often raised so perpendicularly to the head. When they are on occasion held erect, they appear to be single-pointed, but when angled back in the more normal position, each ear tuft appears to have two distinct tips. The plumage is relatively loose and soft but can be tightened against the body as a camouflaging behavior when the need arises. (See Enemies and Defenses.) There is one annual molt of the adults which begins about mid-July and is concluded by early November.

VOICE

Perhaps the most distinctive call issued by *Otus trichopsis trichopsis,* voiced by both sexes, is a somewhat nervous and rapidly delivered series of six to eight notes with usually a distinct emphasis on the next-to-last note uttered and sounding like *whoot-whoot-whoot-whoot-WHOOT-whoot.* This seems to be some sort of recognition call, normally given as the sun is setting or shortly thereafter.

Another common call is a muted, musical, rather syncopated trill run quickly together but with the individual notes detectable and not very much like the tremulous wavering call of the Eastern Screech Owl (*Otus asio naevius*).

The mating call, evidently first uttered by the male in a fairly deep voice and then echoed by the female on a higher tonal level, is a slightly tremulous four-note lyrical delivery with emphasis on the first note and sounding somewhat like *WHOOO-hoo woooo-woo.* Along with this call the birds, especially the male, utter a number of chuckling or clucking sounds.

More often heard in autumn than in spring, just after sunset, is a soft yet rather far-carrying *HOO-OOO,* which is issued in a cadence of three short notes,

a pause, and then one longer concluding note. The sound is very similar to the sound produced by gently blowing across the mouth of an empty pop bottle.

SEXUAL DIFFERENCES: SIZE, COLORATION, VOICE

A slight difference in size, with the female a bit larger, but no detectable difference in coloration or pattern of markings. The voice of the female bird is normally more high pitched and a bit more harsh.

MORTALITY AND LONGEVITY

Little of any real value is known of this aspect of the Whiskered Owl's life history. At least two specimens have been known to live longer than a decade in captivity; one of which was a fledgling when captured, the other an adult.

COLORATION AND MARKINGS: ADULT

As is the case with many of the dichromatic subspecies of *Otus asio,* the gray phase of *Otus trichopsis trichopsis* appears to be much more common than the red phase. In this gray phase the upperparts are a very bold brownish gray, with a distinctly heavy mottled effect and the feathers fringed with a dusky coloration. The ground color of the underparts is grayish white, boldly splashed with deep-gray shaft streakings and multiple parallel crossbars on each feather; these crossbars cross the shafts but do not reach the margin of the webs on either side. The facial rim is normally of two distinct lines, the inner one very dark brown or black, the outer one much lighter and ranging from buffy gray to gray white. The facial rim is not as smoothly round as in most species and there tends to be a distinct inward dip of the dark brown rim toward the eye at about the mid-outer cheek area. Brownish-black markings form something of a broken collar across the throat and sides of the neck, this continuing in broken white markings across the hindneck. In the red-phase bird, the upperparts are a dull-to-bright rufous tone quite boldly marked with black shaft streaks and dusky mottlings. The underparts are a reddish tawny gray, also boldly streaked. The general coloration of both upperparts and underparts is lighter but grayer in tone than in the red-phase birds of the Eastern Screech Owl (*Otus asio naevius*).

XXXIX   TEXAS ELF OWL

Micrathene whitneyi idonea (Ridgway). Female. Vicinity of Rio Grande City, Starr County, Texas, December 11, 1939. A.O.U. Number 381-A

XL   SNOWY OWL

Nyctea scandiaca (Linnaeus). Male. Vicinity of Arlington Heights, Cook County, Illinois, December 8, 1968. A.O.U. Number 376

COLORATION AND MARKINGS: JUVENILE

In the gray phase, the upperparts are a general dull gray brown, rather indistinctly mottled and barred with a murky gray and with gray-white tips on the feathers. The underparts are a dusky white and the feathers are broadly barred with slate brown. In the red-phase bird, the juvenal plumage is much as in the adult red-phase bird, but with the black streaking quite indistinct and sometimes absent in places. The underparts are a very dingy chestnut buff which becomes deeper in tone on the upper breast and throat. Dusky, indistinct bars crossed the flanks, sides, and breast.

GENERAL HABITS AND CHARACTERISTICS

Strangely, *Otus trichopsis trichopsis* seems markedly disinclined to perch or roost in any kind of pine trees, even though its plumage camouflage resembles some pine barks very closely. It much prefers the Arizona white oak (*Quercus arizonica*) not only for perching and roosting, but for nesting and as a place for tearing apart and devouring larger prey. This owl does not seem to care to perch very high in any tree, normally finding a convenient limb only about a dozen feet off the ground. Only on very rare occasions has it been seen to alight higher than 30 feet up in a tree, and far more often 15 feet is the uppermost limit. The Whiskered Owl is not so generally fierce a bird in temperament as are the *Otus asio* subspecies.

HABITAT AND ROOSTING

For the most part, areas of from scattered to rather heavy growths of deciduous trees are preferred. Pine and fir forests are scrupulously avoided, possibly in an effort to avoid the greatest natural enemy, the Western Horned Owl (*Bubo virginianus pallescens*), which favors such habitats. While the sort of cover most favorable for the Whiskered Owl includes oak-scattered slopes, glades, valleys, and canyons, the species is rather tightly regulated by elevation—rarely venturing below an altitude of 4,000 feet or above 7,000 feet. It is most abundant at elevations of between 5,500 and 6,500 feet. In such areas it roosts primarily in the Arizona white oak, but also to some degree in junipers, emory oaks, walnuts, mountain ash, and sycamores.

ENEMIES AND DEFENSES

In addition to falling prey to the Western Horned Owl, the Whiskered Owl will also occasionally become the prey of the Long-eared Owl (*Asio otus* sp.) and, less often, the Barn Owl (*Tyto alba pratincola*). Now and again territorial affrays will take place with the Saw-whet Owl (*Aegolius acadicus acadicus*), and in such altercations, even though the Whiskered Owl is the larger, it is usually the Saw-whet Owl that triumphs.

Not especially bothered by small-bird harassment, the Whiskered Owl is often plagued by extremely heavy infestations of Mallophaga lice. This may occur to such degree that severe debilitation of the bird results and its survival ability is much decreased.

Undoubtedly the greatest defense of *Otus trichopsis trichopsis* lies in its protective coloration. Its plumage has such incredibly barklike patterning that when it perches quietly in the Arizona white oak on a low branch close to the trunk—often even leaning against the trunk as it sleeps—it becomes almost invisible. When perching at night it tends to move farther away from the trunk on a large limb and sit in a stance something like that of the nighthawk, parallel with the branch with head held low and tail touching the limb so that in silhouette, even from very close range, it appears to be no more than a bulge on the limb. As its plumage blends well with the bark of a roosting tree, so too does it serve admirably as camouflage when the bird occasionally perches in the more dense foliage of the outer branches. Here again it tends to sit in a crouched pose with the body leaning forward, as if poised to take flight.

HUNTING METHODS AND CARRYING OF PREY

The Whiskered Owl prefers to perch in a tree near some likely spot and patiently listen and watch for prey. This prey, when detected, is swiftly swooped upon, snatched up in the talons almost without pause, and carried back (usually) to the same tree the bird has just left, there to be swallowed whole or torn into chunks for devouring. When larger insects are snatched up in flight, as often occurs, they are carried in the beak. More often than not, however, the prey is carried in one foot back to a convenient perch.

FOOD, FEEDING HABITS, WASTES

Although mice and other small mammals make up a certain portion of the Whiskered Owl's diet, by far the greatest percentage of food is invertebrate prey, especially insects. Small birds are rarely taken, even during the nesting season. *Otus trichopsis trichopsis* shows a fondness for a diet of black crickets, large moths and beetles, grasshoppers and locusts, praying mantids, roaches, and cicadas. Large caterpillars, fleshy or hairy, are eaten avidly, as are mole crickets and large beetle larvae. Such insects are the staples of the Whiskered Owl's diet most of the year, but during the winter months when they are not so abundant, scorpions and centipedes become important as prey.

Since so few vertebrate animals are ingested, there is less of a need for regurgitation of numerous pellets containing hair, bone, teeth, claws, and other such materials, and thus the Whiskered Owl is nowhere near to being the pellet-casting owl that most other species are. Nevertheless, a certain amount of small and poorly formed pellets are cast, mainly containing the chitinous bits of insects. Such pellets disintegrate very quickly as they dry. A stiff breeze will blow them apart.

Fecal wastes tend to be more liquid than are commonly seen among other owl species. They are generally dropped straight down below the small-branch perch the bird alights on for that specific purpose, and they are generally gray brown with some gray-green marblings of a more viscous nature.

COURTSHIP AND MATING

Some interesting study has been done on the courtship activities of the Whiskered Owl, but hardly anything in respect to the actual mating. Courtship is not as prolonged as among the Screech Owls, but is generally similar. The principal difference seems to be that the female is just about as vociferous as the male, and she will echo nearly every call he makes as he woos her. At sunset the birds begin calling back and forth, and as twilight deepens they draw closer together, all the while repeating at irregular intervals a rather harsh note that sounds almost like the clanging note of a heron. This call then becomes interspersed with the call sounding like *WHOOO-hoo woooo-woo,* as described earlier. (See Voice.) Young, unmated males begin wandering great distances in early spring, repeating these calls until they have located a receptive unmated female. Little male-to-male rivalry has been noted, even over territory.

ANNUAL BROODS, NEST, NESTING HABITS

Single-brooded, the Whiskered Owl normally nests in a natural cavity or abandoned hole of flicker or wood-pecker. There seems to be an especial preference for such holes located in a large branch or stub, rather than in the trunk of the tree itself; although if branch or stub holes are not available, a trunk cavity will suffice. Almost invariably the nest is located in a white oak tree and normally from 10 to 20 feet above ground. Usually there are some dried oak leaves in the bottom of the cavity, but it is not known whether or not the owl is responsible for bringing these in; chances are best that they are the residue of the former occupant. A relatively deep hole is preferred, with the bottom about 14 to 16 inches below the entry.

EGGS

Number per nesting Rarely fewer than three or more than four eggs are laid, though just as often three as four.

Color Pure, unblemished white.

Shape Very close to being globular; never notably ovoid.

Texture Quite smooth but without glossiness.

Size Smaller than the eggs of the Texas Screech Owl (*Otus asio mccallii*). The average size, based on the measurements of 13 eggs, was 32.9 mm. (1.3") in length by 27.3 mm. (1.1") in width. The extreme measurements of these eggs were:

Maximum length:	33.7 mm. (1.3")
Minimum length:	28.7 mm. (1.1")
Maximum width:	31.6 mm. (1.2")
Minimum width:	25.8 mm. (1.0")

Interval of egg-laying This is not known for certain, but eggs are probably laid two or three days apart.

Egg-laying dates Earliest, April 22; latest, May 19; normally between May 1 and May 9.

INCUBATION AND BROODING CHARACTERISTICS

There has been no recorded instance of the male bird aiding in incubation, although he provides food for the incubating female and remains very close at roosting times while incubation is in progress. The female sits very closely on her eggs, leaving them only with the greatest of reluctance and returning to them very quickly when danger is past. On occasion females have allowed themselves to be lifted off the eggs without protest.

WHISKERED OWL

Otus trichopsis trichopsis (Wagler)

Not migratory.

ECONOMIC INFLUENCE

Probably of benefit because of insect-eating habits.

ARIZONA WHISKERED OWL

(COLOR PLATE XXXIV)

SCIENTIFIC NAME AND ORIGINAL DESCRIPTION

Otus trichopsis asperus (Brewster). Original description: *Megascops asperus* Brewster, *The Auk,* Volume 5, Number 1, January 1888, page 87; based on a specimen from El Carmen, Chihuahua, Mexico.

OTHER NAMES

TECOLOTITO MANCHADO DE BREWSTER Mexican-Indian name meaning "Brewster's Little Spotted Owl."

WHISKERED SCREECH OWL Erroneously, as the same name formerly applied to the Whiskered Owl (*Otus trichopsis trichopsis*).

YOUNG AND FAMILY LIFE CHARACTERISTICS

Very little concrete data have been gathered about this aspect of the Whiskered Owl's life cycle, although what little has been recorded seems very closely to resemble similar characteristics among the *Otus asio* subspecies.

DISTINGUISHING FEATURES

Otus trichopsis asperus is primarily located at higher elevations than *Otus trichopsis trichopsis,* usually occurring only within a few hundred feet of the 7,000-foot altitude. It is a somewhat larger and much darker gray bird generally than is the Whiskered Owl, with a distinct buffiness of the plumage around the face, which is lacking in *Otus trichopsis trichopsis.* The streakings of both back and breast are much bolder and more distinctive than are those of the Whiskered Owl. The Arizona Whiskered Owl remarkably parallels the Mexican Screech Owl (*Otus asio cineraceus*) in size, and both that owl and the Saguaro Screech Owl (*Otus asio gilmani*) in coloration, though it more closely approximates the markings of the Whiskered Owl. There is no known red phase.

DISTRIBUTION IN NORTH AMERICA

Primarily in a small portion of southeastern Arizona in the area of the Chiricahua and Huachuca mountains at elevations of from 4,000 to 7,000 feet, but usually below 6,500 feet. The range extends southward through Mexico, Guatemala, and Honduras, though not in Baja California. In Mexico, Chihuahua, Durango, Puebla, Oaxaca, Guerrero, west to Michoacán, Jalisco, Nayarit.

WEIGHT

Subspecies average: 166.1 gr. (5.8 oz.).

TOTAL LENGTH

Subspecies average: 184.2 mm. (7.3″).

WINGSPAN

Subspecies average: 527.1 mm. (20.8″).

INDIVIDUAL WING LENGTH

Subspecies average: 157.8 mm. (6.2″).

TAIL LENGTH

Subspecies average: 81.3 mm. (3.2″).

BEAK LENGTH

Subspecies average: 15.4 mm. (0.6″).

ARIZONA WHISKERED OWL

Otus trichopsis asperus (Brewster)

VOICE

Quite similar to that of *Otus trichopsis trichopsis* except that the female not infrequently issues a brittle, short, whistling sound which rises at the end, sounding like *kiEW! kiEW!*

HABITAT AND ROOSTING

Evinces the same preference for deciduous trees, especially the white oak, as does *Otus trichopsis trichopsis,* but at higher elevations. The Arizona Whiskered Owl rarely ventures below an elevation of 6,800 feet and prefers 7,000 feet or slightly more. It seems, at times, most abundant at elevations of from 7,500 feet to 7,700 feet, but has been known to reach 8,100 feet.

NEST

Much like *Otus trichopsis trichopsis* except that woodpecker and flicker holes are much less often used, the preference being for natural cavities in oak.

DISTRIBUTION IN NORTH AMERICA

In the mountains of southeastern Arizona (Baboquivari, Parajito, and Santa Catalina Mountains to the Chiricahua Mountains) and of northeastern Sonora, Chihuahua, and Durango, Mexico, south to Nayarit (Sierra Madre) and San Luis Potosí (Álvarez).

SPECIES

ORDER: STRIGIFORMES

FAMILY: STRIGIDAE

GENUS: *Otus* Pennant

SPECIES: *flammeolus* (Kaup)

SUBSPECIES

flammeolus (Kaup) FLAMMULATED OWL

FLAMMULATED OWL
(*COLOR PLATE XXXV*)

SCIENTIFIC NAME AND ORIGINAL DESCRIPTION

Otus flammeolus flammeolus (Kaup). Original description: *Scops (Megascops) flammeola "Licht"* Kaup, in *Jardine's Contributions to Ornithology*, 1852 (1853), page 111; based on a specimen from an unnamed locale in northern Mexico.

OTHER NAMES

DWARF SCREECH OWL Because of its small size and its former classification with the Screech Owls.

FLAMMULATED DWARF OWL After the red-phase coloration and the small size.

FLAMMULATED SCREECH OWL Former name when classified with the Screech Owls.

FLAMMULATED SCOPS OWL Former name after the Old World designation.

LE PETIT-DUC NAIN French-Canadian name meaning "The Little Dwarf Duke."

LEAST SCREECH OWL Same reasons as for Dwarf Screech Owl.

SCOPS OWL Former Old World designation.

TECOLOTITO DE FLÁMULAS Mexican-Indian name meaning "Little Flame-colored Owl."

DISTINGUISHING FEATURES

Quite a small owl having red- and gray-color phases, with ear tufts that are distinctly rounded, very short, and barely visible even when held fully erect. The tufts tend to give more of an impression of the head itself having a couple of points, rather than the bird being "eared" as in the *Otus asio* races. The Flammulated Owl has longish wings and tiny feet. Its very soft and gentle-appearing dark-chocolate-colored eyes give the owl a very appealing expression. Hardly larger than a sparrow (though it tends to look larger), it is only slightly larger than the Ferruginous Owl (*Glaucidium brasilianum ridgwayi*). Its distinctive V-shaped reddish bars running down the scapulars in the gray phase and its variegated rufous color pattern in the red phase give it a warm ruddy look from which its name results.

Rank in size among the eighteen species: Fifteenth.

SHAPE AT REST AND IN FLIGHT

When perched it tends to resemble a very small Screech Owl, except for the distinctly modified ear tufts. It tends also to sit rather erect, with tail pointing groundward. In flight the resemblance to a Screech Owl is less distinct, as the wingbeats are more rapid and the wings themselves seem narrower and longer in proportion to the body than do those of the *Otus asio* subspecies.

FLIGHT PATTERN

A rather nervous, darting, and sometimes actually jerky type of flight, interspersed with occasional hoverings as it pauses to check for prey. Little gliding is done except during the first few moments after the bird has left a high perch and angles toward the ground in a

---

Normal perching (left) and roosting (right) postures of the Flammulated Owl (*Otus flammeolus flammeolus*) showing the abundant and fine barrings and pencilings on the plumage, especially of the breast and belly. The ear tufts, unlike those of Screech Owl subspecies, are tiny and often difficult to discern. The feet are not feathered. This species evinces a considerable variety of coloration and markings.

breast feather

Flammulated Owl
(formerly
Flammulated
Screech Owl)
Grant co.,
New Mexico
11 april 1887

Red-phase
all barrings rich
red

Dark eyes

barring fine
and abundant

Feet naked

of 11 skins no two were alike.
some skins without any reddish
Red-phase-only one skin

K.E.K

ear tufts
tiny

sweeping curve. A shorter glide occurs with a slight upswing just prior to alighting. Normal flight is on a comparatively level plane.

Measurements have been based on 13 birds measured: 6 males and 7 females.

WEIGHT

Species average: 131.7 gr. (4.6 oz.).

	Male	Female
Average	126.3 gr. (4.4 oz.)	137.1 gr. (4.8 oz.)
Minimum	113.6 gr. (4.0 oz.)	122.4 gr. (4.3 oz.)
Maximum	143.4 gr. (5.0 oz.)	149.3 gr. (5.2 oz.)

Rank in weight among the eighteen species: Fourteenth.

TOTAL LENGTH

Species average: 165.5 mm. (6.5″).

	Male	Female
Average	157.3 mm. (6.2″)	173.6 mm. (6.8″)
Minimum	151.0 mm. (5.9″)	163.6 mm. (6.5″)
Maximum	163.8 mm. (6.5″)	188.7 mm. (7.4″)

Rank in total length among the eighteen species: Sixteenth.

WINGSPAN

Species average: 457.5 mm. (18.0″).

	Male	Female
Average	452.6 mm. (17.8″)	462.3 mm. (18.2″)
Minimum	379.1 mm. (14.9″)	450.7 mm. (17.8″)
Maximum	462.9 mm. (18.2″)	501.1 mm. (19.7″)

Rank in wingspan among the eighteen species: Fifteenth.

INDIVIDUAL WING LENGTH

Species average: 134.2 mm. (5.3″).

	Male	Female
Average	132.7 mm. (5.2″)	135.6 mm. (5.3″)
Minimum	128.3 mm. (5.1″)	130.8 mm. (5.2″)
Maximum	138.6 mm. (5.5″)	145.1 mm. (5.7″)

Rank in wing length among the eighteen species: Fourteenth.

TAIL LENGTH

Species average: 61.6 mm. (2.4″).

	Male	Female
Average	61.0 mm. (2.4″)	62.2 mm. (2.5″)
Minimum	57.8 mm. (2.3″)	60.9 mm. (2.4″)
Maximum	62.9 mm. (2.5″)	64.9 mm. (2.6″)

Rank in tail length among the eighteen species: Seventeenth.

BEAK LENGTH

Species average: 9.7 mm. (0.4″). The beak is slate black.

	Male	Female
Average	9.4 mm. (0.4″)	10.0 mm. (0.4″)
Minimum	8.7 mm. (0.3″)	9.9 mm. (0.4″)
Maximum	10.5 mm. (0.4″)	11.1 mm. (0.4″)

Rank in beak length among the eighteen species: Fifteenth.

LEGS, FEET, TALONS

The legs of the Flammulated Owl are relatively lightly feathered, but the feet are naked, with the toes a slaty gray in coloration and often with the faintest tinge of yellow. The talons are very sharp and rather long, well curved, and entirely black. Leg and foot muscles are strong and, for the size of the bird, it has a powerful grip.

EYES AND VISION

Otus flammeolus flammeolus, the only small owl with dark-brown eyes, seems to have a very placid and friendly look which can be deceiving, since the bird is rather ferocious in the protection of nest and young. The eyes are large and as brown in the young as in adults. Vision is quite good day or night, but especially adapted to deep twilight.

EARS AND HEARING

The auditory sense is extremely acute. Ear cavities are asymmetrical to some degree in placement and size, and this owl has well-developed sound-location capabilities. Eyes and ears synchronize well in hunting. The authors, using binoculars to observe a Flammulated Owl perched near the top of a conifer fully a quarter mile away just after sunset, noted an instant reaction on the bird's part when the squeaking of a mouse was simulated. With one quick jerk of the head the gaze of the bird was directed at the source of the sound. A second squeak was given, even more faintly, and the owl immediately left its perch and arrowed toward the sound. Only at the last moment, as the authors flinched, did it veer off and take a perch in a nearby tree. It remained there for a considerable while, wholly unafraid.

EAR TUFTS, PLUMAGE, ANNUAL MOLT

The ear tufts are hardly more than rudimentary and less than a quarter the size of those of even the smallest subspecies of *Otus asio*. They tend to peak in sharp little points on each side of the crown, but can be laid practically flat to the head. The plumage of this owl is somewhat tighter than that of the Screech Owls, giving more of an appearance of trimness to the bird. There is one molt annually, beginning in mid-August and completed before November, and at this time of molting the bird tends to increase its calling. This is especially true of the male birds, although the significance of this fact is not known.

VOICE

The most commonly heard call of the Flammulated Owl is a single, quite mellow-toned *WHOOOP* repeated over long periods at about five- to ten-second intervals, the hoot sometimes followed by one or two grace notes distinctly lower in tone. This call is so remarkably ventriloquial that it is virtually impossible to locate the bird by following the sound of its voice. Though it is a rather low-toned call, it has far-carrying qualities and is a delight to hear. Occasionally it is preceded by two rapidly issued lower notes.

The mating call, on the other hand, is not at all ventriloquial. It is uttered in two notes with the emphasis strongly on the second. This call, too, is voiced over prolonged periods and tends to become monotonous. Higher pitched than the single note described above, it sounds like *whoo-WHOOOT*. Occasionally the first note is not given. In the more advanced stages of courtship, the double-note call is sometimes broken at intervals with soft chuckling or chattering sounds.

Another call given primarily by the male but on occasion by the female is a kittenlike *MEEEeee-ooooo* sound, not unlike the call of Whitney's Elf Owl (*Micrathene whitneyi whitneyi*).

When disturbed, especially if nesting, the female Flammulated Owl sometimes gives vent to an outraged sounding little shriek which cannot be emulated in print but which, if it had greater volume behind it, would be a most decidedly frightening sound. The male, when disturbed, issues a single gruff *HOOT!*

Most calling is done in the spring, and the majority of it by the male bird; but after a relatively quiet summer, the birds tend to become more vocal at the time of the molt and the calling may continue for several weeks after the molt has finished. Again, most of this calling is by the male bird.

SEXUAL DIFFERENCES: SIZE, COLORATION, VOICE

There is no evident difference in coloration or markings between the sexes, but the female is slightly the larger bird and her voice is very dissimilar to the male's, being much more highly pitched, quavering, and with the underlying quality of a whine.

MORTALITY AND LONGEVITY

Captive birds have lived for thirteen years, and one wild bird was recovered eight years after it was banded as a fledgling. There seems to be little nest mortality where this species is concerned, and no incidence of cannibalism has ever been recorded.

COLORATION AND MARKINGS: ADULT

This is one of the most difficult of all North American Owls to describe or paint insofar as coloration and markings are concerned. There is great variation in colors and patterns, not only in the two color phases, but between individuals of the same color phase as well. The differences between the actual color phases are often extreme. For example, a red-phase bird may have a very distinctive cinnamon-red general coloration with little mottling or pattern (or sometimes with a great deal of both), while the gray-phase bird may have no trace whatever of rufous tone, not even on the V-shaped scapular markings. There seems to be an inclination for gray-phase birds to be more heavily marked with dark mottling than among the red-phase birds, but this is no hard-and-fast rule. Markings of both phases on the underparts may vary from quite broad and heavy to surprisingly finely drawn pencilings. So far as can be determined, the color and pattern variations are not induced by sex, age, geographical location, or season. The only exceptions are that the most decidedly red birds are from the more southerly parts of the bird's range—primarily in Guatemala—but even there the gray-phase birds, as well as some of the red-phase, cannot be distinguished from more northerly specimens.

Some birds seem to tend distinctly toward melanism, especially on the belly, but with all plumage being very dark. Others will have almost a marbling effect of silvery plumage intermingled with the gray or red. Still others have a decidedly tawny aspect. Quite often in the gray phase, even when rufous coloration is absent from most of the plumage, there will be a decidedly reddish coloration to that portion of the facial disks immediately surrounding the eyes.

COLORATION AND MARKINGS: JUVENILE

There is as much variation among individuals and color phases as among the adults, but with somewhat more coarse and regular barrings on the back.

GENERAL HABITS AND CHARACTERISTICS

More or less reclusive in its habits, the Flammulated Owl is not often seen, even by trained observers, although it frequently flies by day. Essentially a twilight and nighttime hunter, it is most often observed as the bird takes a perch high in a conifer prior to hunting in the evening, or during the early morning hours before sunrise.

HABITAT AND ROOSTING

Rarely if ever seen at elevations lower than 3,000 feet, but has been observed as high as elevations of 10,000 feet. Preference seems to be most pronounced for dense thicket-type cover close to relatively open areas at elevations of from 4,500 to 7,800 feet.

Otus flammeolus flammeolus will be found equally among deciduous or coniferous trees, although it avoids forests of ponderosa pine and areas of extensive forest cuttings. It likes forests of spruce and fir with some intermixing of aspen and Arizona white oak.

Pine trees, with white oak a close second choice, seem to be the favored roosts, and the bird normally settles for the day on a live limb (rarely, if ever, a dead limb) close to the trunk of the tree but only about a quarter of the tree's height from the top. It will also roost in emory oak, madrona, and dense piñon. Except during the nesting season, it rarely roosts in any kind of hollow.

ENEMIES AND DEFENSES

Horned Owls (*Bubo virginianus* sp.) and, to some small extent, Long-eared Owls (*Asio otus* sp.) are dangerous enemies. Because of the rather secretive habits of this bird, man is not as much a threat as he is with other owl species. The Flammulated Owl can, however, become furious when aggravated at the nest, and there are cases on record where parent birds have attacked humans about the face and neck with talons and beak.

The greatest defense seems to be the superb camou-

flage afforded by the variegated plumage this bird wears. The plumage of the upperparts, in particular, of both red-phase and gray-phase birds blends remarkably well with pine or oak bark. The markings of the underparts blend extremely well with the trunk of the white oak; so much so that when the bird is perched close to the trunk and is, in fact, leaning its back against the trunk, it becomes virtually invisible from below. It also makes a concerted effort to keep a branch or other obstruction between itself and an observer.

HUNTING METHODS AND CARRYING OF PREY

As with the Whiskered Owl (*Otus trichopsis trichopsis*), a great deal of prey is spotted from a high perch in a tree and the owl skims swiftly downward and snatches it up in its talons while still in flight, carrying it to a convenient perch—often the very perch it left—for eating. However, the Flammulated Owl seems slightly more inclined to land, when it attacks, and to devour its prey on the spot than does the Whiskered Owl. Prey seems to be just as often carried in the beak as in the talons, and there is some evidence that small prey snatched up in the talons in flight may be transferred to the beak almost immediately while flying.

FOOD, FEEDING HABITS, WASTES

Approximately 90 per cent of the Flammulated Owl's annual diet consists of insects and other invertebrate prey such as spiders, scorpions, and centipedes. It has a surprising taste for ants and has been known to stand on a small anthill, scratch the surface with its feet, and then pluck up and swallow the insects as they come within reach. In addition to insects and other vertebrate life, however, this owl will eat mice of many varieties, shrews, moles, and, during the nesting season only, a few small birds.

Pellets are small and poorly formed, largely made up of bits of chitinous material from insects. Fecal wastes are relatively solid and dull grayish brown.

COURTSHIP AND MATING

Very little is known about this bird's courtship and mating activities, mainly because of the bird's shyness and seclusion. This is probably abetted by the fact that while even though the owl becomes more vociferous during this season, its highly ventriloquial abilities make it extremely difficult to locate for observation.

ANNUAL BROODS, NEST, NESTING HABITS

Single-brooded, *Otus flammeolus flammeolus* almost always nests in a flicker hole in an aspen, oak, or pine. If an abandoned hole is not available, the owl will forcefully evict a flicker from its in-use nest and lay its own eggs atop or beside those of the flicker. What happens to those eggs is not known, although it is supposed that if they hatch, the young flickers are eaten. The nest itself does not have to be very high in the tree to satisfy this owl; holes anywhere from as low as 7 or 8 feet to as high as 25 feet are used. One female was observed nesting in a flicker hole 40 feet above the ground in a pine stub. On rare occasions, if a suitable hole is not available, the Flammulated Owl has been known to nest in the holes of bank swallows.

EGGS

Number per nesting Two to five eggs are laid, but most commonly three or four.

Color Usually pure white, but occasionally with a faint creaminess.

Shape From almost globular to slightly ovate.

Texture Very finely granulated and with some glossiness.

Size Just about midway in size between those of Whitney's Elf Owl (*Micrathene whitneyi whitneyi*) and the Mexican Screech Owl (*Otus asio cineraceus*). On the basis of 44 eggs measured, the average egg size was 27.7 mm. (1.1″) in length by 23.6 mm. (0.9″) wide. The extremes were:

Maximum length:	32.7 mm. (1.3″)
Minimum length:	26.4 mm. (1.0″)
Maximum width:	28.0 mm. (1.1″)
Minimum width:	21.6 mm. (0.9″)

Interval of egg-laying Unknown, but probably about two days.

Egg-laying dates Southern areas: earliest, May 6; latest, June 24; normally between May 18 and June 11.

Northern areas: earliest, May 21; latest, July 2; normally between June 4 and June 21.

INCUBATION AND BROODING CHARACTERISTICS

Incubation probably is by the female entirely, and though the exact term of incubation is not known, it is supposed to be about 25 days. The female sits tightly on her eggs and will usually refuse to budge even if disturbed. However, if attempt is made to lift her off the eggs, she is apt to deliver a most painful bite.

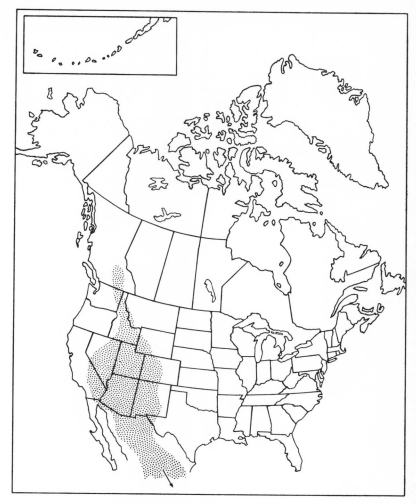

FLAMMULATED OWL

Otus flammeolus flammeolus (Kaup)

YOUNG AND FAMILY LIFE CHARACTERISTICS

When first hatched, the owlets have flesh-colored feet and beaks, but these darken within six days. The tiny babies are covered with a rather dense, snow-white down. Because of restricted in-hole nesting, observation of nestling young is sketchy at best; but in their first full, imperfect plumage of autumn, the young birds have wings and tail similar to those of the adults. Elsewhere they have transverse dusky gray-and-white barrings which are narrow on head and breast but wide on belly and flanks. The facial disks are decidedly ruddy in coloration and lores are usually somewhat rufous, though the superciliaries are white, bordered with dusky gray.

DISTRIBUTION IN NORTH AMERICA

Breeds from southern British Columbia (Kamloops), Idaho (Ketchum), and northern Colorado (Estes Park), southward through the mountains (except near the Pacific coast) to southern California (San Bernardino Mountains) and the highlands of Mexico to the State of Mexico (Chimalpa) and Veracruz (Las Vigas), and south to the Guatemalan highlands.

Winters chiefly south of the United States in the Mexican and Guatemalan highlands, but also rarely in the San Bernardino Mountains of southern California and in the Guadalupe, Franklin, and Chisos mountains of the Trans-Pecos, Texas.

MIGRATION

The Flammulated Owl is one of the more migratory of North American owls but, even at that, the southward movement is quite loose and never occurs in large flocks. Almost all migratory flight is nocturnal, occurring in early autumn and late spring.

ECONOMIC INFLUENCE

Probably valuable as a destroyer of injurious insects and, to a lesser extent, rodents.

SPECIES

ORDER: STRIGIFORMES

FAMILY: STRIGIDAE

GENUS: *Speotyto* Gloger

SPECIES: *cunicularia* (Molina)

SUBSPECIES

---

hypugaea (Bonaparte)   WESTERN BURROWING OWL

floridana Ridgway   FLORIDA BURROWING OWL

WESTERN BURROWING OWL

(*COLOR PLATE XXXVI*)

SCIENTIFIC NAME AND ORIGINAL DESCRIPTION

Speotyto cunicularia hypugaea (Bonaparte). Original description: *Strix hypugaea* Bonaparte, *American Ornithology,* Volume I, 1825, page 72 (note); based on a specimen from the plains of the Platt River, Nebraska.

OTHER NAMES

BILLY OWL   Although this is one of the more common names for both the Western Burrowing Owl and the Florida Burrowing Owl, its derivation and meaning are unclear.

CUCKOO OWL   From one of its more distinctive calls, which has a decided cuckoolike quality. (See Voice.)

GOPHER OWL   Because it lives underground as gophers do, and sometimes in reconditioned gopher holes.

GROUND OWL   For its habit of living on and in the ground.

HILL OWL   Because of the mound of earth at the entrance to the burrow, upon which the owl customarily stands watch.

LA CHOUETTE À TERRIER DE L'OUEST   French-Canadian name meaning "Western Burrowing Owl."

LECHUCILLA LLANERA   Mexican-Indian name meaning "The Little Barn Owl (or simply "Owl") of the Fields."

PRAIRIE DOG OWL   Because of its propensity for using the burrows of the prairie dog for its own underground nesting and because of the erroneous belief that it will share such a hole with the prairie dog.

RATTLESNAKE OWL   Because superstition has it that the owl shares its underground burrow with rattlesnakes, for reasons to be explained. (See Enemies and Defenses.)

SNAKE OWL   Because it frequently kills and eats small snakes, and probably for the same reason it is often called rattlesnake owl.

TUNNEL OWL   Because it nests at the end of an underground tunnel.

DISTINGUISHING FEATURES

The *Speotyto cunicularia* subspecies, including both the Western Burrowing Owl (*Speotyto cunicularia hypugaea*) and the Florida Burrowing Owl (*Speotyto cunicularia floridana*), is the only small owl species that habitually resides on the ground in very open places. The Short-eared Owl (*Asio flammeus flammeus*), for example, is a much larger owl and it inhabits much more heavily grassed areas, generally disliking the bare or only lightly grassed sandy ground favored by the Burrowing Owls.

Very distinctive as it stands on the small mound before its burrow, this owl has a gangly, knock-kneed stance and its facial disks are rather poorly developed. It swivels its head back and forth almost constantly and, upon seeing anything of a suspicious or dangerous nature, goes into a curious bobbing motion. A small, generally darkish-sandy owl without ear tufts and having a very rounded head, it is only slightly larger than the Eastern Screech Owl (*Otus asio naevius*) but seems much larger because of its long legs and upright stance. It is one of the most easily observable—and interesting to watch—of the owls of North America.

Rank in size among the eighteen species: Eleventh.

SHAPE AT REST

The Western Burrowing Owl has an uncommonly awkward appearance when standing on the ground or on a fence post, but seems much less gangly when perching on a telephone wire or low branch and crouching on its own legs. Part of the illusion of awkwardness is created by the very short tail and the fact that the bird stands with a seemingly abnormal erectness.

SHAPE IN FLIGHT

The wings of this bird are long and narrow and certainly very reminiscent of the wings of a sparrow hawk, but with the similarity to the sparrow hawk lessened because of the uncommonly short tail and the head well couched on the shoulders in flight. The wing tips are considerably more sharply pointed than those of most other North American owls and its body seems considerably smaller in flight than when perched.

FLIGHT PATTERN

Just as its outstretched wings bear a likeness to those of the sparrow hawk, the flight of this owl is also markedly similar to that of the little falcon. It is a strong, easy, powerful flight, even though one might at first get the impression that it is rather labored, jerky, and irregular. Some observers compare it with the flight of the woodcock. At any rate, it is a quite distinctive flight, usually fairly close to the ground and highly maneuverable. Also in keeping with the sparrow hawk image it will, as that bird does, frequently hover while scanning the ground below for prey. It frequently makes rather long, low-level glides, interspersed with uncommonly agile turns and rapid wingbeats. At such times the wings will sometimes flap asynchronously. It has the habit, after having caught an insect on the wing, of taking a long downward glide. While normally it makes only short flights at relatively low level, the powerful wingstrokes can carry it great distances without rest, as attested by the occasional reportings of the owl alighting on the rigging or decks of ships far out at sea.

Measurements have been based on 39 birds measured: 18 males and 21 females.

WEIGHT

Species average: 208.2 gr. (7.3 oz.).

	Male	Female
Average	202.6 gr. (7.1 oz.)	213.9 gr. (7.5 oz.)
Minimum	180.5 gr. (6.3 oz.)	194.9 gr. (6.8 oz.)
Maximum	212.0 gr. (7.4 oz.)	222.7 gr. (7.8 oz.)

Rank in weight among the eighteen species: Eleventh.

Burrowing Owl

TOTAL LENGTH

Species average: 241.4 mm. (9.5″).

	Male	Female
Average	229.6 mm. (9.0″)	253.2 mm. (10.0″)
Minimum	212.9 mm. (8.4″)	225.8 mm. (8.9″)
Maximum	267.9 mm. (10.6″)	284.5 mm. (11.2″)

Rank in total length among the eighteen species: Eleventh.

WINGSPAN

Species average: 584.5 mm. (23.0″).

	Male	Female
Average	577.6 mm. (22.8″)	591.5 mm. (23.3″)
Minimum	558.9 mm. (22.0″)	574.8 mm. (23.7″)
Maximum	596.9 mm. (23.5″)	616.3 mm. (24.3″)

Rank in wingspan among the eighteen species: Twelfth.

INDIVIDUAL WING LENGTH

Species average: 163.4 mm. (6.4″).

	Male	Female
Average	155.3 mm. (6.1″)	171.5 mm. (6.8″)
Minimum	147.5 mm. (5.8″)	160.2 mm. (6.3″)
Maximum	175.0 mm. (6.9″)	184.3 mm. (7.3″)

Rank in wing length among the eighteen species: Eleventh.

TAIL LENGTH

Species average: 80.8 mm. (3.2″).

	Male	Female
Average	76.3 mm. (3.0″)	85.3 mm. (3.4″)
Minimum	73.4 mm. (2.9″)	82.3 mm. (3.2″)
Maximum	82.6 mm. (3.3″)	89.1 mm. (3.5″)

Rank in tail length among the eighteen species: Twelfth.

BEAK LENGTH

Species average: 13.9 mm. (0.5″). The beak is a dull but light grayish yellow.

	Male	Female
Average	13.5 mm. (0.5″)	14.3 mm. (0.6″)
Minimum	12.5 mm. (0.5″)	13.5 mm. (0.5″)
Maximum	14.0 mm. (0.6″)	15.3 mm. (0.6″)

Rank in beak length among the eighteen species: Thirteenth.

LEGS, FEET, TALONS

Very long legs for the size of this bird, imparting somewhat the appearance of the Barn Owl (*Tyto alba pratincola*) but rather stubbier in the body and a good bit more knock-kneed and gangly in general aspect. The legs are lightly feathered with short, fine, immaculate plumage and the toes are almost bare, though with small, very bristly feathers more like sparse hair than plumage.

The tarsus is more than twice as long as the middle toe, averaging 47.2 mm. (1.9″), scantily feathered in front and almost bare behind. Where scales of legs and feet can be seen, they are from dull gray or yellowish gray to horn-colored. The feet are not especially powerful in their grip.

EYES AND VISION

The irides are a bright lemon yellow and vision is excellent, probably even better on cloudy days or at twilight than on a dark night, since this owl does a considerable amount of diurnal and crepuscular hunting. It is likely, too, that vision is equally important to hearing in the location of prey for this species.

EARS AND HEARING

Ear cavities are slightly asymmetrical in size and placement, but not pronouncedly so. The auditory sense is acute, and observers have stated that the bird can hear the flight of a beetle or grasshopper at well over one hundred yards. A great deal of prey is located through the rustling of grasses.

EAR TUFTS, PLUMAGE, ANNUAL

The head of the Burrowing Owl is very rounded, with no trace of ear tufts. Plumage is reasonably tight to the body, though tending to be fluffed slightly when standing on the ground and even more so when perched on a wire or branch. In flight the plumage is much closer to the body than that of the Screech Owls, thus imparting a more streamlined appearance. All adult birds have one complete annual molt which begins in late July or early August and is completed by the end of September or early October. While it is evidently not an annual trait of the species as a whole, numerous individual birds have been observed to undergo another molt, primarily of body feathers only, late in winter. This begins in mid-February and lasts for about one month.

VOICE

While its repertoire of calls is nowhere nearly as varied as that of the Barred Owls (*Strix varia* sp.), the Western Burrowing Owl does have a number of different calls and most of them are of a rather soft and mellow nature. One of its more common calls, in fact, is responsible for its nickname of Cuckoo Owl—a deep, melodious *COO-COO-O-O-O*, not unlike the call of the European cuckoo. Generally voiced while the owl is perched on its burrow mound, this song may be continued for several hours at a time. It is similar to, though not exactly like, the courtship song which is voiced by the male only and is a little more softly delivered, sounding like: *Coo-COO-OOO COO COO-OOO*. This call is similar to that of the road runner, though not as penetrating in character.

In addition, the Western Burrowing Owl often engages in a sort of conversation with other owls perched on their own burrow mounds nearby. The calls are somewhat harsher and more abrupt. Normally issued at an even, conversational pace, they can become emphatic and irregular if the bird becomes excited or alarmed. The call sounds something like: *TOOO-whit-tit-tit TOOO-whit-tit-tit,* interspersed with a *TWEEE-CHIKIT-CHIKIT-CHIT CHIKIT-CHIKIT* and, less often, with *TWEEE-ticka-tit TWEEE, TICKA-TICKA-tit-tit TWEEEE tit-tit.*

When badly alarmed, there is a cry given just before the bird disappears into its burrow—a raucous *KAK! KAK! KAK! KAK!* If, however, it flies to a nearby burrow mound or fence post, the call modifies in flight and becomes much less harsh, sounding like *KUK-KUK-KUK-KUK!,* and this may degenerate into a continuous rapid rattling noise.

Beak snappings and hissings are not uncommon when the bird is disturbed at the nest, but both young and adults have a most interesting and unusual defensive call issued at times when an intruder begins disturbing or entering the mouth of the burrow—a sound remarkably like the angry buzzing of a rattlesnake. (See Enemies and Defenses.)

SEXUAL DIFFERENCES:
SIZE, COLORATION, VOICE

There is very little difference in size on the whole, although on very close measurement the female is just barely the larger. As nearly as can be determined, there is no difference in coloration between the sexes and no distinguishable difference in vocal characteristics.

MORTALITY AND LONGEVITY

Because *Speotyto cunicularia* is a ground-nesting species, it is more prone to attack from many predators which do not normally molest tree-nesting owls. Skunks, weasels, large snakes, ferrets, and badgers make significant onslaughts against eggs and nestlings. Cannibalism is not a notable infant-mortality factor except during times of famine, but in recent years mortality in the nest and even among adult birds has sharply increased because of the extensive use by man of bisulphides to poison ground squirrels and other rodent pests. Eating rodents that have ingested such poisons will subsequently cause the death of the owl too, either directly or through such malfunction of bodily activities that the owl can no longer function as it must in order to survive. In such a case, starvation is usually the result.

Numerous captive specimens have lived for well over a decade, and band recoveries indicate that some wild birds live nearly as long. Large clutches of eggs laid by this species help to some degree in offsetting a higher rate of infant mortality than most other North American owl species suffer.

COLORATION AND MARKINGS: ADULT

Generally a speckled, dark sandy appearance at a distance, with distinctive narrow barring on the throat and upper breast. More specifically, the upperparts are generally brown with buff to buffy-white spots. These spots are very small on the crown and mingle with slight streakings of the same. On the hindneck the spots become more elongated oval in shape and slightly larger. The largest of the spots are on the wing coverts, back and shoulders, and these are mainly roundish in shape. The secondaries have similar spottings, but these are arranged in four or five regular transverse series. Larger whitish spots occur on the outer webs of the primaries, becoming most apparent on the three or four longest quills. The rectrices are transversed by four (occasionally five or six) rather narrow and somewhat irregular bands of light grayish buff, suffused with a vague medium buff brown. All tail quills are narrowly tipped with light buff to buff white. The superciliaries are dull brown white and the lores are the same color but with each feather black-shafted.

Facial disks are a slightly deeper sandy buff. The sides of the head are narrowly and indistinctly streaked with buff over deeper brown. Whitish or (often more commonly) light buffy coloration extends from the chin area and malar region to behind the lower half of the ear region. A narrow line of intermingled black and buff across the upper throat is evident. The throat and upper breast are buff, barred with narrow dark brown, the bars sometimes merging at the sides and continuing as a dark area behind the light buffy plumage of the ear region. The center of the breast is more sparsely barred, with this barring sometimes very indefinite or even absent. The belly, thighs, undertail coverts, and leg plumage are usually unmarked medium buff to light buffy white. Some slight general paling of all colors has been observed during late spring and summer.

COLORATION AND MARKINGS: JUVENILE

Wings and tail are identical to those of the adult birds, but the crown, hindneck, and back are mainly buffy gray brown with spotting absent. Underparts are plain, unmarked light buff in the center, shading to a deeper brownish buff toward the sides, with the throat band a solid deeper brown.

GENERAL HABITS AND CHARACTERISTICS

Although most actively on the move from about the period of just before sunset until full darkness, these owls can be seen at almost any time of the day or night. Sometimes they will sit with just their heads protruding from the burrow, but most often they are observed perched on their burrow mounds in the early morning hours and from midafternoon to late afternoon. Their actions on these mounds are most distinctive and very interesting. They stand quite erect with little body movement, but with the head almost continuously moving slowly from side to side as they scan their surroundings. Anything noted that is out of the ordinary causes an immediate reaction. The bird will stand staring gravely and almost regally at the disturbance for a moment, and then it will suddenly bow with a sense of courtliness, recover its erect pose quickly, and begin rolling (or, more rarely, jerking) its head about in a strange and rather comical manner while uttering its alarm cry. (See Voice.) This may

---

XLI AMERICAN HAWK OWL
Surnia ulula caparoch (Muller). Male. Vicinity of Okanagan Landing, British Columbia, Canada, November 4, 1913. A.O.U. Number 377-A

XLII ROCKY MOUNTAIN PYGMY OWL
Glaucidium gnoma pinacola Nelson. Male. Bear Creek near Priest Lake, Bonner County, Idaho, October 26, 1931. A.O.U. Number 379

Karl E. Karalus
1970

be repeated several times or more, along with some gesticulation with half-opened wings. At times the bowings are so low that the breast is practically on the ground. If the danger appears to be approaching, the bird will usually fly a short distance to another burrow mound, a cattle-shed roof peak, or a fence post, and perform the same grave bowings again. Less often it will simply disappear into the burrow. If the danger is of a more severe nature, its calling will become more alarmed, and immediately after it flies off, one or two or even more of these owls will emerge from the burrow and similarly move off.

Speotyto cunicularia is undoubtedly the most continuously gregarious owl species in North America. It has a very peaceable disposition toward other Burrowing Owls, even outside the immediate family—a rare trait among the raptors. In years past the birds often lived in distinct colonies close to or amid colonies of prairie dogs or other ground squirrels. The Burrowing Owl very much dislikes cultivated ground, and so increased agriculture with the resultant extermination of many of these rodents has caused a reduction in the Burrowing Owl colonies, although the inclination toward gregariousness still exists among them. Scores of them once lived in close conjunction, but they now reside in more scattered groups of four or five families or, less often, in colonies as large as a dozen families. In winter particularly, these owls tend to gather in little communal groups of as many as twenty birds within a single burrow. An unusual habit in conjunction with this is that they will store an abundance of food underground for communal subsistence during periods of severe weather when prey is scarce or unavailable.

There are numerous strong superstitions and many more erroneous beliefs in regard to the Burrowing Owl. Foremost among such stories is that it coexists in the same burrow with prairie dogs and rattlesnakes. To the contrary, there is no friendly relationship whatever with either the mammal or the reptile. The rattlesnake is an enemy which may enter the burrow in search of Burrowing Owl eggs or nestlings, or while on the hunt for young prairie dogs or ground squirrels. The prairie dog, when young, is prey for the Burrowing Owl, and certainly the mammal, young or old, will not willingly associate with the owl. On the rare occasions when an owl and prairie dog happen to disappear into the same burrow, it is simply because when danger

threatens, the handiest burrow around will be used as a haven. Though it often perches on power lines, fence wires, poles and fence posts, the Burrowing Owl never perches to avoid detection. Concealment is invariably sought underground.

The Burrowing Owl has the peculiar habit of collecting odds and ends of items which attract its attention, bringing them back to the burrow where they are scattered about equally on the ground surface near the entrance and also in both the tunnel and main chamber of the burrow. Some of the items recorded in these odd collections include bits of charcoal, bird feathers, fragments of colored rags, lost mittens, tufts of hair or hide from decomposed winter-killed cattle, corncobs, fair-sized chunks of bone, and other matter.

Although resident within their range and active all winter, Burrowing Owls tend to remain secluded in their burrows during especially bad weather and perch outside or actively hunt only on the milder days. Throughout their entire range they are relatively abundant, probably because of their mobility and adaptability.

HABITAT AND ROOSTING

Expansive, treeless, unbroken prairies and virgin plains are most preferred, but the bird shows a distinct aversion to cultivated lands and almost equally to the more arid desert regions. Surprisingly, in view of its dislike for cultivation, the bird will sometimes take up residence well within city limits, roosting in sidewalk drains during the day and emerging at night to catch house mice and rats in alleys and vacant lots, or flying in nighthawk manner around arc lights to capture moths and other large insects that have been attracted by the glow. Such behavior, though, is far from common and most often the bird seeks wide-open places, from sagebrush plains to extensive natural prairies, although it is found in scattered numbers in the lightly timbered areas of California, from the western foothills of the Sierras to the Pacific coast. Roosting (as opposed to perching) is almost invariably done underground. Perching, with some occasional light napping, occurs primarily on burrow mounds, telephone wires and poles, fence posts and fencing wires, on isolated cattle sheds, and sometimes on a roadside billboard or the low branch of a leafless bush or tree.

XLIII   CALIFORNIA PYGMY OWL

Glaucidium gnoma californicum Sclater. Female. Vicinity of Okanagan, British Columbia, Canada, November 9, 1913. A.O.U. Number 379-A

XLIV   ARIZONA PYGMY OWL

Glaucidium gnoma gnoma Wagler. Female. Vicinity of Bernardino, Cochise County, Arizona, October 22, 1917. A.O.U. Number 379-D

ENEMIES AND DEFENSES

After the initial grave bowings, head turnings, and chattering when it spies an enemy from its burrow mound (see General Habits and Characteristics), the Burrowing Owl flies low and swiftly to the mound of another burrow not far off. Here it may stand and repeat the bowing act and bob its head in an agitated way, or it may immediately dive underground. When a particularly severe threat of some sort occurs for a communal group, the sentinel bird issues its alarm cry and other owls will often come from all directions and almost bowl one another over in their anxiety to get down into the burrow without even an instant's pause on the mound to see what the danger is.

At times when the still-flightless young are on ground surface near the burrow mouth and danger threatens, the adult birds will wait until the young scurry underground and then themselves fly off to another burrow not far distant to take refuge there.

Where enemies are concerned, man is responsible for the deaths of a great many Burrowing Owls through use of poisons in rodent control. Also, a great many are killed by cars as they catch prey on the highways. Natural enemies include weasels, ferrets, occasional mink, skunks, opossums, snakes, and armadillos—though most of these are more dangerous to eggs and young than to adult birds. In fact, with enemies as fierce as the ferret or weasel, four or five adult Burrowing Owls will attack the animal simultaneously and drive it away, often harassing it unmercifully for fully one hundred yards before giving up and returning to their burrow.

If it has no other choice, *Speotyto cunicularia hypugaea* will attack an enemy, even man, with considerable ferocity. Uttering a shrill shrieking sound, it will roll over onto its back and strike out with great accuracy and effectiveness with its talons. If the bird is wounded, the shriek becomes a weird rattling sound and the talons are used with surprising violence and strength to inflict severe injury on the attacker.

Perhaps the most unusual and certainly one of the most highly effective defensive mechanisms used by the an intruder's attempt to enter, reach into, or dig up the Burrowing Owl, both young and adult, is reserved for burrow. At this time the bird can give an incredibly accurate vocal mimicry of the buzzing rattle of the diamondback rattlesnake. Few, if any, predators will continue coming down the burrow—and few men will continue reaching in or digging—when this sound has been given. Often the rattling is accompanied as well by a hissing which is also reminiscent of a snake.

has pinpointed the source and it takes to wing, flies with uncanny accuracy to the precise location, and pounces with outstretched talons.

Upon contact with flesh, the talons sink in deeply with an initial spasmodic jerk, and in that first brief clutch usually penetrate the vital organs and kill the prey. While this is occurring the owl spreads its wings for balance and uses its tail as a prop against the ground, then administers a series of devastating bites (if the animal has not expired at once) with its beak to hasten the demise by snapping the vertebrae at the nape. The owl will then pick up the dead animal, if not too large, in the beak and will fly with it back to the burrow. It will devour the animal there while perched on the mound outside, or it may take it underground for eating then or later. Only if the prey is too large for convenient carrying in the beak will the talons be used to transport the carcass.

Quite often when a mound-perched Western Burrowing Owl glances skyward and spies a large insect passing, it will launch itself in instant pursuit. With rapid, irregular wingbeats it will climb at a steep angle to a height of 150 feet or more without taking its gaze off the insect. At this point it will go into a relatively steep dive, gliding during the last portion of the dive as it overtakes the prey and grasps it in mid-air with its talons. There is then a brief spate of level flight while the prey is being killed by the talons, followed by a sometimes circular gliding as the dead prey is transferred to the beak. Having accomplished this, the owl turns adroitly, aligns itself with its own burrow, and makes a long gliding approach on set wings.

At times the Burrowing Owl will circle casually above a moving ground animal—cow, deer, dog, fox, or coyote—waiting to swoop down and snatch up any mouse or other rodent or large insect the animal flushes. In most cases when this occurs, the prey animal is snatched up from the ground without pause, often to the bafflement of the animal which may itself have been in pursuit of that very prey.

While most hunting is done during late afternoon and twilight, the parent owls hunt virtually 24 hours a day when there are young birds to feed, pausing only at intervals to take brief naps.

HUNTING METHODS AND CARRYING OF PREY

To some extent, the adult *Speotyto cunicularia hypugaea* will range back and forth across the prairieland, watching and listening for rodents and insect prey. More commonly it will take a perch on some slight elevation and wait until a prey animal on the ground, usually a mouse or ground squirrel, inadvertently betrays its own presence with a sound. Instantly the owl

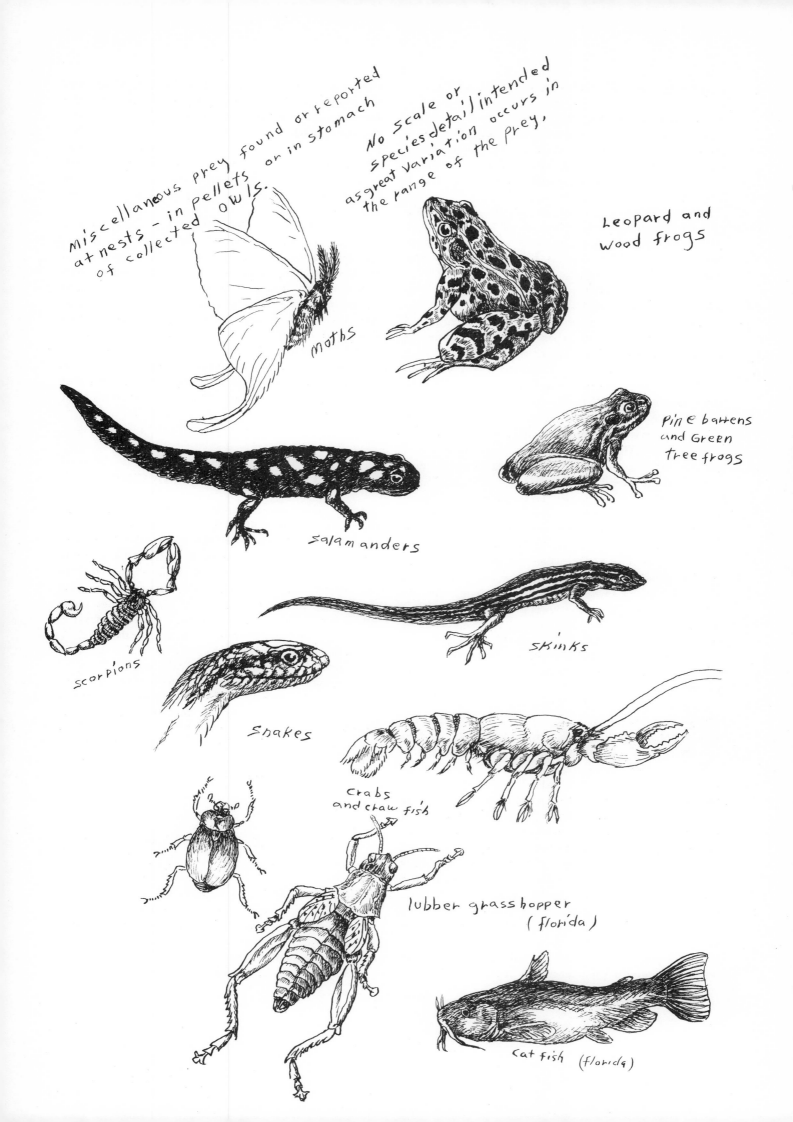

Miscellaneous prey found or reported at nests — in pellets or in stomach of collected owls.

No scale or species detail intended as great variation occurs in the range of the prey.

moths

Leopard and wood frogs

salamanders

Pine barrens and Green tree frogs

scorpions

skinks

snakes

crabs and craw fish

lubber grasshopper (florida)

cat fish (florida)

FOOD, FEEDING HABITS, WASTES

The diet of the Western Burrowing Owl is widely varied and what it eats usually depends upon what happens to be available at any given time. Insects and mice make up by far the majority of what it eats on an annual basis, but pellet analysis has also shown that it will eat the following:

Insects Grasshoppers, cicadas, locusts, black crickets, roaches, dragonflies, beetles of all kinds and their larvae, moth and butterfly adults and larvae, mole crickets and Jerusalem crickets, praying mantids, water bugs, and others.

Additional invertebrates Scorpions, centipedes and other myriapods, crayfish, snails, slugs, earthworms.

Fish Minnows of many varieties, suckers, carp, and other small fish, especially when they become marooned in rapidly drying pools of streams or ponds.

Reptiles and amphibians Lizards of many varieties, small snakes (but not venomous species), horned toads, frogs, salamanders, and toads.

Mammals Banner-tailed rats, young prairie dogs, ground squirrels and house rats as large as themselves, house mice, white-footed mice, grasshopper mice, meadow voles, sage rats, young cottontail rabbits, chipmunks, shrews, moles.

Birds Black terns, horned larks, sparrows of many species, least sandpipers, vireos, grosbeaks, western meadowlarks, and other birds up to their own size, but with all such feeding on birds normally taking place only in the nesting season when the food demands of the young owls are so extreme. There have been cases where Burrowing Owls have been examined with the remains of other Burrowing Owls in their stomachs, but whether this is the result of direct-attack cannibalism or the devouring of highway-killed owls is not known.

Vegetable matter Some fruits and seeds are eaten, especially the succulent fruits of the Tesajilla and prickly pear cacti.

Whenever possible, the Burrowing Owl swallows its prey whole. Large prey is ripped into chunks for swallowing, the head always being eaten first, followed in turn by the viscera, then chunks of the actual meat.

Speotyto cunicularia hypugaea is one of the most perpetually hungry of the owls. It will consume considerably more than its own weight in prey daily, if available. Therefore, it is more persistently on the hunt than most other species. Even when not hungry it will continue to hunt and store what prey it catches for devouring at a later time, especially when bad weather is in the offing. One burrow opened for study yielded the carcasses of 68 mice, one small rabbit, two sparrows, four rats, and a ground squirrel.

Young owls that are not yet able to fly well but nevertheless wait outside the burrow, keep a sharp watch for parent birds returning with prey for them. At sight of an adult approaching with prey, the young will run in a comical hop-and-flutter manner to intercept the parent bird, bowling each other over in their eagerness. The parent flies directly to the mound, and the young birds turn and run back in the same way; they never seem to learn to stand and wait at the burrow. Despite their avidity, there is little fighting over prey at any time; whichever young bird is fortunate enough to claim it first is usually left alone to devour it in peace.

Western Burrowing Owl pellets are relatively small—about an inch long and three-fourths of an inch wide—and are usually smooth and brown. They are regurgitated without any apparent difficulty anywhere the bird happens to be, in the burrow or outside, and as a result the main chamber and tunnel as well as the outside area around the mouth of the burrow are usually well littered with pellets in various stages of decomposition.

Defecation is performed more often in flight than while standing, usually occurring immediately after the bird has taken wing. Fecal droppings are somewhat dry and quite dark, looking like short, twisted twigs of charcoal.

COURTSHIP AND MATING

Some aerial maneuverings occur on the part of the male over the ground-perched female, but these are usually brief and not especially spectacular in nature. They are more in the nature of circling flights interspersed with gliding. When the male alights close to the female and walks up beside her on a burrow mound, she tends to move toward him and they stand side by side with shoulders touching for several minutes. Then there follows a short interval of rubbing their heads together. Actual copulation almost always occurs underground, but there are occasional instances of above-ground mating. When this takes place, the two birds normally walk off the mound onto level ground and copulation follows, swiftly accomplished. It is believed that copulation is repeated several times daily for from several days to a week. The Western Burrowing Owl mates for life, but if the mate of one is killed, the survivor will seek another.

ANNUAL BROODS, NEST, NESTING HABITS

The Burrowing Owl is single-brooded, but will usually lay a second set of eggs if the first is destroyed, and sometimes even a third laying if the second set is also destroyed. If a second or third set is laid, the eggs are normally smaller than the first.

The nest itself is invariably underground in an enlarged chamber at the end of a tunnel which may have been constructed by the owl itself or, far more likely, may have been the burrow of a prairie dog or other mammal which the owl has enlarged or modified for its own use. The burrow entrance is usually somewhat oval-shaped, about six inches by four or five inches. The tunnel is a minimum of five inches in diameter and often as much as eight inches, though usually about six. Although the hole may sometimes go straight down, it often angles diagonally downward for two or three feet before leveling off and continuing for another five or six feet to the nest chamber. Tunnel lengths tend to vary greatly, and though for some birds a tunnel may be as much as eighteen or twenty feet, for others it may be a mere four or five feet from entry to nest. Close to the nesting chamber the tunnel begins angling upward, and in many cases the chamber itself will be only ten or twelve inches below ground. Sometimes the tunnel will make a sharply angled turn; at other times it will follow a sort of U-curve for ten or twelve feet and the nesting chamber will be within a couple of feet of the entry hole.

The nesting chamber is usually from a minimum of eight inches to as much as eighteen inches in diameter and about six to eight inches from the floor of the chamber to its somewhat domed roof.

The nest is always pretty disreputable. In addition to all the strange odds and ends the owl finds to bring in (see General Habits and Characteristics), it also brings in considerable quantities of dried cattle dung until there may be a layer of it as deep as two inches on the bottom of the den. With this material, along with bits of bone, cloth, grasses, pellet debris, and other material, the nest more often than not has an extremely unpleasant odor and practically without exception is infested with fleas.

If the Western Burrowing Owl is improving the existing burrow or constructing its own, which it may do on rare occasions, it will loosen the dirt of the tunnel walls with both beak and feet and then kick this dirt backward, gradually moving it toward the mouth of the burrow and then kicking it outside, in much the way a chicken will scratch in the soil. This results in the well-raised mound of earth around the entry hole. Both male and female work at the digging and the bringing-in of nest-bed material, when such is introduced by the owl. The preference seems to be for level ground for the hole, but this is not a prerequisite, since nesting burrows are often located on slopes.

EGGS

Number per nesting Normally at least six eggs are laid and sometimes as many as twelve. Seven, eight, or nine eggs seem to be the most common-sized clutches. These eggs are usually laid in a single layer, but de-

liberately moved into a sort of horseshoe formation. Even so, there are often such a number of them that it is difficult to understand how all can be effectively incubated. Yet, hatching is nearly always 100 per cent successful.

Color Pure white or, sometimes, white with just the faintest tinge of bluish. The eggs are often stained with flea excrement.

Shape Usually a rounded oval but frequently very nearly globular.

Texture Quite variable. At times they can be very smooth shelled; at other times they may be heavily granulated. But they are either all one way or the other within a single clutch. The eggs are always very glossy; more so than in any other North American owl species.

Size Roughly about the size of pigeon eggs, a measurement of 42 eggs yielded the averages of 32.9 mm. (1.3″) in length and 27.3 mm. (1.1″) in width. Extremes included:

Maximum length:	33.1 mm.	(1.3″)
Minimum length:	28.4 mm.	(1.1″)
Maximum width:	28.0 mm.	(1.1″)
Minimum width:	24.8 mm.	(1.0″)

Interval of egg-laying While two eggs may be laid on the same day, the interval is more often at least 36 hours between layings and sometimes as much as 72 hours apart.

Egg-laying dates Northern area (Dakotas): earliest, April 22; latest, July 18; normally between May 1 and June 16.

Middle area (Kansas/Colorado): earliest, March 29; latest July 1; normally between May 14 and June 6.

Western area (California): earliest, March 20; latest, June 17; normally between April 14 and May 2.

INCUBATION AND BROODING CHARACTERISTICS

Incubation is almost equally divided between the parent birds and there are times on a fairly regular basis when both birds are brooding at the same time, side by side. However, since incubation may not begin until the laying of the third, fourth, or fifth egg, the term of incubation is not accurately established. Some authorities have stated as short a time as 21 days, but the consensus seems to be that it is either 28 or 29 days.

YOUNG AND FAMILY LIFE CHARACTERISTICS

Newly hatched birds are very scantily feathered—primarily on the main feather tracts—with a soft,

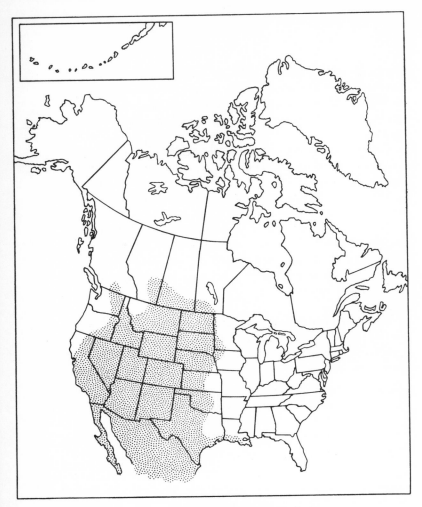

WESTERN BURROWING OWL
Speotyto cunicularia hypugaea (Bonaparte)

DISTRIBUTION IN NORTH AMERICA

Breed from southern interior British Columbia (Okanagan), southern Alberta (Munson), Saskatchewan (Livelong; Rush Lake; Nipawin), and central southern Manitoba (Kildonan), south through eastern Washington and Oregon (Rogue River Valley) and California (including coastal islands and Guadalupe Island), eastward to the eastern border of the Great Plains in Minnesota (Swift and Martin counties), northwestern Iowa (Paton), central Kansas (Sedgwick County), Oklahoma, central Texas (Bonham; Austin), and Louisiana (Baton Rouge), southward to at least central Mexico, but southernmost extremity of breeding range has not been definitely established. May include Baja California.

Winters over much of the breeding range except in the northernmost Great Basin and Great Plains regions. In what migration actually occurs, it will move into southern Louisiana, southern Mississippi, and the western panhandle of Florida, and southward through southern Mexico and western Central America to western Panama (Chiriquí), Chile, and Argentina.

Accidental in Indiana, Michigan, southern Ontario, New Hampshire, Massachusetts, New York, and Virginia.

MIGRATION

Migrational to some extent, though not at all on a regular annual basis. Most birds in the central and southern portions of the breeding range are year-round residents. Northern birds make a definite movement southward in midautumn, migrating at night only. Generally speaking, birds located southward of a line from Oregon to northern Kansas do not migrate although, oddly enough, the owl is said to be absent from northeastern Arizona from November through April.

ECONOMIC INFLUENCE

Because of the enormous numbers of rodents and insects eaten by *Speotyto cunicularia hypugaea,* it is ranked as the second most economically beneficial owl of North America, surpassed only by the Barn Owl (*Tyto alba pratincola*).

fairly short gray-white down which is darker at the base, but so sparse that the bare skin shows through, even after the juvenile plumage has begun sprouting.

By about the sixth to eighth day, the first soft juvenile plumage appears on wings, tail, and the principal feather tracts. This gradually spreads and broadens until, by the fourth week, the young bird is well clad in distinctive first juvenal plumage (see Coloration and Markings: Juvenile) which is worn until about early August. At this time there is begun a complete molt of the contour plumage to first-winter plumage, beginning on the sides, scapulars, and wing coverts. By the time this molt is completed in mid-September, the young birds are virtually indistinguishable from adults.

The young birds are still flightless when they first leave the burrow, and they tend to gather in a circular formation on the mound around the hole, ready at an instant's notice to tumble back into the hole if danger threatens or to rush to meet a parent bird approaching with food. They are most comical in their actions and very interesting to watch.

A variety of attitudes and posturings of the Florida Burrowing Owl (*Speotyto cunicularia floridana*) at the mouth of its burrow in De Soto County, Florida.

Burrowing Owl

Burrowing owls
Florida

Long Legs very
apparent

K.E.K.

FLORIDA BURROWING OWL

(COLOR PLATE XXXVII)

SCIENTIFIC NAME AND ORIGINAL DESCRIPTION

Speotyto cunicularia floridana Ridgway. Original description: *Speotyto cunicularia* var. *Floridana* Ridgway, *American Sportsman*, Volume 4, Number 14 (n.s. No. 40), July 4, 1874, page 216; based on a specimen taken 16 miles east of Sarasota Bay, Manatee County, Florida. In recent years there has been considerable discussion concerning the possibility of reclassifying this owl as a species distinct in its own right, rather than as a *Speotyto cunicularia* subspecies, since the differences are quite pronounced. Should such a change in the classification be made, the new name proposed for the species would be *Speotyto floridana*.

OTHER NAMES

CATTLE OWL   Because its habitat in Florida coincides with beef-producing ranches and it is often seen close to cattle.

PALMETTO OWL   Since it often nests in open areas adjacent to extensive growths of low palmetto.

SANDHILL OWL   Because of the mound of sand it deposits and stands upon at the entrance to its burrow.

DISTINGUISHING FEATURES

The upperparts of this owl are much darker and far less sandy-colored than those of any other form of *Speotyto cunicularia,* and the spots and general coloration of the underparts are a dull white rather than buff-colored. The only distinct buffiness of the underparts occurs on the thighs and underwing coverts, and these coverts are spotted with brown toward the wing edges.

The legs are not only considerably shorter than those of *Speotyto cunicularia hypugaea,* but they are much less feathered, the tail and wings are shorter, and the beak is larger.

FLIGHT PATTERN

The flight pattern of the Florida Burrowing Owl differs in many respects from that of the Western Burrowing Owl. Where the flight of the latter bird is relatively level and direct, if somewhat irregular, that of the Florida Burrowing Owl is considerably less direct and distinctly undulative—not as strongly so as that of the pileated woodpecker, but with more dips and rises and more expansive wanderings. It does not glide as often or for as long distances as does *Speotyto cunicularia hypugaea*, although it does hover in a similar manner for prey location. Rarely will it fly for more than forty or fifty yards in one flight. Most often, when startled from the mound in front of its burrow, it will fly in a semicircular pattern, returning to another burrow perhaps twenty yards from its own.

WEIGHT

Subspecies average: 186.7 gr. (6.5 oz.).

TOTAL LENGTH

Subspecies average: 222.6 mm. (8.8″)—nearly an inch shorter than the Western Burrowing Owl.

WINGSPAN

Subspecies average: 529.6 mm. (20.9″) as compared to 590.6 mm. (23.3″) for *Speotyto cunicularia hypugaea*.

INDIVIDUAL WING LENGTH

Subspecies average: 157.7 mm. (6.2″).

TAIL LENGTH

Subspecies average: 76.0 mm. (3.0″).

BEAK LENGTH

Subspecies average: Slightly broader than that of the Western Burrowing Owl, and longer, averaging 15.5 mm. (0.6″) as compared to 13.9 mm. (0.5″) for the Western form.

LEGS

The tarsi average 36.8 mm. (1.5″) and are nearly naked. What little plumage there is, is much shorter than that worn by the Western Burrowing Owl.

VOICE

Essentially similar to *Speotyto cunicularia hypugaea* except that the alarm cry has a much higher quality and differs in structure, being a series of one long note followed by two short notes and sounding like: *WHIII-IIT whit-whit,* or by two short notes to begin with and a sort of stuttering cry following, as in *whit-whit whoodle-oodle-oodle-ittt!,* with the final note slightly more emphatic. Sometimes this call is given with the final note absent.

Another slightly different call from those given by the Western form is a tremulous ploverlike cry often voiced at sight of a distant, unfamiliar object.

SEXUAL DIFFERENCES: SIZE, COLORATION, VOICE

Unlike the Western Burrowing Owl, which shows remarkably little sexual difference in color, markings, size, or voice, the Florida Burrowing Owl female is quite definitely more deeply reddish on the upperparts, especially in the center of the back, than the male, and her spottings on breast and belly have more distinct margins and are therefore much more sharply defined. In flight the female appears generally darker, particularly on the upperparts, than the male.

MORTALITY

Considerably more cannibalistic in the nest than the Western Burrowing Owl. Because the young birds are such voracious feeders, they will tax their parents to the utmost to provide enough to reasonably satisfy their appetites. If one parent bird should be killed, almost certainly the remaining parent will not be able to supply enough food for the young. In such a case, the larger nestlings will fall upon the smallest and devour it. This can and will continue until only one bird remains, if sufficient food is not provided by the parent.

COLORATION AND MARKINGS: ADULT

All upperparts are a rather deep brownish—grayish brown in the male birds—and both spotted and barred in whitish. The throat is narrowly white and the remainder of the underparts are barred in equal rows with grayish brown and white, becoming less distinct toward mid-belly, and practically indistinguishable in the area of the vent.

GENERAL HABITS AND CHARACTERISTICS

Considerably more diurnal than is *Speotyto cunicularia hypugaea,* but still principally active in late afternoon and evening. Communal to some extent, but not as numerously as in the Western Burrowing Owl. There are rarely more than two to five families in a colony, and often a bird will make an isolated nest and establish only a single-family group.

Generally speaking, the Florida Burrowing Owl is less easily frightened than the western subspecies, and therefore more easily approached and observed. It is less inclined to take flight from its burrow, but much more inclined to bend far over after standing erect, and then run a dozen feet or more as a robin might, before standing erect again. It tends to preen itself extensively and often as it stands on the burrow mound, yet it gives the impression of being more actively alert than the Western Burrowing Owl. Curiously, this Florida subspecies has the habit of gaping widely, as if yawning, frequently during the day.

HABITAT

Mostly prefers treeless, expansive areas of sand and sparse grasses. Although often nesting within a dozen feet of the standing water of a lake, pond, or canal, the burrow is always on a high point well above the waterline. It especially likes wide-open tracts which are spotted here and there with small marshes, hammocks, and interconnecting ponds.

ENEMIES AND DEFENSES

The male Florida Burrowing Owl is generally far more aggressive than the female, especially where protection of young birds is concerned. When danger threatens, the female is apt to move some distance away and stand in what seems to be a worried manner with several other adult females, murmuring softly among themselves. The male, on the other hand, will attack the intruder with vigor, and is often aided in this endeavor by neighboring males.

Because the soils of the nesting grounds are generally loose and soft, the nests are more vulnerable than those of the Western Burrowing Owl, and numerous eggs are destroyed by skunks, opossums, raccoons, and armadillos.

Unfortunately, many of these little owls are shot by ranchers who object to the holes they make, into which cattle may step with resultant injury.

FLORIDA BURROWING OWL
Speotyto cunicularia floridana Ridgway

HUNTING METHODS AND CARRYING OF PREY

Speotyto cunicularia floridana feeds mostly on insects, especially beetles and grasshoppers, along with small snakes, some anoles and skinks, and occasional frogs. This owl will also stand in shallow water at times and snag fish up to six inches long with its talons. Some mice are eaten, along with spiders, centipedes, and scorpions. Unlike the Western race, which swallows whole whatever prey it can, the Florida Burrowing Owl has a strong tendency to dissect its prey and eat it in smaller bits, as a sparrow hawk does. It rarely regurgitates well-developed pellets but coughs up small bones or other undigestibles by themselves, and these materials are often scattered about the entrance to the burrow.

NEST, NESTING HABITS

Differing considerably from the Western Burrowing Owl, far more often than not the Florida Burrowing Owl digs its own nesting burrow, although sometimes it will use abandoned armadillo holes. It has few helpful mammal associates to compare with prairie dogs, which are so helpful to the Western race. Burrowing is usually begun during the first half of March, and the sand scratched out by the bird makes a quite conspicuous mound at the entry hole. Unafraid of vehicles, this owl is nevertheless rarely struck by one. This is all the more surprising in view of the fact that not at all infrequently it will dig its burrow within a few feet of a busy road. In 1971, the authors closely observed the nesting activities of a pair of Florida Burrowing Owls which built their burrow exactly 28 inches from the edge of the pavement of State Route 74 in the vicinity of La Belle, Florida, a highway heavily used by cross-state truck traffic, including tractor-trailer rigs moving at high speed. At times the sentinel owl would literally be blown off its feet by the blast of wind from a passing semivan but, unruffled, it would immediately regain its feet, preen itself carefully and continue standing guard. It was possible to stop an auto less than fifty feet away without alarming the bird into flight, although a walking human could get no closer than about 100 feet before the bird chattered its warning cry and fled.

EGGS

Generally, fewer eggs are laid by *Speotyto cunicularia floridana* than by *Speotyto cunicularia hypugaea,* with five or six being the most common clutch. Rarely, if ever, fewer than four or more than eight eggs are laid. The average egg size, based on the measurements of 50 eggs, was slightly smaller than that of the Western Burrowing Owl, averaging 32.5 mm. (1.3″) in length by 26.3 mm. (1.0″) in width. Egg-laying dates from about March 15 at the earliest to May 25 at the latest, the height of the egg-laying occurring between April 4 and April 23.

DISTRIBUTION IN NORTH AMERICA

In the prairies of central and southern Florida, from the upper St. Johns River area westward through the Gainesville area and southward through the Kissimmee area, in the area surrounding Lake Okeechobee, to the Miami and Coral Gables area, and westward to the vicinity of Immokalee, and northwesterly from there to the area of Punta Gorda. It is also found in the Bahamas from Grand Bahama Island to Great Inagua Island.

MIGRATION

Non-migratory.

ECONOMIC INFLUENCE

Of benefit in its predation upon mice and insects, but disliked by cattle ranchers because of the holes it makes, which can cause cattle to break their legs. The owl also causes some problems by interfering with aircraft at major Florida airports.

SPECIES

ORDER: STRIGIFORMES

FAMILY: STRIGIDAE

GENUS: *Micrathene* Coues

SPECIES: *whitneyi* (Cooper)

SUBSPECIES

---

whitneyi (Cooper)   WHITNEY'S ELF OWL

idonea (Ridgway)   TEXAS ELF OWL

WHITNEY'S ELF OWL
(COLOR PLATE XXXVIII)

SCIENTIFIC NAME AND ORIGINAL DESCRIPTION

Micrathene whitneyi whitneyi (Cooper). Original description: *Athene whitneyi* Cooper, *Proceedings of the California Academy of Sciences*, Series 1, Volume 2 (before December), 1861, page 118; based on a specimen from Fort Mojave, Lat. 35°, Colorado River Valley, Arizona. Former scientific names: *Athene whitneyi*, *Micropallas whitneyi whitneyi*.

OTHER NAMES

ELF OWL   For its diminutive size.

TECOLOTE ENANO DE COOPER   Mexican-Indian name meaning "Cooper's Dwarf Owl."

DISTINGUISHING FEATURES

This is the smallest owl species in North America, being much smaller in over-all size than the Screech Owls (*Otus asio* sp.) and even smaller than the Pygmy Owls (*Glaucidium gnoma* sp.). It is distinctive from the Pygmy Owls in that the tail is much shorter and, though coloration is similar, it is generically more like the Burrowing Owls (*Speotyto cunicularia* sp.). It is dichromatic, with a brown phase and a gray phase. Whitney's Elf Owl is little larger than a chickadee and can comfortably perch upon a drinking straw.

Rank in size among the eighteen species: Eighteenth.

SHAPE AT REST

Whitney's Elf Owl perches in a relatively upright position and, though hardly the size of a house sparrow, it seems larger than that bird because of the fluffy nature of its plumage. The head is quite round with no trace of ear tufts and, while it does not stand quite as erect as the Burrowing Owl, it has the same knock-kneed stance. Whether perched or on the wing, the tail is very short and rather square-cut in appearance.

SHAPE IN FLIGHT

In flight the tail appears especially stubby and the wings have distinctly rounded tips. This little owl gives the impression of being a bat when in flight, although not quite as erratic in its movements.

FLIGHT PATTERN

The wings beat very rapidly as it flies swiftly from one perch to another. It tends to drop slightly from its perch before actually beginning to fly, then wings quickly along with little or no gliding and fairly low to the ground, making a slight rise as it nears the next perching spot.

Measurements have been based on 41 measured birds: 11 males and 30 females.

WEIGHT

Species average: 25.7 gr. (0.9 oz.).

	Male	Female
Average	25.2 gr. (0.9 oz.)	26.1 gr. (0.9 oz.)
Minimum	17.0 gr. (0.6 oz.)	17.3 gr. (0.6 oz.)
Maximum	28.9 gr. (1.0 oz.)	30.6 gr. (1.1 oz.)

Rank in weight among the eighteen species: Eighteenth.

TOTAL LENGTH

Species average: 151.5 mm. (6.0").

	Male	Female
Average	147.9 mm. (5.8")	155.0 mm. (6.1")
Minimum	135.5 mm. (5.3")	152.4 mm. (6.0")
Maximum	157.1 mm. (6.2")	167.1 mm. (6.6")

Rank in total length among the eighteen species: Eighteenth.

WINGSPAN

Species average: 373.5 mm. (14.7").

	Male	Female
Average	369.7 mm. (14.6")	377.2 mm. (14.9")
Minimum	353.1 mm. (13.9")	373.8 mm. (14.7")
Maximum	379.7 mm. (15.0")	382.3 mm. (15.1")

Rank in wingspan among the eighteen species: Eighteenth.

INDIVIDUAL WING LENGTH

Species average: 99.7 mm. (3.9").

	Male	Female
Average	99.1 mm. (3.9")	100.3 mm. (4.0")
Minimum	98.8 mm. (3.9")	100.0 mm. (4.0")
Maximum	100.4 mm. (4.0")	102.0 mm. (4.0")

Rank in wing length among the eighteen species: Eighteenth.

TAIL LENGTH

Species average: 54.8 mm. (2.2").

	Male	Female
Average	53.0 mm. (2.1")	56.5 mm. (2.2")
Minimum	50.8 mm. (2.0")	54.4 mm. (2.1")
Maximum	56.6 mm. (2.2")	60.3 mm. (2.4")

Rank in tail length among the eighteen species: Eighteenth.

BEAK LENGTH

Species average: 8.6 mm. (0.3").

	Male	Female
Average	8.5 mm. (0.3")	8.7 mm. (0.3")
Minimum	8.1 mm. (0.3")	8.2 mm. (0.3")
Maximum	9.2 mm. (0.4")	9.3 mm. (0.4")

Rank in beak length among the eighteen species: Eighteenth.

LEGS, FEET, TALONS

The legs are rather sparsely feathered and the toes have only scattered hairlike bristles and appear virtually naked. The feet are small and rather weak and yellowish gray in coloration. The slate-gray-to-black talons are fairly short, only moderately curved, and quite weak for an owl.

EYES AND VISION

The irides are a bright lemon yellow, occasionally shading into orangish yellow. Because of the wide manner in which the eyes are usually opened, Whitney's Elf Owl wears a constantly startled expression. Vision is quite good, but nowhere nearly as important as hearing in the location of prey. This tiny owl can see well enough during the day and probably even better at night, but twilight is the ideal condition for its vision.

EARS AND HEARING

Ear cavities are markedly asymmetrical, though placement on the head is very nearly the same on both sides. There is a slight difference in size of the ear coverts, and the owl seems to have great control over the degree of extension of the ear coverts, to aid in sound locating. As a result, hearing is superb.

EAR TUFTS, PLUMAGE, ANNUAL MOLT

Whitney's Elf Owl has no ear tufts whatever, and the head shape seems almost perfectly round. Plumage is not quite as tightly held to the body as in the Pygmy Owl and, as a result, the Elf Owl tends to look more bulky, even though smaller. Well-fluted feathers and soft plumage give it a somewhat more silent style of flight than is true of the Pygmy Owl. There is one complete annual molt of the adults which begins in early September and is usually completed by late October.

MORTALITY AND LONGEVITY

Very little banding has been accomplished with these owls, and not a great deal is known in respect to infant or adult mortality or longevity. A few captive birds have lived for over five years.

A field study of a family of Whitney's Elf Owls (*Microthene whitneyi whitneyi*). Sketched on the New Mexico-Arizona-Mexico border.

Whitney's Elf owl
M.w. whitneyi

young
Gray with
very fine
barring

♀

♂

K.E.K.

COLORATION AND MARKINGS:
ADULT

Gray phase: The upperparts are generally grayish brown to brownish gray, with irregular small spottings of buff, shading to a more ruddy buff on the forehead. There is an interrupted collar of whitish-buff spotting across the lower hindneck. Outer webs of the shoulder feathers are white with thin black margins. Middle coverts and greater coverts have largish half-oval spottings on the outer webs of each feather, causing a tear-shaped white outline with a comma-shaped line extending from the tip of that. (See Color Plate XXXVIII.) The outer webs of the primaries have six (sometimes five or seven) conspicuous buffy-reddish spots which do not touch the shaft. The rectrices are crossed by four or five narrow and often interrupted bands of pale whitish buff which do not touch the shaft on either web. Superciliaries and lores are white, each feather barely tipped with black. Facial disks are buffy to cinnamon buff, darker around the eyes and in the outer-eye corner area than in the suborbital and malar areas. There is sometimes a whitish spot on the cheek. The throat is buffy with a reddish cast much more pronounced in some individuals than in others.

The underparts are generally duskily barred with narrow lines on the reddish feathering, but breast and belly are primarily unmarked buff to dusky or cinnamon buff. Undertail coverts are white with narrow, somewhat dusky center streaks or irregular spots. Underwing coverts are whitish buffy, irregularly spotted with slaty gray to slaty brown, but pure white on the wing edges.

Brown phase: markings are quite similar to those of the gray phase, but generally more—considerably more —of a dark-brownish coloration, particularly on the back.

COLORATION AND MARKINGS:
JUVENILE

Like adults, but with the crown unspotted and deep brownish gray. The facial disks in particular are much grayer without ruddy buffiness. Marbled and rather cloudy gray or gray-brown underparts, narrowly barred with darker gray.

GENERAL HABITS AND
CHARACTERISTICS

Quite decidedly crepuscular and nocturnal in its habits, spending the day at rest. Throughout the year this owl becomes very active at dusk and will often ap-proach close to campfires and chase insects attracted by the glow. Has a strong dislike for flying during brisk winds.

HABITAT AND ROOSTING

Prefers very arid, low-elevation desert terrain overgrown with cacti, mesquite, and creosote bush growing in hard, stony ground, but often ventures to slightly higher elevations to the canyons, ravines, and grasslands, especially among well-grown walnuts, sycamores, and oaks on the more northerly rises. While it can be found at elevations of as much as 7,000 feet, this is rare and more often it is found below 5,500 feet and seems especially to favor areas between 3,000 and 5,000 feet in elevation. It frequently inhabits creek valleys and roosts in a hole during the day, either a natural tree cavity or an old woodpecker hole. Just as often, though, it spends the day perched amid very heavy foliage in dense thickets. Generally the holes it finds in saguaro cacti are not used except during the nesting season. While females brood the eggs and young, the males become somewhat gregarious and perch together well hidden in thick cover.

ENEMIES AND DEFENSES

The greatest defense of this petite owl is its protective coloration, which makes it virtually invisible, even at close range, as it perches in heavy foliage. If danger threatens, the roosting bird straightens and brings one wing forward, bent at the wrist, and spread so that the speckled coverts and primaries shield the light underparts, which would be much more visible. It tends to turn slightly sideways on the perch, but still facing the intruder, with only the tops of the pupils peering over the wing edge.

While it generally prefers to flee rather than fight, it will occasionally attack the larger Whiskered Owl (*Otus trichopsis trichopsis*) in territorial dispute. Almost always the smaller owl emerges triumphant. Oddly, such disputes have almost invariably been witnessed in stands of well-grown sycamore.

Now and again Whitney's Elf Owl will squabble with woodpeckers over who has the right to inhabit a particular hole, but for the most part there is little harassment by other birds.

A variety of field sketches made in Arizona of the Whitney's Elf Owl (*Micrathene whitneyi whitneyi*) in posturings at and near its nesting hole in a saguaro cactus.

Elf Owl
Micrathene
whitneyi whitneyi

Tiny, short-tailed

Some
Museum skins
Tend To be Long-
Tailed

Tail very
short.

K.E.K.

HUNTING METHODS AND CARRYING OF PREY

Because of its rapid and highly maneuverable flight, much of its prey—almost entirely insects—is captured in flight in the outstretched talons. Insects are also often plucked off trees, brush, or the ground without the bird alighting. These are almost always carried in the talons to a nearby perch to be eaten. Likes to perch relatively low in tree or bush or on cactus and wait for prey to advertise its presence by movement or sound, at which it attacks at once.

FOOD, FEEDING HABITS, WASTES

Most prey, even smaller insects, are ripped apart before being swallowed, much as a sparrow hawk eats its prey piecemeal. Although by far the greater majority of prey is made up of insects and other invertebrate life such as scorpions, spiders, and centipedes, this little owl will occasionally prey upon small mice, shrews, and very rarely a small bird. Mainly it eats caterpillars, moths, beetles, crickets, grasshoppers, cicadas, locusts, and various insect larvae. Pellets are poorly formed, relatively dry and loose, and disintegrate quickly after regurgitation. Light brownish to grayish, they contain mainly of the undigestible chitinous materials of the insects and other invertebrates devoured.

Fecal wastes are viscous, gray brown, and generally dropped below the bird during flight.

COURTSHIP AND MATING

Because of the almost strictly nocturnal or late crepuscular habits of the bird, data on courtship and mating are still largely wanting. Some muted calling originates during this time from the males, but these calls are rather ventriloquial, increasing the difficulty of close observation.

ANNUAL BROODS, NEST, NESTING HABITS

Single-brooded, *Micrathene whitneyi whitneyi* almost always nests in abandoned woodpecker holes, favoring those in hardwoods—sycamores, oaks, willows, walnuts—but using those in saguaro cactus when nothing else is available. The nest hole is generally about twenty feet in height, but may be as low as ten feet or as high as thirty. This little owl has been known to nest without aggression only a few feet from nesting flickers and woodpeckers in the same tree or cactus.

EGGS

Number per nesting Two to five eggs are laid, but only rarely either two or five. Usually there are three and somewhat less commonly, four.

Color Pure, unblemished white.

Shape Roundly ovate.

Texture Finely granulated and moderately glossy. On rare occasions the eggs will be highly glossy.

Size A total of 31 measured eggs yielded average egg-size figures of 27.5 mm. (1.1″) in length and 23.5 mm. (0.9″) in width. Extreme measurements included:

Maximum length:	30.1 mm.	(1.2″)
Minimum length:	25.0 mm.	(1.0″)
Maximum width:	26.3 mm.	(1.0″)
Minimum width:	22.5 mm.	(0.9″)

Interval of egg-laying From 48 to 54 hours between eggs.

Egg-laying dates Earliest, April 28; latest, June 16; normally between May 14 and May 28.

INCUBATION AND BROODING CHARACTERISTICS

It is very likely that incubation begins with the first egg laid, since from the time it is laid one or the other of the parents is on the nest, with incubation shared equally between them. The incubation period of 14 days is the shortest of any North American owl species. The male rarely brings food to the incubating female, allowing her to hunt for herself while he takes his turn at incubating.

XLV COAST PYGMY OWL (*Above*)

Glaucidium gnoma grinnelli Ridgway. Female. Vicinity of Seattle, King County, Washington, December 25, 1916. A.O.U. Number 379-C

XLVI VANCOUVER PYGMY OWL (*Below*)

Glaucidium gnoma swarthi Grinnell. Male. Cedar Hill, Vancouver Island, British Columbia, Canada, November 30, 1922. A.O.U. Number 379-B

XLVII FERRUGINOUS OWL

Glaucidium brasilianum ridgwayi (Sharp). Male. One mile northwest of Dog Springs, Hidalgo County, New Mexico, November 19, 1970. Number 380-A

XLVIII CACTUS OWL

Glaucidium brasilianum cactorum van Rossem. Male. San Blas Territory, Tepic, Mexico, April 19, 1905. A.O.U. Number 380

Karl E. Karalus

Karl E Karalus
1971

Karl E. Karalus
1971

YOUNG AND FAMILY LIFE CHARACTERISTICS

Disappointingly little is known about the nest life of this dainty little owl. When first hatched the babies are about the size of the first joint of a man's thumb and are well covered with a short, pure-white down. The intermediate plumage begins to appear before the end of the first week, with the down being pushed out and clinging to the tips of the new feathers. This new plumage is usually pure gray on the head and body (both upperparts and underparts), with some very in-distinct mottling and barring of slightly darker gray on the underparts. Practically no indication of buffiness or brown anywhere on the young bird. A final postnuptial molt occurring in June and July results in plumage practically indistinguishable from that of the parent birds.

DISTRIBUTION IN NORTH AMERICA

This is the most abundant owl in Arizona, and it breeds from the lower Colorado River Valley of California and Arizona (Fort Mojave), southern Arizona (Prescott, Oracle), southwestern New Mexico, and southwestern Texas (Chisos Mountains), southward to Sonora (Guirocoba), Guanajuato, and Puebla, Mexico.

Winters primarily south of the United States.

On rare occasions it is found in the Big Bend country of Texas.

MIGRATION

Migratory in the more northerly parts of its range. Almost all birds of this species in the United States move southward into Mexico in late October and probably winter as far south as the Rio Balsas Basin of south-

WHITNEY'S ELF OWL

Micrathene whitneyi whitneyi (Cooper)

ern Mexico. Spring migration northward commences in late February and early March. As far as is known, all migrational flying is done at night.

ECONOMIC INFLUENCE

Although Whitney's Elf Owl is a useful destroyer of injurious insects, the effects are relatively negligible since its range is mostly confined to non-agricultural areas.

XLIX   GREAT HORNED OWL

Bubo virginianus virginianus (Gmelin). Male. Vicinity of Dayton, Montgomery County, Ohio, January 1, 1970. A.O.U. Number 375

L   ST. MICHAEL HORNED OWL

Bubo virginianus algistus (Oberholser). Male. Near the mouth of Tubutulik River at Norton Bay, Moses Point, Seward Peninsula, Alaska. A.O.U. Number 375-G

LI   LABRADOR HORNED OWL

Bubo virginianus heterocnemis (Oberholser). Male. Vicinity of Charlottetown, Prince Edward Island, Canada, March 7, 1938. A.O.U. Number 375-F

TEXAS ELF OWL

(COLOR PLATE XXXIX)

SCIENTIFIC NAME AND ORIGINAL DESCRIPTION

Micrathene whitneyi idonea (Ridgway). Original description: *Micropallas whitneyi idoneus* Ridgway,

TEXAS ELF OWL

Micrathene whitneyi idonea (Ridgway)

U. S. National Museum Bulletin, Number 50, Part 6, 1914, pp. 807 (in key), 810; based on a specimen from near Hidalgo, Texas.

DISTINGUISHING FEATURES

Considerably grayer in general coloration than Whitney's Elf Owl (*Micrathene whitneyi whitneyi*), with all light markings considerably whiter and without cinnamon or buffy traces, and with all grays generally darker and more contrasting against ground coloration than in the gray phase of Whitney's Elf Owl.

GENERAL HABITS AND CHARACTERISTICS

Without doubt this is the least known of all North American owls. Robert Ridgway had only two specimens of this owl to work with when he named and described the race. The type specimen was taken on April 5, 1889, just five miles outside Hidalgo, Texas, and while a fair number of specimens have been taken since then, little comprehensive study of the bird's natural history has been accomplished. It is, however, believed to be considerably more aggressive in nature than Whitney's Elf Owl.

DISTRIBUTION IN NORTH AMERICA

Resident in the lower Rio Grande Valley of Texas (Hidalgo, Brownsville), southward to Guanajuato, Valley of Mexico, and Puebla (Tehuacán).

SPECIES

ORDER: STRIGIFORMES

FAMILY: STRIGIDAE

GENUS: *Nyctea* Stephens

SPECIES: *scandiaca* (Linnaeus)

SNOWY OWL

SNOWY OWL

(COLOR PLATE XL)

SCIENTIFIC NAME AND ORIGINAL DESCRIPTION

Nyctea scandiaca (Linnaeus). Original description: *Strix scandiaca* Linnaeus, *Systematica Natura*, Edition 10, Volume 1, 1758, page 92; based on a specimen from Alpibus Lapponiae (Lapland). Former scientific names: *Strix nyctea, Strix arctica, Nyctea nivea, Nyctea nyctea, Nyctea scandiaca arctica.*

OTHER NAMES

AMERICAN SNOWY OWL Used more in former times than at present, to show difference between American, European, and Asiatic birds, although all are of the same race without subspecific classification.

ARCTIC OWL For geographical location.

ERMINE OWL Probably as much for black-and-white ermine colors as for the fact that it frequently dines on ermine.

GHOST OWL For its ghostly white appearance as it flies or perches in the twilight.

GREAT WHITE OWL For its coloration and size.

LE HIBOU BLANC French-Canadian name meaning "The White Owl."

OOKPIKJUAK (ALSO OKPIK) Eskimo name for this owl.

TUNDRA GHOST For its appearance and habitat.

WHITE OWL After its general coloration.

DISTINGUISHING FEATURES

Nyctea scandiaca is not only the largest North American owl, but one of the most strikingly beautiful owls in the entire world. Though differing from both considerably, there are only two other birds within its range for which it might be mistaken. One of these is the Arctic Horned Owl (*Bubo virginianus subarcticus*) which, in its lightest coloration, bears some resemblance to the Snowy Owl. The Arctic Horned Owl, however, is generally darker, has highly distinctive ear tufts which are lacking in the Snowy Owl, and has a considerably more erect posture. The other bird to some degree similar is the White Gyrfalcon (*Falco rusticolus obsoletus*) which is a smaller bird with much narrower wings and a more aquiline shape. The Willow Ptarmigan (*Lagopus lagopus albus*) in its winter garb has a similar coloration, but really looks nothing at all like the Snowy Owl. Streamlined in a rather bulky way, the Snowy Owl is essentially pure white, more or less speckled with slate-colored spots, depending upon age and sex. (See Sexual Differences: Size, Coloration, Voice and Coloration and Markings: Juvenile.)

Rank in over-all size among the eighteen species: First.

SHAPE AT REST

The Snowy Owl is most often seen squatting on the ground or on a slight rise (except during migrations when it tends to perch on low rooftops, haystacks, mounds of earth, stumps, and fence posts). It has a very heavy but smooth-lined shape and though there are vestigial ear tufts, the head appears perfectly round and very large. It rarely perches in the stiffly upright posture so often assumed by the Horned Owls (*Bubo virginianus* sp.) but rather tends to lean its body well forward, sometimes to the extent that the belly and even lower breast are on the ground. It actually squats rather than sits and practically never stands high on its legs, as does the more slender White Gyrfalcon.

SHAPE IN FLIGHT

Again there is that sense of great heaviness along with streamlining; the head melding smoothly into the body and no visible neck shape. The extended wings are remarkably broad, very long, and rounded at the tips rather than narrow and decidedly pointed, as are those of the White Gyrfalcon. In flight it might be mistaken for the Arctic Horned Owl, but the wingbeat is considerably different and the body of the Snowy Owl in flight undulates more than does that of the Arctic Horned Owl.

FLIGHT PATTERN

In most circumstances the Snowy Owl's flight is quite direct, very strong and steady, and not unlike that of a falcon, though much slower. The wings make a long, full, powerful, and deliberate downstroke, but the upstroke is much faster and not as smoothly executed. The body will at times seem to undulate in flight, sinking slightly with each upstroke of the wings and rising with each downstroke. It is a very silent and graceful flight which, at times, can be surprisingly swift, but it is far more often characterized by its easy sailing nature. Almost always as it flies, even during the migrational flights, the head constantly swivels back and forth and the eyes are ever watchful. Not uncommonly it will swivel its head so far around that it appears to be facing in the exact opposite direction of its flight. When it first rises from the ground the wingbeat is very steady, but soon the owl goes into long glides low to the ground and sweeps upward, still in a glide, to some slight rise of the landscape. When attacking prey or enemy, the wings are abruptly folded in flight and the bird drops with surprising speed. Often during hunting it will hover over one spot, waiting for sight or sound of suspected prey.

Measurements have been based on 74 measured birds: 34 males and 40 females.

WEIGHT

Species average: 1,659.8 gr. (58.1 oz.).

	Male	Female
Average	1,612.9 gr. (56.5 oz.)	1,706.7 gr. (59.7 oz.)
Minimum	1,448.0 gr. (50.7 oz.)	1,593.0 gr. (55.8 oz.)
Maximum	1,839.9 gr. (64.4 oz.)	2,002.6 gr. (70.1 oz.)

Rank in weight among the eighteen species: First.

TOTAL LENGTH

Species average: 628.1 mm. (24.7").

	Male	Female
Average	592.8 mm. (23.4")	663.4 mm. (26.1")
Minimum	531.1 mm. (20.9")	629.9 mm. (24.8")
Maximum	707.2 mm. (27.9")	766.9 mm. (30.2")

Rank in total length among the eighteen species: Second.

WINGSPAN

Species average: 1,610.6 mm. (63.5").

	Male	Female
Average	1,577.4 mm. (62.1")	1,643.8 mm. (64.8")
Minimum	1,316.7 mm. (51.9")	1,567.5 mm. (61.8")
Maximum	1,656.4 mm. (65.3")	1,816.5 mm. (71.6")

Rank in wingspan among the eighteen species: First.

INDIVIDUAL WING LENGTH

Species average: 423.2 mm. (16.7").

	Male	Female
Average	409.0 mm. (16.1")	437.4 mm. (17.2")
Minimum	395.3 mm. (15.6")	414.0 mm. (16.3")
Maximum	439.7 mm. (17.3")	477.3 mm. (18.8")

Rank in wing length among the eighteen species: First.

TAIL LENGTH

Species average: 242.0 mm. (9.5").

	Male	Female
Average	233.7 mm. (9.2")	250.3 mm. (9.9")
Minimum	230.4 mm. (9.1")	248.3 mm. (9.8")
Maximum	240.3 mm. (9.5")	261.7 mm. (10.3")

Rank in tail length among the eighteen species: Second.

BEAK LENGTH

Species average: 26.7 mm. (1.1"). Although the beak is wide and black, it is short for the size of the bird and almost hidden by the dense feathering of the lores.

	Male	Female
Average	25.5 mm. (1.0")	27.9 mm. (1.1")
Minimum	24.6 mm. (1.0")	26.7 mm. (1.1")
Maximum	25.7 mm. (1.0")	28.2 mm. (1.1")

Rank in beak length among the eighteen species: Fourth.

SNOWY OWL FIELD SKETCHES

A large Snowy Owl observed perched on a low stub near the south end of one of the O'Hare International Airport runways, not far from Chicago, Illinois, allowed the artist to approach very closely. Obviously fatigued from its long migratory flight, the owl sat quietly for fully twenty minutes while field sketches were made. It showed agitation only when the artist moved to within six feet; shortly afterward it took wing and, flying low to the ground, disappeared from sight to the southwest.

Snowy Owl

Studies from life at O'hare airport, Illinois
Jan. 1949.

under side of wings and tail
show little or no
barring.

K. E. K.

LEGS, FEET, TALONS

The leg muscles are very strong and the grip of the Snowy Owl is quite powerful. Legs and feet, right to the base of the talons, are heavily covered with quite long, hairlike white plumage; so long that even the long, curved, jet-black talons are nearly hidden from view. The feet are not abnormally large for this bird's size, although the toes are rather thick. In not-so-distant history, the northern Indian tribes often made anklets and bracelets from numerous talons of these birds strung on rawhide. The birds, incidentally, were killed by the Indians as a source of food, not merely for the decorative value of the talons.

EYES AND VISION

The vision of the Snowy Owl is probably as good at night as that of almost any other North American owl, and undoubtedly better in the daytime than most. This owl has brilliant, startlingly lemon-yellow irides and deep black pupils. The eyes are set slightly closer to the top of the head than in other species, and though they can be opened widely at will, more often than not they are partially lidded, tending to give the bird a sleepy or dreamy appearance—or, according to some, an insipid, fatuous, or even stupid expression. When angry, the owl narrows its eyes in a distinctly glaring, horizontally elongated oval shape.

EARS AND HEARING

The ear openings are only about one-half inch in diameter, which is rather small for the size of the bird, especially when compared to the diminutive Saw-whet owl (*Aegolius acadicus acadicus*) whose ear openings are not much smaller. The ear cavities and their placement on the skull are not nearly so asymmetrical as in other species, and there is no anterior ear flap; yet the hearing of this owl is extremely keen.

EAR TUFTS, PLUMAGE, ANNUAL MOLT

Although there are indeed rudimentary ear tufts, they are very tiny, practically buried in the head plumage, and rarely raised even a little. For all intents and purposes, insofar as external appearances go, *Nyctea scandiaca* may be considered as being a tuftless owl. Its plumage is probably the most luxurious of any North American owl's, being very heavy, remarkably dense, and yet still reasonably tight to the body contour (as opposed to the notable fluffiness of the Great Gray Owl [*Strix nebulosa nebulosa*]) so as to permit the smoothly streamlined appearance. Adults have a complete molt each year, beginning as early as late June (but more often in early July) and completed by early October to mid-October. The four outermost primaries are quite distinctly emarginated.

VOICE

Nyctea scandiaca has a very distinctive voice, uttering great booming notes which carry phenomenal distances over the barren tundra. Mostly the calls are given while the bird is perched on the ground. It leans well forward, swells out its throat enormously, raises its tail, and rather violently belches out four (usually) bellowing hoots, bowing deeply with each note given and sounding like: *WHOOOO-WHOOOO-WHOOOO-WHOOOO,* with each note of equal pitch and volume. The sound is rather wild and often frightening in the wastelands of the tundra. At times, dozens of the birds will be calling back and forth simultaneously and the crisp air seems to throb with the resonance of it. These hoots, incidentally, can be quite ventriloquial if the owl wishes them to be and will sound as if they are coming from high in the sky above the spot where the bird is actually calling from.

Even more disturbing is the cry of anger made by this bird, most often heard when an intruder is threatening the nest or young. It is a loud, gravelly sort of barking growl with the notes distinctly separated at the beginning of the cry, but degenerating into a hoarse quaver at the conclusion, sounding like *WHOOO-uh WHOOO-uh WHOOO-uh WHOOO-uh WUH-WUH-WUH-WUHWUHWUH.* Not infrequently this call will be preceded or succeeded by a very piercing whistle, almost like a boy whistling shrilly through his fingers. If the bird decides to attack, the actual onslaught is most often preceded by a guttural and fierce sound something like *KRUFFF-GUH-GUH-GUK,* rapidly sounded. Less often, when the bird or its young are endangered, it will make an unwritable sound similar to that of teeth grinding together heavily and will occasionally accompany this with a rattling sound deep in its throat.

One other call, possibly a mating cry, is worthy of note. It is a series of remarkably doglike barkings, usually in three syllables but repeated numerous times and sounding like *WUFFF-WUFFF-WUCK WUFFF-WUFFF-WUCK.*

Despite these distinctive cries, the Snowy Owl is most often a rather silent bird throughout much of the year. It appears to be particularly mute during its cyclic migrations southward.

Snowy Owl

SEXUAL DIFFERENCES: SIZE, COLORATION, VOICE

There is a more distinctive sexual difference among Snowy Owls than among any other owl species on the North American continent. Adult males are decidedly smaller than adult females and, as a rule, the males are a much purer white, sometimes to the point of being entirely lacking in spots. The males can almost always be easily recognized at a distance because the females (and juveniles) are much more heavily spotted and barred on the body and wings. The very darkest males and the lightest of females will be reasonably alike in coloration and marking, but most often the males are very much lighter. Adult birds with heavy markings are almost always females and they tend to look grayish from a distance. The males, when not pure white, usually have a scattering of slaty spots on the back and near the tips of the primaries and rectrices. The voice of the male may be just a bit deeper than that of the female, but the difference is slight at best and undependable as a device for sexual indentification.

MORTALITY AND LONGEVITY

There is a rather high mortality rate—roughly 30 per cent—of nestling birds. (See Young and Family Life Characteristics.) Snowy Owls have been known to live for nearly 35 years in captivity. Adult birds in the wild which were captured and banded, have been recaptured as much as 17 years later.

COLORATION AND MARKINGS: ADULT

ADULT MALE Pure white occasionally, with no marks whatever; more often some scattered or transverse spots or bars of slate gray (sometimes with a brownish cast) on crown, back, and greater coverts, with primaries and rectrices having dusky spots close to the tips. Usually some narrow and indistinct barrings on the sides, flanks, and belly, but on occasion these can be rather clearly defined. Spotting on the male will occasionally be much more extensive than usual. On extremely rare occasions a male bird will become suffused over its entire plumage with a clear lemon-yellow coloration. This is distinctly aberrative in nature and the color is so fugitive that it disappears entirely soon after the bird's death.

ADULT FEMALE Decidedly darker than the male everywhere except on the facial disks, sides of neck, chin, throat, center of breast, legs, and feet. Elsewhere it is rather heavily barred and speckled with deep slate gray which sometimes has a vague brownish cast.

COLORATION AND MARKINGS: JUVENILE

The juveniles are generally a uniform dusky brown to sooty gray, which is only slightly lighter on legs and feet. Young birds are always much more heavily barred and spotted than adults of the same sex, and this coloration and marking persists until the first postnuptial molt of the first-winter plumage, which occurs about thirteen or fourteen months after hatching.

GENERAL HABITS AND CHARACTERISTICS

Where human intruders are concerned, especially in the treeless tundra areas, the Snowy Owl is very shy, usually taking flight while the person is still several hundred yards distant. But otherwise it is a very bold, extraordinarily patient, and sometimes extremely ferocious bird. Often if a mouse, lemming, or hare finds a hiding place among rocks while the owl is watching, the bird will quietly alight close by and stand waiting in utter silence for hours for the animal to reappear.

Nyctea scandiaca will sometimes attack and kill animals of surprisingly large size. On numerous occasions, for example, it has been known to kill and eat foxes that have been caught in traps, and there are even unverified reports that it will attack animals as fierce and large as badgers and young wolverines—though how successful such attacks might be, if they occur, is a matter of conjecture. It is not at all unusual for Snowy Owls to rip apart and devour great quantities of fur-bearing animals which they find dead in traps, and for this reason they are not held in very high regard by professional trappers. During the periodic southward migrations they have been known actually to enter chicken houses and kill full-grown hens which outweigh them by two or three times.

A powerful flier, especially during migrations, the Snowy Owl in most cases is nonetheless inclined to make rather short, hopping flights from one rise in the ground to another. In the tundra, these rises are called *pingaluks*. They are frost-heaves which raise a section of ground up to several yards in diameter as much as two or three feet above the surrounding flat terrain. It is also ordinarily on such pingaluks that this owl species nests.

Individual birds have territories that encompass several square miles, but they are not territorially aggressive among themselves and it is not unusual for the territories of several birds to overlap. A highly diurnal owl, though not exclusively so, most of its hunting in the north country—and much of it in the south—is done during daylight hours, often when the sun is brightly shining.

While it can be ferocious on occasion, the Snowy Owl tends to have a reasonably gentle disposition where humans are concerned and, unlike the Horned Owls (*Bubo virginianus* sp.), submits without great protest to confinement as an adult and soon becomes gentled enough to be fed by hand, stroked, and even carried about on the arm.

When squatting on a pingaluk, this owl wears its seemingly dreamy, sleepy expression and appears wholly devoid of interest in anything around it, but this is deceptive because it is always very alert, especially for sounds. Almost constantly its head swivels from side to side as it listens and watches. The slightest hint of prey will send it arrowing to the attack with startling abruptness.

HABITAT AND ROOSTING

Roosting, as noted, is almost always on pingaluks when the bird is in the northern barrens. During migrations, however, it favors any abrupt rise in the ground, roof peaks of low buildings, posts, stumps, low tree branches, haystacks, earth mounds, and similar prominences. Its habitat preference is for treeless, moss- and lichen-covered tundra flatlands which are reasonably well dotted with scattered pingaluk mounds. As a matter of fact, it will not remain in northern areas where such mounds are absent. While now and again it will hunt in wooded areas during the southern migration, even during those periods it prefers more open areas such as prairies, marshes, lakeshores, riverbanks, weed fields and pastures, and (particularly while migration is in progress) coastal beaches and the shores of small islands. Its most normal habitat, however, is north of the tree line in circumpolar arctic tundra areas where the ground is not perpetually covered by ice and snow, and where there is an abundance of prey.

ENEMIES AND DEFENSES

Aggressiveness is most often displayed when nest, eggs, and young are threatened, and this is more true of the male Snowy Owl than of the female, although both will be actively defensive in protecting the young. Parent birds will often fall onto the ground and perform the broken-wing act to lure intruders away from the nest area; but if the intruder persists and refuses to be lured away, direct attack by one or both adult birds is a distinct likelihood, and both are formidable foes. The attacking owl will fly directly at the head of the intruder from a considerable distance away, and the powerful talons and beak will slash viciously and with great accuracy as the bird whizzes past, inflicting severe injury.

At times other than the nesting season, however, the birds will more often fly away from potential danger long before it gets too close to them. Dense plumage acts as a protective device, too, in case a hunter gets near. Extra-heavy shotgun loads must be used to penetrate the plumage; ordinary bird shot will not normally bring the bird down unless one of the pellets chances to penetrate the brain through eye or ear.

Man, as usual, is the worst enemy of the Snowy Owl. Great numbers of these magnificent owls are killed as trophies by hunters while the birds are making their southern migrations, and even in the normal northern habitat they are not entirely safe. The Eskimos still regularly seek the owl's eggs as a source of food and kill the bird itself for its meat. Trophy hunting remains the greatest threat, however. At one time it was fashionable for practically every tavern in the city of Chicago to have several mounted Snowy Owls. Many still have them.

Where natural enemies are concerned, the adult bird has little to fear, but such is not the case with eggs and nestlings. Arctic foxes and husky dogs will destroy the nests and eat the eggs of absent parent birds, although the adults can usually drive them off if their presence is detected in time. Skuas and jaegers are also a menace to eggs and young alike and usually far more successful in their depredations against Snowy Owls than are the four-legged predators. There have even been cases where a pair of jaegers will simultaneously attack an adult Snowy Owl and peck it to death. Equally, there have been cases where an adult Snowy Owl, caught in the act of stealing nestling duck hawks, has been killed by the parent falcon as it stoops and strikes the owl's head a crushing blow with its tight-fisted foot. Such occurrences are rare, however.

HUNTING METHODS AND CARRYING OF PREY

Even though much of the hunting done by *Nyctea scandiaca*, both day and night, is accomplished by simply perching on a pingaluk and waiting for prey to come within sight or hearing, the owl will sometimes hunt lemmings by ranging back and forth on the wing, much in the manner of the marsh hawk, relatively low to the ground, occasionally hovering and then plunging swiftly downward with outstretched talons when prey is detected. The owl has also been known to watch hunters from a distance, and when a grouse or ptarmigan is downed by a shot, to fly in swiftly, snatch up the bird and carry it away before the hunters can reach it. Al-

There is a considerable difference in the markings between male and female Snowy Owls (*Nyctea scandiaca*). The male bird (left) is normally much less heavily marked and may be completely white at times. The female (right) and immature birds tend to have considerably more extensive markings and may tend to look light gray rather than white, especially from a distance.

Snowy Owl

♂

♀

K.E.K.

Female tends to
have more barred
Plumage

though it is neither agile enough nor swift enough to pursue and catch a bird like the ptarmigan on the wing (though on rare occasions this does occur), once it flushes such a bird it almost always catches it eventually. When the prey bird flushes, the owl watches it carefully until it alights, then flies quickly to the spot and puts it to flight again. Over and over this act is repeated until the ptarmigan becomes too weary to flush any more, at which time the owl launches its attack.

Often the Snowy Owl will keep a regular watch on the snares set by Indians for snowshoe hares. Its struggles to get the captive animal out will usually destroy the snare. Similarly, fur bearers caught in steel traps are quickly killed by the owl in a fierce attack. Even when the trapped animal is, for example, an Arctic fox, the owl will make repeated attacks on the animal's head while itself staying out of range. As the fox weakens, the attacks become bolder and even more savage until finally the fox is killed, usually by the talons penetrating the brain.

In its normal hunting method of perching on a pingaluk, where it sits quietly for hours watching and listening, the slightest sound will cause the head to snap and lock the gaze on the exact spot the sound came from, and at once the attack is launched. Sometimes the owl acts strangely lazy in its hunting methods. It will perch on a pingaluk and watch a mouse or lemming approach. As long as the little animal is heading in its direction the owl will remain still. As the animal gets closer to the edge of the mound the owl will leap at it, scarcely using its wings, and pursue it with comical hops and runs until it snatches the animal by one foot. At that point the owl may fly off with it, but most often it is simply transferred to the beak and swallowed whole. Ground squirrels are caught in the same manner, except that the owl will use its wings more.

When attacking a larger animal, such as a fully grown hare, the owl lands on the fleeing animal's back with the talons of one or both feet outstretched. As the feet make contact, the talons drive inward through the flesh. If the owl still has one foot free, it may use it as an anchor to help stop the plunging of the hare. At the same time it will flap its wings with reverse strokes to stop the hare's forward progress and, as soon as the animal is exhausted and stops, the owl breaks its neck with a savage bite at the nape.

Nyctea scandiaca quite often fishes as well as hunts. When fishing it will lie on a rock with its body parallel to the water's edge, head held very low but facing the water. The eyes are very nearly closed and the bird seems to be asleep, but it is watching carefully. As a fish rises close by, the leg of the owl which is closest to the water darts out with amazing speed and the talons close on the fish, dragging it flopping from the water. The owl will also fish this way through holes in the ice.

Most smaller prey, if not devoured on the spot, is carried away by the owl in the beak. For larger prey the feet are put to use and the ability of the bird to fly long distances while carrying creatures weighing far more than itself is little short of incredible. Snowy Owls have been known to fly with ease while carrying below them in the talons a full-grown hen twice their own weight or a hare weighing half again as much as the owl. Once one was seen carrying a half-grown emperor goose which it had evidently killed.

FOOD, FEEDING HABITS, WASTES

Although lemmings and mice are eaten in abundance, a wide variety of other mammals and birds make up the diet of the Snowy Owl. It is probably one of the most destructive of North American owl species to birds, especially waterfowl, game birds, and poultry. Among the mammals, this owl has been known to kill and eat mice of many varieties, lemmings, rats, moles, ground squirrels, prairie dogs, Arctic hares, snowshoe hares, cottontail rabbits, muskrats, woodchucks, entrapped foxes, squirrels, and jack rabbits.

Birds known to have been killed and eaten include ring-necked pheasants, domestic chickens, ducks, pigeons, and guinea fowl; curlews, plovers, snipe, young geese, coots, sage grouse, ruffed grouse, mourning doves, old squaw ducks, mallards, longspurs, buntings, grebes, crows, Short-eared Owls, Long-eared Owls, Screech Owls, fledgling gyrfalcons, and duck hawks; ptarmigans, ravens, quail; and other varieties of shorebirds, songbirds, upland game birds, waterfowl, and gulls.

Fish and small marine animals of almost any type that the owl can catch will be taken readily, and the Snowy Owl is known to seek out and devour carrion, meat scraps, fish refuse, and animal matter of almost any kind, fresh or not.

All prey up to the size of a small rabbit is swallowed whole. Prey larger than this is torn apart to be swallowed in enormous chunks. A full-grown snowshoe hare may be devoured in as few as five or six huge swallowings. Often the facial disks and breast plumage of the bird are badly bloodstained from tearing apart large prey. This is particularly true of the female who, during the nesting season, does most of the feeding of the young, ripping up the prey brought by the male and feeding chunks of it (without bones, fur, or feathers) to the hatchling owls.

In swallowing prey whole, the owl mouths it a few times, turning it around usually to a headfirst position, then throws its own head back and swallows the prey in convulsive gulpings. Often the bird will gape widely several times after swallowing, as if clearing its mouth and throat of residue.

COURTSHIP AND MATING

Beginning about mid-May, the unmated male begins actively seeking a female, often flying long meandering distances among the tundra pingaluks as he searches. Occasionally he voices his booming call as he flies and if a receptive female is within hearing, she will usually reply. At once the big white bird flies to where she is and alights within a few feet of her. Here he bows in a rather courtly way, fluffs his feathers, struts about a bit (sometimes dragging his wing tips as he does so), and pausing often to issue his great throat-swelling hoots. Courtship is brief and copulation is not prolonged, normally occurring on the pingaluk where the owls met. It is repeated numerous times for about a week. It is believed that the birds, once mated, remain mated for life, since pairs of the birds remain more or less in company the year around, even during migrations. The same pair will also return to the same pingaluk to nest year after year if not disturbed.

ANNUAL BROODS, NEST, NESTING HABITS

Snowy Owls are single-brooded and will rarely lay a second clutch of eggs if the first is destroyed. Nesting is almost invariably done in a shallow depression atop a pingaluk. This depression may be lined with scattered feathers and a few grasses or bits of moss, but more often than not there is no real attempt at nest-building. There are cases on record where the Snowy Owl has used the abandoned nest of an eagle high in a tree, but this happens so infrequently that mention is made of it only as a matter of curiosity. Sometimes eggs are laid on a gravel bank, on a tidal flat, or on the slopes above a salt-water marsh or lake. At times the eggs are laid on a bare, flat outcrop of rock which has a small depression that will prevent the eggs from rolling. Such nests often get water in them, so that the eggs may be sitting in as much as half an inch of icy water, yet this seems to have little effect on their hatching. The earlier layings of eggs are often covered by late snowfalls, but this too seems to have no deterrent effect on the hatching of the owls. On the whole, the Snowy Owl is a messy nester, regurgitating pellets, defecating, and scattering prey refuse in and around the nest with abandon.

EGGS

Number per nesting As few as three eggs may be laid, but normally there are not fewer than five. Equally, while as many as thirteen have been laid, it is unusual that there are more than ten. The average clutch is from seven to ten eggs.

Color Pure white to rich creamy white, but invariably badly nest-soiled.

Shape Rather more elongated than those of most other owls of this continent. They are generally an oblate oval.

Texture Quite roughly granulated in shell texture and without glossiness. A peculiarity exists in that about seven out of every ten Snowy Owl eggs will bear a few raised corrugations which begin close to the center of the shell and converge at the longer axis. What significance this may have is not yet known.

Size The eggs of *Nyctea scandiaca* are the largest of all owl eggs in North America. Based on the measurements of 59 eggs, they average 59.5 mm. (2.3") in length and 45.5 mm. (1.8") in width, with extreme measurements of:

Maximum length:	60.5 mm.	(2.4")
Minimum length:	47.8 mm.	(1.9")
Maximum width:	50.6 mm.	(2.0")
Minimum width:	41.6 mm.	(1.6")

Interval of egg-laying The average duration between eggs is 41 hours, but this varies considerably, and eggs may be laid as close together as several hours, or as far apart as one week. As a rule, the last egg to be laid is deposited from 15 to 16 days after the rest.

Egg-laying dates Arctic Alaska: earliest, May 28; latest July 6; normally between June 8 and June 25.

Arctic Canada: earliest, May 19; latest, June 30; normally between June 13 and June 23.

INCUBATION AND BROODING CHARACTERISTICS

Incubation is said to begin with the first egg laid, but some authorities hold that it does not commence until the third egg appears. Term of incubation is also a matter of some dispute, with claims made of as short a duration as 28 days, or as long as 39 days. Most authorities now cite the figures of 32 or 33 days. There is said to be some inadvertent brooding of the later eggs by the heavily downed nestlings, the oldest of which may be two weeks old before the last egg hatches. For the most part, incubation is strictly by the female, while the male provides food for her and takes care of most of the defense of the family.

YOUNG AND FAMILY LIFE CHARACTERISTICS

The newly hatched young are downy white and so weak they can scarcely raise their heads, and then only for brief periods. However, they gain strength with the first feeding and by the end of the third day are able to sit relatively erect. At this early age, as soon as they can use their stubby wings to push along the ground and aid their feet in moving them, they tend to wander. Many will fall off the pingaluk and perish from exposure. The mortality rate among young birds from this cause alone may run as high as three or even four birds for each clutch of eight or nine eggs laid.

The babies are clad in their white down for about nine days, at which time the down begins to be pushed out by the appearance of a long, fluffy, deep sooty-gray down. It is particularly long on the sides, flanks, and thighs. The natal down remains on the tips of this sooty

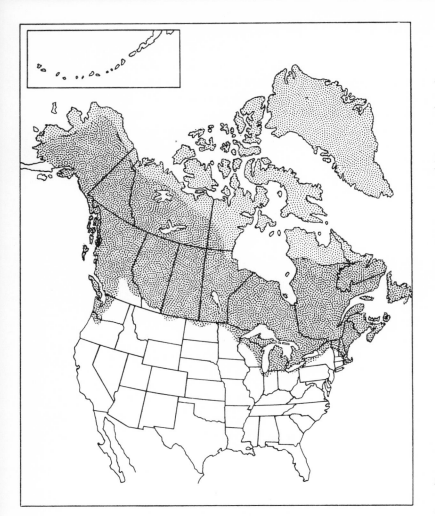

SNOWY OWL

Nyctea scandiaca (Linnaeus)

down until finally worn off by the movements of the babies, but even before it is completely worn away, the first-winter plumage begins emerging—apparent first at the wrist of the wing and around the eyes, then followed by the wing quills and a general spread of new body plumage. The sooty plumage, however, is not lost; it remains beneath the first-winter plumage until the following summer when it finally disappears with the first postnuptial molt. The young birds are fully fledged in the first-winter plumage by the end of the seventh week after hatching. The family tends to remain loosely together during the remainder of summer, but the young wander off on their own with the coming of autumn.

DISTRIBUTION IN NORTH AMERICA

Circumpolar in its Arctic distribution, *Nyctea scandiaca* in North America breeds from northern Alaska (Point Hope, Barrow), Yukon (Herschel Island), Melville Island, northern Devon Island (Grinnell Peninsula), northern Ellesmere Island (Fort Conger), and northernmost Greenland (Peary Land), southward to Hall Island, Bering Sea, the coastal area of western Alaska to Hooper Bay, across northern Alaska, northern Northwest Territories, northeastern Manitoba (Chur-

chill), northern Quebec (Fort Chimo), northern Labrador (Okak), and northern Greenland (south to Humboldt Glacier on the west and Scoresby Sound on the east).

Irregular winter migrant to northern Alaska, Saskatchewan, North Dakota, Minnesota, Ontario, New York, southern Quebec, southern Labrador, and Newfoundland.

Occasionally migrates as far south as southern California (Los Angeles County), Nevada (Clark County), Utah (Provo), Colorado (Denver), Oklahoma, central Texas (Austin), Missouri, Louisiana, Tennessee, Georgia, South Carolina.

Casual in Bermuda.

MIGRATION

Sometimes the migration of the Snowy Owl is very extensive and far-reaching, but mostly it is negligible or even absent. Migration is extremely cyclic and predicated upon availability or nonavailability of prey. The normal cycle is once about every four years, but this does not always hold true. The migrations have been as much as eight years apart. Sometimes there will be migrations two years in succession, although as a rule when this occurs, the second migration is made by considerably fewer birds. In some years so many of the white owls descend into the northern tier of states that they create newspaper headlines. Occasionally they will summer far south of their normal breeding range, but this usually follows a heavy southward migration the preceding winter. Migrating birds anywhere near the ocean will usually follow the coastlines southward. Some will wander far out to sea, and often they have landed on ships 300 miles or more from land. It is believed that a certain number are lost at sea when they become confused in heavy fog.

ECONOMIC INFLUENCE

Indisputably, the Snowy Owl does considerable damage to game bird populations in the far north and sometimes causes extensive economic losses to professional trappers because of the trap-robbing proclivities of the bird. Equally, heavy damages may sometimes be incurred by poultry raisers along the migrational routes of the big bird of prey. These bad features, however, are rather well offset by the enormous amount of good the owl does in reducing populations of lemmings, mice, and rats throughout its range. The bird also continues to serve a useful purpose to the Indians of the North who still rely on its flesh and eggs for food. Esthetically, it is a truly beautiful bird which it is a shame to destroy. In most areas of North America, it is now a protected species.

SPECIES

ORDER: STRIGIFORMES

FAMILY: STRIGIDAE

GENUS: *Surnia* Dumeril

SPECIES: *ulula* (Linnaeus)

SUBSPECIES

caparoch (Muller) AMERICAN HAWK OWL

AMERICAN HAWK OWL

(COLOR PLATE XLI)

SCIENTIFIC NAME AND ORIGINAL DESCRIPTION

Surnia ulula caparoch (Muller). Original description: *Strix caparoch* P. L. S. Muller, *Natursystema*, Supplement, 1776, page 69; based on the Little Hawk Owl of Edwards, *Natural History of Birds*, Part 2, page 62, plate 62; from a specimen of the Hudson Bay area. Former scientific names: *Strix caparoch, Strix funerea, Strix hudsonica, Strix canadensis, Strix ulula hudsonica.*

OTHER NAMES

CANADIAN OWL Because of general geographic location.

DAY OWL After its normally diurnal habits.

FALCON OWL For the superficial resemblance to a falcon.

HAWK OWL Without specific geographical location name.

HUDSONIAN OWL After its life-zone range.

LA CHOUETTE ÉPERVIÈRE D'AMÉRIQUE French-Canadian name meaning "The Sparrow Hawk Owl of America."

STUB OWL After its predilection for roosting on bare stubs, especially at the very top of a tree.

DISTINGUISHING FEATURES

The most hawklike owl in general appearance and habits in North America, *Surnia ulula caparoch* is a medium-sized, slender bird which bears quite a remarkable resemblance to the sparrow hawk both in flight and at rest, although it is a good bit larger. A neat, rather streamlined owl with small head, tight plumage, and long tail, it rarely sits erect like most owls but tends to sit in a hawklike pose, intent and alert. It somehow gives the impression of being formally and impeccably dressed. It also lacks the vague or sometimes vacant expression adopted by many owls. Breast and belly are distinctly, neatly, and regularly barred, as is the tail.

Rank in over-all size among the eighteen species: Ninth.

SHAPE AT REST

Decidedly falconlike in aspect, the American Hawk Owl has no ear tufts, a very small head for an owl, a long tail held at an angle to the body rather than straight downward when the bird is perched. Even its habit of perching adds to the hawklike similarity, since it likes to sit in bright daylight atop the uppermost dead stub of a pine or other conifer, as hawks do. It frequently flicks its tail when perched and lacks the sedate nature of most perched owls. The tail jerking is not in a regular cadence but performed in what seems to be a rather absentminded manner; it is raised rather jerkily and then slowly lowered, and most often held at a distinct angle to the body.

SHAPE IN FLIGHT

Here the similarity to a hawk continues, since its outspread wings have tips that are rather pointed and its tail in flight is decidedly wedge-shaped. In flight silhouette it resembles most an overgrown sparrow hawk, or a prairie falcon.

FLIGHT PATTERN

The wingbeat is quite suggestive of that of a falcon, with rapid and somewhat erratic strokes, and the line of flight is with a straight-line directness. Although occasionally it will hover like a sparrow hawk, in normal flight the wings beat almost ceaselessly and there is little gliding. When leaving its perch high atop a conifer stub, it throws itself forward and down, drops swiftly nearly to ground level and then skims along rapidly only a few feet above the ground until it nears its next perch, at which time it rises in a smooth, graceful arc which carries it to the leafless stub-top of another conifer. Its flight when hunting through dense woodland is much like that of the sharp-shinned hawk, with a highly developed maneuverability. The flight is always quite strong and direct, rarely meandering even when it is skimming low over the borders of bogs or meadows as it hunts.

Measurements have been based on 28 birds measured: 19 males and 9 females.

WEIGHT

Species average: 238.6 gr. (8.4 oz.).

	Male	Female
Average	225.6 gr. (7.9 oz.)	251.6 gr. (8.8 oz.)
Minimum	194.1 gr. (6.8 oz.)	202.3 gr. (7.1 oz.)
Maximum	265.8 gr. (9.3 oz.)	273.5 gr. (9.6 oz.)

Rank in weight among the eighteen species: Ninth.

TOTAL LENGTH

Species average: 427.8 mm. (16.9").

	Male	Female
Average	423.2 mm. (16.7")	432.3 mm. (17.0")
Minimum	363.5 mm. (14.3")	401.2 mm. (15.8")
Maximum	424.0 mm. (16.7")	446.7 mm. (17.6")

Rank in total length among the eighteen species: Seventh.

WINGSPAN

Species average: 838.5 mm. (33.0").

	Male	Female
Average	835.9 mm. (32.9")	841.0 mm. (33.1")
Minimum	777.5 mm. (30.6")	833.3 mm. (32.8")
Maximum	859.5 mm. (33.9")	891.8 mm. (35.1")

Rank in wingspan among the eighteen species: Ninth.

INDIVIDUAL WING LENGTH

Species average: 222.9 mm. (8.8").

	Male	Female
Average	218.4 mm. (8.6")	227.3 mm. (9.0")
Minimum	212.7 mm. (8.4")	213.6 mm. (8.4")
Maximum	224.5 mm. (8.9")	229.7 mm. (9.1")

Rank in wing length among the eighteen species: Ninth.

TAIL LENGTH

Species average: 178.3 mm. (7.0").

	Male	Female
Average	177.9 mm. (7.0")	178.6 mm. (7.0")
Minimum	173.0 mm. (6.8")	175.5 mm. (6.9")
Maximum	180.4 mm. (7.1")	184.8 mm. (7.3")

Rank in tail length among the eighteen species: Seventh.

BEAK LENGTH

Species average: 19.4 mm. (0.8").

	Male	Female
Average	19.2 mm. (0.8")	19.5 mm. (0.8")
Minimum	18.2 mm. (0.7")	18.3 mm. (0.7")
Maximum	20.0 mm. (0.8")	20.1 mm. (0.8")

Rank in beak length among the eighteen species: Eighth.

LEGS, FEET, TALONS

The legs and feet of the American Hawk Owl are quite fully feathered, though the plumage of the feet is quite close, even though thick. The legs are comparatively short, with the tarsus not quite equaling the length of the middle toe. Talons are not quite as distinctly curved as in most owls and are of an almost uniform coloration of deep slate gray.

EYES AND VISION

The irides are clear lemon yellow in most birds, but with some specimens having a vague suggestion of orange in the iris coloration. The eyes are slightly smaller than one might expect for an owl of this size, which is another factor lending to the over-all impression of the hawklike characteristic in this bird. Vision, especially in the daytime and at twilight, is excellent. It is not, however, as good at night as that of most of the other North American owls. Very likely, vision plays an even more important part in the American Hawk Owl's hunting than does hearing.

AMERICAN HAWK OWL FIELD STUDIES

For ten days, as the artist has observed, the American Hawk Owl pictured here fed on lemmings and red squirrels near Mud Lake, Labrador, during the autumn of 1953. The owl was finally captured by one foot, in a steel trap baited with meat and set atop a pole about eight feet high.

American Hawk Owl

Hawk owl
S. ulula

Goose bay,
Labrador,
1952.

eyes smallish

this bird was feeding
on lemmings and
red squirrels, The
artist watched the bird
for 10 days until one
of the mud Lake Indians
pole-trapped and killed
the bird, and fed it to
a dog.

feet small
Legs Longish

studies made
in field,
mud Lake, Labrador,
1953.

tail very long when bird is at
rest.

Tail
Long

Luk
1953

EARS AND HEARING

Although the hearing of *Surnia ulula caparoch* is good, it lacks much of the extreme acuteness of the auditory sense possessed by the other North American owls. The ear cavities are not covered by an operculum (ear flap) as in other owls, and the ear cavities themselves are no larger than in any other bird of similar size; neither are the cavities particularly asymmetrical in size or placement. This owl is sensitive to the faint sounds made by prey, but it is not so remarkably adept at pinpointing the exact sound location as other owls.

EAR TUFTS, PLUMAGE, ANNUAL MOLT

There are no ear tufts, the head being small, rounded, and hawklike in structure. The plumage is tight, closely fitted to the body contours, and much harder than the plumage worn by the majority of other owls. The flutings on the leading edges of the flight feathers are minute and sometimes virtually absent; thus, the flight of the American Hawk Owl is not as silent as that of the more nocturnal owls, although neither is it particularly noisy. On the whole, the plumage has more the crisp, well-laid aspect of the hawk, especially on back, wings, and tail, than the general soft fluffiness of appearance in the other owls. The complete annual molt begins in late June or early July and is finished by mid-October.

VOICE

This owl has a rather wide variety of vocal utterances and, as might be expected, most of them are hawklike in quality, being harsh, high-toned, and rather screaming sounds. The most common cry is a high-pitched *tuh-WITTA-WITT tuh-WITTA-tuh-WITT tuh-WITTA-WITTA-WITTA,* which is reminiscent of a call from a soaring falcon. Another relatively common call is a whistled cadence not unlike the sparrow hawk's cry, sounding like *ILLY-ILLY-ILLY-ILLY-ILLY.* This latter call is sometimes modulated to a deeper, rolling tone not too unlike the call of the Long-eared Owl (*Asio otus wilsonianus*) and without the final uplifted inflection at the end of each note, sounding similar to a steady, not quite tremulous *ILL-ILL-ILL-ILL-OOOOOOOO,* with the last note sometimes taking two or three seconds to fade away. When on the wing, the American Hawk Owl often issues a single harsh scream not very different from that of the red-tailed hawk—*KWHEEEEEEEE!*

In addition to these more common calls, there are many variations of them as well as a wide variety of single or multiple-note calls too numerous to attempt to record here, but essentially similar to one another and universally more hawklike than owl-like in tone and delivery.

SEXUAL DIFFERENCES: SIZE, COLORATION, VOICE

The female is slightly the larger, but there is no apparent color variation nor vocal difference between the sexes.

MORTALITY AND LONGEVITY

Infant mortality among American Hawk Owls is quite low, and most nestings are completely successful. The birds have lived to ten years of age in captivity, and several banded specimens have been recovered that also survived for a decade.

COLORATION AND MARKINGS: ADULT

In general coloration, the upperparts are a very deep, rich, pure brown, well flecked with neatly aligned spottings of white. The spottings on the scapulars are particularly thick and loosely or rather irregularly arranged in rows, much smaller near the shoulder than toward the rear. White tippings on the near terminal outer web of the primaries and secondaries, and middle and greater coverts, also create about five rows of white spots, these becoming somewhat more irregularly placed on the folded wing primaries and secondaries than on the coverts, where they are quite neatly arranged. The back is pure brown, but the rump is speckled with irregular, narrow, rather broken white barrings; these becoming more regular and distinct on the uppertail coverts. The dark brown rectrices are marked with seven or eight narrow white lines on each web, but broken by the brown quill in the center. Each

---

LII NORTHWESTERN HORNED OWL

Bubo virginianus lagophonus (Oberholser). Male. Vicinity of Spokane, Spokane County, Washington, November 4, 1926. A.O.U. Number 375-I

LIII MONTANA HORNED OWL

Bubo virginianus occidentalis Stone. Female. Wind River in vicinity of Dubois, Wind River County, Wyoming, December 30, 1961. A.O.U. Number 375-J

Karl E. Karalus
1972

Karl E. Karalus

tail feather terminates in a narrow margin of dingy buff white.

Irregularly edged semicircles of deep brown black begin at the outer edge of the facial disks and encircle the imperfect facial disks to just below the middle point on each side, giving the appearance of dark sideburns. Facial disks are buffy white, becoming very dark around the eyes, especially supraorbitally, and showing some faint degree of concentric circling of deeper buff. Superciliaries and lores are white to grayish buff white, but with the dark brown of the forehead very narrowly separating them to the base of the beak.

The chin is dark brown with tiny vague pepperings of lighter brown. The gular area is an unblemished white, wide but not deep. The upper breast is very densely barred in dark brown, with the barrings becoming more widely spaced toward the lower breast and belly and the white becoming clearer, though broken in each feather by narrow central shafting of brown. Thighs, legs, and feet are tawny buff to light buff, indistinctly mottled with deeper buff.

COLORATION AND MARKINGS: JUVENILE

Plumage of young American Hawk Owls is very similar to that of the adult birds, but with considerably less spotting on the upperparts. The rectrices are more broadly terminating in white than on the adult birds, and the brown of the underparts is more a chestnut red brown than deep-umber brown black.

GENERAL HABITS AND CHARACTERISTICS

One of the most distinctive and recognizable habits of *Surnia ulula caparoch* is its proclivity to perch on the uppermost spike of a tall living fir or spruce, or on the uppermost stub or spike of any dead conifer. An extremely bold and fearless bird, it can be approached quite closely without its taking alarm and fleeing—even to the point where at times it has been

LIV PACIFIC HORNED OWL

Bubo virginianus pacificus Cassin. Female. Six miles upstream on Witch Creek from the mouth, San Diego County, California, December 5, 1906. A.O.U. Number 375-D

LV WESTERN HORNED OWL

Bubo virginianus pallescens Stone. Male. Vicinity of Skidmore, Bee County, Texas, February 27, 1910. A.O.U. Number 375-A

caught by hand. It seems to have an utter lack of fear where man is concerned, especially in the more remote portions of its range. While it is almost entirely diurnal or crepuscular in its habits, occasionally it will fly at night to a campfire and hover for long periods a dozen feet above the flames. If shot at and missed while perched on a conifer spike, it will take a short, circling flight and return to the very same perch. This may be done over and again until either the perch is struck and shattered or the bird itself is shot.

HABITAT AND ROOSTING

The American Hawk Owl shows a decided preference for more brushy, tangled areas of tamarack and swamp as well as forest fringe. It seems to like areas of dead trees as well, almost always finding the highest and most open stub, branch, or spire as its lookout perch. Burnt lands choked with scrubby second growth are also well favored. The owl likes muskeg, swamps, scrubby spruce growths, forest glades, and well-grown woodlands of mixed hardwoods and conifers, including willows, poplars, spruce, tamarack, birch, pine, and fir. When it finds a perch it especially likes, it will return there regularly, often using it for a period of years. Sometimes it will sit on such a perch for several consecutive hours. Actual roosting is done almost entirely at night, in the same type of trees but usually lower, closer to the trunk, and somewhat more hidden by foliage or branches. Rarely it will roost in a large hollow stub.

ENEMIES AND DEFENSES

Because of its almost total lack of fear of man, this graceful owl is very frequently killed by hunters who are able to approach very close and shoot the bird as it rests atop an exposed perch. Some are killed as trophies, others as "sport," or merely because they are something at which to shoot. Fortunately the bird resides in primarily uninhabited areas and so it is not particularly endangered because of this form of vulnerability.

Among natural enemies, larger owls—especially the Horned Owls (*Bubo virginianus* sp.)—frequently kill adult roosting American Hawk Owls at night. Martens, fishers, and weasels kill a certain number of fledgling birds, although the furious attack of the enraged parent bird will usually discourage any such interloper. Even a human disturbing the nest or young will be attacked without hesitation by one or both parent birds, although the male is more often the most vigorous protector. When attacking, the bird arrows in with rapid wingbeats and accurately snatches at the intruder's head with its talons as it flashes past.

The American Hawk Owl is less often bothered with fleas and bird lice than most other owls.

HUNTING METHODS AND CARRYING OF PREY

Uncommonly swift and certain in its attack, *Surnia ulula caparoch* tends to range through brushy cover much in the manner of the Cooper's hawk or the sharp-shinned hawk, with spectacular exhibitions of maneuverability as it dodges obstructions in its path. Almost all hunting is done in the daytime and especially in the morning until about nine o'clock, and again in the afternoon from about three o'clock until sunset.

While hunting is often done in the ranging method described above, more often this owl prefers to sit high on one of its favored perches and watch with great intensity for the movement of prey below. When prey is seen, the bird drops from its perch and bullets to the spot, nailing the animal with outstretched talons if it is large or, with smaller prey, snatching it up and carrying it back to the perch without pause. Rarely does it miss in its attack. Not uncommonly it will streak in and speed away with snipe or woodcock that have been downed by hunters.

When it is ranging over plains, muskeg areas, and blueberry barrens, its hunting techniques are closely emulative of the sparrow hawk. Prey is almost never carried in the beak. The grip of the talons is quite strong, and this owl can lift and carry with ease prey weighing several times its own weight. On numerous occasions American Hawk Owls have been seen flying rapidly and well while carrying in their talons full-grown ruffed grouse much larger than themselves. Although it rarely kills and eats small birds, those that are taken are often caught on the wing.

FOOD, FEEDING HABITS, WASTES

In summer, the diet of *Surnia ulula caparoch* consists primarily of lemmings, mice, rats, ground squirrels, chipmunks, and rabbits, along with lesser numbers of squirrels, hares, weasels, and insects. In winter the ptarmigan is the most important prey, along with sharp-tailed grouse, snowshoe hares, and mice, and in the more southerly parts of its range, cottontail rabbits. A less ravenous eater than most owls, it generally does not swallow whole any prey larger than a mouse. Bigger prey, and often even the small prey, is eaten piecemeal, much in the manner of a hawk eating its

prey, but with more swallowing of undigestibles. Pellets are relatively small, grayish in color, coated with mucus, and regurgitated easily. Fecal wastes are more liquid than viscous and rather dark chalky in color. They are usually expelled as the bird leaves its perch.

COURTSHIP AND MATING

Despite the fact that the American Hawk Owl is primarily diurnal and easily observable, strangely little has been recorded about its courtship or mating habits. The male does become quite vociferous as courtship begins, usually about mid-March, but sometimes as early as February. His mating call is a high-pitched, rather melodious trilling whistle followed by a distinctly uttered musical series of two-syllable notes followed closely by a single note at almost the same tonal level, sounding like: *WITTA-TIT WITTA-TIT WITTA-TIT WITTA-TIT*. It may also, especially late in the day, give voice to a much more gentle and owl-like call similar to: *WHUT-TU-TU-OOO-ooo-ooo*.

ANNUAL BROODS, NEST, NESTING HABITS

Again unlike most other owls, the American Hawk Owl more often than not will construct its own nest; usually a rather poorly built affair of interlocked twigs lined with a few grasses, bits of moss, and much plumage from the breast of the female bird, and located sometimes in a low crotch of a living tree or, more often, in the hollow stub or a crotch of a dead tree about ten or twelve feet above the ground. Only on rare occasions will it use an abandoned nest of a hawk or crow as its own, though more often it will nest in an old pileated woodpecker hole or natural hollow, usually in a dead tree.

This owl shows a marked preference for the hollow end of a broken-off dead tree leaning at an angle of about 45°, with the top of the stub about eight to fifteen feet above ground. Occasionally it will even nest in a hollow stump within four or five feet of the ground. The female bird will often pluck her lower breast nearly bare, line the nest with the feathers, and incubate the eggs against her bare skin. In all cases, the American Hawk Owl is single-brooded.

A variety of field sketches made near Goose Bay, Labrador, of the American Hawk Owl (*Surnia ulula caparoch*). Note the unusually long tail which, especially in profile, gives this owl the aspect of a kestrel. The sketch at upper left was from a specimen skin in the Field Museum of Natural History in Chicago.

American Hawk Owl

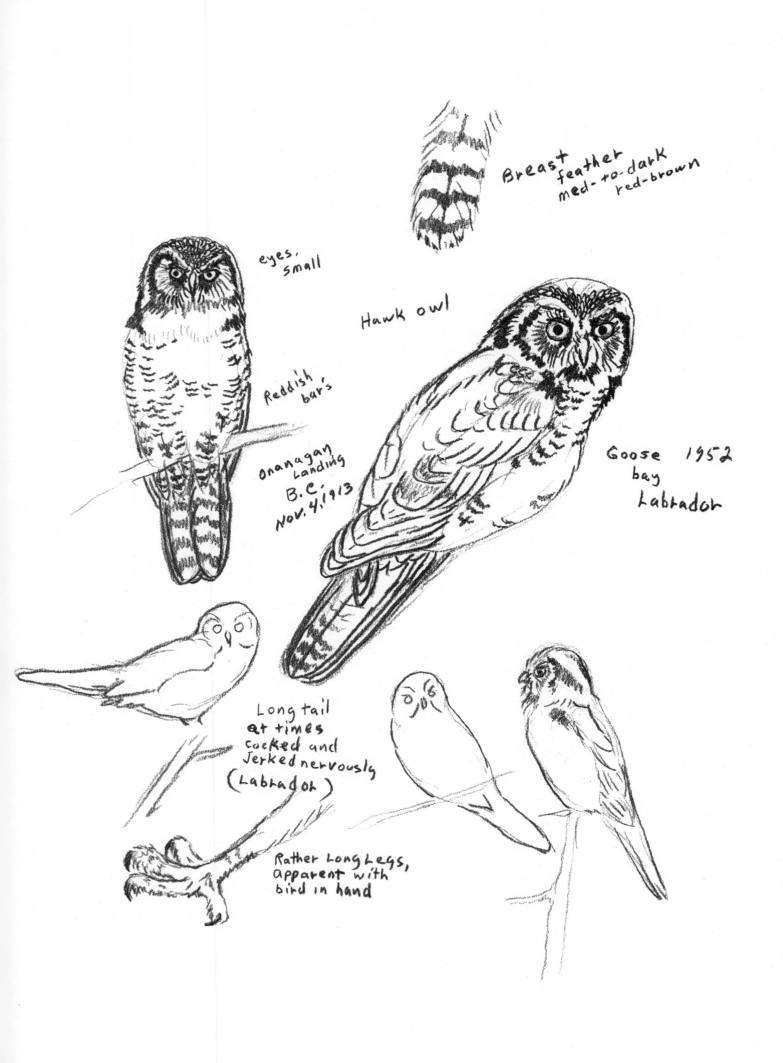

Breast feather
med-to-dark red-brown

eyes, small

Hawk owl

Reddish bars

onanagan Landing
B.C.
Nov. 4, 1913

Goose 1952
bay
Labrador

Long tail at times cocked and Jerked nervously
(Labrador)

Rather Long Legs, apparent with bird in hand

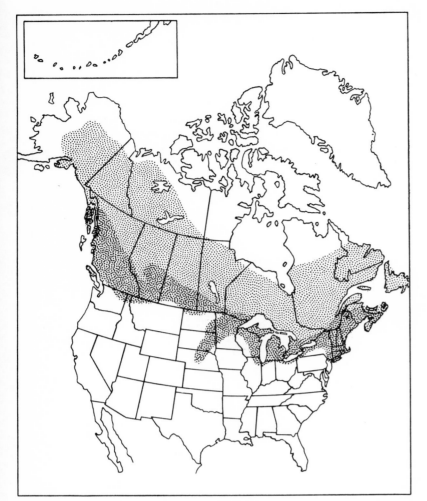

AMERICAN HAWK OWL

Surnia ulula caparoch (Muller)

EGGS

Number per nesting As few as two eggs (but very rarely only two eggs) and as many as nine, but usually between four and eight, and at most five or six.

Color Pure unblemished white. Infrequently the eggs may have a vague yellowish tinge.

Shape Rather variable; sometimes an oblate globe, sometimes distinctly oval; less often an elongated oval.

Texture Very smooth without trace of granulation, but with only a slight gloss.

Size From 56 eggs measured, the average length was 39.3 mm. (1.5″) and the average width was 31.5 mm. (1.2″).

Extreme measurements included:

Maximum length:	43.9 mm.	(1.7″)
Minimum length:	34.3 mm.	(1.4″)
Maximum width:	36.6 mm.	(1.4″)
Minimum width:	30.3 mm.	(1.2″)

Interval of egg-laying Not positively known, but believed to be no less than 24 hours apart and probably closer to twice that duration.

Egg-laying dates Northern Areas (Alaska and Arc-tic Canada): earliest, April 25; latest, June 26; normally between May 4 and May 18.

Southern Areas (Alberta and central to southern Canada): earliest, March 22; latest, June 22; normally between March 30 and June 5.

Eastern Areas (Labrador and Newfoundland): earliest, April 21; latest June 30; normally between May 9 and June 11.

INCUBATION AND BROODING CHARACTERISTICS

Mainly, incubation is taken care of by the female while the male bird brings food and defends against intruders. Incubation is believed to begin with the first egg to be laid and has a duration of 25 days.

YOUNG AND FAMILY LIFE CHARACTERISTICS

Newly hatched American Hawk Owls are very downy and their eyes are sealed. Almost immediately after hatching they begin issuing an irritated wheezing hiss and high-pitched little whistlings. These sounds can be heard quite distinctly by someone standing as far as 20 or 30 feet away from the base of the nest tree. They are uttered almost continuously during the day-time for the first week but then begin to slacken, although the wheedling nature of the cries continues even as the birds have reached fledgling size. An angry fledgling will issue a brittle cackle followed by a star-tlingly loud hissing and some beak snapping.

Before the nestlings are fully grown—about late June or early July—the wings and tail are well developed and similar to an adult's as the first-winter plumage begins to sprout on back and sides. The last of the downy plumage to be replaced by first-winter plumage is the grayish-drab plumage of the crown.

Family groups tend to remain together until the following early spring when the parent birds begin nesting activities again.

DISTRIBUTION IN NORTH AMERICA

Breeds from northern Alaska (Jade Mountains, Coldfoot), Yukon (La Pierre House), northwestern and central Mackenzie (Good Hope, Lake Hardisty), northern Saskatchewan (Fond du Lac), northern Manitoba, northern Quebec (Whale River, Fort Chimo), Labrador (Okak), and Newfoundland, southward to northern British Columbia (Atlin), central Alberta (Jasper, Glenevis), east-central Saskatchewan (Hudson Bay Junction), northern Michigan (Isle Royale), central Ontario (Lake Temiskaming), southern Quebec (Lochaber), and New Brunswick (Tabusintac). Casual in summer in Idaho (Stanley Butte) and Montana (Summit, Madison River).

Winters southward to southern Canada and northern United States; casually to Washington (Martin), northwestern Montana, northeastern North Dakota (Grafton), Nebraska (Raymond), Minnesota, Wisconsin (Lake Koshkonong), Illinois (Chicago), southern Michigan (Port Huron), northern Ohio, western New York (Conquest), and New Jersey (Mercer County), and New England.

Accidental in Scotland and England.

MIGRATION

Surnia ulula caparoch is not regularly migratory in its habits, but during especially severe winters or when a great scarcity of prey occurs, it gradually moves much farther southward than its normal breeding range.

ECONOMIC INFLUENCE

Wintertime feeding on ptarmigan and grouse is offset more than sufficiently by its summertime feeding on rodents and insects. Since most of the bird's range is in largely uninhabited area or in areas of grain production where rodents are a distinct economic threat, the bird's economic influence is either immaterial or leaning toward the beneficial side.

SPECIES

ORDER: STRIGIFORMES

FAMILY: STRIGIDAE

GENUS: *Glaucidium* Boie

SPECIES: *gnoma* Wagler

SUBSPECIES

---

pinacola Nelson   ROCKY MOUNTAIN PYGMY OWL

californicum Sclater   CALIFORNIA PYGMY OWL

gnoma Wagler   ARIZONA PYGMY OWL

grinnelli Ridgway   COAST PYGMY OWL

swarthi Grinnell   VANCOUVER PYGMY OWL

ROCKY MOUNTAIN PYGMY OWL
(COLOR PLATE XLII)

SCIENTIFIC NAME AND ORIGINAL DESCRIPTION

Glaucidium gnoma pinacola Nelson. Original description: *Glaucidium gnoma pinacola* Nelson, *Proceedings of the Biological Society of Washington,* Volume 23, June 24, 1910, page 103; based on a specimen from Alma, New Mexico.

OTHER NAMES

PYGMY OWL   Without specific geographical significance.

MOUNTAIN PYGMY OWL   After the type of terrain inhabited.

DISTINCTIVE FEATURES

Next to the Elf Owl (*Micrathene whitneyi* sp.), the Pygmy Owl (*Glaucidium gnoma* sp.) is the smallest owl in North America, but considerably unlike the Elf Owl in many aspects of its natural history. The Pygmy Owl is a pert little bird, scarcely as large as a bluebird, with an alert, intelligent expression, a long tail normally held at a distinct angle to the body, and a generally excitable attitude. Despite its diminutive size, this is one of the boldest, most aggressive, and fierce of North American owls. The Rocky Mountain Pygmy Owl is the easternmost race of the five Pygmy Owl subspecies north of Mexico, and it is generally much lighter in coloration than the more westerly forms.

Rank in over-all size among the eighteen species: Seventeenth.

SHAPE AT REST

The Pygmy Owl is quite distinguishable from the only slightly smaller Elf Owl, in that its tail is held at such an expressive angle when the bird is perched and tends to twitch and flick when the bird becomes excited. The wings, too, are often flicked open briefly at such times. This bird is rarely recognized as an owl, even when seen by good observers, since it is primarily a day flier and swiftly whisks out of heavy cover upon being disturbed and disappears rapidly from view. Much smaller than a robin, it has perching habits quite similar to those of the considerably larger American Hawk Owl (*Surnia ulula caparoch*). Like that bird, it enjoys sitting high atop the uppermost spire of a conifer or dead tree. The perching movements of its round, tuftless head are very quick and constant.

SHAPE IN FLIGHT

The rounded wing tips become very noticeable, but at twilight, when it is merely silhouetted against the sky, it is most often mistaken for a bat. It is not a silent flier. Much like the American Hawk Owl, it leaves its lofty perch with a swift plummeting action, leveling off just above the ground and skimming along with unusually rapid wingbeats, only to rise in a sweeping curve to settle on the next suitable treetop. Its flight has been compared to that of the sparrow hawk and the shrike, but it is probably a little less direct in its flight than the former and a little less undulative than the latter.

Measurements have been based on 18 birds measured: 8 males and 10 females.

WEIGHT

Species average: 42.8 gr. (1.5 oz.).

	Male	Female
Average	40.8 gr. (1.4 oz.)	44.8 gr. (1.6 oz.)
Minimum	34.6 gr. (1.2 oz.)	36.9 gr. (1.3 oz.)
Maximum	46.8 gr. (1.6 oz.)	50.7 gr. (1.8 oz.)

Rank in weight among the eighteen species: Seventeenth.

TOTAL LENGTH

Species average: 175.2 mm. (6.9 oz.).

	Male	Female
Average	165.5 mm. (6.5″)	184.9 mm. (7.3″)
Minimum	160.0 mm. (6.3″)	181.3 mm. (7.1″)
Maximum	174.1 mm. (6.9″)	190.6 mm. (7.5″)

Rank in total length among the eighteen species: Fifteenth.

WINGSPAN

Species average: 382.0 mm. (15.1″).

	Male	Female
Average	377.7 mm. (14.9″)	386.3 mm. (15.2″)
Minimum	368.4 mm. (14.5″)	381.1 mm. (15.0″)
Maximum	379.0 mm. (14.9″)	400.9 mm. (15.8″)

Rank in wingspan among the eighteen species: Seventeenth.

INDIVIDUAL WING LENGTH

Species average: 101.2 mm. (4.0″).

	Male	Female
Average	100.9 mm. (4.0″)	101.5 mm. (4.0″)
Minimum	99.8 mm. (3.9″)	101.3 mm. (4.0″)
Maximum	106.0 mm. (4.2″)	106.8 mm. (4.2″)

Rank in wing length among the eighteen species: Seventeenth.

TAIL LENGTH

Species average: 64.0 mm. (2.5″).

	Male	Female
Average	61.0 mm. (2.4″)	66.9 mm. (2.6″)
Minimum	58.8 mm. (2.3″)	63.6 mm. (2.5″)
Maximum	64.0 mm. (2.5″)	71.3 mm. (2.8″)

Rank in tail length among the eighteen species: Sixteenth.

BEAK LENGTH

Species average: 9.6 mm. (0.4″). The coloration of the beak varies from a dull yellowish green to a rather pale greenish yellow, but always darker at the base than at the tip.

	Male	Female
Average	9.4 mm. (0.4″)	9.8 mm. (0.4″)
Minimum	8.6 mm. (0.3″)	8.9 mm. (0.4″)
Maximum	10.1 mm. (0.4″)	10.3 mm. (0.4″)

Rank in beak length among the eighteen species: Sixteenth.

LEGS, FEET, TALONS

The legs are fully feathered, but the toes are covered only with fine bristlelike feathers and the scales showing through are usually a dull greenish yellow, not unlike the beak color, although there are times when the feet tend toward a light yellowish-brown coloration. The well-curved talons are needle sharp and horn-colored at the base, shading into a very deep slate gray, almost black, at the tips.

EYES AND VISION

Glaucidium gnoma pinacola has very keen vision in the daytime and at twilight, but not as sharp as the more nocturnal owls at night. The irides are a pale yellow.

EARS AND HEARING

The auditory sense of the Rocky Mountain Pygmy Owl is very well developed and probably more useful than vision in the location of prey, although both senses work well in concert. There is only a vague suggestion of asymmetricism to the placement and relative size of the ear cavities. This bird has been decoyed from quite considerable distances by the simulated squeak of a mouse.

EAR TUFTS, PLUMAGE, ANNUAL MOLT

This little owl has no ear tufts. The plumage is quite tight to the body contour—much more so than in most other North American owl species—but not quite as much as that of either the Barn Owl (*Tyto alba pratincola*) or the American Hawk Owl (*Surnia ulula caparoch*). There is one complete annual molt which takes about three weeks, beginning in late August or early September.

VOICE

The voice of this little owl is characterized by a strong ventriloquism, general mellowness and musicality of tone, and surprisingly far-carrying qualities. Even the softer calls can be heard for a mile, and some of the louder calls can be heard for two or three miles. As with most owls, it is more vocal in the spring and early summer than at other times of the year, though slightly more vocal in autumn than the majority of other owl species on the continent. Calls from this owl are apt to be heard at any time of the day or night, but most often in the twilight of morning or evening.

Many of the notes uttered by *Glaucidium gnoma pinacola* have a distinctly dovelike cooing quality to them, though more penetrating. The most common of these is a low trill with rolling timbre and sounding like *OOOOoooo-oooo-ooo-oo-o-o-o-o-o*.

Another sound, more distinctive to this species, is a peculiar wood-knocking sound, not too unlike that of a wooden mallet tapping on a short length of two-by-four, and making the sound of *POOOK POOOK POOK POOK POOK*, and sometimes continuing virtually without pause for hours. This, however, is one of the more ventriloquial of its calls, and it is extremely difficult to locate the bird by trying to follow the call to its source. This call is not too unlike the similar call of the Saw-whet Owl (*Aegolius acadicus acadicus*), but it is higher pitched and with a more whispered quality.

When the male brings food to the nesting female, he often gives a three-note call as he approaches the nest and takes a perch somewhere nearby. She leaves the nest immediately, flies to him, takes the food, and returns with it to the nest.

The courtship call by the male (and possibly answered in kind by the female) is a series of *PHOOOOT* sounds with mourning dove quality. Usually eight of these notes will be sounded in succession, then a slight pause, followed by three similar final notes that are a bit more extended.

A number of other odd whistlings and occasional shrill squeakings are issued by the Rocky Mountain Pygmy Owl, but these do not lend themselves to transliteration.

SEXUAL DIFFERENCES: SIZE, COLORATION, VOICE

There are more sexual differences between the male and female Rocky Mountain Pygmy Owls than is usual among most other owls. The female not only tends to be a good bit larger, her general coloration has a more reddish tone than the male's (although the markings are the same) and her voice is lower pitched and less emphatically staccato than the male's. A recent study has also indicated that for some reason not yet fully understood, males feed much more often on birds (on an annual basis) than do the females.

MORTALITY AND LONGEVITY

There are reports of some occurrence of cannibalism in the nest, but evidently of such infrequency that this cannot be rated as a significant infant-mortality factor. It is not known for certain how long this little owl can live in the wild, but a captive specimen was kept in perfect health for six years until it finally escaped. It was an adult bird when captured.

COLORATION AND MARKINGS: ADULT

The Rocky Mountain Pygmy Owl (as well as the other Pygmy Owl subspecies) has on the hindneck and nape a distinctive plumage pattern unlike that of any other owl species in North America. The illusion given by this pattern is that of two huge dark eyes rimmed with white and separated by a white beak. Evidently this serves some function as a protective device. (See Enemies and Defenses.) Other than that, this owl is dichromatic, with a gray phase and a reddish phase—and the female, as noted, more inclined to reddishness than the male. The reddish phase of *Glaucidium gnoma pinacola* has a tendency to overlap the coloration of the grayish phase of the California Pygmy Owl (*Glaucidium gnoma californicum*), but its gray phase is much more distinctly gray than is the gray phase in the California race, and the reddish phase is not as intense. In neither color phase are the colors as pronounced as they are in the Coast Pygmy Owl (*Glaucidium gnoma grinnelli*).

Generally, the underparts are white, streaked with dark brown. The sides (but not the flanks) are a lighter olive-brown speckled with buffy-white or grayish-white feathers having black tips. The upperparts are dark slaty brown in the gray phase and almost chestnut in the red phase. The tail is very dark brown, almost black, distinctly but narrowly barred with white. The crown, forehead, and sides of the head are liberally speckled with white over darker brown. Superciliaries are white and the lores slightly duskier. The facial disks are fairly dark brown, spotted in four concentric circles with white—the innermost circle usually being imperfect. The brown of the upper sides tends to stretch into narrow bars at the throat, these bars approaching each other from opposite sides but not touching, and the center of the throat area is white.

COLORATION AND MARKINGS: JUVENILE

Juvenile plumage is essentially like adult plumage except for being mainly unspotted. The top of the young bird's head is a plain, unspotted, dull gray. A few indistinct spots may be on the forehead, but nowhere else, and the plumage of upperparts and sides is entirely unspotted. The spots everywhere gradually appear as the bird grows older.

GENERAL HABITS AND CHARACTERISTICS

This is undoubtedly one of the most fierce and bloodthirsty little birds in the world for its size. Astoundingly bold and savage, it will not hesitate to attack creatures a great many times its own size. Because of its size it looks quite innocently harmless, and one expects it to have a very gentle disposition. This is a mistake. Without a moment's hesitation this little owl will hurl itself at the throat of a bird as large as fully grown quail, flickers, and doves, and sometimes even half-grown chickens, or at mammals as large as good-sized ground squirrels and full-grown rats. One was observed as it arrowed directly to the throat of a full-grown hen weighing just over six pounds, plunged its talons home and grimly held on until it had killed the bird—a fowl over 64 times its own weight. This would be equivalent to a man weighing about 200 pounds attacking an animal that weighed over six tons!

The Pygmy Owl is extremely determined and self-sufficient, dauntless almost beyond belief. It can bring real terror to the community of bird life wherever it lives. It is almost entirely diurnal. Its flight is noisy for an owl, and the whirring of its wings can easily be heard from about a dozen feet away. For these reasons, as well as the fact that the long tail and tiny size of the bird make the observer confuse it with a songbird, the Rocky Mountain Pygmy Owl is rarely recognized by the casual observer, especially since the little owl

flits away so swiftly and so well camouflages itself when it alights.

When taking a perch, the bird generally lands in a low, leafy bush and then works its way from branch to branch until reaching the top. It rarely lands right at the top where it intends to sit. If danger threatens, it becomes perfectly immobile and so well hidden in the foliage that even the sharpest-eyed observer is apt to miss it. If seen at all, it is probably when the bird perches, as it so likes to do, atop the uppermost tip of a low tree and suns itself. Although not particularly wary, it will, if disturbed, jerk its head about nervously and continuously, often turning it incredibly far around.

During the midday hours it likes to perch in deep shade, where it naps fitfully. And, just like the Eastern Screech Owl (*Otus asio naevius*), it is very fond of bathing. Rarely does a day pass that it does not take time to bathe itself thoroughly and sometimes for prolonged periods.

HABITAT AND ROOSTING

The Rocky Mountain Pygmy Owl is almost always found at elevations of between 5,000 feet and 10,000 feet within its range, especially where there are trees—from dense pine forests to open areas with well-scattered trees. It frequently hunts in meadows and over grasslands, but it likes these to be adjacent to roosting areas of forest growth. Daytime perches are more often than not well exposed, but at night when most of the actual roosting is done, it prefers perching at the outermost tips of dense conifer branches, but well hidden. Occasionally it will roost in a natural cavity or woodpecker hole in a tree.

ENEMIES AND DEFENSES

Probably no other owl—not even the Horned Owl (*Bubo virginianus* sp.)—is so thoroughly hated by small birds. At least once and often as many as a dozen times each day the Rocky Mountain Pygmy Owl will be wildly harassed by a shrieking mob of wrens, hummingbirds, titmice, orioles, juncos, blackbirds, and many others. However, because of its speed and maneuverability in flight and its well-developed ability to camouflage itself, the little owl can usually escape its tormentors easily. In addition to being able to conceal itself peculiarly well in foliage, this owl can also stretch out lengthwise on a rough branch and seem almost to merge with the bark. Jays, crows, ravens, some hawks, and larger owls are all enemies that have been known to kill the Pygmy Owl, but none is able to catch and kill the little owl with any degree of regularity. The distinctive, rather frightening illusion of a face on the hindneck of the Pygmy Owl undoubtedly helps discourage would-be attackers coming up from behind, and it must be listed as a protective device.

HUNTING METHODS AND CARRYING OF PREY

Because of its great ferocity, hardly any bird of robin size or smaller within its range is safe when the Rocky Mountain Pygmy Owl is actively hunting. Yet, this little owl, savage and destructive to bird life though it is, nevertheless kills far fewer birds annually than the California Pygmy Owl (*Glaucidium gnoma californicum*). Even many larger birds are killed by the Rocky Mountain Pygmy Owl—flickers, meadowlarks, occasional grouse. Similarly, mice, chipmunks, ground squirrels, shrews, rats, and even weasels are attacked and killed.

In hunting, *Glaucidium gnoma pinacola* sometimes arrows back and forth across the meadows in a shrike-like manner, bulleting to the attack the instant prey is seen. More often than not, though, it prefers perching on a high, isolated branch and watching carefully until prey comes into sight, then speeding to the attack with great directness and savagery. It almost always attempts to drive its talons deep into the throat of its intended prey, and once attached it is most difficult to dislodge, despite the violent thrashings of the victim. Most hunting is done in the earlier hours of the morning and from midafternoon until sunset.

Now and then insect prey will be carried in the beak, but most often any prey to be transported is carried by the feet. The little owl has unusual strength and can lift and fly with dead prey weighing two or possibly even three times as much as itself. With very heavy prey it often will take short flights, pausing frequently to rest until it has finally managed to bring the carcass to the nest tree, and then go up to the nest with the prey branch by branch.

FOOD, FEEDING HABITS, WASTES

In addition to the birds and mammals already mentioned as prey, the Rocky Mountain Pygmy Owl will kill and eat moles, bats, young rabbits, numerous insects (especially grasshoppers), and other invertebrates such as spiders, scorpions, and centipedes. It will also prey upon small snakes, lizards, toads, and frogs.

This owl is a more fastidious eater than most other owls. Not infrequently it will hold a bird it has caught against the branch with one foot and completely pluck it with its beak before beginning to eat. At times the air will be full of lightly drifting feathers as it does so. Similarly, many small mammals are stripped of fur and skin before being consumed.

The Rocky Mountain Pygmy Owl eats slowly and rather delicately, taking dainty bites and pausing often to look around casually as it feeds. Almost without exception it will eat the head of its prey first. If not hungry enough to eat all of the animal, it may hide the remainder in a hole or crotch and return for it later— or perhaps not return at all. It can and will eat twice its own weight in food daily.

Nearly always, it will take wing immediately after it feeds, discharge glistening white feces as it does so, and fly to a favored perch to doze for a while. Defecation also very often occurs if the bird is alarmed.

There is very little pellet formation in this owl, but pellets that are formed are very small and unstable, often falling apart even as they are regurgitated. They are rarely, if ever, regurgitated anywhere near the nest.

COURTSHIP AND MATING

With an owl so difficult to observe or even identify in the field, it is perhaps understandable that much information is still lacking in what we know about the courtship and mating of the species. It is known that the male and female will often snuggle close together in a shoulder-to-shoulder manner. The male has been observed passing bits of food to the female and, less frequently, she to him. When time for copulation nears, the female attracts the male with a soft little call. At such times he is usually inside a woodpecker hole, but he emerges at this inducement, after first looking out for a moment, and, repeating the same note she issued to call him, flies to her side. He snuggles his shoulder against hers for a brief while before the actual copulation begins. There is no protest whatever from the female, and following copulation they will often snuggle together some more.

ANNUAL BROODS, NEST, NESTING HABITS

Pygmy Owls are single-brooded. The Rocky Mountain subspecies ordinarily uses the abandoned hole of a hairy woodpecker or flicker as a nest, usually about 15 feet off the ground, but as low as 8 feet or as high as 24. The same nest will often be used several years in succession. Almost all nesting is done at elevations above 6,000 feet and below 9,500 feet, usually between 8,000 and 9,000 feet.

EGGS

Number per nesting Three to six eggs, but usually four.

Color Pure white to occasionally creamy white.

Shape Very nearly globular.

Texture Normally smooth, but now and again pitted with odd little pocks which look like puncture marks. The shells are normally dull, but on some occasions have a vague gloss to them.

Size Twenty-one measured eggs yielded average figures of 26.7 mm. (1.1″) in length and 23.8 mm. (0.9″) in width, and the extremes were:

Maximum length: 30.5 mm. (1.2″)
Minimum length: 24.1 mm. (1.0″)
Maximum width: 25.4 mm. (1.0″)
Minimum width: 22.6 mm. (0.9″)

Interval of egg-laying Believed to be in the vicinity of 30 hours apart.

Egg-laying dates Earliest, May 2; latest, July 4; normally between May 8 and June 24.

INCUBATION AND BROODING CHARACTERISTICS

Incubation The term of incubation is not definitely known but is believed to be about 22 days. It begins with the first or second egg laid and is carried on primarily by the female while the male procures food and guards the nest area.

ROCKY MOUNTAIN PYGMY OWL
Glaucidium gnoma pinacola Nelson

YOUNG AND FAMILY LIFE CHARACTERISTICS

At hatching, the young Rocky Mountain Pygmy Owls are practically all head and stomach and very repulsive in appearance, being naked and very weak, with their bulbous, thin-lidded eyes sealed. Within just a few days, however, they are well covered with down and their eyes are opening. From the beginning they are voracious feeders and keep their parents very busy bringing prey. The male bird in particular is extremely busy providing enough food during the early days after the young hatch and brooding is still in progress by the female. He normally brings his catch to a perch near the nest and issues a trilling, whistled call repeated three times, and the female leaves the nest hole and comes to him. She takes the food, strips it quickly of feathers or fur, and returns to the nest with it, where she tears it into little bits and feeds only digestible meat portions to the babies. A little more fastidious in nesting habits than the majority of owls, the

female will occasionally house-clean and carry away accumulated debris. At about the age of one month, the young emerge from the nesting hole and venture out onto a branch—usually with some parental coaxing—and they are fed there. At this time they are well fledged and begin flapping and strengthening their wings with little hopping flights from branch to branch. Within a few days all the young birds are flying and learning to hunt for themselves. From this point on they are not long dependent upon the parent birds. The first prey they normally catch by themselves is grasshoppers.

DISTRIBUTION IN NORTH AMERICA

Throughout the Rocky Mountains and westward, from northwestern Montana in the north to extreme eastern Washington, Oregon, and California in the west, and southward through New Mexico and into the Sierra Madre of Mexico.

MIGRATION

Essentially non-migratory, although there is a certain amount of movement from the higher elevations to the lower elevations as winter approaches.

ECONOMIC INFLUENCE

The Pygmy Owls (*Glaucidium gnoma* sp.) are probably the most destructive of small bird life of any North American owl species, but this is offset to some degree by the numerous rodents and insects devoured by the little owls each year.

CALIFORNIA PYGMY OWL
(COLOR PLATE XLIII)

SCIENTIFIC NAME AND ORIGINAL DESCRIPTION

Glaucidium gnoma californicum Sclater. Original description: *Glaucidium californicum* Sclater, *Proceedings of the Zoological Society of London,* Volume 15, Number 237 (May 26), 1857, page 4; based on a specimen from Calaveras County, California.

OTHER NAMES

LA CHOUETTE NAINE   French-Canadian name meaning "The Dwarf Owl."
LA CHOUETTE PYGMÉE DE CALIFORNIE   French-Canadian name meaning "The California Pygmy Owl."

DISTINGUISHING FEATURES

Browner in general coloration than the Rocky Mountain Pygmy Owl (*Glaucidium gnoma pinacola*) but about the same size. There are two color phases—red and gray—but with the gray phase less gray and somewhat overlapping the red-phase coloration of *Glaucidium gnoma pinacola* and the red phase much redder than that of the latter owl.

SHAPE AT REST AND IN FLIGHT

Quite similar to the Rocky Mountain Pygmy Owl except that its perching posture is a bit more erect and

the tail is shorter, so that in flight the bird has an even more pronounced batlike appearance. The tail averages about a fifth of an inch shorter than that of *Glaucidium gnoma pinacola.*

SEXUAL DIFFERENCES

More nearly alike in size and coloration than are the sexes of *Glaucidium gnoma pinacola.* The breast plumage of *Glaucidium gnoma californicum* males is slightly lighter than that of the females as a general rule.

COLORATION AND MARKINGS: ADULT

Upperparts are rusty brown to grayish brown, and the lower flanks are heavily streaked with black. The remainder of the underparts are generally a slaty buff.

GENERAL HABITS AND CHARACTERISTICS

The California Pygmy Owl has the peculiar habit, when emerging from its nest hole or roosting hole, of seeking out another bird of its own subspecies, either male or female, and chasing it; during this time, a series of wild maneuverings are engaged in by both birds. This seems to be more in the nature of a game than any kind of territorial dispute.

HABITAT AND ROOSTING

Glaucidium gnoma californicum is found from sea level to elevations of about 6,000 feet. It is not as fond of dense forest growth as the Rocky Mountain Pygmy Owl, although it does want some trees around, especially mixed, scattered hardwoods and conifers. It does not often perch for its daytime naps as much exposed as does *Glaucidium gnoma pinacola,* instead preferring quiet, shady alder thickets.

ENEMIES AND DEFENSES

Similar to those of the Rocky Mountain Pygmy Owl, but the California subspecies frequently falls prey to the California Spotted Owl (*Strix occidentalis occidentalis*) and the Northern Spotted Owl (*Strix occi-*

dentalis caurina). Every now and again an individual bird will be killed while struggling with its prey, this occurring most often with snakes and weasels.

HUNTING CHARACTERISTICS

Somewhat more aggressive as a hunter than the Rocky Mountain Pygmy Owl and a considerably more voracious feeder on small birds. It is far more adept at catching flying insects than the Rocky Mountain subspecies.

FOOD, FEEDING HABITS

Glaucidium gnoma californicum feeds on fewer mammals than does *Glaucidium gnoma pinacola,* but much more heavily on insects and birds. It is also more wasteful in its feeding habits, quite often eating only the brains of the birds it kills and the abdomens of the insects.

NEST

As a rule, the nest is located higher than that of the Rocky Mountain Pygmy Owl, averaging about 40 feet off the ground, but sometimes as high as 75 feet.

EGGS

The eggs will sometimes have a more distinctly yellowish cast than those of *Glaucidium gnoma pinacola,* but are otherwise similar in size, shape, texture, and number.

DISTRIBUTION IN NORTH AMERICA

Northern interior of British Columbia (Doch-da-on Creek, Stikine River, Driftwood River), and western Alberta southward through central and eastern Washington and Oregon (east of the lower Willamette Valley but including the upper Rogue River Valley) to the inner coastal ranges of northern California (Yolly Bolly Mountains), Sierra Nevada, and mountains of southern California (San Luis Obispo County to San Diego County); the Great Basin Ranges and Rocky Mountains from northern Idaho and western Montana through Wyoming, Utah, and western and central Colorado (Colorado Springs) to Arizona (except the

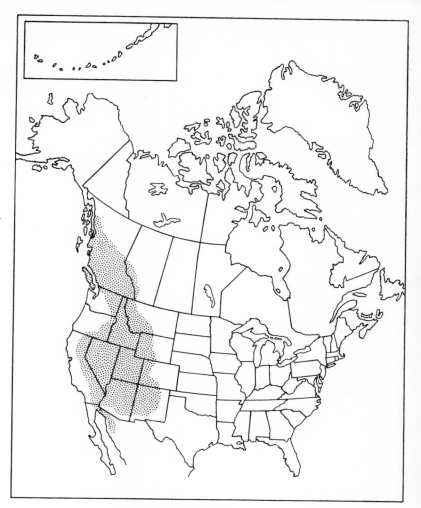

CALIFORNIA PYGMY OWL
Glaucidium gnoma californicum Sclater

southern border country) and northern Coahuila (Sierra del Carmen) in Mexico.

ARIZONA PYGMY OWL

(COLOR PLATE XLIV)

SCIENTIFIC NAME AND ORIGINAL DESCRIPTION

Glaucidium gnoma gnoma Wagler. Original description: *Glaucidium gnoma* Wagler, *Isis von Oken,* 1832, Heft 3, Column 275; based on a specimen from an undesignated locale in Mexico.

OTHER NAMES

PICAMETATE DE WAGLER Mexican-Indian name meaning "Wagler's Metate-pecker." (A metate is a curved stone for corn grinding.)

ARIZONA PYGMY OWL

Glaucidium gnoma gnoma Wagler

INDIVIDUAL WING LENGTH

Subspecies average: 81.4 mm. (3.2″)

TAIL LENGTH

Subspecies average: 58.6 mm. (2.3″).

BEAK LENGTH

Subspecies average: 7.6 mm. (0.3″).

VOICE

The Arizona Pygmy Owl has less of a repertoire than the Rocky Mountain Pygmy Owl; its voice is possibly more muted and the calling is mainly low, double-noted cooings interspersed with single notes.

HABITAT

Glaucidium gnoma gnoma, within its range, is found at elevations of from as low as 4,000 feet to as high as 13,000 feet. It dislikes desert terrain and keeps mainly to intermixed oak and pine areas on south-facing slopes. At the higher elevations it tends to frequent coniferous forests exclusively.

DISTINGUISHING FEATURES

The coloration of the Arizona Pygmy Owl is basically similar to that of the Rocky Mountain Pygmy Owl (*Glaucidium gnoma pinacola*), but in all respects *Glaucidium gnoma gnoma* is the smaller owl.

EGGS

Subspecies average: 25.2 mm. (1.0″) in length by 24.0 mm. (1.0″) in width.

WEIGHT

Subspecies average: 36.9 gr. (1.3 oz.).

DISTRIBUTION IN NORTH AMERICA

Found from extreme southern Arizona (Atasco, Parajito, Santa Rita, Huachuca, and Chiricahua Mountains) and the highlands of Mexico from Chihuahua, Nuevo León, and Tamaulipas (Galindo) southward through Nayarit and Morelos to Guerrero (Omilteme, Venta de Zopilote), and Chiapas.

TOTAL LENGTH

Subspecies average: 140.3 mm. (5.5″).

WINGSPAN

Subspecies average: 367.2 mm. (14.5″).

COAST PYGMY OWL

(COLOR PLATE XLV)

SCIENTIFIC NAME AND ORIGINAL DESCRIPTION

Glaucidium gnoma grinnelli Ridgway. Original description: *Glaucidium gnoma grinnelli* Ridgway, *U. S. National Museum Bulletin,* Number 50, Part 6, 1914, pages 781 (in key), 791; based on a specimen from the mouth of the Mad River at Humboldt Bay, California.

OTHER NAME

LA CHOUETTE PYGMÉE CÔTIERE French-Canadian name meaning "The Coast Pygmy Owl."

DISTINGUISHING FEATURES

Glaucidium gnoma grinnelli is considerably darker brown—almost a black brown—on the back and other upperparts than either *Glaucidium gnoma pinacola* or *Glaucidium gnoma gnoma,* and with the dichromatism more pronounced than in any other of the Pygmy Owl subspecies. Unlike the other races, it tends to keep its tail widespread in flight. Its size approximates the Rocky Mountain Pygmy Owl. Perched, it tends to hold its tail at right angles to the body and to twitch it frequently, giving the illusion of a kingbird at perch. In flight, except for the widespread tail, it resembles a woodpecker.

COAST PYGMY OWL
Glaucidium gnoma grinnelli Ridgway

VOICE

The voice of the Coast Pygmy Owl is generally heard for about three hours beginning at dawn, and again for the last few hours preceding nightfall. Calls are seldom given during the night or midday.

GENERAL HABITS AND CHARACTERISTICS

Somewhat more crepuscular than other Pygmy Owl subspecies, it is nevertheless still considerably diurnal. On the whole, it is the wariest of the five subspecies and thus very difficult to observe. It tends to live the majority of its life in the middle reaches of the trees of its range and rarely comes to the ground except to bathe.

HABITAT

This Pygmy Owl is found only in the dense humid forests of fir, redwood, and cedar along the Pacific coast, although now and again one will be observed in the cut-over or burned-over timberlands and alder swamps in heavily timbered areas. Spends almost its entire life far above ground in the middle to upper reaches of the great trees. Most of its prey is caught in those trees.

FOOD

Primarily small birds and some tree frogs and lizards along with other small, tree-living vertebrates and invertebrate animals.

ENEMIES

In addition to Spotted Owls, Coast Pygmy Owls will also occasionally be killed by a mob of attacking Steller's jays.

NEST

Almost invariably in a woodpecker hole at least 50 or 60 feet high, but possibly as high as 100 feet.

EGGS

The eggs of the Coast Pygmy Owl are slightly larger and more oval in shape than those of the California Pygmy Owl; they average 29.4 mm. (1.2″) in length and 23.0 mm. (0.9″) in width.

DISTRIBUTION IN NORTH AMERICA

Pacific coast from southeastern Alaska (Wrangell), through western coastal British Columbia (exclusive of Vancouver Island), western coastal Washington and Oregon, to the coastal districts of California northward from Monterey County. Inland it is found to the lower Willamette River Valley of Oregon, and extreme western Trinity County, Napa County, and eastern Alameda County in California.

VANCOUVER PYGMY OWL

(COLOR PLATE XLVI)

SCIENTIFIC NAME AND ORIGINAL DESCRIPTION

Glaucidium gnoma swarthi Grinnell. Original description: *Glaucidium gnoma swarthi* Grinnell, *The Auk,* Volume 30, Number 2, April (March 31), 1913, page 224; based on a specimen from Errington, Vancouver Island, British Columbia, Canada.

OTHER NAME

LA CHOUETTE PYGMÉE DE VANCOUVER French-Canadian name meaning "Pygmy Owl of Vancouver."

DISTINGUISHING FEATURES

The Vancouver Pygmy Owl is darker in general coloration everywhere than the California Pygmy Owl. It is slightly smaller and very much darker than the Rocky Mountain Pygmy Owl, averaging about a half-inch shorter in total length.

WEIGHT

Subspecies average: 40.8 gr. (1.4 oz.).

TOTAL LENGTH

Subspecies average: 163.8 mm. (6.5″).

WINGSPAN

Subspecies average: 377.2 mm. (14.9″).

INDIVIDUAL WING LENGTH

Subspecies average: 91.4 mm. (3.6″).

TAIL LENGTH

Subspecies average: 62.2 mm. (2.5″).

BEAK LENGTH

Subspecies average: 11.0 mm. (0.4″). This is larger than is ordinarily found in other Pygmy Owl races in relation to the size of the bird. The Vancouver Pygmy Owl's beak averages 0.057″ longer than that of the Rocky Mountain Pygmy Owl, even though the latter is the larger of the two subspecies.

LVI   DUSKY HORNED OWL

Bubo virginianus saturatus Ridgway. Male. Victoria, British Columbia, Canada, January 13, 1967. A.O.U. Number 375-C

LVII   ONTARIO HORNED OWL

Bubo virginianus scalariventris Snyder. Female and two young. South Fork Roseau River near Malung, Roseau County, Minnesota, March 1, 1927. Not included in the 1957 A.O.U. Check-list

Karl E. Karalus

Karl E. Karalus

SEXUAL DIFFERENCES

The females are more distinctly larger than the males than is apparent in the other Pygmy Owl races.

VOICE

Unlike the other *Glaucidium gnoma* subspecies, the Vancouver Pygmy Owl does more calling in the autumn than during spring or summer.

GENERAL HABITS AND CHARACTERISTICS

There seems to be a considerably closer year-round relationship between male and female Vancouver Pygmy Owls than among the other Pygmy Owl subspecies, and at almost any time of year they tend to perch side by side, snuggling together often.

This is probably the shyest, most reclusive of the Pygmy Owls; much more so than even the Coast Pygmy Owl.

HABITAT AND ROOSTING

Mostly comparable to that of the Coast Pygmy Owl (*Glaucidium gnoma grinnelli*) but with a slight preference for more open areas of scattered trees. It rarely roosts in vacated woodpecker holes or natural tree cavities, preferring dense foliage for all roosting.

HUNTING METHODS

This is the most strictly insectivorous of the Pygmy Owl races, though it will take mice, shrews, and some small birds. Oddly, in view of its dietary preference, it has never been observed to capture an insect on the wing. Invariably it lands upon a stationary or crawling insect, pinning it with its talons while tearing it apart and eating it.

VANCOUVER PYGMY OWL

Glaucidium gnoma swarthi Grinnell

FOOD

Chiefly grasshoppers, crickets, beetles, moths, and butterflies; and, in late winter and early spring, some small mammals and small birds.

EGGS

Subspecies average: 25.4 mm. (1.0″) in length and 22.9 mm. (0.9″) in width.

DISTRIBUTION IN NORTH AMERICA

Glaucidium gnoma swarthi is thought to be confined entirely to Vancouver Island, British Columbia; however, there have been some fairly recent unconfirmed sightings of the subspecies in coastal areas of the adjoining British Columbia mainland.

LVIII ARCTIC HORNED OWL

Bubo virginianus subarcticus (Hoy). Male. Outskirts of Miles City, Custer County, Montana, April 4, 1963. Not included in the 1957 A.O.U. Check-list

SPECIES

ORDER: STRIGIFORMES

FAMILY: STRIGIDAE

GENUS: *Glaucidium* Boie

SPECIES: *brasilianum* (Gmelin)

SUBSPECIES

---

ridgwayi (Sharp) FERRUGINOUS OWL

cactorum van Rossem CACTUS OWL

FERRUGINOUS OWL
(COLOR PLATE XLVII)

SCIENTIFIC NAME AND ORIGINAL DESCRIPTION

Glaucidium brasilianum ridgwayi (Sharp). Original description: *Glaucidium brasilianum Ridgwayi* Dearborn, *Field Museum of Natural History,* Publication 125, November 1907, page 84; based on a specimen from El Rancho, Guatemala.

OTHER NAMES

FERRUGINOUS PYGMY OWL Former common name before reclassification.

STREAKED PYGMY OWL Former Pygmy Owl designation, and because of distinctive scattered dark streaking of the underparts, especially the sides and flanks.

TECOLOTILLO RAYADO DE SHARP Mexican-Indian name meaning "Sharp's Streaked Pygmy Owl."

DISTINGUISHING FEATURES

This is a very pert and extremely attractive little owl which often seems to be trying, without a great deal of success, to look very fierce. It is closely related to the Pygmy Owls (*Glaucidium gnoma* sp.), with which it and the Cactus Owl (*Glaucidium brasilianum cactorum*) were previously classed; its beak is more bulbous, the wings slightly shorter and more rounded, the head proportionately smaller than that of most other North American owl species. There are two distinct color phases of this owl—red and gray—as well as a ruddy-gray intermediate coloration which occurs on very rare occasions and appears to be a combination of the two, but which is not generally accepted as a third color phase in its own right.

Rank in over-all size among the eighteen species: Sixteenth.

SHAPE AT REST

Although the Ferruginous Owl is very similar to the Pygmy Owls in size and general shape, its head is proportionately just a bit smaller and it usually perches with the tail held straight down rather than at an angle to the body as in the Pygmy Owls.

SHAPE IN FLIGHT

It is extremely difficult at twilight to differentiate between this owl and the bats which also fly in the same general area of its range; an impression given because of the general configuration of the silhouette of the bird.

FLIGHT PATTERN

The wingbeats are quite rapid and there is a bare minimum of gliding. Gliding, in fact, is mostly absent from the flight and there is rarely, if ever, any hovering. The flight line is usually very direct and slightly undulative, although not quite so pronouncedly dipping and rising as that of a woodpecker.

Measurements have been based on 7 birds measured: 2 males and 5 females.

WEIGHT

Species average: 80.4 gr. (2.8 oz.).

	Male	Female
Average	78.5 gr. (2.8 oz.)	82.2 gr. (2.9 oz.)
Minimum	65.5 gr. (2.3 oz.)	71.4 gr. (2.5 oz.)
Maximum	85.1 gr. (3.0 oz.)	88.2 gr. (3.1 oz.)

Rank in weight among the eighteen species: Sixteenth.

TOTAL LENGTH

Species average: 159.1 mm. (6.3″).

	Male	Female
Average	150.2 mm. (5.9″)	167.9 mm. (6.6″)
Minimum	146.1 mm. (5.8″)	158.9 mm. (6.3″)
Maximum	155.0 mm. (6.1″)	183.2 mm. (7.2″)

Rank in total length among the eighteen species: Seventeenth.

WINGSPAN

Species average: 383.4 mm. (15.1″).

	Male	Female
Average	377.5 mm. (14.9″)	389.2 mm. (15.3″)
Minimum	361.9 mm. (14.3″)	373.7 mm. (14.7″)
Maximum	373.3 mm. (14.7″)	405.9 mm. (16.0″)

Rank in wingspan among the eighteen species: Sixteenth.

INDIVIDUAL WING LENGTH

Species average: 98.2 mm. (3.9″).

	Male	Female
Average	91.8 mm. (3.6″)	104.6 mm. (4.1″)
Minimum	89.4 mm. (3.5″)	89.5 mm. (3.5″)
Maximum	96.8 mm. (3.8″)	116.8 mm. (4.6″)

Rank in wing length among the eighteen species: Sixteenth.

TAIL LENGTH

Species average: 72.9 mm. (2.9″).

	Male	Female
Average	62.2 mm. (2.5″)	83.5 mm. (3.3″)
Minimum	56.7 mm. (2.2″)	80.5 mm. (3.2″)
Maximum	68.0 mm. (2.7″)	88.9 mm. (3.5″)

Rank in tail length among the eighteen species: Sixteenth.

BEAK LENGTH

Species average: 9.0 mm. (0.4″).

	Male	Female
Average	8.9 mm. (0.4″)	9.1 mm. (0.4″)
Minimum	8.2 mm. (0.3″)	8.6 mm. (0.3″)
Maximum	9.4 mm. (0.4″)	9.9 mm. (0.4″)

Rank in beak length among the eighteen species: Seventeenth.

LEGS, FEET, TALONS

The legs of the Ferruginous Owl are well covered with short, close plumage, and on the feet are bristly feathers to the base of the talons. The feet are unusually large in proportion to the size of the bird, and the talons are a light horn color for most of their length but shading into dusky yellowish gray at the tips.

EYES AND VISION

Vision is extremely good, best during morning and evening twilight, but better during the day than during the night. The irides are a very brilliant, penetrating, clear yellow.

EARS AND HEARING

The hearing of the Ferruginous Owl is excellent, though not as extremely sensitive as that of the more nocturnal owl species. Nevertheless, this bird has been decoyed for unusually great distances by the simulated squeak of a mouse. There is no marked degree of asymmetricism in placement or size of the ear cavities.

EAR TUFTS, PLUMAGE, ANNUAL MOLT

The plumage is fairly tight to the body, though not quite so much so as that of the Pygmy Owls. The flight feathers are slightly more fluted on *Glaucidium brasilianum ridgwayi* than those of the *Glaucidium gnoma* subspecies and, while not completely soundless in flight, the Ferruginous Owl flies much more quietly than the Pygmy Owls. The annual molt does not begin until early September (sometimes not until mid-September) and it is usually all finished by early December at the latest. Flight is not in any way impaired by this progressive molting.

VOICE

The most common call of this pretty little owl occurs in the early evening and is a twice-repeated-per-second sound like *CHOOOK-CHOOOK-CHOOK-CHOOOK-CHOOOK-CHOOOK,* voiced with the head held upward and the tail jerking spasmodically at each note uttered. The voice is not quite as mellow as that of the Pygmy Owl, and it carries a bit more inflection. At times the notes are drawn out for two to three seconds each, but usually they are more rapidly uttered than those of the Pygmy Owls. A variety of less frequently voiced calls is also given, most of which do not lend themselves to reproduction in the written word, including a long clear whistling voice by the male.

SEXUAL DIFFERENCES: SIZE, COLORATION, VOICE

The calls of the male are lower in tone than are those of the female and somewhat less wheezing in their quality. Female birds are slightly the larger, but there is no detectable difference in coloration or markings between the sexes.

MORTALITY AND LONGEVITY

No data have been ascertained in these respects insofar as the Ferruginous Owl is concerned, although mortality rates and longevity would probably be along similar lines to those of the Pygmy Owls.

COLORATION AND MARKINGS: ADULT

The common red phase and gray phase, along with the less often occurring brownish-red-gray phase, are each distinctive in their own right; the gray phase is quite decidedly grayish throughout, with a slight brownish cast on the upperparts and the very distinctly slate-gray tail barred in black; the red phase is a very distinct reddish, but reddish gray on a tail banded with black; the brownish-red-gray phase is more decidedly a mixture of the two prime color phases and with the tail slaty and barred with black. Superciliaries and

lores are a very light buff white or gray white, and the same colors run very narrowly across the throat and on the chin.

COLORATION AND MARKINGS: JUVENILE

Similar to adults except that the crown is not marked.

GENERAL HABITS AND CHARACTERISTICS

Glaucidium brasilianum ridgwayi is not so shy as are the Pygmy Owls (*Glaucidium gnoma* sp.), and it can sometimes be rather easily approached in the open. If, however, it is in its hole, it becomes very nervous at the approach of a human and will usually emerge from the hole at once. The Ferruginous Owl is very fond of perching atop the uppermost knob of a saguaro cactus and closely watching the ground below. The owl rarely flies at all during the night; mostly in early morning and evening, but with a certain amount of daylight activity as well. This is a very appealing little owl, delightful to observe when an opportunity presents itself.

HABITAT AND ROOSTING

The Ferruginous Owl is almost entirely a bird of the desert terrain, although it will enter well-wooded creek valleys at times. Mesquite forests and areas abundant in saguaro and cholla cacti are most favored, ranging from sea level to elevations of 4,000 feet. Perching is almost always done in the open on an outermost or uppermost branch, twig, or cactus spike. Roosting, however, is more often undertaken in the dense foliage of the outer branches of cottonwood trees or creek-bottom brush, or else in woodpecker holes high in saguaro cactus.

Field sketches of (center) the Ferruginous Owl (*Glaucidium brasilianum ridgwayi*) and the closely related Arizona Pygmy Owl (*Glaucidium gnoma gnoma*), observed and sketched on the same day in extreme southeastern Arizona.

Ferruginous Owl

Ferruginous

K.C.K.

Pygmy owls

Tail long for an owl
abroad by day also at times
rests with much tail jerking

G. gnoma

ENEMIES AND DEFENSES

A fantastically courageous and fierce little owl, this tiny creature will without hesitation attack a human who comes too near the nest or young. The attack is accompanied with flailing wings, biting beak, and graspings of the needle-sharp talons. With the exception of the larger owl species, the bird has few natural enemies and there are even cases on record where it has dauntlessly attacked the Western Horned Owl. As with the Pygmy Owls, there is a plumage pattern resembling a rather fierce face on the hindneck of the bird, and this may afford some degree of protection. Equally, in all three color phases the bird can camouflage itself with astounding facility amidst foliage.

HUNTING METHODS AND CARRYING OF PREY

The hunting methods of *Glaucidium brasilianum ridgwayi* are much along the lines of those practiced by the Pygmy Owls, and with an equal degree of ferocity. The Ferruginous Owl, too, will attack birds much larger than itself, including even fryer-sized chickens. Driving its talons deeply and firmly into the larger bird's throat, the little owl hangs on, keeping its balance with flapping wings as the prey struggles, squeezing with its feet ever more tightly until the larger bird dies, and sometimes even helping to hurry the demise by tearing at the head of the prey bird with the sharp little beak at the same time.

The Ferruginous Owl has never been observed to carry any kind of prey in its beak—not even insects. It has amazing lifting power and can carry in its talons birds and mammals weighing more than twice its own weight.

FOOD, FEEDING HABITS, WASTES

In a feeding habit similar to that of the Pygmy Owls, the Ferruginous Owl will often pluck a smaller prey bird clean of feathers before eating it piecemeal. However, it is a more ravenous feeder than the Pygmy Owls and will often begin tearing out chunks of meat from its still-living prey and wolfing them down. The head of the prey animal is almost always eaten first, and there is a slightly greater degree of whole-prey swallowing, especially with small mice and insects, than occurs among the *Glaucidium gnoma* subspecies. As a result, there is more pellet regurgitation as well, and the pellets are better formed and more tightly bound in small elongated-oval bundles. Almost any desert creature—bird, insect, mammal, invertebrate, reptile, amphibian—is prey for this owl if it can be handled.

COURTSHIP AND MATING

There seems to be little difference in the known courtship and mating activities of the Ferruginous Owl from those of the Pygmy Owl subspecies, but considerable study is still needed in these areas where both species are concerned.

ANNUAL BROODS, NEST, NESTING HABITS

Glaucidium brasilianum ridgwayi has only one brood per year, with very little likelihood of a second set of eggs being laid if the first are destroyed. The nests are invariably in abandoned woodpecker holes in cottonwoods, mesquite and, most often, saguaro cactus, usually between 10 and 40 feet in height. The bird is very clean in its nesting habits, carrying away debris regularly and usually not defecating or regurgitating pellets anywhere in or near the vicinity of the nest hole.

EGGS

Number per nesting Three to five eggs are laid, but far more often just three rather than four or five.

Color Pure white with no trace of discoloration or even nest staining.

Shape Very roundly ovoid.

Texture The shells are thicker than are the shells of the eggs laid by Pygmy Owls (*Glaucidium gnoma* sp.), and they are more granulated but less glossy than those laid by the Elf Owls (*Micrathene whitneyi* sp.). In addition, the eggshells sometimes are characterized by a few slight knobby protuberances.

Size Fifty measured eggs have yielded an average length of 29.0 mm. (1.1″) and an average width of 23.6 mm. (0.9″). The extremes included:

Maximum length:	30.3 mm. (1.2″)
Minimum length:	24.8 mm. (1.0″)
Maximum width:	25.5 mm. (1.0″)
Minimum width:	21.9 mm. (0.9″)

Interval of egg-laying Not authenticated, but believed to be in the vicinity of 30 hours apart.

Egg-laying dates Earliest, March 13; latest, May 30; normally between April 1 and May 14.

Field sketches rendered on two successive days in **May in north-central Sonora, Mexico, of the Cactus Owl (*Glaucidium brasilianum cactorum*).

Over-all ground color on back
Warm Olive-To-reddish

Crown and nape
striped with creamy
white

Cactus owl
G. b. cactorum

bird from
Sonora, Mex.

Toes bare

dark stripe   warm
brown

breast feather

Tail Long
reddish with
brown bars

Primaries
very dark
brown

Tarsus
Reddish
barred with
Tan

K.E.K

FERRUGINOUS OWL

Glaucidium brasilianum ridgwayi (Sharp)

still being fed to some extent by the parent birds. In less than a week after leaving the nest they are flying off on their own.

DISTRIBUTION IN NORTH AMERICA

The Ferruginous Owl has a very restricted range in North America north of Mexico. It inhabits a narrow stretch of the southernmost portion of Arizona and a similar area in southern New Mexico and southwestern Texas, especially in the lower Rio Grande Valley area from the vicinity of Del Rio to the Gulf of Mexico. South of the United States border it occurs in much greater abundance through Mexico, most of Central America, and into Brazil.

MIGRATION

Non-migratory.

ECONOMIC INFLUENCE

Negligible.

INCUBATION AND BROODING CHARACTERISTICS

Incubation is probably entirely by the female, with the male keeping guard over the area and providing food for the female and newly hatched nestlings.

YOUNG AND FAMILY LIFE CHARACTERISTICS

Much observation still needs to be recorded here, but insofar as can be determined from what limited observations have been made, the development of the young birds and the characteristics of family life are reasonably parallel to those of the Rocky Mountain Pygmy Owl (*Glaucidium gnoma pinacola*). It is known that the young Ferruginous Owls do not linger long in family groups once they have acquired the ability to fly. Within two or three days of leaving the nesting hole they are capturing their own insect prey, though

CACTUS OWL

(COLOR PLATE XLVIII)

SCIENTIFIC NAME AND ORIGINAL DESCRIPTION

Glaucidium brasilianum cactorum van Rossem. Original description: *Glaucidium brasilianum cactorum* van Rossem, *Proceedings of the Biological Society of Washington,* Volume 50, February 23, 1937, page 27; based on a specimen from between Guaymas and Empalme in Sonora, Mexico.

OTHER NAMES

CACTUS PYGMY OWL For the size of the owl and its favored nesting site, although the term "Pygmy" is now misapplied.

TECOLOTILLO RAYADO DE LOS ÓRGANOS Mexican-Indian name meaning "Streaked Owl of the Organ Cactus."

Cactus Owl

DISTINGUISHING FEATURES

Very similar in size to the Ferruginous Owl (*Glaucidium brasilianum ridgwayi*) but a much paler gray in general coloration and, on the whole, the markings somewhat more clearly defined against the ground color. The tail is always a deep reddish in color with wide but rather faint crossbarrings of a dusky brown gray. The crown is not spotted as in the Ferruginous Owl; rather, it is streaked, but the streakings are always faint.

HABITAT

Not very different from that of the Ferruginous Owl, but with less inclination to frequent cottonwood creek valleys.

DISTRIBUTION IN NORTH AMERICA

Southern and south-central Arizona (Phoenix and Tucson west to Agua Caliente), western and northwestern Sonora, and the lowermost portion of the Rio Grande Valley in Texas (Hidalgo County, Brownsville), and southward to Michoacán, Nuevo León, and Tamaulipas.

CACTUS OWL

Glaucidium brasilianum cactorum van Rossem

SPECIES

ORDER: STRIGIFORMES
FAMILY: STRIGIDAE
GENUS: *Bubo* Dumeril
SPECIES: *virginianus* (Gmelin)

SUBSPECIES

virginianus (Gmelin)	GREAT HORNED OWL
algistus (Oberholser)	ST. MICHAEL HORNED OWL
heterocnemis (Oberholser)	LABRADOR HORNED OWL
lagophonus (Oberholser)	NORTH-WESTERN HORNED OWL
occidentalis Stone	MONTANA HORNED OWL
pacificus Cassin	PACIFIC HORNED OWL
pallescens Stone	WESTERN HORNED OWL
saturatus Ridgway	DUSKY HORNED OWL
scalariventris Snyder	ONTARIO HORNED OWL
subarcticus (Hoy)	ARCTIC HORNED OWL
wapacuthu (Gmelin)	TUNDRA HORNED OWL

SCIENTIFIC NAME AND ORIGINAL DESCRIPTION

Bubo virginianus virginianus (Gmelin). Original description: *Strix virginianus* Gmelin, *Systematica Natura,* Volume 1, Part 1, 1788, page 287, based mainly on the Virginia Eared Owl of Latham, *Gen. Syn.,* Volume 1, Part 1, page 119, on a specimen from an undesignated location in Virginia. Former scientific names: *Asio magellanicus virginianus, Strix maximus, Strix virginiana, Bubo pinacola.*

OTHER NAMES

BIG-EARED OWL   After the large, significant ear tufts.

CAT OWL   Because of the catlike features of the head when the ear tufts are held erect, giving the general aspect of a sitting cat when the owl is perched. Also called BIG CAT OWL to differentiate it from the Screech Owl, which is sometimes referred to as the Little Cat Owl.

HOOT OWL   From the deep, booming call it makes, but this same term is often used for the Barred Owl, though to differentiate between the two, the Great Horned Owl is sometimes called BIG HOOT OWL.

LE GRAND-DUC   French-Canadian name meaning "The Grand Duke," as opposed to the Screech Owl, which is called "The Little Duke."

LE GRAND-DUC D'AMÉRIQUE   French-Canadian name for the Horned Owl species in general, rather than subspecifically.

LE GRAND-DUC DE L'EST (sometimes spelled "LE GRAND-DUC DU L'EST")   French-Canadian name for the Great Horned Owl specifically, meaning "The Grand Duke of the East."

TECOLOTE CORNUDO   Indian-Mexican name for the species in general, meaning "The Horned Owl."

DISTINGUISHING FEATURES

Beyond any doubt whatever, the Great Horned Owl is the fiercest, most aggressive, and most impressive owl of North America. A book could easily be written on this bird alone, so varied and interesting are its habits and natural history. Here we will only discuss the most distinctive and salient features. The various subspecies of *Bubo virginianus* are the only large owls in North America with very distinctive ear tufts. It is by far the largest of the common resident owls of the United States and second in over-all size on this continent only to the Snowy Owl (*Nyctea scandiaca*) of more northerly climes. It is easily distinguishable from the Great Gray Owl (*Strix nebulosa nebulosa*) and the Northern Barred Owl (*Strix varia varia*) in that neither of those large species have ear tufts, and the Great Horned Owl is generally darker than the Northern Barred Owl and buffier brown than the Great Gray Owl. The latter owl is longer in total length and may look as large or even larger, but this is not the case—it is simply that the plumage of the Great Gray Owl is looser and fluffier than that of the Great Horned Owl and thus gives the impression of greater bulk. The general aspect of the Great Gray Owl is one of placidity, as compared to the Great Horned Owl, which perpetually wears a glaring, angry expression. The feet and talons of the Great Horned Owl are large and extremely powerful and its eyes are a highly conspicuous yellow, though often narrowed to mere slits.

Rank in over-all size among the eighteen species: Second.

SHAPE AT REST

When perched, *Bubo virginianus virginianus* normally sits very erect and almost always with its ear tufts fully raised and quite prominent. The body, despite a fairly tight plumage, always appears heavy and powerfully built. The plumage is generally dark on the upperparts and somewhat lighter on the underparts. There is always a characteristic white patch in the gular area of the throat and upper breast. On its perch, this bird has a magnificent bearing and seems to exude an aura of fierce regality, strength, and condescending dignity.

SHAPE IN FLIGHT

Here the impression of great strength and size continues. The wings are long and broad, rather more pointed toward the tips than those of the Great Gray Owl or Barred Owls. The ear tufts are almost invariably flattened to the head in flight and the head is well tucked in, so that it appears to have no neck and the body seems somewhat shortened and compacted. The tail, too, appears in flight to be rather short and it is, indeed, much shorter than the tail of the Great Gray Owl.

FLIGHT PATTERN

Even though a somewhat heavy flier, the Great Horned Owl never fails to exhibit a sense of great power in flight. The wings are sometimes flapped with methodical deliberation, and yet at other times, especially when attacking or fleeing, they beat with amazing rapidity. For a short span after it first launches itself from its perch, the huge feet of the Great Horned Owl dangle below the bird, but soon they are drawn up and tucked firmly against the lower-belly plumage. Every now and again this owl will climb to an extraordinary altitude—upward of several thousand feet—and soar on motionless wings much in the manner of one of the large *Buteo* hawks. Normally, though, it does not fly much higher than treetop height or below. When diving on prey it will almost completely close its wings and not reopen them until the last possible moment, thus achieving great speed and accuracy in its attack. Low-level gliding is frequently engaged in, but only for relatively short distances at a time. The Great Horned Owl has great maneuverability for its size and can weave its way with incredible skill through the interlocked branches and trees of very dense forest growth. On occasion it deliberately bulls its way through brushy cover, striking twigs and brittle branches with the wing edges and snapping them off. Incredibly, for such an enormous bird, its deeply fluted flight feathers and generally soft plumage allow it to fly with absolute silence.

Measurements have been based on 84 birds measured: 33 males and 51 females.

WEIGHT

Species average: 1,523.0 gr. (53.3 oz.).

	Male	Female
Average	1,448.9 gr. (50.7 oz.)	1,597.0 gr. (55.9 oz.)
Minimum	1,383.8 gr. (48.4 oz.)	1,454.2 gr. (50.9 oz.)
Maximum	1,691.7 gr. (59.2 oz.)	1,876.0 gr. (65.7 oz.)

Rank in weight among the eighteen species: Second.

TOTAL LENGTH

Species average: 553.9 mm. (21.8").

	Male	Female
Average	509.4 mm. (20.1")	598.3 mm. (23.6")
Minimum	468.1 mm. (18.4")	548.8 mm. (21.6")
Maximum	602.4 mm. (23.7")	651.5 mm. (25.7")

Rank in total length among the eighteen species: Third.

WINGSPAN

Species average: 1,382.5 mm. (54.5″).

	Male	Female
Average	1,335.7 mm. (52.6″)	1,429.3 mm. (56.3″)
Minimum	1,242.6 mm. (49.0″)	1,260.3 mm. (49.7″)
Maximum	1,409.7 mm. (55.5″)	1,575.0 mm. (62.1″)

Rank in wingspan among the eighteen species: Second.

INDIVIDUAL WING LENGTH

Species average: 386.8 mm. (15.2″).

	Male	Female
Average	370.8 mm. (14.6″)	402.7 mm. (15.9″)
Minimum	355.8 mm. (14.0″)	362.5 mm. (14.3″)
Maximum	373.6 mm. (14.7″)	430.5 mm. (17.0″)

Rank in wing length among the eighteen species: Second.

TAIL LENGTH

Species average: 213.8 mm. (8.4″).

	Male	Female
Average	211.7 mm. (8.3″)	215.8 mm. (8.5″)
Minimum	208.2 mm. (8.2″)	207.9 mm. (8.2″)
Maximum	224.3 mm. (8.8″)	231.6 mm. (9.1″)

Rank in tail length among the eighteen species: Fifth.

BEAK LENGTH

Species average: 39.0 mm. (1.5″). Beak is slate gray black.

	Male	Female
Average	36.8 mm. (1.5″)	41.2 mm. (1.6″)
Minimum	30.8 mm. (1.2″)	36.1 mm. (1.4″)
Maximum	42.4 mm. (1.7″)	46.6 mm. (1.8″)

Rank in beak length among the eighteen species: Second.

LEGS, FEET, TALONS

The legs, feet, and talons of the Great Horned Owl are all enormously well developed; the legs impressively muscled, the feet and talons extremely powerful in grasping and lifting. The legs are well feathered and the feet are moderately well covered with short, thick bristly feathers which become nearly absent on the outermost balls of the toes. Here the scaling is brownish gray in color. The great curved talons are very thick at the base and taper to heavy but sharp points. They are a brownish-yellow horn color at the base but gradually darken until they are jet black at the tips. These talons are indeed murderous weapons, whether used in hunting, offense, or defense.

EYES AND VISION

These are the largest eyes of all North American owls—markedly convex, very piercing in their glare, and with an iris coloration that is brilliant yellow. As in the other owls, a rather heavy, translucent, nictitating membrane is drawn protectively over the eye as the owl struggles with prey and, according to some authorities, when the owl flies through very heavy cover. The expansion or contraction of the pupil changes automatically with light intensity, as it does in the other owls, but there is in addition good reason for believing that the Great Horned Owl can consciously control expansion or contraction of one eye at a time or both eyes simultaneously, especially when the focus of the eye moves from a near object to one farther distant. The eye itself is partially covered at its upper inner edge by the heavy brows as they form the V of the forehead. Vision is extremely keen, day or night—quite probably better on a 24-hour rating than any other North American Owl. A Great Horned Owl, with ears plugged with dampened cotton, stiffens into alert attention when a mouse almost a hundred yards away runs through short meadow grasses which all but hide it. Similarly, even in very bright sunlight, it will look upward into the sky and watch intently the flight of birds passing, which the human eye cannot detect without the aid of binoculars. This owl has also been known to look directly at the sun, enduring without seeming discomfort or ocular damage a glare that the human eye cannot.

EARS AND HEARING

As superb as the vision is, the auditory sense is even better. It may not quite surpass that of the Barn Owl (*Tyto alba pratincola*) but certainly it must come very close to equaling it. The eyes and ears together make the location of prey a very simple matter for *Bubo virginianus virginianus,* whether under the brightest or darkest of lighting conditions. It is virtually impossible, irrespective of what pains are taken, to creep up behind a roosting Great Horned Owl without that owl abruptly waking and turning its head to impale the intruder with its fierce stare. The ear cavities are enormous and more asymmetrical than are those of the Barn Owl. The ear coverts—auriculars—are extremely mobile and of tremendous benefit to this owl in pinpointing the location of any sound, near or far.

Customary threatening posture of the Great Horned Owl (*Bubo virginianus virginianus*).

Horned Owl

Karalus

from life – ♂
Live bird given artist
by E. J. Koestner – Dayton Museum

EAR TUFTS, PLUMAGE, ANNUAL MOLT

The ear tufts are very large, erect, and distinctive at most times when the bird is perched, though they are flattened or very nearly flattened to the crown in flight. At times when the perched bird becomes very angry, they may be tilted backward at a considerable angle. They are fully two inches in length.

The plumage is heavy and soft, but not as thick and bulky as that of the Great Gray Owl. Emargination of the outermost primaries is quite distinct and all flight feathers are deeply fluted to afford entirely soundless flight. The pure white feathers of the gular region are especially thick and fluffy, sometimes giving the distinct impression of an ascot. (See Color Plate LVI.) There is a complete molt of all plumage once each year, beginning in late June or early July and usually completed around late October. Flight is in no way affected by this progressive molt.

VOICE

The Great Horned Owl comes close to equaling the Northern Barred Owl (*Strix varia varia*) in the amazingly wide variety of sounds it can make, ranging from deep booming hoots to whistles, shrieks, screams, and hisses. The hooting it makes is quite different in tonal quality from that of the Barred Owl, being in a much lower bass range and more mellow in tone, but yet carrying much power. On a still night, the hooting of the Great Horned Owl can be heard for several miles or more. It is a resonant call, generally of five notes, the first two and the last two rather quickly given and the middle note prolonged. It sounds like *WHOOO-WHOOO WHOOOOOOOO WHOO-WHOOO,* with sometimes the elongated middle note inflected to a lower pitch during delivery. The whole call, heard from a distance, bears resemblance to a far-off foghorn.

Another *WHOOO* note, but with a sort of angry growling sound issued at the beginning of it, and much more abruptly uttered, has a sound like *G-G-G-GGG-RROOOOO!* This call sometimes has a distinct deep rattling quality. If the bird is very excited it may precede this note by an expressively harsh cry of *WAAAaaa!* There are other variations of this and nearly all other calls the owl makes—so many, in fact, they could not all be listed here. But, briefly, a listing of some of the more basic call structures includes these:

. . . from the female, a sound like *KEEE-uh KEEE-uh,* most reminiscent of a large soaring hawk.

. . . a sound made while incubating, rather softly voiced, which can be written as *Urrrrr-Urrrrr.*

. . . an explosively laughing scream, uttered by an angry female, sounding like *WHAAA WHHAAAAA-A-A-A-AARRRRK!*

. . . a remarkably catlike cry of *MEEE-OWwwww.*

. . . a barking call like a hound baying deep in a distant woods.

. . . a piercing, unwritable, hair-raising shriek.

. . . soft, cooing notes of almost dovelike quality.

. . . a gargled, gasping sound like someone being choked.

. . . a tremulous, wavering cry not unlike that uttered by the Eastern Screech Owl (*Otus asio naevius*), but much louder and somewhat harsher.

. . . a variety of hissings of different intensity, usually accompanied by angry snappings of the beak.

By far the greater majority of utterances made by the Great Horned Owl have an unearthly quality to them and are often very much feared by the superstitious. The birds are most vociferous during the mating season, in December, January, and February, and generally most quiet, at least in the vicinity of the nest, where there are young birds in the nest, in late February, March, and April. As with other owls, many of the calls are quite markedly ventriloquial. Calling is most frequently engaged in during the hours from dusk until midnight and again during a brief period just before dawn, although it is not too uncommon to hear this owl call during the daytime.

SEXUAL DIFFERENCES: SIZE, COLORATION, VOICE

There is a considerable sexual difference in the vocal quality and delivery of the birds. The calls given by the male are generally quite a bit lower, more elaborate, mellower, longer-lasting, and more musical than those issued by the female. In coloration and markings, the sexes are identical, but the female is decidedly the larger bird. Compared with a fully developed but small male, a large female may be almost seven inches longer, over a pound heavier, and with a wingspan greater by more than a foot.

Some attitude sketches of a captive Great Horned Owl procured from E. J. Koestner, director of the Dayton Museum of Natural History, Dayton, Ohio. This specimen of *Bubo virginianus virginianus,* though raised from hatchling to adulthood in captivity with excessive care and gentleness, remained unalterably savage throughout its life.

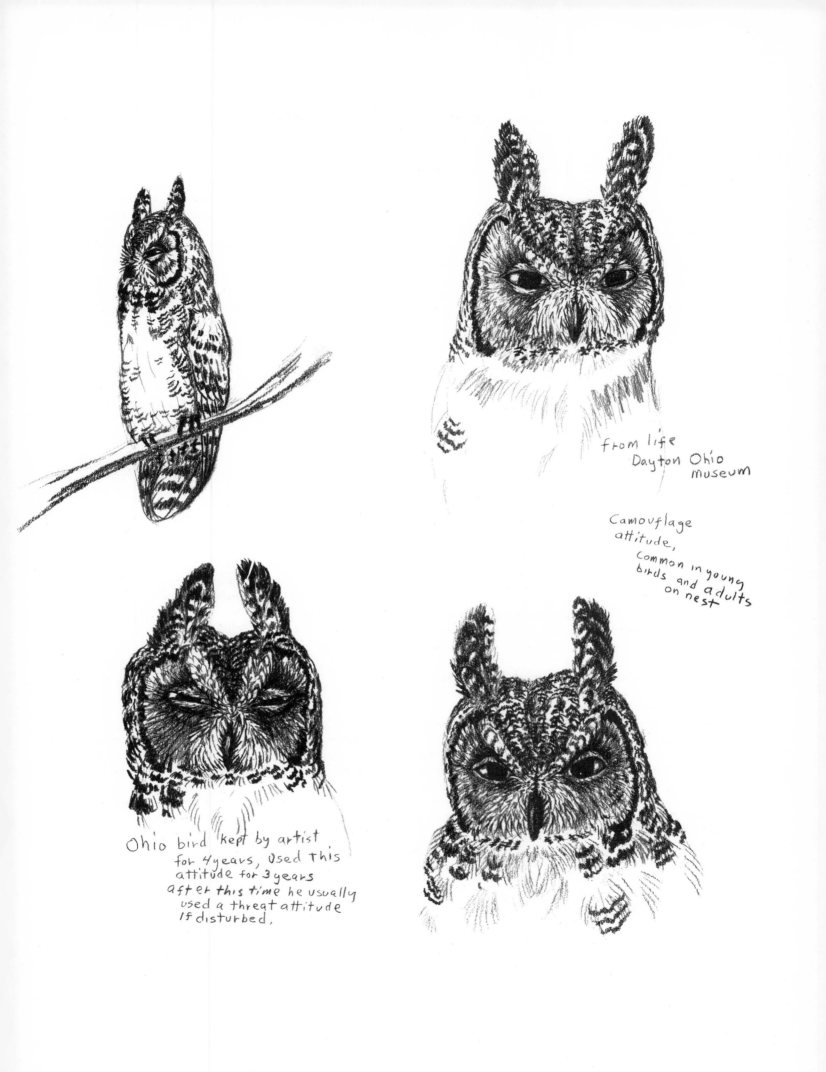

from life
Dayton Ohio
museum

Camouflage
attitude,
common in young
birds and adults
on nest

Ohio bird kept by artist
for 4 years, used this
attitude for 3 years
after this time he usually
used a threat attitude
if disturbed.

MORTALITY AND LONGEVITY

There is a high degree of infant mortality, from numerous causes—not the least of which are cannibalism and severe weather—during the first year. Approximately 50 per cent of the Great Horned Owls which hatch in late winter each year do not live to see the end of the following winter. It is not known for certain how long a Great Horned Owl can live in the wild, but the oldest recovered banded bird (which had been banded as a nestling) was thirteen years old. It is likely that some will live considerably longer, since numerous captive birds have lived for well over twenty years. One reliable report is on record of a captive Great Horned Owl living for twenty-nine years and another, not as verifiable, was said to have been accidentally killed in a fire at the age of thirty-eight.

COLORATION AND MARKINGS: ADULT

Bubo virginianus virginianus has a distinctly gray-brown appearance when perched, but seems to be very light in coloration when viewed from beneath while it is in flight. There is much variation in color, especially from a geographical standpoint, with more northerly birds being more markedly gray, and southern birds being so reddish they appear almost to be a red-phase bird. This is particularly true of the Great Horned Owls living in southern Florida, with the ruddy coloration and generally smaller size differential being so distinct from specimens of the same species from more northern parts of the range that there is some belief that the Florida Great Horned Owl should have subspecies classification.

Because of the wide color variation, even of birds in the same geographical area, it is difficult to verbalize an accurate representation of the Great Horned Owl's coloration, but in a rather general way the coloration and markings are as follows:

Almost all feathers are lighter at the base than terminally, which becomes apparent if the feathers are parted or the bird itself ruffles its feathers. The underparts are generally a slightly sooty gray buff broken by very bold and somewhat erratic transverse barrings of brownish black, much more pronounced on the sides, flanks, and lower belly than on the breast. The median line is usually unmarked from throat to at least mid-breast, this whiteness tending to rise from belly to throat in an elongated V-shape which broadens abruptly in the gular area. There are often (but not always) a series of very dark, irregular vertical blotches in the upper gular area. (See Color Plate LVIII.)

The upperparts are generally a darkly mottled sooty brown, broken by transverse mottlings of tawny gray

white. The generally darkest coloration prevails on crown and hindneck. The greater wing coverts, some of the middle wing coverts, and the shoulders are speckled with mottlings and irregular spottings or blotches of buffy white to grayish white. Tail, primaries, and secondaries are very distinctly and regularly barred in dark slate gray to brown black. The outer webs of the ear tufts are black, but becoming orangish sooty brown on the inner webs. Superciliaries and lores are dull white with fine black central shafting in each feather. The facial disks range from a dull tawny buff (especially in more northerly specimens) to a distinct orange buff (in the more southerly specimens), becoming whiter and duller around the eyes. The facial rim is black, becoming broken by gray-buff fleckings in the lower arc. Leg and foot plumage is generally unmarked and from grayish buff to tawny buff.

COLORATION AND MARKINGS: JUVENILE

In first-winter plumage, the wings and tail of young birds are identical to those of adult birds. The remainder of the plumage is somewhat ruddier brown orange than in adults, and the barrings are farther apart. The white throat patch is duller and much less extensive, and the ear tufts are shorter. Although first-winter plumage is complete on the young birds by their twentieth week—about September—there persists a certain amount of the downy plumage, especially on the lower underparts and around the neck, which is not entirely displaced until the bird undergoes the first postnuptial molt the following summer.

GENERAL HABITS AND CHARACTERISTICS

It has been said of the Great Horned Owl that it is wholly untamable if it has been allowed to stay in the nest until its eyes have opened, several days after hatching, even if taken into captivity only shortly after that. This is largely true, for the bird has a fierce and generally antagonistic temperament. It will survive well in captivity but rarely, or never, adapt to human handling

---

LIFE SKETCHES OF CAPTIVE GREAT HORNED OWL

The Great Horned Owl pictured here was raised from an approximate ten-day-old nestling to adulthood at the Dayton (Ohio) Museum of Natural History, but never became tame and scarcely was able to be handled—and then by only one of the museum staff members.

Great horned owl,
Dayton, Ohio.

or companionship, irrespective of how gentle. There are cases where captive birds became capable of being handled to some degree, but always with the sense that one instant of carelessness or unalertness on the handler's part could result in a lost eye or other injury. The bird, once its eyes have opened in the wild, tends to remain savage and unpredictable. As a pet it invariably tends to be generally bad-tempered and definitely dangerous, pointedly resisting attempts at familiarity. The strength and tenacity of this owl sometimes border on the incredible. In one well-documented case, a Great Horned Owl was seen to have a steel trap locked about one ankle for a week or so, and was evidently little inconvenienced; but abruptly it was seen in a still more desperate situation, with a second steel trap gripping the foot that had previously been unfettered, and the chains and rings of both traps trailing beneath as the bird flew. Despite this tragic state of affairs, which rendered useless the bird's most important hunting tools, the owl managed to survive for well over a month longer before finally being found dead, with the trap chains having become inextricably entangled in a barbed-wire fence. That the Great Horned Owl has frequently been referred to as a "winged tiger" is by no means a misplaced comparison. As untamably savage a spirit as one might expect to see anywhere, it remains dauntless as long as the spark of life remains within it, and one cannot help admiring and respecting such a wild nature.

It is believed that the Great Horned Owl's sense of smell is rather poorly developed, since it is not especially bothered by the vile stench of skunk scent, with which it is often sprayed. This is one of the only birds of prey which will regularly kill and eat skunks.

Bubo virginianus virginianus and the Red-tailed Hawk often inhabit and hunt the same territory—the owl by night and the hawk by day. But while the hawk will not prey upon the owl, the Great Horned Owl will attack and kill the hawk without hesitation if it locates the hawk's nighttime roost.

Not especially wary in temperament, the Great Horned Owl will nevertheless prefer to move away if danger threatens, rather than fight. However, if its young are jeopardized, it is another story altogether and the appellation of "winged tiger" becomes well-earned indeed. (See Enemies and Defenses.)

Mostly solitary in its habits, the Great Horned Owl rarely shows any real degree of affection for its mate, even during the height of the mating season; it remains relatively aloof and mates as if it were doing so as an unavoidable chore. The birds are almost never seen in pairs except during the mating season, and then much more briefly than other North American owl species. A caged pair, even if well fed, cannot live in peace for long and eventually the female will fall upon her mate, kill, and devour him.

Although essentially a nocturnal hunter, *Bubo vir-*

ginianus virginianus is apt to be seen on the wing at almost any time of night or day, and it is quite commonly abroad on moderately cloudy to heavily overcast days. During those times, when it soars high on motionless wings during daylight hours (see Flight Pattern), it is usually mistaken for an eagle.

HABITAT AND ROOSTING

A wide variety of terrain is frequented by the Great Horned Owl, but it is primarily a resident of rather densely forested regions. The forest may be all coniferous or all hardwoods or mixed, seemingly making no difference whatever to the owl, as long as prey is abundant. In addition to heavy woodlands, it also likes more open woodlands, orchards, parks, marshes (especially those adjacent to woodlands), swamps, rivers, creek valleys, canyons and ravines, partially wooded slopes, cliff areas, grainfield areas (especially immediately after the harvest), isolated woodlots, tamarack areas, and brushy hillsides. In the deepest south it likes cypress hammocks and expansive areas of dense palmetto interspersed with scattered slash pine and occasional dense clumps of Australian pine. For roosting purposes there is always a very definite preference for dense evergreens of any kind. In such trees it tends to camouflage itself by perching very close to the trunk (often leaning against it), with ear tufts erect, body shape slightly elongated, and the eyes completely closed or else narrowed to mere slits.

ENEMIES AND DEFENSES

There is no dearth of tales about the incredible savagery with which the Great Horned Owl attacks a foe or defends itself, nor is there need for exaggeration of any kind. There are scores of well-authenticated cases on record where men have been blinded and suffered severe injuries to head, throat, chest, back, and groin by enraged attacking Great Horned Owls. The attacks are bold, slashing, and very dangerous, made even more so by the total unexpectedness with which they strike. The soundlessness of their flight allows them to arrow in unseen and unheard by the intruder, with the first indication of danger being nearby when the great talons are driven deeply into flesh with power enough to knock a man out of a tree or drive him to his knees on the ground. Such attacks, which are more

Some threatening posturings and facial expressions of a captive Great Horned Owl (*Bubo virginianus virginianus*).

Horned Owl

Great Horned Owl
In threatening
attitude

Karalus

the rule than the exception, generally occur when the young of a pair of Great Horned Owls are endangered; at such time both parent birds will attack simultaneously and usually from different directions with positively devastating results.

For all intents and purposes, once the Great Horned Owl becomes an adult, it has no natural enemies which are any real threat to it. It is, of course, soundly hated by almost all other birds and often harassed unmercifully by them in the daytime, but only to the irritation of the owl, not to its physical detriment. Would-be enemies such as roving dogs, cats, lynxes, wolves, and even bears are forced to flee very quickly because of the concerted attacks of this aggressive bird. Only man proves to be an enemy who can and frequently does kill the Great Horned Owl.

The attack of a Great Horned Owl is a fearsome thing to witness and even worse to experience. The intruder approaching the nest will usually be warned by a series of harsh cries, hissings, beak snappings, and wing flappings of the adult birds. If he keeps coming, the birds may fly toward him in an extremely threatening way, veering off only at the last possible instant and with snapping beak; the grasping talons and bludgeoning wings only barely miss the intruder. That is the last warning. If the man persists, the next attack is in deadly earnest, coming always from an unexpected quarter and wholly without sound. Suddenly the intruder is struck a heavy, painful blow in some area of head, neck, or chest. Talons dig in almost their full length and grip tightly, while the beak tears at the flesh and the hard wing edges beat the intruder unmercifully. The second owl may attack while the first is still in the midst of its fight. The contact usually lasts only 10 or 15 seconds, but much damage is done in that time. Immediately upon breaking away, the owls wheel and circle and dive in for another attack. This continues until the intruder flees or is killed.

Only rarely will the Great Horned Owl utilize the broken-wing act to draw an intruder away from its nest. An outright attack always provides a much greater encouragement for an intruder to leave.

Attacks against people by *Bubo virginianus virginianus* do not always occur merely because of a close approach to nest or young. In numerous cases, campers have been struck by these owls while moving about their campsites in the late evening or after dark. Similarly, people walking past wooded areas at night have occasionally been struck by this owl, though the reason for such attack is unclear.

Probably the greatest cause of death among adult Great Horned Owls, next to being deliberately killed by man, is by being accidentally killed on highways by passing vehicles. No figures are available in regard to how many may be killed this way annually, but the occurrence is frequent enough that this form of death must be considered as being significant.

HUNTING METHODS AND CARRYING OF PREY

Just as the Great Horned Owl is a fantastic fighting machine, so too it is a deadly hunter, combining keenly alert senses and absolute silence in flight with amazing strength and audacity, a ravenous appetite, and a willingness to attack nearly any kind of animal as prey up to as large as a fox or small dog.

Two hunting methods are favored and utilized about equally. In the first, the owl perches fairly high, watching and listening intently for anything that might be considered prey to move in the vicinity. This is particularly true along the edges of forest clearings, along creek valleys, near lake shores, and in similar areas where the owl can observe both woodland and open stretches. When prey does appear, the owl leaves its perch, plunging head foremost nearly straight down, leveling off just above the ground and arrowing directly to the prey with unerring accuracy and total silence. Most prey struck by *Bubo virginianus virginianus* is wholly unaware of the danger until suddenly a set of talons is driven deeply into the flesh, and then it is much too late.

The second hunting method so common is ranging. Flapping and gliding smoothly over cover where prey is likely to be, constantly watching and listening, the owl plunges to the attack the instant prey is detected or flushed, effectively nailing a rabbit, quail, or pheasant to the ground, or a squirrel against the trunk of a tree, or a sleepy grouse against the branch upon which it has been roosting.

An unusual hunting method this owl employs occasionally is to alight and walk about on foot looking for prey, and even this mode of hunting can be extremely effective. One Great Horned Owl which was closely observed by the authors was hunting on the wing over a tree-dotted pasture area late in the afternoon on a cloudy day not far from Sycamore, Illinois. In an area where there were some scattered pieces of bark and tufts of cut dried grasses on the ground, the owl alighted and began marching along in a purposeful, brisk, almost military manner. At each piece of bark it would stop and, sometimes with beak but more often with one foot, jerk the wood aside, exposing whatever was underneath. An amazing number of larvae, earthworms, mice, and shrews were discovered and gobbled up in a very short time. At the small clumps of grasses

---

MAINSTAY IN THE DIET OF THE GREAT HORNED OWL

Although the Great Horned Owl will catch, kill, and eat a phenomenal variety of animals—birds, mammals, amphibians, reptiles, fish, insects, and other invertebrates—probably its most favored form of prey is the common cottontail rabbit.

Karl Eugene Karalus
1970

the owl would take a little hop and land in the middle of the pile, freeze as it listened closely, and then suddenly duck its head and snatch up a mouse or some other creature that had been frightened into movement.

The audacity of the Great Horned Owl is often extreme. It is not uncommon to hear of Great Horned Owls landing in chicken yards, walking up the little ramp the chickens use to enter the henhouse, going inside the building, stalking to the nearest roosting or brooding chicken, killing it, walking back outside with the fowl clutched in one talon, and then flying off with it.

Along with its great hunting ability, the Great Horned Owl is an adept fisherman as well. Quite frequently it will wade into the water of a marsh, creek, or lake until its own stomach is touching the surface, and then snatch fish, turtles, crayfish, frogs, and other creatures. It has even been known to wade out into six inches of water in order to rip a dead muskrat out of a steel trap in which it was caught and drowned.

When attacking larger prey, the owl is occasionally hurt or inconvenienced. Often it becomes well sprayed with skunk scent during a struggle to kill that mammal. The smell itself does not seem to bother the owl (Great Horned Owls have often been captured with the stench of skunk very strong on their plumage), but the bird takes care to close its nictitating membrane as it attacks, to protect the eyes from the spray which might otherwise blind it. The same is true when it attacks a porcupine; if it is not able to get an immediate paralyzing and fatal grip on the porcupine, the owl itself may be in danger. One owl was found suffering severely from a total of 84 quills embedded in its flesh, mostly in side, flanks, and legs, but several in the side of the head and even in the facial disk.

Sometimes it takes a considerable while for the owl to kill its prey. Domestic cats, which are sometimes taken by the Great Horned Owl, put up strong fights for their lives. Once in a while, especially with a very large feral cat, the owl is forced to relinquish its hold because of the savagery of the cat's defense. More often than not, however, the owl has driven its talons deep into the neck or shoulders and it merely hangs on grimly, tearing at the animal with its beak, beating it with its wings and gradually forcing the talons ever deeper until at last a vital organ is punctured or the slashing beak is able to sever the spine. At times this may take upward of half an hour to accomplish.

Bubo virginianus virginianus, with its great strength of wings and feet, is able to lift and carry prey a great deal heavier than itself. A Great Horned Owl weighing about three pounds can lift and fly with prey weighing as much as eight or nine pounds, though it rarely chooses to do so. Very large prey is often brought to the nest as food for the young birds; prey may include large barnyard hens, full-grown mallard ducks, skunks, opossums, cats, small dogs, snowshoe rabbits, woodchucks, young foxes, half-grown turkeys, muskrats, and

other such relatively large animals. This sort of prey, if it can be carried at all, is carried in the talons. Smaller prey, up to about the size of a large rat, cottontail rabbit, or pheasant, will normally be carried in the beak. The authors, while preparing this very section of the book, watched with interest as a Great Horned Owl arose from an area heavily overgrown with palmetto scrub, near the town of Placida, Florida, and flew to the top of a telephone pole with a large indigo snake dangling from the talons of one foot. The snake was fully six feet in length and was gripped just behind the head, its rather heavy body trailing out below the flying owl. It appeared that the snake was dead, but as the owl alighted with it atop the pole, the snake began writhing as if in an effort to coil around the bird. Methodically, standing on one foot and continuing to grip the reptile with the other, the owl half-spread its wings to maintain balance and swiftly, expertly, tore off the snake's head and swallowed it. The bird continued to perch there for several minutes until most of the movement of the snake's body had ceased, then flew off with the long dark body of the snake still trailing below.

Usually when lifting prey its own weight or heavier, the owl will make several preliminary attempts at rising, changing its foot grip perhaps two or three times until it finds just the right balance point on the prey before flying off in earnest with it. The flight is low and heavy at first, but with speed and height gradually increasing.

FOOD, FEEDING HABITS, WASTES

When it is possible to do so, the Great Horned Owl will swallow its prey whole. The size of the prey that it can ingest without first tearing it apart is little short of astounding. Full-grown Norway rats are swallowed without undue difficulty, as are young rabbits. One of the largest of prey swallowed whole was recorded when

---

PREY BIRDS

Practically any bird below the size of a young turkey or large duck will be caught and eaten by some North American owl species, but the smaller owls—from the size of the American Hawk Owl downward—normally confine themselves to sparrow-sized birds or smaller, with most prey birds being taken during the nesting period when the parent birds are hard pressed to provide food enough for their demanding young.

REPRESENTATIVE PREY MAMMALS (*Overleaf*)

These are some of the mammals which North American owls customarily take as prey—the larger species, such as mink, skunk, marmot, muskrat, and jack rabbit, normally being taken only by Horned Owl species and occasionally by Snowy Owls, Great Gray Owls, and both Barred and Spotted Owls.

Horned Owl

* taken by Great horned and Snowy owls mainly.

all thumb-nail sketches
of prey for owls for
suggestion only. No detail
intended
or scale
on all plates of prey

Grouse * all

Ducks *

bob white
Quail all

Pheasant *

Crow *

small owls are
taken by G. Horned
and Barred owls.

small birds
especially
house sparrows

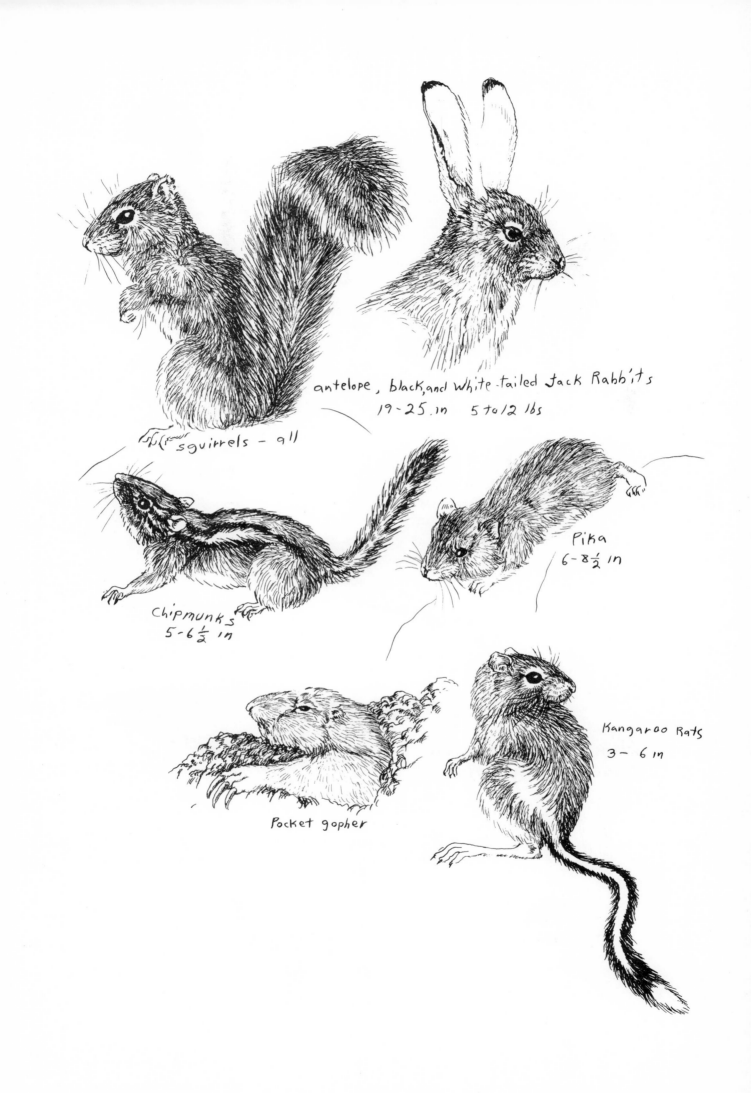

antelope, black, and white-tailed Jack Rabbits
19-25 in   5 to 12 lbs

squirrels - all

Pika
6-8½ in

Chipmunks
5-6½ in

Pocket gopher

Kangaroo Rats
3- 6 in

Mink
1½ to 4 lbs

(white
winter coat)

weasel
2 to 5 ozs

Marmots
all
4 to 17 lbs

Skunks
2 to 14 lbs

Bats

muskrat and water rat
(florida)

K.E.K.

Shrew

Mole

a Great Horned Owl was killed and found to contain an entire muskrat weighing just over a pound, although the owl itself had a body weight of a fraction under three pounds. Another was seen to swallow, with some difficulty, a half-grown cottontail rabbit. Birds up to the size of quail are swallowed whole in many cases.

Larger prey is torn apart, with the powerful beak of the owl snapping the bones, separating large sections of meat and viscera from the prey and swallowing it whole. If plenty of prey is available, it may eat only a portion of a large animal it has killed and then abandon it. Where prey is less abundant it may do the same thing, but return later on to eat more of it. With fowl as large as geese, chickens, large pheasants, or turkeys, the owl will often walk along dragging its prey to a nearby spot having more protective cover and there virtually pluck the entire bird with its beak. It may then fly with the denuded bird to a favored feeding platform or branch some distance away, bite off and discard the ends of the wings and the bony feet, and then devour the bird in great ripped-off chunks.

Where manner of prey is concerned, probably no other bird of prey in North America has a diet so varied. Especially when providing for young in the nest, it will kill practically any animal that it feels it can kill, from a cricket to a turkey or porcupine. Almost any living creature (but rarely carrion of any sort) that walks, swims, crawls, or flies within the range of *Bubo virginianus virginianus* is considered prey, although certain preferences are obvious. Rats, mice, cottontail rabbits, skunks, crows, and other owls rank very high on the list of preferred foods, as do pigeons, chickens, ducks, grouse, and pheasants. The following list of animals—which could be greatly expanded—includes just a sampling of what the Great Horned Owl is known to eat.

Mammals Rats, mice, ground squirrels of many species, hares, rabbits, chipmunks, gray squirrels, fox squirrels, red squirrels, mink, weasels, skunks, opossums, woodchucks, small dogs, porcupines, domestic cats, shrews, moles, armadillos, bats, young raccoons, muskrats, nutrias, and some others.

Birds Owls of any other species, including even Northern Barred Owls and Barn Owls, but rarely if ever Snowy Owls or Great Gray Owls, woodpeckers, crows, pheasants, quail, grouse, turkeys, geese, ducks, chickens, pigeons, guinea fowl, hawks up to the size of Red-tailed Hawks, grebes, bitterns, great blue herons, snipe, swans, kingfishers, blue jays, ravens, rails, gallinules, phalaropes, gulls, and virtually any other birds within its range.

Reptiles Almost any snake, including even some smaller venomous species and snakes as large as well-grown indigo snakes, turtles (especially soft-shelled), lizards of any kind (including, at times, young alligators in Florida).

Amphibians Frogs, toads, and salamanders of any species.

Fish Practically any fish, including even garfish, up to about three or four pounds in weight.

Invertebrates Insects of any kind large enough to be worth the effort of snatching up, centipedes, scorpions, crabs, crayfish, worms, and spiders.

The Great Horned Owl frequently regurgitates quite large pellets, averaging from three to four inches in length and upward of an inch and a half thick. These pellets are normally very dense, filled with bones, feathers, teeth, fur, claws, and other undigestibles, all bound tightly and compactly by the hair of the prey. The resultant pellet is a dark grayish-brown-black mass well coated with a slimy mucus which helps regurgitation. The pellets remain damp and very dark for a day or two after falling, and even when dry they retain their shape for long periods unless discovered by carrion beetles, which will mine through them and hasten disintegration. As they dry they become an almost uniform slate gray in color. Oddly, considering how completely the owl's digestive juices will dissolve all food matter of the ingested prey, microscopic examination has shown that feathers and hair are totally unaffected by the digestive processes, except that the feather quills become splintered and the hair and feathers well compacted. Pellets are usually regurgitated between six and ten hours after prey has been swallowed.

The Great Horned Owl also expels unusually large amounts of feces in a rather heavily viscous state; usually whitish with specklings or marblings of black, deep gray, and brown. The defecation usually occurs while the bird is perching, but more often immediately after it takes wing.

COURTSHIP AND MATING

The first mating calls generally begin long before winter has even set in in earnest—as early as late November or early December, but more often in late December or early January. Mate location is evidently done primarily by voice. Once the vocal response of a female has attracted him, the male sails in and alights (more often on the ground than in a tree) relatively close to her. At once he begins bowing his head in a curious manner, ruffling and fluffing his feathers and half-spreading his wings, often dragging the wing tips on the ground. Other than occasionally giving him a rather disdainful glance, the female outwardly pays little attention to him. This makes the male that much more determined to make her aware of his presence, and he struts and hops all around her, edging continually closer, sometimes throwing his head back and snapping his beak, wheezing, groaning as if in great pain. When he evidently feels she has been well primed and is taking an interest in him, he comes even closer and makes an effort to caress her with his beak. Sometimes she will let him do so. More often she ruffles her

Horned Owl

own feathers and savagely drives him off. This whole scene may be repeated three or four times before the female finally gives in and lets him come very close.

Occasionally the turning point in her affections comes when, after having been driven off briefly, he returns with some small manner of prey for her, which he may attempt to give to her with his beak or which, more often, he flips to the ground in front of her. If she picks it up and swallows it, he seems to realize she is accepting him and he becomes greatly emboldened. At this stage he approaches her with care and she, no longer exhibiting antagonism, tends to half-turn away in a manner that in human terms would be called coy. He stops, almost pressed against her, and strokes her nape, shoulder, and breast feathers with his beak, from time to time moving to a new position. Sometimes she responds in kind, but more often merely accepts the caresses.

While all this is occurring, the male is usually making a deep bass humming sound or, less often, a sound deep in his throat like teeth grinding together. Occasionally the pair will fly to a perch in a tree or to another ground perch a short distance away and repeat the caressings. The female finally indicates her full acceptance of him as her mate by joining him in an odd series of wing openings, hoppings, and shufflings. The actual copulation, almost always occurring on the ground, takes place soon after, but now the female seems to accept his attentions with ill-concealed impatience. Mating may be accomplished in as little time as 15 or 20 seconds, but more likely it will last upward of a minute, sometimes even longer. It is generally repeated a half dozen times or more in the ensuing days. The birds thereafter stay relatively close together, but with little further exhibition of any kind of affection on the part of either.

ANNUAL BROODS, NEST, NESTING HABITS

The Great Horned Owl is single-brooded and will rarely lay a second clutch of eggs, even if the first is destroyed. The nest is practically always an abandoned nest of a Red-tailed Hawk, at a height of 40 to 70 feet, firmly placed in a principal upper crotch of the tree. Occasionally it will be much lower. At times, too, the owl will nest in a large natural hollow without sticks or nesting material of any kind, these hollows being as low as 10 or 12 feet, or as high as 50 feet. If food is plentiful in the area, it may use the same nest two or three years in succession, but rarely more than that because by then it has severely depleted the prey of the area.

The Great Horned Owl does virtually nothing to improve the old nest it has taken as its own, and some-times such a nest is in so disreputable a condition that eggs or young will fall through holes and perish. Once in a great while the female will merely lay her eggs on the bare surface of the bark in a particularly low, broad crotch of a huge tree, but such nestings have very limited chances of success. Other unusual nestings occur on bare silo ledges, in cliff crannies, and in hollow logs lying on the ground. Very rarely, the nest will be on open ground surrounded by deep grasses, or in an artificial nesting box.

While nest selection is most often made immediately following courtship, sometimes it occurs much earlier. A female bird (rarely a male and female) will select a nest as early as September or October and remain in the area guarding it against intrusion until ready to put it to use after courtship.

Nesting is undertaken so early in the year that in the more northerly portions of its range, it is not at all unusual for the brooding female to be incubating her eggs while at the same time the ground and branches surrounding her may be covered with a foot or more of snow and the temperature may well be subzero. This seems to inconvenience the female very little and does not have any appreciable deleterious effect upon the eggs.

Both male and female owl will vigorously protect their chosen nest against usurpation by other large birds of prey such as hawks, eagles, or other owls. Even if the bird that built the nest in the first place tries to come back and repossess it, they will drive it off or sometimes kill it. In fact, the nesting Great Horned Owl likes seclusion and will drive away other hawks or owls which may attempt to nest anywhere within a rather wide radius around her nest.

EGGS

Number per nesting Almost always there are two eggs, but there may be only one or, on rare occasions, as many as four or five. On at least three occasions, authenticated reports have been written of nestings in which six eggs were laid.

Color White to slightly dusky white, occasionally with a vague yellowish tinge; even less often with a faint bluish cast.

Shape Quite roundly oval; at times nearly spherical.

Texture The shell is quite thick and coarse to the touch, with very distinct granulation and little or no gloss. On rare occasions, for which there is no adequate explanation, the eggs will be imbued with a rather distinctive glossiness.

Size Based on the measurements of 69 eggs, the average length of the egg was 56.8 mm. (2.2") and its average width was 48.0 mm. (1.9"). Extreme measurements included:

Maximum length: 60.2 mm. (2.4″)
Minimum length: 50.3 mm. (2.0″)
Maximum width: 50.8 mm. (2.0″)
Minimum width: 43.1 mm. (1.7″)

Interval of egg-laying Eggs are laid at an average interval of 72 hours.

Egg-laying dates Southern (Florida): earliest, December 7; latest, April 3; normally between December 28 and January 31.

Middle (Carolinas, Virginia, Tennessee, etc.): earliest, January 12; latest, May 1; normally between January 24 and March 6.

Midwest (Ohio through Iowa): earliest, February 1; latest, May 28; normally between February 8 and March 9.

Northern (New York through New England): earliest, January 17; latest, May 17; normally between February 20 and March 25.

INCUBATION AND BROODING CHARACTERISTICS

Incubation is entirely by the female Great Horned Owl, and her incubation of the eggs is very close because of extreme low temperatures at that time, along with severe weather changes. Even then there are times when the eggs freeze and fail to hatch. Incubation probably begins with the first egg laid in most cases but, if mild weather is prevailing, possibly not until the second or third. The term of incubation is not definitely established and has been recorded as being from as short a time as 21 days to as long as 34 days. Most authorities agree on the figures of 28 to 30 days.

YOUNG AND FAMILY LIFE CHARACTERISTICS

Until the time of hatching, both parent birds stay very close to the nest and guard it well. The protective nature of the parents increases as soon as the young birds hatch. These are about the size of newly hatched chickens and well covered with soft, thick, gray-white down tinged with buff or grayish buff on mid-back and wings. At first the hatchling is barely able to raise his head and peep faintly. The eyes are sealed and the hatchling tends to shiver violently against the cold. Some observers believe that at this stage the young gain a certain amount of protection from the surrounding cold from the fur of the animals that have accumulated in the nest. The parent birds supply a great abundance of food for their young. In one nest in which there were two babies no more than four days

old, there were also 25 different items of prey, all with the head gone; they included one muskrat, one mouse, one cottontail rabbit, one woodcock, two American eels, four ruffed grouse, and eleven rats—the whole assemblage of food weighing just over 18 pounds!

The eyes of the baby birds begin opening on the seventh day but do not become wide open until the end of the ninth or tenth day. During this time, too, the down has become a more buffy gray. At about the eleventh to fourteenth day after hatching, the natal down begins being replaced by the secondary down, which is a dingy buff in color and grayer on the underparts. The eyes are now open wide and the irides are a rather unappealing brownish yellow. By this time, too, the nest has become quite a mess: smeared with excrement, cluttered with pellets, bones, feathers, very often smelling strongly of skunk, putrid meat, and rotted fish.

By the end of the fourteenth day after hatching, the young have attained about one-third their ultimate size. Within another day or two the irides have become a bright lemon yellow and the young birds begin taking an interest in more than just the food being brought by the parents.

Half-growth is attained about the third week, at which time the primaries begin bursting their sheaths and the young birds become decidedly aggressive and even belligerent in their manner, quarreling almost incessantly among themselves. Some young birds fall or are pushed out of the nest by fellow nestlings at this time. They may survive on the ground, as the parent birds will continue feeding them there, but more often they succumb to exposure. By this time, too, the secondary body growth of down is quite long, soft and fluffy, creamy buff in color.

In the fourth week the baby owls are approaching full growth but they are still very definitely fledgling birds. The feathers of wings and back are fairly well developed and the rectrices are sprouting well. Under the secondary down is appearing the soft downy plumage which will be worn, at least in part, until replaced in early autumn by the first-winter plumage. This present new plumage is a more grayish buff and distinctly barred with sooty gray, heavily on the back and slightly less so on the underparts. Ear tufts begin showing at this stage and the facial disks are irregularly mottled with grayish, black, and dark brown. There is quite a good bit of individual color variation in this soft plumage and for the first time it is possible, without seeing the parent birds, to determine that these are fledgling Great Horned Owls and not some other Horned Owl subspecies.

A pair of young Great Horned Owls (*Bubo virginianus virginianus*) about six weeks of age, sketched in a stand of pines near Englewood Dam, Montgomery County, Ohio.

Horned Owl

Great Horned
Owlets

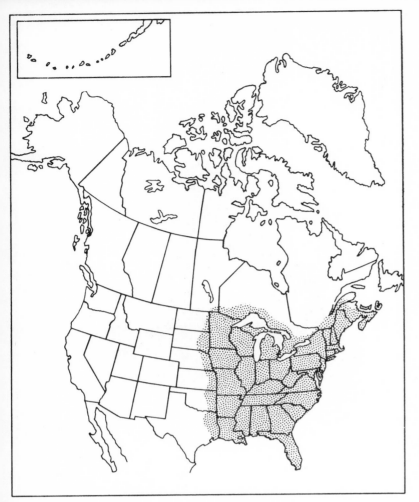

GREAT HORNED OWL

Bubo virginianus virginianus (Gmelin)

In another few days—usually about 32 days after hatching—the young birds begin venturing out onto the surrounding limbs. Some fall and flutter to the ground, but are cared for there by the parent birds and still have an excellent chance of survival. Occasionally, as some recent observations have proved, the young owl that has fallen will walk back to the nest tree and slowly climb back up to the perch from which it fell, gripping with its talons and sometimes with its beak as it goes up the trunk of the tree in a somewhat woodpeckerlike manner.

By the sixth week the young are well feathered and ready to begin testing their wings. They usually wind up on the ground but continue to hop and flap there and make little further effort to climb back up into the tree. They are still incapable of actual flight and, though the parents are still bringing them food, the young begin catching some small creatures on the ground themselves—mostly insects.

At the close of the ninth week the tail is sufficiently developed, along with the wings, to permit flight. The body plumage at this time is still soft and downy. The young birds have now reached their full growth, but their flights are very short at best.

During the twelfth week the young birds are flying quite well and the supply of food being brought by the parent birds tapers off sharply, forcing the young birds

to hunt vigorously for themselves. All summer long the families remain loosely together, the young following their parents and often still screaming demands for food, which are even less often filled.

In the twentieth week the first-winter plumage is coming in well, but the talons at this age are still only half-size. It is not until the twenty-sixth week that the young have fully acquired their first-winter plumage (see Coloration and Markings: Juvenile) and are good fliers and hunters. Autumn is in the air and the young birds either scatter voluntarily or, as sometimes occurs, are driven away by the adults. The young bird will ordinarily establish his own territory within about 20 or 30 miles of where he was hatched. It is believed that the Great Horned Owl does not breed until it is two years old.

DISTRIBUTION IN NORTH AMERICA

From Minnesota, southern Ontario, southern Quebec, western New Brunswick, Prince Edward Island, northern Cape Breton Island, and Nova Scotia southward through southeastern South Dakota, eastern Kansas, eastern Oklahoma, and eastern Texas to the Gulf Coast, and Florida (to Cape Sable).

MIGRATION

The Great Horned Owl is essentially non-migratory, although during especially severe winters when prey becomes extremely difficult to find, there is some slight movement of the more northerly birds.

ECONOMIC INFLUENCE

In some places *Bubo virginianus virginianus* is relatively beneficial because of the large numbers of rodents which make up much of its diet, but everywhere it is quite destructive of game birds, songbirds, game mammals, poultry, and sometimes domestic pets. A single Horned Owl will quite systematically empty a henhouse of all its occupants, one after another, night after night, unless forcefully driven off or killed. Great Horned Owls have caused severe economic losses to breeders of goldfish, bullfrogs, muskrats, and poultry of all kinds.

ST. MICHAEL HORNED OWL

(COLOR PLATE L)

SCIENTIFIC NAME AND ORIGINAL DESCRIPTION

Bubo virginianus algistus (Oberholser). Original description: *Asio magellanicus algistus* Oberholser, *Proceedings of the U. S. National Museum*, Volume 27 (January 22), 1904, pages 178 (in key), 190; based on a specimen from St. Michael, Alaska.

DISTINGUISHING FEATURES

This is a considerably darker bird than the Great Horned Owl (*Bubo virginianus virginianus*) but vaguer in coloration, with fewer barrings on the underparts than is seen on the Northwestern Horned Owl (*Bubo virginianus lagophonus*), its closest relative geographically, and with legs and feet not so conspicuously mottled. In general coloration it is more similar to the Montana Horned Owl (*Bubo virginianus lagophonus*) and the Pacific Horned Owl (*Bubo virginianus pacificus*) than it is to the Northwestern subspecies, though not actually identical in these respects to either the Montana or Pacific subspecies. Its upperparts, especially the wings, are darker and it is less heavily barred on breast, sides, and belly than the Montana race; and it is not only larger than the Pacific race, its facial disks have considerably less brownish yellow and its upperparts are paler.

ST. MICHAEL HORNED OWL
Bubo virginianus algistus (Oberholser)

VOICE

Two distinctive cries of this race are a close mimicry of the yapping bark of the arctic fox, and a squeal uncommonly similar to that voiced by an arctic hare which has been caught by a predator.

GENERAL HABITS AND CHARACTERISTICS

While it prefers dense coniferous forests, especially spruce, somewhat inland from coastal areas, it often frequents the bleak, open coastline of the Bering Strait, perching on the roosting in piles of tree branches which collect on the shoreline.

FOOD

Primarily hares, ground squirrels, red squirrels, and a smaller number of birds and fish. This subspecies is reported to feed, on occasion, on fish carrion.

WASTES

The St. Michael Horned Owl regurgitates extraordinarily large pellets—some of them measuring fully six inches in length and two inches thick.

NEST

Bubo virginianus algistus almost always adopts the abandoned nest of a hawk or eagle, but on extremely rare occasions it has been known to build a nest of its own of sticks loosely interwoven high in a tall spruce standing in the midst of a dense forest of similar trees.

EGGS

Generally two, averaging slightly larger than those of the Great Horned Owl. Average length, 57.2 mm. (2.3″); average width, 48.4 mm. (1.9″). The eggs are normally laid about mid-April.

YOUNG

Well-fledged young are ready to leave the nest toward the latter portion of June.

DISTRIBUTION IN NORTH AMERICA

The coastal region of western Alaska from Kotzebue Sound to Bristol Bay.
Casual at Point Barrow.

LABRADOR HORNED OWL

(COLOR PLATE LI)

SCIENTIFIC NAME AND ORIGINAL DESCRIPTION

Bubo virginianus heterocnemis (Oberholser). Original description: *Asio magellanicus heterocnemis* Oberholser, *Proceedings of the U. S. National Museum,* Volume 27 (January 22), 1904, pages 178 (in key), 187; based on a specimen from Lance au Loup, Labrador.

OTHER NAME

· LE GRAND-DUC DU LABRADOR French-Canadian name meaning "The Grand Duke of Labrador."

DISTINGUISHING FEATURES

The Labrador Horned Owl is larger than the Great Horned Owl (*Bubo virginianus virginianus*), with similar markings but darker all over to quite a degree; the darker underparts and the barring of these underparts often obliterating the white and giving the bird a rather dark-breasted appearance. It is considerably paler in over-all coloration, however, than the Dusky Horned Owl (*Bubo virginianus saturatus*), but with a larger beak.

TOTAL LENGTH

Subspecies average: 560.1 mm. (22.1″).

WINGSPAN

Subspecies average: 1,409.8 mm. (55.6″).

BEAK LENGTH

Subspecies average: 44.5 mm. (1.8″).

GENERAL HABITS AND CHARACTERISTICS

The Labrador Horned Owl has a much keener sense of smell than most other Horned Owl subspecies. The olfactory sense is so sharp that this bird has been known to detect and fly to well-hidden carrion deposits from considerable distances.

HABITAT

Heavily timbered areas are favored, especially if they have an abundance of broken and tangled pines.

FOOD

Mostly ptarmigan, hares, as well as some other birds and fish; equally, a certain amount of carrion is eaten, and the bird has occasionally been caught in steel traps as it has tried to take the dead-animal bait from them.

ANNUAL BROODS, NEST, NESTING HABITS

Only one annual brood, but the Labrador Horned Owl will almost always lay a second clutch of eggs if the first is destroyed. This bird not uncommonly nests on the ground—sometimes in a hollow log, but more often in a shallow depression among deep grasses. It has, in fact, been known to make use of old goose nests on the ground. Sometimes the nest will be in a cavity of a stump, but more often it is a coarse twig nest in a dense spruce at a height of about 40 feet.

A variety of sketches of a nesting Labrador Horned Owl (*Bubo virginianus heterocnemis*) rendered near Goose Bay, Labrador.

This bird struck
when nest was approached
to make drawings
K.E.K

very dark
Facial discs
deep brown

dark
buff

Breast feather

Goose Bay, Labrador
1952

Labrador Horned owl
B. v. heterocnemis

K.E.K

feet buff with dark bars

NORTHWESTERN HORNED OWL

(COLOR PLATE LII)

LABRADOR HORNED OWL

Bubo virginianus heterocnemis (Oberholser)

SCIENTIFIC NAME AND ORIGINAL DESCRIPTION

Bubo virginianus lagophonus (Oberholser). Original description: *Asio magellanicus lagophonus* Oberholser, *Proceedings of the U. S. National Museum,* Volume 27 (January 22), 1904, pages 178 (in key), 185; based on a specimen from Fort Walla Walla, Washington.

OTHER NAMES

BRITISH COLUMBIA HORNED OWL   After its geographical location.

LE GRAND-DUC DU NORD-OUEST   French-Canadian name meaning "The Grand Duke of the Northwest."

DISTINGUISHING FEATURES

The Northwestern Horned Owl is a medium-colored bird which is less tawny and buffy than the Great Horned Owl (*Bubo virginianus virginianus*) and a good bit grayer but much darker than the Arctic Horned Owl (*Bubo virginianus subarcticus*). It is probably the closest in its coloration to the Montana Horned Owl (*Bubo virginianus occidentalis*), but larger and with more contrast between the black-and-white and buffy markings of the underparts. It is lighter generally, and with more yellowish brown and reddish brown in the facial disks than the Dusky Horned Owl (*Bubo virginianus saturatus*). It is both larger and darker than the Pacific Horned Owl (*Bubo virginianus pacificus*), with feet and legs more heavily mottled and the facial disks more reddish dark.

EGGS

Two or three eggs are laid which are just barely larger than those of *Bubo virginianus virginianus.* They are laid about the first week of May.

DISTRIBUTION IN NORTH AMERICA

Wooded portions of northern Quebec (Fort Chimo), Labrador (Okak), and Newfoundland.

Casual in some winters to the south and west as far as Ontario, New Brunswick, and Connecticut (Black Hall).

VOICE

Often heard at dawn with a quite distinctive hooting which sounds like *WHOO-TO-WHOOO WHOOO WHOOO.*

MIGRATION

More of a migratory movement than is seen in most other Horned Owl subspecies, but still by no means a general or regular movement.

A Labrador Horned Owl (*Bubo virginianus heterocnemis*) abroad and hunting during the daylight hours was sketched as it was attacked and severely harassed by crows near Goose-Bay, Labrador, in 1952.

K.E.K

Goose Bay, Labrador
1952

NORTHWESTERN HORNED OWL

Bubo virginianus lagophonus (Oberholser)

NEST AND NESTING HABITS

This owl nests rather earlier than others of the more northerly Horned Owl subspecies. It is considerably more inclined to nest in cliff cuts, on ledges, and in small caves than other *Bubo virginianus* races, but its preference still lies with abandoned hawk or magpie nests fairly high in poplar trees.

EGGS

Seemingly irrespective of whatever bad weather conditions may prevail, the usual two eggs are laid by late February. They are a little smaller than those of the Great Horned Owl, averaging 53.4 mm. (2.1″) in length by 44.5 mm. (1.8″) in width.

DISTRIBUTION IN NORTH AMERICA

Cook Inlet, interior of Alaska (Yukon drainage), and Yukon southward through northern British Columbia (except for the Peace River parklands) to eastern Washington, northeastern Oregon (the Blue and Wallowa mountains), northern Idaho (to the Salmon River drainage), and extreme northwestern Montana (Kalispell).

Casual in winter to Utah (St. George), Colorado, and Nebraska.

GENERAL HABITS AND CHARACTERISTICS

Bubo virginianus lagophonus is rather shy and retiring for a Horned Owl, though at times it can be approached by a man afoot with surprising ease. It has the facility for building up extensive fatty deposits under the skin as winter approaches; thus, a late autumn specimen is apt to weigh easily a third more than the same bird in spring.

MIGRATION

The Northwestern Horned Owl wanders considerably, especially from higher elevations to lower country, along with some southward movement, during the harsher winters.

HABITAT AND ROOSTING

The Northwestern Horned Owl prefers heavily timbered interior areas, especially going well up into the mountains where there are numerous craggy cliff areas. The most preferred types of timber are yellow pine, alpine fir, and black hemlock. In any one of these trees it will roost well concealed very near the top.

MONTANA HORNED OWL

(COLOR PLATE LIII)

SCIENTIFIC NAME AND ORIGINAL DESCRIPTION

Bubo virginianus occidentalis Stone. Original description: *Bubo virginianus occidentalis* Stone, *The Auk*, Volume 13, Number 2, April 1896, page 155; based on a specimen from Mitchell County, Iowa.

FOOD

Mainly rabbits, mice, and rats, but also some grouse, poultry, squirrels, and rarely some snakes.

Horned Owl

DISTINGUISHING FEATURES

Larger and darker than the Western Horned Owl (*Bubo virginianus pallescens*) and, though roughly similar to the Pacific Horned Owl (*Bubo virginianus pacificus*) in size, it has darker feet and legs. It is also somewhat more heavily barred with black, and it lacks (or has considerably less of) the buffy tinge of coloration on both upperparts and underparts.

GENERAL HABITS AND CHARACTERISTICS

The Montana Horned Owl has a peculiar habit of making the motions of hooting but without issuing any sound. Not particularly wary, it is sometimes extraordinarily curious and will visit campsites and stare with great interest at the campers. It also seems to be far more affectionate in courtship and mating than the other Horned Owl subspecies. It is almost always on the hunt during cloudy days.

HABITAT AND ROOSTING

This owl especially favors well-wooded creek bottoms grown up in cottonwood and willow cover. Although it will hunt quite extensively over plains, this is almost always done within sight of the favored creek bottoms. It can be found to elevations of 10,000 feet, and it is the only Horned Owl subspecies that will roost in plain view atop a telephone pole or even on the ground at times.

HUNTING METHODS AND CARRYING OF PREY

Bubo virginianus occidentalis has a habit of swooping down on a running rabbit, snatching the animal up without pause, and killing it with its talons while in flight. It is also an especial hazard to the Long-eared Owls (*Asio otus* sp.).

FOOD

Primarily ground squirrels, rats, mice, rabbits.

EGGS

Normally two eggs, which are just a shade smaller than those of the Great Horned Owl (*Bubo virginianus*

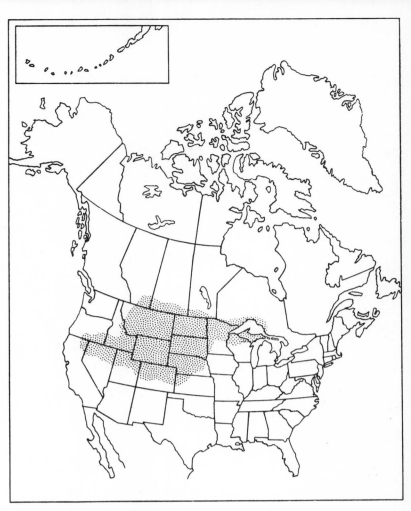

MONTANA HORNED OWL
Bubo virginianus occidentalis Stone

virginianus) and just a bit larger than those of the Northwestern Horned Owl (*Bubo virginianus lagophonus*).

INCUBATION

Unlike other Horned Owl races, the male Montana Horned Owl rather commonly shares in the incubation of the eggs and also in the brooding of hatchlings.

DISTRIBUTION IN NORTH AMERICA

Montana (extreme northwestern section excepted), southern Alberta, southern Saskatchewan, southern Manitoba, northern and western Minnesota, and Isle Royale, Lake Superior; southward through eastern and southern Idaho to southeastern Oregon, northeastern California (Modoc area), central Nevada, central Utah, Colorado, and western and central Kansas.

Casual in winter to Iowa and southern British Columbia.

MIGRATION

There is some movement during especially bad winters, but it is never a general movement of the subspecies and it is highly irregular at best. The most usual movement is simply from higher to lower elevations during the winter months, and even this does not always occur.

ECONOMIC INFLUENCE

Considered beneficial because of its rodent-eating habits in grain-belt areas.

PACIFIC HORNED OWL

(COLOR PLATE LIV)

SCIENTIFIC NAME AND ORIGINAL DESCRIPTION

Bubo virginianus pacificus Cassin. Original description: *Bubo virginianus* var. *pacificus* Cassin, *Illustrated Birds of California, Texas* . . . etc., Part 6 (September 12), 1854, page 178; based on a specimen from Sacramento, California.

OTHER NAMES

CALIFORNIA HORNED OWL   After part of its geographical distribution.
TECOLOTE CORNUDO CALIFORNIANO   Mexican-Indian name meaning "California Horned Owl."

DISTINGUISHING FEATURES

This is the most commonly seen and recorded owl in California. It is a relatively small Horned Owl subspecies, lighter in general coloration than the Dusky Horned Owl (*Bubo virginianus saturatus*) but darker generally than the Western Horned Owl (*Bubo virginianus pallescens*). The Pacific Horned Owl tends to have a general buffy-colored wash to the plumage tone, especially on the upperparts, and there is a tendency in this race toward albinism. It does not have the very dark black-and-white barring which characterizes the Montana Horned Owl (*Bubo virginianus*

PACIFIC HORNED OWL
Bubo virginianus pacificus Cassin

occidentalis). Even though this is one of the smallest races among the Horned Owls, its ear tufts are among the largest, averaging more than two inches in height.

WEIGHT

Subspecies average: 1,383.8 gr. (48.4 oz.).

TOTAL LENGTH

Subspecies average: 504.2 mm. (19.9″).

WINGSPAN

Subspecies average: 1,274.4 mm. (50.2″).

INDIVIDUAL WING LENGTH

Subspecies average: 351.9 mm. (13.9″).

Horned Owl

TAIL LENGTH

Subspecies average: 210.8 mm. (8.3″).

BEAK LENGTH

Subspecies average: 26.9 mm. (1.1″).

HABITAT

Dry forests, wooded foothills, well-wooded river bottoms, and forested canyons from sea level to elevations of 7,000 feet. The Pacific Horned Owl dislikes and avoids the humid coastal-belt forests.

FOOD

Mainly rodents, but also a fair number of brush rabbits, jack rabbits, waterfowl, and pigeons.

NEST

Occasionally in natural hollows in trees. More often, *Bubo virginianus pacificus* prefers abandoned hawk, crow, or magpie nests. Now and again it will nest in an exposed eagle nest or on a protected cliff ledge.

EGGS

The nest of the Pacific Horned Owl, along with the eggs that are in it—usually two—is invariably very badly stained with blood and excrement. The eggs themselves average 53.3 mm. (2.1″) in length by 43.9 mm. (1.7″) in width.

DISTRIBUTION IN NORTH AMERICA

California west of the Great Basin and desert areas (but exclusive of the northern humid coastal forest belt), and southward to Latitude 30° North in northwestern Baja California, and east to extreme west-central Nevada (the Lake Tahoe area).

MIGRATION

None.

WESTERN HORNED OWL
(COLOR PLATE LV)

SCIENTIFIC NAME AND ORIGINAL DESCRIPTION

Bubo virginianus pallescens Stone. Original description: *Bubo virginianus pallescens* Stone, *American Naturalist*, Volume 31, Number 363, March 1, 1897, page 237; based on a specimen from the Watson Ranch, 18 miles southwest of San Antonio, Texas.

OTHER NAMES

DESERT HORNED OWL Because of its habitat near (but not too often directly within) desert areas.
PALLID HORNED OWL After its generally light coloration.
TECOLOTE CORNUDO PÁLIDO Mexican name meaning "Pallid (or Pale) Horned Owl."

DISTINGUISHING FEATURES

About the same size as the Great Horned Owl (*Bubo virginianus virginianus*) but generally much lighter, as it is also lighter than the Pacific Horned Owl (*Bubo virginianus pacificus*). This is a very clearly marked, bleached subspecies of Horned Owl.

HABITAT

Relatively arid but grassy areas, interwoven with well-wooded dry creekbeds, ravines, bluffs, brushy slopes, and cliffs. The Western Horned Owl especially likes areas having large cottonwood trees in the creek bottoms.

FOOD

Mainly rabbits and ground squirrels.

NEST

Sometimes located on the ground in a protected area of rocks or brush, but more often in an aban-

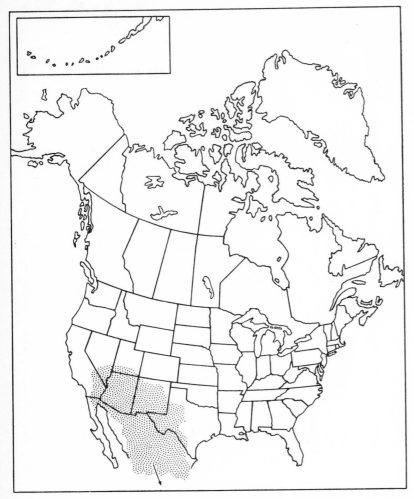

WESTERN HORNED OWL

Bubo virginianus pallescens Stone

doned crow or hawk nest high in a cottonwood, oak, or mesquite. There is some nesting in hollow trees and caves, as well as on cliff ledges and crannies.

EGGS

Almost identical in size to those of the Montana Horned Owl.

DISTRIBUTION IN NORTH AMERICA

Arid regions of southeastern California (from the Inyo District), southern Nevada (Clark County), southern Utah (Virgin River), northern New Mexico, and north-central Texas, southward to extreme northeastern Baja California, northern Sonora (Hermosillo), Chihuahua, Durango, Coahuila, Nuevo León, and northern Tamaulipas, Mexico.

Horned Owl

DUSKY HORNED OWL

(*COLOR PLATE LVI*)

SCIENTIFIC NAME AND ORIGINAL DESCRIPTION

Bubo virginianus saturatus Ridgway. Original description: *Bubo virginianus saturatus* Ridgway, *U. S. Geological Exploration of the 40th Parallel,* Volume 4, Part 3, Ornithology, 1877, page 572 (note); based on a specimen from Sitka, Alaska.

OTHER NAME

LE GRAND-DUC NOIRÂTRE French-Canadian name meaning "The Dusky Grand Duke."

DISTINGUISHING FEATURES

Living up to its common name, the Dusky Horned Owl is by far the darkest Horned Owl subspecies in North America. It is also one of the largest. This owl is similar in its markings to the Western Horned Owl (*Bubo virginianus pallescens*) and the Montana Horned Owl (*Bubo virginianus occidentalis*), but very much darker than either, with the facial disks a deep sooty orange brown, the barring of the upperparts and underparts very close, very dark, and almost excluding light undertones of yellowish brown. From even a short distance away, this bird tends to look black.

WEIGHT

Subspecies average: 1,691.6 gr. (59.2 oz.).

TOTAL LENGTH

Subspecies average: 616.0 mm. (24.3″).

Some posture sketches of the Dusky Horned Owl (*Bubo virginianus saturatus*) along with a detail of one of the primary feathers, showing fluting on the leading edge for soundless flight, and distinct emargination of the tip.

B.V. saturatus

DUSKY HORNED OWL

Bubo virginianus saturatus Ridgway

WINGSPAN

Subspecies average: 1,460.6 mm. (57.6″).

INDIVIDUAL WING LENGTH

Subspecies average: 403.9 mm. (15.9″).

TAIL LENGTH

Subspecies average: 234.1 mm. (9.2″).

BEAK LENGTH

Subspecies average: 42.0 mm. (1.7″).

VOICE

The mating call of the Dusky Horned Owl is a deeply hollow booming sound which carries for great distances and sounds like *WHOOO-WHOOO HOO-HOO WHOOOOO*. This owl—and quite possibly the male only—utters a peculiar and distinctive laughing bark, sometimes at a medium tonal level and at other times lower in pitch toward the end until it seems to fade into inaudibility. It sounds like *HOO-HOO-HOO-HOO-HOO HOO-HOO-hoo-hoo-hoo*.

GENERAL HABITS AND CHARACTERISTICS

Bubo virginianus saturatus is very fond of a daytime perch at a high elevation and with a commanding view of the surrounding country, but will flee at the first suggestion of approach by man. This bird is noted as having an especially powerful grip with its talons and great lifting power for carrying prey.

HABITAT

Strictly the more humid northerly Pacific coastal forest districts.

FOOD

The Dusky Horned Owl rarely if ever smells of skunk, and so it probably does not prey upon *Mephitis* as much as the other Horned Owl races. It is, however, a decided killer of waterfowl—ducks, geese, and swans in particular. If prey is abundant, it will often kill a great many and eat only the heads of each. It is more regularly a feeder on birds than most other Horned Owl races.

NEST

Usually an old hawk nest about 45 feet high in a fir or spruce tree.

EGGS

Despite the fact that this is the largest of the Horned Owls, its eggs are about the same size or perhaps even a trifle smaller than those of the Great Horned Owl (*Bubo virginianus virginianus*). They are usually laid in the latter half of February to the middle of March.

Horned Owl

DISTRIBUTION IN NORTH AMERICA

Humid region of the Pacific coast from southeastern Alaska (Glacier Bay) through coastal British Columbia, Washington, and Oregon, from the Cascade Range westward, and a narrow coastal belt in California south to Monterey Bay (Santa Cruz).

Occasional winter visitor to interior British Columbia (Okanagan).

MIGRATION

The Dusky Horned Owl makes very little of a southerly migrational movement, but great numbers do move from the higher elevations to the lowlands in late autumn and early winter. Oddly, female birds seem to predominate in these migrations, and the movement seems to have little to do with weather or food availability, since it is as pronounced during mild winters as during the more severe winters.

ONTARIO HORNED OWL

(COLOR PLATE LVII)

ONTARIO HORNED OWL
Bubo virginianus scalariventris Snyder

SCIENTIFIC NAME AND ORIGINAL DESCRIPTION

Bubo virginianus scalariventris Snyder. Original description: *Bubo virginianus scalariventris* Snyder, *Royal Ontario Museum Publication*, Volume 54, Number 5, Cont.; based on a specimen taken in 1961 in northeastern Manitoba. Until 1961 this owl was classed with the Tundra Horned Owl (*Bubo virginianus wapacuthu*), which is listed in the 1957 A.O.U. Check-list.

DISTINGUISHING FEATURES

The Ontario Horned Owl subspecies is a very light-colored race, much lighter generally than even the lightest of the Great Horned Owls (*Bubo virginianus virginianus*) or the Western Horned Owl (*Bubo virginianus pallescens*), yet substantially darker buff gray than the Tundra Horned Owl from which it was considered separable in 1961. The validity of this reclassification is still under discussion, but the differences are believed to be racially strong enough to support inclusion of the form in this volume as a separate subspecies.

HABITAT

Muskeg and tamarack swamps and areas of partial tundra relatively adjacent to treed areas.

DISTRIBUTION IN NORTH AMERICA

Breeding data on this race are still sketchy at best, but as nearly as can be ascertained, breeding is rather closely limited to northern and western Ontario, with some possible extension westward into north-central Manitoba, from the Hudson Bay region near the mouth of Kettle River to the Churchill River basin.

MIGRATION

None.

ARCTIC HORNED OWL

(COLOR PLATE LVIII)

Dusky/Ontario/Arctic Horned Owl

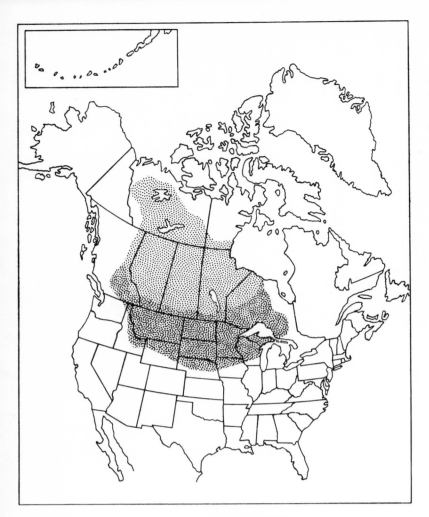

ARCTIC HORNED OWL
Bubo virginianus subarcticus (Hoy)

SCIENTIFIC NAME AND ORIGINAL DESCRIPTION

Bubo virginianus subarcticus (Hoy). Original description: *Bubo virginianus arcticus* Hoy, *Proceedings of the Academy of Natural Sciences of Philadelphia*, Volume 6, 1852, page 211; based on a specimen taken near Racine, Wisconsin.

OTHER NAMES

WHITE HORNED OWL After generally light coloration.

LE GRAND-DUC ARCTIQUE French-Canadian name meaning "The Grand Duke of the Arctic."

DISTINGUISHING FEATURES

The Arctic Horned Owl is a very stately, extremely pale and extensively white Horned Owl subspecies, similar to the Tundra Horned Owl (*Bubo virginianus*

wapacuthu), but with rather narrower barring on both upperparts and underparts, and more extensively barred on sides and flanks. There is a definite lack of brownish or orangish coloration in the general plumage ground color. There is a broad median line connected to the gular region, the whole of immaculate white plumage. Scattered irregular blotches of jet black are on the sides of the gular region, and there is a narrow broken line of black across the throat. The facial disks are almost pure white, with a slight orangish cast close to the eyes, and the facial rim is jet black. Quite similar in pattern to the Montana Horned Owl (*Bubo virginianus occidentalis*), but much lighter. Closer in general coloration to the Ontario Horned Owl (*Bubo virginianus scalariventris*) but markedly lighter generally, with more pure white and less black, and possibly a little larger.

FOOD

Almost exclusively ptarmigan, arctic hares, and waterfowl.

NEST

Mostly in abandoned hawk nests in dense tamarack, but sometimes in deep ground grass, well hidden, in muskeg areas.

DISTRIBUTION IN NORTH AMERICA

Mackenzie, central-eastern British Columbia, Alberta (except in the mountains), Saskatchewan, Manitoba, northern and western Ontario, Hudson Bay, and the northern tree limits to the valley of the Mackenzie.

Winters to southern British Columbia and the northern United States from Idaho to Nebraska and Wyoming.

Casual in New York, Massachusetts, and Oregon.

MIGRATION

The Arctic Horned Owl undertakes some irregular southerly movement and considerably more easterly movement during particularly harsh winters.

Some sketches of the Ontario Horned Owl (*Bubo virginianus scalariventris*) observed in a heavily wooded area of northwestern Roseau County, Minnesota, with some details of facial feathers and foot.

Horned Owl

Ear covert feather

Lores feather

Ontario
Horned Owl
B.V. scalariventris

Roseau Co., ♀
Minnesota
March 1-1957

malar region feather

Facial disc
on some specimens
Pale buff

barred
sepia

feet white
heavily feathered

N.E.K.

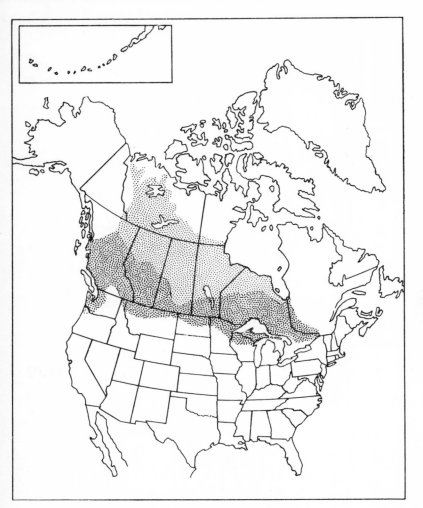

TUNDRA HORNED OWL

Bubo virginianus wapacuthu (Gmelin)

TUNDRA HORNED OWL

(COLOR PLATE LIX SEE

FRONTISPIECE)

SCIENTIFIC NAME AND ORIGINAL DESCRIPTION

Bubo virginianus wapacuthu (Gmelin). Original description: *Strix wapacuthu* Gmelin, *Systematica Natura,* Volume 1, Part 1, 1788, page 290; based on the Wapacuthu Owl of Pennant, *Arctic Zoology,* Volume 1, 1785, page 231, from a specimen taken in the woods about Hudson Bay.

DISTINGUISHING FEATURES

Considerable confusion and scientific discussion still reign over whether or not the Ontario Horned Owl (*Bubo virginianus scalariventris*), the Arctic Horned Owl (*Bubo virginianus subarcticus*), and this Tundra Horned Owl are all valid subspecies. The most recent

(1957 Edition) American Ornithological Union Checklist includes only the latter, with the Ontario Horned Owl and the Arctic Horned Owl included as a part of the *Bubo virginianus wapacuthu* classification. The difference in the three, however, seems to the authors to be significant enough to include each as a separate subspecies for the purpose of this volume, although the reader should bear in mind the nebulosity of the classification.

Generally speaking, the Tundra Horned Owl is lighter grayish than the Ontario Horned Owl, but slightly darker than the Arctic Horned Owl. The lines of demarcation become difficult in the extreme light or dark specimens of each race. Some Tundra Horned Owl specimens, for example, are very nearly as white as the Snowy Owls—a whiteness which the Arctic Horned Owl does not approach, even though the Arctic Horned Owl is generally lighter in coloration than the Tundra Horned Owl.

HABITAT

Bubo virginianus wapacuthu generally prefers somewhat less forested areas than the Ontario Horned Owl or the Arctic Horned Owl, although some scattered trees are essential.

FOOD

Arctic hares, lemmings, ptarmigans, waterfowl.

DISTRIBUTION IN NORTH AMERICA

Breeds from the tree limit in the Mackenzie Valley to Hudson Bay, and in northeastern British Columbia (Peace River), southward to central Alberta, Saskatchewan, central Manitoba, and northern Ontario.

Winters south to western Washington, southern British Columbia, northern Idaho, Wisconsin, and southern Ontario.

MIGRATION

There is a slight tendency to southerly and easterly migrational movements on a highly irregular basis, when winters are the most vicious.

Some attitude and posture sketches of the Arctic Horned Owl (*Bubo virginianus subarcticus*).

Horned Owl (Tundra)

B. V. Subaratius

KBK

COMPARISON TABLE 1

Relative Size of North American Owl Species

There is no accurate way to rank birds of the same Family according to size except by combining the figures of total length, wingspan, and weight. For example, the Great Gray Owl (*Strix nebulosa nebulosa*) surpasses both the Snowy Owl (*Nyctea scandiaca*) and the Great Horned Owl (*Bubo virginianus virginianus*) in total length, yet both Snowy Owl and Great Horned Owl surpass the Great Gray Owl not only in weight, but in wingspan as well. Therefore, to say that one owl is bigger than another on the basis of one factor alone can be very misleading. The authors, however, have discovered that by adding together the measurement figures for weight, total length, and wingspan, carried to three decimal places, a quite accurate number will result for comparison purposes. For example, the measurements of the Snowy Owl totaled 171.877 points (derived by adding the ounces of maximum weight (70.091), the inches of total length (30.216), and the inches of wingspan (71.570). Lengths of beak and tail are, of course, included in the total length figure for the bird and not added separately. The system has worked quite well and the authors recommend it highly for establishing relative-size listings within any particular Family of birds.

In the following Comparison Table, rank in size as largest has been determined by adding together the figures for maximum weight, maximum total length, and maximum wingspan, thereby arriving at the point count as described above. Rank in size as smallest has been determined by adding together the figures for minimum weight, minimum total length, and minimum wingspan.

Smallest

Rank	Species	Points
1st	Whitney's Elf Owl	19.842
2nd	Rocky Mountain Pygmy Owl	22.030
3rd	Ferruginous Owl	22.308
4th	Flammulated Owl	24.862
5th	Whiskered Owl	26.439
6th	Saw-whet Owl	28.073
7th	Eastern Screech Owl	31.656
8th	Richardson's Owl	34.668
9th	Western Burrowing Owl	36.727
10th	American Hawk Owl	51.750
11th	Long-eared Owl	56.780
12th	Short-eared Owl	60.631
13th	California Spotted Owl	63.377
14th	Northern Barred Owl	65.599
15th	Barn Owl	65.672
16th	Great Gray Owl	112.680
17th	Great Horned Owl	115.834
18th	Snowy Owl	123.483

COMPARISON TABLE 2

Average Egg Size

Species	Millimeters	Inches
Snowy Owl	59.5×45.5	2.3×1.8
Great Horned Owl	56.8×48.0	2.2×1.9
Great Gray Owl	55.3×43.9	2.2×1.7
Northern Barred Owl	50.0×41.9	2.0×1.7
California Spotted Owl	50.0×41.3	2.0×1.6
Barn Owl	42.4×32.4	1.7×1.3
Long-eared Owl	40.1×33.3	1.6×1.3
Short-eared Owl	39.6×31.9	1.6×1.3
American Hawk Owl	39.3×31.5	1.6×1.2
Eastern Screech Owl	35.8×30.0	1.4×1.2
Whiskered Owl	32.9×27.3	1.3×1.1
Western Burrowing Owl	32.9×27.3	1.3×1.1
Richardson's Owl	32.2×26.9	1.3×1.1
Saw-whet Owl	30.5×25.1	1.2×1.0
Ferruginous Owl	29.0×23.6	1.1×0.9
Flammulated Owl	27.7×23.6	1.1×0.9
Whitney's Elf Owl	27.5×23.5	1.1×0.9
Rocky Mountain Pygmy Owl	26.7×23.8	1.1×0.9

RANK IN SIZE OF THE OWLS

Largest

Rank	Species	Points
1st	Snowy Owl	171.877
2nd	Great Horned Owl	153.384
3rd	Great Gray Owl	146.719
4th	Northern Barred Owl	91.856
5th	California Spotted Owl	89.119
6th	Barn Owl	86.163
7th	Short-eared Owl	76.296
8th	Long-eared Owl	71.021
9th	American Hawk Owl	62.310
10th	Richardson's Owl	46.162
11th	Western Burrowing Owl	43.326
12th	Eastern Screech Owl	42.519
13th	Saw-whet Owl	35.068
14th	Whiskered Owl	34.099
15th	Flammulated Owl	32.404
16th	Ferruginous Owl	26.298
17th	Rocky Mountain Pygmy Owl	25.080
18th	Whitney's Elf Owl	22.717

COMPARISON TABLE 3

Maximum Weight

Species	Grams	Ounces
Snowy Owl	2,002.6	70.1
Great Horned Owl	1,876.0	65.7
Great Gray Owl	1,523.9	53.3
Northern Barred Owl	651.2	22.8
California Spotted Owl	591.1	20.7
Barn Owl	573.2	20.1
Short-eared Owl	429.4	15.0
Long-eared Owl	333.4	11.7
American Hawk Owl	273.5	9.6
Richardson's Owl	235.2	8.2
Western Burrowing Owl	222.7	7.8
Eastern Screech Owl	222.4	7.8
Whiskered Owl	186.7	6.5
Flammulated Owl	149.3	5.2
Saw-whet Owl	124.1	4.3
Ferruginous Owl	88.2	3.1
Rocky Mountain Pygmy Owl	50.7	1.8
Whitney's Elf Owl	30.6	1.1

COMPARISON TABLE 4

Average Weight

Species	Grams	Ounces
Snowy Owl	1,659.8	58.1
Great Horned Owl	1,522.9	53.3
Great Gray Owl	1,339.9	46.9
Northern Barred Owl	450.9	15.8
California Spotted Owl	446.9	15.6
Barn Owl	442.2	15.5
Short-eared Owl	311.8	10.9
Long-eared Owl	275.2	9.6
American Hawk Owl	238.7	8.4
Richardson's Owl	217.5	7.6
Western Burrowing Owl	208.3	7.3
Eastern Screech Owl	204.0	7.1
Whiskered Owl	163.0	5.7
Flammulated Owl	131.8	4.6
Saw-whet Owl	104.3	3.7
Ferruginous Owl	80.4	2.8
Rocky Mountain Pygmy Owl	42.8	1.5
Whitney's Elf Owl	25.6	0.9

COMPARISON TABLE 5

Minimum Weight

Species	Grams	Ounces
Whitney's Elf Owl	17.0	0.6
Rocky Mountain Pygmy Owl	34.6	1.2
Ferruginous Owl	65.5	2.3
Saw-whet Owl	84.3	3.0
Flammulated Owl	113.6	4.0
Whiskered Owl	145.6	5.1
Eastern Screech Owl	166.0	5.8
Western Burrowing Owl	180.5	6.3
Richardson's Owl	192.7	6.7
American Hawk Owl	194.1	6.8
Long-eared Owl	215.4	7.5
Short-eared Owl	261.3	9.2
Barn Owl	311.9	10.9
California Spotted Owl	312.1	10.9
Northern Barred Owl	330.0	11.6
Great Gray Owl	1,056.8	37.0
Great Horned Owl	1,383.8	48.4
Snowy Owl	1,448.0	50.7

COMPARISON TABLE 6

Maximum Total Length

(Outstretched, tip of beak to tip of tail feathers)

Species	Millimeters	Inches
Great Gray Owl	845.3	33.3
Snowy Owl	766.9	30.2
Great Horned Owl	641.5	25.3
Northern Barred Owl	613.7	24.2
California Spotted Owl	606.3	23.9
Barn Owl	534.7	21.1
American Hawk Owl	446.7	17.6
Short-eared Owl	434.7	17.1
Long-eared Owl	407.7	16.1
Richardson's Owl	308.6	12.2
Western Burrowing Owl	284.5	11.2
Eastern Screech Owl	264.4	10.4
Saw-whet Owl	217.2	8.6
Whiskered Owl	190.6	7.5
Rocky Mountain Pygmy Owl	190.6	7.5
Flammulated Owl	188.7	7.4
Ferruginous Owl	183.2	7.2
Whitney's Elf Owl	167.1	6.6

COMPARISON TABLE 7

Minimum Total Length

(Outstretched, tip of beak to tip of tail feathers)

Species	Millimeters	Inches
Whitney's Elf Owl	135.5	5.3
Ferruginous Owl	146.1	5.8
Flammulated Owl	151.0	6.0
Rocky Mountain Pygmy Owl	160.0	6.3
Whiskered Owl	166.4	6.6
Eastern Screech Owl	176.3	7.0
Saw-whet Owl	179.1	7.1
Richardson's Owl	209.6	8.3
Western Burrowing Owl	212.9	8.4
Long-eared Owl	328.9	13.0
Short-eared Owl	336.3	13.3
Barn Owl	360.7	14.2
American Hawk Owl	363.5	14.3
California Spotted Owl	389.3	15.3
Northern Barred Owl	407.9	16.1
Great Horned Owl	468.1	18.4
Snowy Owl	531.1	20.9
Great Gray Owl	617.3	24.3

COMPARISON TABLE 8

Maximum Wingspan

(Outstretched, tip of wing to tip of wing)

Species	Millimeters	Inches
Snowy Owl	1,816.5	71.6
Great Horned Owl	1,575.0	62.1
Great Gray Owl	1,524.8	60.1
Barn Owl	1,143.0	45.0
Northern Barred Owl	1,139.2	44.9
California Spotted Owl	1,130.5	44.5
Short-eared Owl	1,120.3	44.1
Long-eared Owl	1,098.7	43.3
American Hawk Owl	891.8	35.1
Richardson's Owl	654.1	25.8
Eastern Screech Owl	617.2	24.3
Western Burrowing Owl	616.3	24.3
Saw-whet Owl	562.6	22.2
Whiskered Owl	509.0	20.1
Flammulated Owl	501.1	19.7
Ferruginous Owl	405.9	16.0
Rocky Mountain Pygmy Owl	400.9	15.8
Whitney's Elf Owl	382.3	15.1

COMPARISON TABLE 9

Minimum Wingspan

(Outstretched, tip of wing to tip of wing)

Species	Millimeters	Inches
Whitney's Elf Owl	353.1	13.9
Ferruginous Owl	361.9	14.3
Rocky Mountain Pygmy Owl	368.4	14.5
Whiskered Owl	375.3	14.8
Flammulated Owl	379.1	14.9
Saw-whet Owl	458.5	18.1
Eastern Screech Owl	479.7	18.9
Richardson's Owl	499.1	19.7
Western Burrowing Owl	558.9	22.0
American Hawk Owl	777.5	30.6
Long-eared Owl	920.9	36.3
California Spotted Owl	942.0	37.1
Northern Barred Owl	963.9	38.0
Short-eared Owl	970.9	38.3
Barn Owl	1,029.0	40.5
Great Horned Owl	1,242.6	49.0
Great Gray Owl	1,303.8	51.4
Snowy Owl	1,316.7	51.9

COMPARISON TABLE 10

Maximum Individual Wing Length

(Carpal joint to outstretched wing tip)

Species	Millimeters	Inches
Snowy Owl	447.3	18.8
Great Horned Owl	430.5	17.0
Great Gray Owl	426.2	16.8
Barn Owl	356.6	14.1
Northern Barred Owl	355.6	14.0
California Spotted Owl	355.5	14.0
Short-eared Owl	336.7	13.3
Long-eared Owl	301.0	11.9
American Hawk Owl	229.7	9.1
Richardson's Owl	190.9	7.5
Western Burrowing Owl	184.3	7.3
Eastern Screech Owl	177.8	7.0
Whiskered Owl	148.8	5.9
Flammulated Owl	145.1	5.7
Saw-whet Owl	144.9	5.7
Ferruginous Owl	116.8	4.6
Rocky Mountain Pygmy Owl	106.8	4.2
Whitney's Elf Owl	102.0	4.0

COMPARISON TABLE 11

Minimum Individual Wing Length

(Carpal joint to outstretched wing tip)

Species	Millimeters	Inches
Ferruginous Owl	89.4	3.5
Whitney's Elf Owl	98.8	3.9
Rocky Mountain Pygmy Owl	99.8	3.9
Whiskered Owl	124.3	4.9
Saw-whet Owl	127.0	5.0
Flammulated Owl	128.3	5.1
Western Burrowing Owl	147.5	5.8
Eastern Screech Owl	156.2	6.2
Richardson's Owl	158.9	6.3
American Hawk Owl	212.7	8.4
Long-eared Owl	269.2	10.6
Short-eared Owl	284.9	11.2
Northern Barred Owl	307.3	12.1
Barn Owl	311.2	12.3
California Spotted Owl	322.8	12.7
Great Horned Owl	355.8	14.0
Great Gray Owl	358.2	14.1
Snowy Owl	395.3	15.6

COMPARISON TABLE 12

Maximum Tail Length

(Longest rectrix from flesh to outermost tip)

Species	Millimeters	Inches
Great Gray Owl	344.8	13.6
Snowy Owl	261.7	10.3
Northern Barred Owl	260.4	10.3
California Spotted Owl	254.5	10.0
Great Horned Owl	231.6	9.1
Barn Owl	192.6	7.6
American Hawk Owl	184.8	7.3
Long-eared Owl	168.9	6.7
Short-eared Owl	158.8	6.3
Richardson's Owl	119.9	4.7
Eastern Screech Owl	95.5	3.8
Western Burrowing Owl	89.1	3.5
Ferruginous Owl	88.9	3.5
Whiskered Owl	76.3	3.0
Saw-whet Owl	74.0	2.9
Rocky Mountain Pygmy Owl	71.3	2.8
Flammulated Owl	64.9	2.6
Whitney's Elf Owl	60.3	2.4

COMPARISON TABLE 13

Minimum Tail Length

(Longest rectrix from flesh to outermost tip)

Species	Millimeters	Inches
Whitney's Elf Owl	50.8	2.0
Ferruginous Owl	56.7	2.2
Whiskered Owl	57.2	2.3
Flammulated Owl	57.8	2.3
Rocky Mountain Pygmy Owl	58.8	2.3
Saw-whet Owl	66.9	2.6
Western Burrowing Owl	73.4	2.9
Eastern Screech Owl	75.1	3.0
Richardson's Owl	88.1	3.5
Barn Owl	124.8	4.9
Short-eared Owl	135.9	5.4
Long-eared Owl	143.1	5.6
American Hawk Owl	173.0	6.8
Great Horned Owl	208.2	8.2
California Spotted Owl	210.1	8.3
Northern Barred Owl	212.3	8.4
Snowy Owl	230.4	9.1
Great Gray Owl	287.0	11.3

COMPARISON TABLE 14

Maximum Beak Length

(From cere on straight line to tip)

Species	Millimeters	Inches
Great Gray Owl	47.1	1.9
Great Horned Owl	46.6	1.8
Barn Owl	30.5	1.2
Snowy Owl	28.2	1.1
Northern Barred Owl	24.6	1.0
California Spotted Owl	23.5	0.9
Long-eared Owl	20.6	0.8
American Hawk Owl	20.1	0.8
Short-eared Owl	19.9	0.8
Eastern Screech Owl	18.7	0.7
Whiskered Owl	18.1	0.7
Richardson's Owl	16.6	0.7
Western Burrowing Owl	15.3	0.6
Saw-whet Owl	13.0	0.5
Flammulated Owl	11.1	0.4
Rocky Mountain Pygmy Owl	10.3	0.4
Ferruginous Owl	9.9	0.4
Whitney's Elf Owl	9.4	0.4

COMPARISON TABLE 15

Minimum Beak Length

(From cere on straight line to tip)

Species	Millimeters	Inches
Whitney's Elf Owl	8.1	0.3
Ferruginous Owl	8.2	0.3
Rocky Mountain Pygmy Owl	8.6	0.3
Flammulated Owl	8.7	0.3
Saw-whet Owl	11.5	0.5
Western Burrowing Owl	12.5	0.5
Richardson's Owl	13.3	0.5
Whiskered Owl	13.5	0.5
Eastern Screech Owl	14.1	0.6
Long-eared Owl	15.2	0.6
Short-eared Owl	15.8	0.6
American Hawk Owl	18.2	0.7
California Spotted Owl	20.3	0.8
Northern Barred Owl	21.1	0.8
Barn Owl	21.1	0.8
Snowy Owl	24.6	1.0
Great Gray Owl	28.0	1.1
Great Horned Owl	30.8	1.2

Comparison Tables

GLOSSARY

ADULT   An owl of breeding age; fully mature in all respects, including plumage.

ALBINISM   The complete absence of color pigmentation in plumage, skin, and eyes. A true albino will have white feathers and pinkish eyes, beak, and feet. (See also Melanism.)

ALULA   Also called "the bastard wing"; a group of three to six small stiff feathers growing on the pollex (or thumb) of the owl's wing.

ANAL AREA   The area immediately surrounding the anus or vent; also called the crissum.

ARBOREAL   Associated with or residing in trees of any kind.

ASYMMETRICAL   Not symmetrical; that is, not the same in size or placement on opposite sides of the owl, as in asymmetrical ears, meaning ears with openings, cavities, or placement not the same on opposing sides of the head.

AUDITORY   Pertaining to the sense of hearing.

AURICULARS   The feathers covering the ear openings; usually movable to some degree through muscular control.

AXILLARIES   The rather longer feathers of the owl's axilla or armpit area.

BARRINGS   The transverse (side-to-side) markings on the owl's plumage. (See also Streaks.)

BEAK (OR BILL)   The horny mouthparts (or jaws), comprised of the upper mandible and lower mandible.

BEAK LENGTH   The straight-line length of the upper beak (or upper mandible) from cere to tip, as measured with calipers.

BOREAL   Of a northern geographical area, chiefly the Nearctic subregion.

BRISTLE   A hairlike feather, usually short and stiff, such as those located on the feet and near the mouth corners of some owls.

BROODING   The act of the parent bird sitting over young to keep them at a proper temperature. (See also Incubation.)

CARPAL JOINT   The wrist; the upper bend of the owl's wing; often mistakenly referred to as the elbow.

CASUAL   Occurring in a geographical area more as the exception than as the rule.

CERE   The fleshy area at the base of the owl's upper beak, in which the nostrils are located.

CLOACA   The common cavity inside the vent or anus, through which wastes are expelled, copulation occurs, and eggs are laid.

CLUTCH   The total group of eggs deposited by one owl in its nest in one laying period.

CONCENTRIC   Circular (or largely circular) rings within one another, not joined but having a common center.

CONIFEROUS   Pertaining to trees bearing cones, such as pines, firs, cedars, cypress, spruce.

CONTOUR FEATHERS   The general body feathering of the owl which forms the outline shape, as distinguished from wing and tail feathers.

COSMOPOLITAN   Having a world-wide range rather than being restricted to a smaller geographical location.

COVERTS   A patch or area of overlying feathers which cover the base of other feathers.

CREPUSCULAR   Distinctly active at the twilight periods of the day, both morning and evening, but especially evening. (See also Diurnal and Nocturnal.)

CROWN   The uppermost area of the owl's head.

CULMEN   The upper curve of the upper beak (or upper mandible) of the owl, from point of beak to cere; sometimes incorrectly used to signify the entire upper beak including the cere.

DECIDUOUS   Trees (or shrubs) which lose their leaves seasonally; especially hardwood trees: oaks, elms, maples, cottonwoods, willows.

DEFECATION   The act of expelling bodily wastes through the vent or anus.

DICHROMATIC   Having two distinct color phases within one race of owls; these color phases not normally predicated upon sex, age, season, climate, or geographical location.

DISTRIBUTION   The normal geographical range within which the owl is resident, and to which it may migrate in a regular way.

DIURNAL   Distinctly active during the daylight hours, especially between sunrise and sunset. (See also Crepuscular and Nocturnal.)

DORSAL   Pertaining to the back or the upper portion of a part or the whole.

DOWN   Soft, fluffy feathers, often of short duration; the first (and sometimes successive) feathering of the baby owl.

EAR   The auditory openings and inner structure on each side of the owl's skull, ordinarily not visible without parting the plumage or lifting the auriculars toward the outer rim of the facial disks.

EAR TUFTS   The earlike, erectile feathers on each side of the crown; always paired and symmetrical on the individual owl; often called ears, but having nothing whatever to do with the sense of hearing.

EMARGINATE   Feathers (especially outer primaries) which have a distinctly indented or notched margin on the terminal portion of the inner webbing.

FACIAL DISKS   The distinctly saucerlike rounded areas of short (usually lighter-colored) plumage on the owl's face surrounding the eyes.

FACIAL RIM   The narrow line of feathers (usually darker and slightly larger) which encircles the facial disks.

FAMILY   A group of Genera (see Genus) which agree in certain characteristics but which differ in one or more other characteristics from other Families belonging to the same Order. In North America there are two owl Families: the *Tytonidae* (Barn Owls) and *Strigidae* (typical owls), both of which belong to the Order *Strigiformes* (Owls).

FECES   The solid or semisolid digestive wastes expelled by the owl through the vent.

FERRUGINOUS   Reddish brown in color, like rusty iron.

FLANKS   The longish plumes overlying the legs and lower sides of the owl.

FLUSH   To disturb any bird into a run or flight.

FLUTINGS   The toothlike formations on the leading edges of the feathers, especially the flight feathers; these comblike feather edges muffle the sound of wind passage over the feather's edge, thus permitting the soundless flight for which owls are noted.

GAPE   The opening of the mouth, usually to its widest extent.

GENUS   (*plural* Genera). A single species or group of species sufficiently unlike other species in certain physical characteristics to justify separate classification from other genera of the family to which they belong. In North American Owls, the Long-eared Owl and the Western Long-eared Owl both belong to the genus *Asio* and the species *otus*, and the Short-eared Owl also belongs to the genus *Asio*, but to the species *flammeus*.

GRANULATED   A grainy or granular texture, as of a minute lumpiness on the shells of some owl eggs.

GREATER WING COVERTS   The largest wing coverts on the owl; those which overlie the base of the secondaries.

GREGARIOUS   Tending to gather together in groups or flocks, especially during migratory periods.

GROUND COLOR   The basic, most immediately apparent general coloration of the visible surface of the owl's plumage.

GULAR AREA   The region of the throat, extending toward the sides, but especially the upper and central portions of the throat.

HEEL   The backward-bending joint of the leg above the tarsus; often erroneously referred to as the knee.

IMMACULATE   Pertaining to plumage (or sometimes some other physical aspect) that is of solid color or whiteness, unspotted or otherwise unmarked.

IMMATURE   Pertaining to an adult-sized owl that is not yet of breeding age and that usually has some degree of plumage difference from adult owls of the same species.

INCUBATION   The act of the parent bird in setting over the eggs to maintain an even temperature which allows development of the embryo and subsequent hatching. (See also Brooding.)

INCUBATION PERIOD   The duration of time from the beginning of incubation until the egg hatches; among owls this is not necessarily from the time of laying to the time of hatching, since incubation is often delayed in the first or second eggs laid.

IRIS   (*plural* Irides). The colored portion of the eye surrounding the pupil.

JUVENAL PLUMAGE   A specific feather covering worn by an immature bird at one stage in its period as a juvenile.

JUVENILE   An owl which has not yet acquired adult plumage.

LENGTH   The total length of an owl outstretched to its fullest limit, measured in a straight line from the outermost tip of the beak to the outermost tip of the longest tail feather.

LESSER WING COVERTS   The coverts nearest the bend of the wing and overlying the base of the middle (or median) coverts.

LINEAR   Narrow and long, like a line.

LORES   The space between eyes and beak, feathered or unfeathered.

MACULATE   Marked, spotted, or blotched. (See also Immaculate.)

MALAR REGION   The general lower cheek area of the owl's facial disk, running to the base of the lower mandible.

MANDIBLE   Either of the horny jaws of an owl's beak.

MATURE   Pertaining to an owl that has acquired full adult plumage and the ability to reproduce.

MEDIAN   (also Medial). The center line of the owl from head to tail; also the center line of any particular part; most often associated with breast, belly, and back.

MELANISM   An abnormal darkness of the plumage to black or near black, usually most apparent on breast and belly plumage. (See also Albinism.)

MIDDLE WING COVERTS   (or Median Wing Coverts). The middle coverts of the upperpart of the wing, overlying the base of the greater wing coverts, and overlaid at their own base by the lesser wing coverts.

MIGRATION   The movement from one geographical location to another, often due to conditions of food supply or climate.

MOLT   The process (usually annual among owls) of replacing old feathers with new; generally occurring among owls in late summer and autumn.

NAPE   The back of the neck, below the occiput.

NOCTURNAL   Distinctly active at night. (See also Crepuscular and Diurnal.)

OCCIPUT   The upper-back part of the owl's head, below the crown and above the nape.

OLFACTORY   Pertaining to the sense of smell.

ORDER   A group of families with like characteristics, but differing in certain other characteristics from other orders belonging to the same Class. Owls and Hawks both belong to the Class *Aves* (Birds), but Owls belong to the Order *Strigiformes* and Hawks to the Order *Falconiformes*.

ORNITHOLOGY   The study of birds as a separate branch of zoology.

PELLET   A usually compact and initially mucus-coated, oval-shaped bundle of hair, feathers, skulls and other bones, teeth, claws, and other undigestible materials which are regurgitated by the owl.

PENCILING   A set of fine, relatively straight, pencil-like lines (usually transverse) on the owl's plumage, often divergent or convergent at the sides. (See also Vermiculation.)

PLUMAGE   The complete feather covering of any bird.

POSTNUPTIAL   Following the breeding season; for example, applied to the molt and the plumage acquired when the breeding season ends.

POSTORBITAL   Behind or in back of the eye.

PRIMARIES   (*singular* Primary). The principal outer flight feathers of each wing; the quills. (See also Secondaries and Rectrices.)

PUPIL   The central black of the eye, which is surrounded by the iris.

QUILL   Usually a primary wing feather, but sometimes a larger tail feather; the central horny shaft of any feather.

RACE (OR FORM)   See Subspecies.

RECTRICES   (*singular* Rectrix). The tail feathers of any bird.

REGURGITATION   The act of oral ejection by the owl of previously swallowed compact bundles (called pellets) of undigestible materials.

RESIDENT   An owl native to a particular geographical location.

RUFESCENT   Reddish in color.

RUMP   The dorsal portion of the owl between back and tail.

SCAPULARS   Longish feathers, usually broader than others around them, which overlie the shoulder blade.

SECONDARIES   The inner, principal flight feathers of the wing, which are shorter than the primaries. (See also Primaries and Rectrices.)

SHAFT   The central, horny stem of each feather; also called the quill.

SHOULDER   That portion where the leading edge of the wing joins the body.

SPECIES   A group of subspecies (or a distinct single race) with like characteristics among one another, but dissimilar in certain characteristics to others of the same Genus. The Northern Barred Owl, the California Spotted Owl, and the Great Gray Owl all belong to the genus *Strix,* but respectively they belong to the species *varia, occidentalis,* and *nebulosa.*

STREAKS   Longitudinal markings, running generally in a head-to-tail direction. (See also Barrings.)

SUBORBITAL   Below the eye.

SUBSPECIES   A geographical subdivision of a species; also called a race. Generally speaking, an owl with certain characteristics all its own; characteristics not shared with other owls of its species. The Eastern Screech Owl and the Florida Screech Owl both belong to genus *Otus* and species *asio,* but the former is subspecies *naevius* and the latter is subspecies *floridanus.*

SUPERCILIARIES   The line of feathers above each facial disk of the owl, converging in a V-shape above the beak. Roughly, the eyebrows.

SUPRAORBITAL   Above the eye.

TAIL LENGTH   The length of the longest rectrix or tail feather from where it enters the flesh to its outermost point.

TALONS   The strong, curved toenails; the claws.

TARSUS   (*plural* Tarsi). The shank of an owl's leg, above the foot and below the heel, sometimes feathered, sometimes bare; often erroneously referred to as the shin.

TERTIARIES   The inner secondaries; those secondary feathers which are closest to the owl's body.

TRANSVERSE   From side to side; crosswise.

TYPE SPECIMEN   The individual owl which was used as the original description basis for the establishment of a new subspecies, or species; often called the Type Form.

UNDERTAIL COVERTS   The feathers which overlie the base of the underside of the tail feathers (rectrices).

UNDERWING COVERTS   The feathers which overlie the base of the primaries, secondaries, and other coverts on the underside of the wing.

UPPER-TAIL COVERTS   The feathers which overlie the base of the upperside of the rectrices (tail feathers).

VENT   See Anus.

VENTRAL   The underside of the entire owl; or the underside of any individual portion of the owl.

VERMICULATION   Marked with very thin and wavy lines which are usually transverse.

WEBS   The filaments (or barbs) of a feather which grow outward from the central shaft; those closest to the body being called the inner web, and those on the other side of the shaft being called the outer web.

WEIGHT   The total weight of the whole live bird or a freshly dead bird, including the feathers, feet, beak, viscera, and all other parts.

WING LENGTH   The length of the outstretched individual wing from the carpal joint or wrist to the outermost tip of the longest primary feather.

WINGSPAN   The distance from the outermost outstretched wing tip on one wing to the outermost outstretched wing tip of the other wing.

BIBLIOGRAPHY OF PRINCIPAL SOURCES

It is not possible to list here every source consulted by the authors in the preparation of *The Owls of North America*. Often certain books, papers, theses, leaflets, and similar materials provided only a single minor datum which was incorporated into this volume; to list these, except in the most unusual of cases, would be virtually pointless. The following works listed, therefore, are those upon which the authors relied somewhat more heavily in their research into published works.

Abbott, C. G. URBAN BURROWING OWLS, *The Auk,* Vol. 47, 1930, pp. 564–65.

Alcorn, J. R. FOOD OF THE BARN OWL AT SODA LAKE, NEVADA, *The Condor,* Vol. 44, 1942, pp. 128–29.

——— NOTES ON THE FOOD OF THE HORNED OWL NEAR FALLON, NEVADA, *The Condor,* Vol. 44, 1942, pp. 284–85.

Aldrich, J. W. BIRDS OF WASHINGTON STATE (with Stanley G. Jewett, W. P. Taylor, and W. T. Shaw), University of Washington Press, Seattle, 1953.

Allard, Harry A. ACTIVITY OF THE SCREECH OWL, *The Auk,* Vol. 54, 1937, pp. 300–3.

Allen, Arthur A. A CONTRIBUTION TO THE LIFE HISTORY AND ECONOMIC STATUS OF THE SCREECH OWL, *The Auk,* Vol. 41, 1924, pp. 1–16.

Allen, Glover M. BIRDS OF LABRADOR (with Charles W. Townsend), Boston Society of Natural History, Boston, 1907.

——— BIRDS AND THEIR ATTRIBUTES, Dover Publications, New York, 1962.

Anderson, S. H. COMPARATIVE FOOD HABITS OF THREE OWL SPECIES IN CENTRAL OREGON (with C. Maser and E. W. Hammer), *The Murrelet,* Vol. 51, No. 3, Sept.–Dec. 1970, pp. 29–33.

Andrews, Edith BARN OWL NESTING ON NANTUCKET ISLAND, MASSACHUSETTS, *The Auk,* Vol. 87, 1970, p. 573.

American Ornithologists' Union THE A.O.U. CHECK-LIST OF NORTH AMERICAN BIRDS, Fifth Edition, Lord Baltimore Press, Inc., Baltimore, Md., 1957.

Arnold, M. L. RARE PIGMY (THE), *Yellowstone National Park Nature Notes,* Vol. 7, 1930, p. 6.

Ashworth, C. CALIFORNIA OWLS, *The Oölogist,* Vol. 45, 1928, pp. 153–54.

Austing, Ronald ECOLOGICAL NOTES ON LONG-EARED AND SAW-WHET OWLS IN SOUTHWESTERN OHIO, *Ecology,* Vol. 33, 1952, pp. 422–26.

Aymar, Gordon C. BIRD FLIGHT, Garden City Publishing Co., Garden City, 1938.

Bailey, F. M. BIRDS OF NEW MEXICO, U. S. Dept. of Agriculture, Washington, D.C., 1928.

——— HANDBOOK OF BIRDS OF THE WESTERN UNITED STATES, Houghton Mifflin Co., Boston, 1927.

Bailey, H. H. OWL FOOD, *The Oölogist,* Vol. 39, 1922, p. 164.

Baird, S. F. A HISTORY OF NORTH AMERICAN BIRDS (with T. M. Brewer and Robert Ridgway), Little, Brown & Co., Boston, 1874.

Baldwin, S. P. VARIATIONS IN BIRD WEIGHTS (with S. Charles Kendeigh), *The Auk,* Vol. 55, 1938, pp. 416–17.

Banfield, A. A STUDY OF THE WINTER FEEDING HABITS OF THE SHORT-EARED OWL (*Asio flammeus*) IN THE TORONTO REGION, University of Toronto, 1946, *Canada Journal of Research, Sec. D,* 25(2), April 1947, pp. 46–65.

Bangs, O. A NEW BARRED OWL FROM CORPUS CHRISTI, TEXAS, *Proc. of the New England Zool. Club,* Vol. 1, 1899, pp. 31–32.

——— SCREECH OWLS OF EASTERN NORTH AMERICA (THE), *The Auk,* Vol. 47, 1930, pp. 403–4.

Banks, R. C. SOME INFORMATION FROM BARN OWL PELLETS, *The Auk,* Vol. 82, 1965, p. 506.

Barnes, I. R. SNOWY OWL AND THE CRUMBLING PYRAMID (THE), *American Forests,* Vol. 60, 1954, p. 19.

Barrows, W. B. MICHIGAN BIRD LIFE, Michigan Agricultural College Press, Lansing, 1912.

Baumgartner, F. A STUDY OF THE AMERICAN HORNED OWLS (*Bubo virginianus*), Cornell University Press, Ithaca, N.Y., 1938.

——— TERRITORY AND POPULATION IN THE GREAT HORNED OWL, *The Auk,* Vol. 56, 1939, pp. 274–82.

Bent, A. C. LIFE HISTORIES OF NORTH AMERICAN BIRDS OF PREY, Part 2, *U. S. Nat. Mus. Bull.* No. 170, Washington, D.C., 1938.

Bishop. L. B. BIRDS OF THE YUKON REGION (THE), *North American Fauna No. 18,* Washington, D.C.

Black, C. T. ENIGMA OF THE NORTH, *Michigan Conservation,* Vol. 15, Jan. 1946, pp. 3, 11.

Blakemore, L. A. BARRED OWL'S FOOD HABITS IN GLENWOOD PARK, MINNEAPOLIS, MINNESOTA, *The Flicker,* Vol. 12, 1940, pp. 21–23.

Bolander, Gordon BARN OWL PELLETS, *The Gull,* Vol. 21, 1939, p. 76.

Bond, R. M. FOOD HABITS OF HORNED OWLS IN THE PAHRANAGAT VALLEY, NEVADA, *The Condor,* Vol. 42, 1940, pp. 164–65.

——— FOOD OF THE BURROWING OWL IN WESTERN NEVADA, *The Condor,* Vol. 44, 1942, p. 183.

Bowles, J. H. KENNICOTT SCREECH OWL (THE), *The Condor,* Vol. 8, 1906, pp. 143–44.

——— NOTES ON THE FEEDING HABITS OF THE DUSKY HORNED OWL, *The Oölogist,* Vol. 33, 1916, pp. 151–52.

Boyd, E. M. NESTING AND FOOD OF THE BARN OWL (*Tyto alba*) IN HAMPSHIRE COUNTY, MASSACHUSETTS (with Joan Shriner), *The Auk,* Vol. 71, 1954, pp. 199–201.

Bradford, C. H. A RECORD SET OF PACIFIC HORNED OWLS, *The Oölogist,* Vol. 47, 1930, pp. 18–20.

Braly, J. C. NESTING OF THE CALIFORNIA PYGMY OWL IN OREGON, *The Condor,* Vol. 32, 1930, p. 304.

Breckenridge, W. MINNESOTA'S LARGER OWLS, *Conservation Volunteer,* Vol. 9, March–April 1946, pp. 16–22.

——— MINNESOTA'S SMALLER OWLS, *Conservation Volunteer,* Vol. 9, May–June 1946, pp. 36–42.

——— SCIENCE JUDGES THE OWL, *Minnesota Conservation,* Vol. 31, Dec. 1935, pp. 5–6, 16.

Breninger, G. F. FERRUGINOUS PIGMY OWL (THE), *The Osprey,* Vol. 2, 1898, p. 128.

Brewer, T. M. A HISTORY OF NORTH AMERICAN BIRDS (with S. F. Baird and Robert Ridgway), Little, Brown & Co., Boston, 1874.

Brewster, W. AGGRESSIVE SCREECH OWLS, *The Auk,* Vol. 24, 1907, pp. 215–17.

———— BREEDING OF THE ACADIAN OWL IN MASSACHUSETTS, *Nuttall Ornithological Bull.,* Vol. 6, 1881, pp. 143–45.

Brodkorb, P. NOTES ON THE FOOD OF SOME HAWKS AND OWLS, *The Auk,* Vol. 45, 1928, pp. 212–13.

Brooks, A. SOME NOTES ON THE BIRDS OF OKANAGAN, BRITISH COLUMBIA, *The Auk,* Vol. 26, 1909, pp. 60–63.

———— TWO SMALL PREDATORS, *Canadian Nature,* Vol. 7, 1945, pp. 158–61.

Bryant, E. J. AN INTERESTING GREAT HORNED OWL OBSERVATION, *Iowa Bird Life,* Vol. 50, No. 1, March 1970, p. 22.

Burns, B. J. FOOD OF A FAMILY OF GREAT HORNED OWLS (*Bubo virginianus*) IN FLORIDA, *The Auk,* Vol. 69, 1952, pp. 86–87.

Calderwood, A., Jr. NESTING OF THE PIGMY OWL, *The Oölogist,* Vol. 6, 1889, pp. 110–11.

Cameron, A. NIGHTWATCHERS (THE) (with Peter Parnall), Four Winds Press, New York, 1971.

Campbell, B. BIRD NOTES FROM SOUTHERN ARIZONA, *The Condor,* Vol. 36, 1934, pp. 201–3.

Campbell, J. M. OWLS OF THE CENTRAL BROOKS RANGE, ALASKA (THE), *The Auk,* Vol. 86, 1969, pp. 565–68.

Carter, J. D. BEHAVIOR OF THE BARRED OWL, *The Auk,* Vol. 42, 1925, pp. 443–44.

Chapman, F. M. COLOR KEY TO NORTH AMERICAN BIRDS, D. Appleton & Co., New York, 1912.

———— HANDBOOK OF BIRDS OF EASTERN NORTH AMERICA, D. Appleton & Co., New York, 1929.

Chitty, D. A LABORATORY STUDY OF PELLET FORMATION IN THE SHORT-EARED OWL (*Asio flammeus*), *Proc. Zool. Soc. London,* Ser. A., Vol. 108, 1938, pp. 267–87.

Clark, J. R. A FIELD STUDY OF THE SHORT-EARED OWL (*Asio flammeus*) IN NORTH AMERICA, Cornell University Press, Ithaca, N.Y., 1970.

Clay, C. I. SPOTTED OWL IN NORTHERN CALIFORNIA (THE), *The Condor,* Vol. 13, 1911, p. 75.

Cook, G. L. NOTES ON THE WESTERN HORNED OWL, *The Oölogist,* Vol. 43, p. 18.

Cooper, W. A. NOTES ON THE BREEDING HABITS OF THE CALIFORNIA PYGMY OWL, WITH A DESCRIPTION OF ITS EGGS, *Nuttall Ornith. Bull.,* Vol. 4, 1879, pp. 86–87.

Cory, Charles B. BIRDS OF ILLINOIS AND WISCONSIN (THE), *Field Mus. Nat. Hist.,* Publ. No. 131, Vol. 9, Chicago, Ill., 1909.

Coues, E. BIRDS OF THE NORTHWEST, U. S. Geological Survey, U. S. Dept. of Interior, Washington, D.C., 1874.

———— KEY TO NORTH AMERICAN BIRDS, Sixth Ed., Page Co., Boston, 1923.

———— NOTES ON THE ORNITHOLOGY OF LABRADOR, *Proc. Phila. Acad. Nat. Sci.,* 1861, pp. 215–57.

Craighead, J. and *F.* HAWKS, OWLS, AND WILDLIFE, Stackpole Co., Harrisburg, Pa., 1959.

Dawson, W. L. BIRDS OF CALIFORNIA, Vol. III, South Moulton Co., San Diego, Calif., 1923, pp. 1070–1136.

Deignan, H. G. TYPE SPECIMENS OF BIRDS IN THE U. S. NATIONAL MUSEUM, *U. S. Nat. Mus. Bull.* No. 221, Washington, D.C., 1961.

Dice, L. R. MINIMUM INTENSITIES OF ILLUMINATION UNDER WHICH OWLS CAN FIND DEAD PREY BY SIGHT, *American Naturalist,* Vol. 79, 1945, pp. 385–416.

Dickey, D. R. NESTING OF THE SPOTTED OWL (THE), *The Condor,* Vol. 16, 1914, pp. 193–202.

Dixon, J. B. HISTORY OF A PAIR OF PACIFIC HORNED OWLS, *The Condor,* Vol. 16, 1914, pp. 47–54.

Doerksen, G. P. AN ANALYSIS OF BARN OWL PELLETS FROM PITT MEADOWS, BRITISH COLUMBIA, *The Murrelet,* Vol. 50, 1969, pp. 4–8.

Dubois, A. D. NUPTIAL SONG-FLIGHT OF THE SHORT-EARED OWL (THE), *The Auk,* Vol. 41, 1924, pp. 260–63.

Dunn, H. H. PACIFIC HORNED OWL (THE), *The Oölogist,* Vol. 16, 1899, pp. 116–18.

———— SPOTTED OWL (THE), *The Oölogist,* Vol. 18, 1901, pp. 165–67.

Dunstan, T. C. POST-FLEDGLING ACTIVITIES OF JUVENILE GREAT HORNED OWLS AS DETERMINED BY RADIO-TELEMETRY, University of South Dakota Press, Vermillion, 1970.

Earhart, C. M. SIZE, DIMORPHISM, AND FOOD HABITS OF NORTH AMERICAN OWLS (with N. K. Johnson), *The Condor,* Vol. 72, No. 3, July 1970, pp. 251–64.

Earl, T. M. OBSERVATIONS ON OWLS IN OHIO, *Wilson Bull.,* Vol. 46, 1934, pp. 137–42.

Eaton, S. W. FOOD HABITS OF OWLS ON THE NIAGARA FRONTIER (with J. A. Grzybowski), *The Kingbird,* Vol. 19, 1969, pp. 135–38.

Eaton, W. F. RICHARDSON'S OWL IN VERMONT IN SUMMER, *The Auk,* Vol. 41, 1924, pp. 155–56.

Edwards, H. M. BEHAVIOR OF A FLORIDA SCREECH OWL, *Bird Lore,* Vol. 34, 1932, pp. 130–31.

Ekblaw, S. E. NESTING OF AMERICAN LONG-EARED OWL, *Wilson Bull.,* Vol. 31, 1919, pp. 99–100.

Emerson, W. O. CALIFORNIA MOTTLED OWL (THE), *Ornithologist and Oölogist,* Vol. 10, 1885, pp. 173–74.

Errington, P. L. GREAT HORNED OWL AS AN INDICATOR OF VULNERABILITY IN PREY POPULATIONS (THE), *Journal of Wildlife Management,* Vol. 2, October 1938, pp. 190–205.

———— STUDIES ON THE BEHAVIOR OF THE GREAT HORNED OWL, *Wilson Bull.,* Vol. 44, 1932a, pp. 212–20.

———— GREAT HORNED OWL AND ITS PREY IN NORTH-CENTRAL UNITED STATES (THE), (with F. and F. M. Hamerstrom, Jr.), *Iowa Agric. Expr. Station Bull.* No. 277, Sept. 1940, pp. 758–850.

———— CONCLUSIONS AS TO THE FOOD HABITS OF THE BARRED OWL IN IOWA (with Malcolm McDonald), *Iowa Bird Life,* Vol. 7, 1937, pp. 47–49.

———— FOOD HABITS OF BURROWING OWLS IN NORTH-WESTERN IOWA, *Wilson Bull.,* Vol. 47, 1935, pp. 125–28.

Esten, S. R. BIRD WEIGHTS, *The Auk,* Vol. 48, 1931, pp. 572–73.

Evermann, B. W. AMERICAN BARN OWL, *Ornithologist and Oölogist,* Vol. 7, 1882, pp. 97–98.

Farley, J. A. FOOD HABITS OF OWLS, *The Auk,* Vol. 41, 1924, p. 156.

Finley, W. L. BARN OWL AND ITS ECONOMIC VALUE (THE), *The Condor,* Vol. 8, 1906, pp. 83–88.

Fischer, R. B. DATA ON THE FOOD HABITS OF LOCAL OWLS, *Proc. Linnaean Soc. N. Y.,* Nos. 58–62, 1951, pp. 46–48.

Fisher, A. K. HAWKS AND OWLS FROM THE STANDPOINT OF THE FARMER, *U. S. Biol. Surv. Circ.* No. 61, U. S. Interior Dept., Washington, D.C., 1907.

Fitch, Henry S. PREDATION BY OWLS IN THE SIERRAN FOOT-

HILLS OF CALIFORNIA, *The Condor,* Vol. 49, 1947, pp. 137–51.

———— SOME OBSERVATIONS ON HORNED OWL NESTS, *The Condor,* Vol. 42, 1940, pp. 73–75.

Fleming, J. H. SAW-WHET OWL OF THE QUEEN CHARLOTTE ISLANDS (THE), *The Auk,* Vol. 33, 1916, pp. 420–23.

Forsman, E. SAW-WHET OWL PREYS ON RED TREE MICE (with C. Maser), *The Murrelet,* Vol. 51, No. 1, Jan.–April 1970, p. 10.

Foster, M. AN EARLY REFERENCE TO THE TECHNIQUE OF OWL CALLING, *The Auk,* Vol. 82, 1965, pp. 651–53.

Franks, E. C. GREAT HORNED OWL NESTING IN A POPULATED AREA (with J. E. Warnock), *Wilson Bull.,* Vol. 81, 1969, pp. 332–33.

Frazar, A. M. MOTTLED OWL AS A FISHERMAN (THE), *Nuttall Ornith. Bull.,* Vol. 2, 1877, p. 80.

Freemyer, H. PROXIMAL NESTING OF HARRIS' HAWK AND GREAT HORNED OWL, *The Auk,* Vol. 87, 1970, p. 170.

Friedmann, H. DISTRIBUTIONAL CHECK-LIST OF THE BIRDS OF MEXICO (with Ludlow Griscom and Robert T. Moore), Cooper Ornithological Club, Berkeley, Calif., 1950.

Fuertes, L. A. AMERICAN BIRDS OF PREY, *National Geographic,* 1920, pp. 460–67.

Gabrielson, I. BIRDS OF OREGON (with S. G. Jewett), Oregon State College Press, Corvallis, 1940.

———— HELPING THE USEFUL BARN OWL, *Game & Gun and The Angler's Monthly,* Vol. 16, 1939, pp. 147–50.

Geis, A. D. WINTER FOOD HABITS OF A PAIR OF LONG-EARED OWLS, *The Jack-Pine Warbler,* Vol. 30, 1952, p. 93.

Gessamon, J. A. METABOLISM AND THERMOREGULATION OF THE SNOWY OWL, Univ. of Illinois Press, Urbana, 1968.

Getz, L. L. HUNTING AREAS OF THE LONG-EARED OWL, *Wilson Bull.,* Vol. 73, 1961, pp. 79–82.

Gilliard, E. T. TYTO ALBA, Part I, *Natural History,* May 1958, pp. 239–45.

Gilman, M. F. SOME OWLS ALONG THE GILA RIVER IN ARIZONA, *The Condor,* Vol. 11, 1909, pp. 145–50.

Glover, Fred A. SUMMER FOODS OF THE BURROWING OWL, *The Condor,* Vol. 55, 1953, p. 275.

Godfrey, W. E. BIRDS OF CANADA (THE), National Museum of Canada, Ottawa, 1966.

Grimm, R. J. PELLET FORMATION IN A GREAT HORNED OWL, *The Auk,* Vol. 80, 1963, pp. 301–6.

Grinnell, J. A NEW SUBSPECIES OF SCREECH OWL FROM CALIFORNIA, *The Auk,* Vol. 32, 1915, pp. 59–60.

———— TWO NEW RACES OF THE PIGMY OWL FROM THE PACIFIC COAST, *The Auk,* Vol. 30, 1913, pp. 222–24.

Griscom, L. DISTRIBUTIONAL CHECK-LIST OF THE BIRDS OF MEXICO (with Herbert Friedmann and Robert T. Moore), Cooper Ornithological Club, Berkeley, California, 1950.

Grosman, M. L. BIRDS OF PREY OF THE WORLD (with John Hamlet), Bonanza Books, New York, 1964.

Gross, A. O. CYCLIC INVASIONS OF THE SNOWY OWL AND THE MIGRATION OF 1945–1946, *The Auk,* Vol. 64, 1947, pp. 584–601.

———— FOOD OF THE SNOWY OWL, *The Auk,* Vol. 61, 1944, pp. 1–7.

Grzybowski, J. A. FOOD HABITS OF OWLS ON THE NIAGARA FRONTIER, (with S. W. Eaton), *The Kingbird,* Vol. 19, 1969, pp. 135–38.

Hamerstrom, F. GREAT HORNED OWL AND ITS PREY IN NORTH-CENTRAL UNITED STATES (THE), (with Paul L. Er-

rington and F. N. Hamerstrom, Jr.), *Iowa Agric. Expr. Station Bull.* No. 277, Sept. 1940, pp. 758–850.

Hamilton, W. J. A NOTE ON THE FOOD OF THE WESTERN BURROWING OWL, *The Condor,* Vol. 43, 1941, p. 74.

Hamlet, J. BIRDS OF PREY OF THE WORLD (with Mary L. Grosman), Bonanza Books, New York, 1964.

Hammer, E. W. COMPARATIVE FOOD HABITS OF THREE OWL SPECIES IN CENTRAL OREGON (with S. H. Anderson and C. Maser), *The Murrelet,* Vol. 51, No. 3, Sept.–Dec. 1970, pp. 29–33.

Hanson, W. C. SNOWY OWL INCURSION IN SOUTH-EASTERN WASHINGTON AND THE PACIFIC NORTHWEST (1966–67), *The Condor,* Vol. 73, No. 1, Spring, 1971, pp. 114–16.

Hausman, L. A. OWLS OF NEW JERSEY (THE), *New Jersey Agric. Expr. Station Bull.* No. 690, 1941.

Hayse, A. ELF OWL REDISCOVERED IN LOWER RIO GRANDE DELTA OF TEXAS (with Pauline Jackson), *Wilson Bull.,* Vol. 75, 1963, pp. 179–82.

Henderson, A. D. NESTING OF THE AMERICAN HAWK OWL, *The Oölogist,* Vol. 36, 1919, pp. 59–63.

———— NESTING OF THE GREAT GRAY OWL IN CENTRAL ALBERTA, *The Oölogist,* Vol. 32, 1915, pp. 2–6.

Hendrikson, G. WINTER NOTES ON THE SHORT-EARED OWL (with Charles Swan), *Ecology,* Vol. 19, 1938, pp. 584–88.

Henny, C. J. GEOGRAPHICAL VARIATION IN MORTALITY RATES AND PRODUCTION REQUIREMENTS OF THE BARN OWL (*Tyto alba*), *Bird-Banding,* Vol. 40, No. 4, Oct. 1969, pp. 277–90.

Hermes, R. C. SAW-WHET OWL IN ACTION [Pictorial], *The Auk,* Vol. 72, 1955, Plates 8 and 9.

Hickey, J. C. SURVIVAL STUDIES OF BANDED BIRDS, Special Scientific Report, Wildlife No. 15, U. S. Dept. of Interior, Washington, D.C., June 1952.

Holland, H. M. WHO WOULD HAVE THOUGHT IT OF BUBO?, *Bird Lore,* Vol. 38, 1926, pp. 1–4.

Hollister, N. BREEDING OF THE ACADIAN OWL IN NEWTON COUNTY, INDIANA, *The Auk,* Vol. 25, 1908, p. 221.

Hope, C. E. STUDYING OWL PELLETS, *Canadian Nature,* Vol. 6, Jan.–Feb. 1944, pp. 22–23.

Hosking, E. BIRDS OF THE NIGHT (with C. Newberry), London, England, 1945.

Hough, F. TWO SIGNIFICANT CALLING PERIODS OF THE SCREECH OWL, *The Auk,* Vol. 77, 1960, pp. 227–28.

Howard, W. E. FOOD INTAKE AND PELLET FORMATION OF A HORNED OWL, *Wilson Bull.,* Vol. 70, 1958, pp. 145–50.

Howell, A. H. FLORIDA BIRD LIFE, U. S. Dept. of Agric., Washington, D.C., 1932.

Howell, T. R. NOTES ON INCUBATION AND NESTLING TEMPERATURES AND BEHAVIOR OF CAPTIVE OWLS, *Wilson Bull.,* Vol. 76, 1964, p. 28.

Huey, L. M. SKUNKS AS PREY FOR OWLS, *Wilson Bull.,* Vol. 43, 1931, p. 224.

———— BATS EATEN BY SHORT-EARED OWL, *The Auk,* Vol. 43, 1926b, pp. 96–97.

Humphrey, P. S. AN APPROACH TO THE STUDY OF MOLTS AND PLUMAGES, *The Auk,* Vol. 76, 1959, pp. 1–31.

Huxley, T. H. ON THE CLASSIFICATION OF BIRDS, AND ON THE TAXONOMIC VALUE OF THE MODIFICATIONS OF CERTAIN CRANIAL BONES OBSERVABLE IN THAT CLASS, *Proc. Zool. Soc. London,* 1867.

Ingram, C. IMPORTANCE OF JUVENILE CANNIBALISM IN THE

BREEDING BIOLOGY OF CERTAIN BIRDS OF PREY (THE), *The Auk,* Vol. 76, 1959, pp. 218–26.

——— CANNIBALISM BY NESTLING SHORT-EARED OWLS, *The Auk,* Vol. 79, 1962, p. 715.

Irving, L. BIRDS OF ANATUVUK PASS, KOBUK, AND OLD CROW, *U. S. Nat. Mus. Bull.* No. 217, Washington, D.C. 1960.

Jacot, E. C. NOTES ON THE SPOTTED AND FLAMMULATED SCREECH OWLS IN ARIZONA, *The Condor,* Vol. 33, 1931, pp. 8–11.

Jackson, P. ELF OWL REDISCOVERED IN LOWER RIO GRANDE DELTA OF TEXAS, *Wilson Bull.,* Vol. 75, 1963, pp. 179–82.

James, R. F. A STUDY OF SCREECH OWLS IN SOUTHERN ONTARIO (with N. D. Martin), *The Canadian Field Naturalist,* Vol. 64, Sept.–Oct. 1950, pp. 177–80.

Jewett, S. G. BIRDS OF WASHINGTON STATE (with J. W. Aldrich, W. T. Shaw, and W. P. Taylor), Univ. of Washington Press, Seattle, 1953.

Johnson, N. K. FOOD OF THE LONG-EARED OWL IN SOUTHERN WASHOE COUNTY, NEVADA, *The Condor,* Vol. 56, 1954, p. 52.

Johnson, N. K. SIZE, DIMORPHISM, AND FOOD HABITS OF NORTH AMERICAN OWLS (with C. M. Earhart), *The Condor,* Vol. 72, No. 3, July 1970, pp. 251–64.

——— SUPPOSED MIGRATORY STATUS OF THE FLAMMULATED OWL (THE), *Wilson Bull.,* Vol. 75, 1963, pp. 174–78.

Jones, J. K., Jr. NOTES ON THE FOOD HABITS OF THE GREAT HORNED OWL IN CHERRY COUNTY, NEBRASKA, *Nebraska Bird Review,* Vol. 20, 1952, pp. 10–11.

Kelso, L. H. A STUDY OF THE SCREECH OWL, Unpubl. MS. Thesis, Cornell Univ., Ithaca, N.Y., 1938.

——— VARIATIONS OF THE EXTERNAL EAR OPENING IN THE STRIGIDAE, *Wilson Bull.,* Vol. 52, 1940, pp. 24–29.

Kendeigh, S. C. VARIATIONS IN BIRD WEIGHTS (with S. P. Baldwin), *The Auk,* Vol. 55, 1938, pp. 416–67.

Kenyon, K. W. CAUSE OF DEATH OF A FLAMMULATED OWL, *The Condor,* Vol. 49, 1947, p. 88.

Lansdowne, J. F. BIRDS OF THE NORTHERN FORESTS (with J. A. Livingston), Houghton Mifflin Co., Boston, 1966.

LeDuc, P. NESTING ECOLOGY OF SOME HAWKS AND OWLS IN SOUTHEASTERN MINNESOTA (THE), *The Loon,* Vol. 42, No. 2, June 1970, pp. 48–62.

Lesser, F. H. OCCURRENCE OF THE SAW-WHET OWL IN FLORIDA, *The Auk,* Vol. 84, 1967, p. 425.

Ligon, J. D. BREEDING RANGE EXPANSION OF THE BURROWING OWL IN FLORIDA, *The Auk,* Vol. 80, 1963, pp. 367–68.

——— HABITS OF THE SPOTTED OWL, *The Auk,* Vol. 43, 1926, pp. 421–29.

——— SOME ASPECTS OF TEMPERATURE RELATIONS IN SMALL OWLS, *The Auk,* Vol. 86, 1969, pp. 458–72.

Lippincott, J. BARN OWL'S VOICE (THE), *Bird Lore,* Vol. 19, 1917, p. 275.

Little, R. GREAT HORNED OWLS, *The Cardinal,* Vol. 3, 1931, pp. 17–18.

Livingston, J. BIRDS OF THE NORTHERN FORESTS (with James F. Lansdowne), Houghton Mifflin Co., Boston, 1966.

Lockie, J. D. BREEDING HABITS AND FOOD OF SHORT-EARED OWLS AFTER A VOLE PLAGUE (THE), *Bird Study,* Vol. 2, 1955, pp. 53–69.

Lowry, G. H. LOUISIANA BIRDS, Louisiana State Univ. Press, 1955.

Lumley, E. D. OWLS, Emergency Conservation Commission Publication No. 67, U. S. Dept. of the Interior, Washington, D.C., 1937.

Macoun, J. and *J.* CATALOG OF CANADIAN BIRDS, Canada Dept. of Mines, Ottawa, 1909.

Marshall, J. T. FOOD AND HABITAT OF THE SPOTTED OWL, *The Condor,* Vol. 44, 1942, pp. 66–67.

——— BIRDS OF ARIZONA (with Gale Monson and Allan Phillips), Univ. of Arizona Press, Tucson, 1964.

——— PARALLEL VARIATION IN NORTH AND MIDDLE AMERICAN SCREECH-OWLS, *Monographs of the Western Found. of Vert. Zool.,* No. 1, July 1967.

Marti, C. D., Jr. FEEDING ECOLOGY OF FOUR SYMPATRIC OWLS IN COLORADO, Colorado State Univ. Press, Denver, 1970.

——— RENESTING BY BARN AND GREAT HORNED OWLS, *Wilson Bull.,* Vol. 81, No. 4, Dec. 1969, pp. 467–68.

Martin, D. J. A TRAPPING TECHNIQUE FOR BURROWING OWLS, *Bird-Banding,* Vol. 42, No. 1, Jan. 1971, p. 46.

Maser, C. COMPARATIVE FOOD HABITS OF THREE OWL SPECIES IN CENTRAL OREGON, *The Murrelet,* Vol. 51, No. 3, Sept.–Dec. 1970, pp. 29–33.

——— SAW-WHET OWL PREYS ON RED TREE MICE, *The Murrelet,* Vol. 51, No. 1, Jan.–April 1970, p. 10.

Mayr, E. and *M.* TAIL MOLT OF SMALL OWLS (THE), *The Auk,* Vol. 71, 1954, pp. 172–78.

McDonald, M. CONCLUSIONS AS TO THE FOOD HABITS OF THE BARRED OWL IN IOWA (with Paul L. Errington), *Iowa Bird Life,* Vol. 7, 1937, pp. 47–49.

McDowell, R. D. GREAT HORNED OWL (THE), *Pennsylvania Game News,* Vol. 11, Nov. 1940, pp. 10–11, 29.

McLean, D. D. SPEED OF FLIGHT IN CERTAIN BIRDS (THE), *The Gull,* Vol. 12, No. 3, 1930.

Michael, C. W. CALIFORNIA SPOTTED OWL IN YOSEMITE VALLEY, CALIFORNIA (THE), *The Condor,* Vol. 35, 1933, pp. 202–3.

Miller, L. SAGUARO SCREECH OWL IN CALIFORNIA (THE), *The Condor,* Vol. 30, 1928, p. 192.

Monson, G. BIRDS OF ARIZONA (with Joe T. Marshall and Allan Phillips), Univ. of Arizona Press, Tucson, 1964.

Moorejohn, G. V. BARN OWLS WITH TWO BROODS OF YOUNG, *The Auk,* Vol. 72, 1955, p. 298.

Morse, D. H. GREAT HORNED OWLS AND NESTING SEABIRDS, *The Auk,* Vol. 88, 1971, p. 426.

Munro, J. A. SHORT-EARED OWL EATING BIRDS, *The Auk,* Vol. 35, 1918, p. 223.

Murie, O. J. NESTING OF THE SNOWY OWL, *The Condor,* Vol. 31, 1929, pp. 3–12.

Murray, J. J. GREAT HORNED OWL (THE), *Virginia Wildlife,* Vol. 8, June 1947, pp. 7–9.

Neilson, J. A. WESTERN GREAT HORNED OWL, *The Oölogist,* Vol. 47, 1930, pp. 53–54.

Nero, R. W. STATUS OF THE GREAT GRAY OWL IN MANITOBA, WITH SPECIAL REFERENCE TO THE 1968–1969 INFLUX (THE), *The Blue Jay,* Vol. 27, 1969, pp. 191–209.

Newberry, C. BIRDS OF THE NIGHT (with Eric Hosking), London, England, 1945.

Nicholson, D. J. HORNED OWL SHREWDNESS AND FEROCITY, *The Oölogist,* Vol. 43, 1926, p. 14.

Nitsch, C. L. PTERYLOGRAPHY (translated by Dr. P. L. Sclater), Ray Society of London, England, 1867.

Oberholser, H. A REVISION OF THE AMERICAN GREAT HORNED OWLS, *Proc. U. S. Nat. Mus.,* Vol. 27, 1904, pp. 177–92.

Ohlendorf, H. M. ARTHROPOD DIET OF A WESTERN HORNED OWL, *Southwestern Naturalist,* 23 July 1971, Vol. 16, No. 1, pp. 124–25.

O'Reilly, R. A. BENEFICIAL FEEDING HABITS OF THE BARN OWL, Bird Calendar of the Cleveland Bird Club, Cleveland, Ohio, March–May 1940.

Owen, D. F. POLYMORPHISM IN THE SCREECH OWL IN EASTERN NORTH AMERICA, *Wilson Bull.,* Vol. 75, 1963, pp. 183–90.

Parmalee, P. W. FOOD OF THE GREAT HORNED OWL AND BARN OWL IN EAST TEXAS, *The Auk,* Vol. 71, 1954, pp. 469–70.

Patton, F. A. BURROWING OWLS, HORNED LARKS, *The Oölogist,* Vol. 43, 1926, p. 14.

Payne, R. S. TYTO ALBA, PART II (with William H. Drury), *Natural History,* June–July 1958, pp. 316–23.

Peabody, P. B. RICHARDSON'S OWL, *Bird Lore,* Vol. 1, 1899, pp. 190–92.

Pearson, T. G. HOO'S HOO!, *Field and Stream,* Vol. 48, Nov. 1943, pp. 32–33, 78–79.

Peterson, R. T. A FIELD GUIDE TO THE BIRDS, Houghton Mifflin Co., Boston, 1947.

——— A FIELD GUIDE TO THE BIRDS OF TEXAS, Houghton Mifflin Co., Boston, 1960.

——— A FIELD GUIDE TO WESTERN BIRDS, Houghton Mifflin Co., Boston, 1941.

Pool, E. L. WEIGHTS AND WING AREAS IN NORTH AMERICAN BIRDS, *The Auk,* Vol. 55, 1938, pp. 511–17.

Potter, J. K. OBSERVATIONS ON THE DOMESTIC BEHAVIOR OF THE BARN OWL, *The Auk,* Vol. 42, 1925, pp. 177–92.

Preston, E. and F. GLOSS OF EGGS (THE) (with N. Wilson), *The Auk,* Vol. 75, 1958, pp. 456–64.

Price, H. F. CONTENTS OF OWL PELLETS, *American Midland Naturalist,* Vol. 28, 1942, pp. 524–25.

Putnam, W. L. USE OF CONCEALING POSTURE BY A SCREECH OWL, *The Auk,* Vol. 75, 1958, pp. 477–78.

Red Eagle, Chief A GLIMPSE OF OWL LIFE, *Bird Lore,* Vol. 31, 1929, pp. 261–62.

Reynolds, R. T. NEST OBSERVATIONS OF THE LONG-EARED OWL IN BENTON COUNTY, OREGON, WITH NOTES ON THEIR FOOD HABITS, *The Murrelet,* Vol. 51–1, April 1970, p. 196.

Rhoads, S. N. BREEDING HABITS OF THE FLORIDA BURROWING OWL, *The Auk,* Vol. 9, 1892, pp. 1–8.

Richard, C., Jr. CANNIBALISM IN OWLS, *The Condor,* Vol. 8, 1906, p. 57.

Ridgway, R. A HISTORY OF NORTH AMERICAN BIRDS (with S. F. Baird and T. M. Brewer), Little, Brown & Co., Boston, 1874.

——— BIRDS OF NORTH AND MIDDLE AMERICA, *U. S. Nat. Mus. Bull.* No. 50, Part VI, Washington, D.C., 1914.

Roberts, T. S. BIRD PORTRAITS IN COLOR, Univ. of Minneapolis Press, Minneapolis, Minn., 1934.

——— GREAT GRAY OWL NESTING IN MINNESOTA, *Minnesota Jour. of Minne. Ornith.,* Vol. 1, 1936, pp. 65–66.

Robertson, J. M. SOME OBSERVATIONS ON THE FEEDING HABITS OF THE BURROWING OWL, *The Condor,* Vol. 31, 1929, pp. 38–39.

Robertson, W. B. BARRED OWL NESTING ON THE GROUND, *The Auk,* Vol. 76, 1959, pp. 227–30.

Rockwell, R. B. GLIMPSES OF THE HOME LIFE OF THE SAW-WHET OWL, *Natural History,* Vol. 21, 1921, pp. 628–38.

——— NESTING OF THE WESTERN HORNED OWL IN COLORADO, *The Condor,* Vol. 10, 1908, pp. 14–17.

——— SOME COLORADO NOTES ON THE ROCKY MOUNTAIN SCREECH OWL, *The Condor,* Vol. 9, 1907, pp. 140–45.

Ross, A. ECOLOGICAL ASPECTS OF THE FOOD HABITS OF INSECTIVOROUS SCREECH OWLS, *Proc. Western Found. Vert. Zool.,* Vol. 1, 1969, pp. 301–44.

Ruhl, H. D. BRANDING BARRED OWLS, *Wilson Bull.,* Vol. 38, 1926, p. 175.

Rusling, W. J. FOOD HABITS OF NEW JERSEY OWLS, *Proc. Linnaean Soc. N. Y.,* Nos. 58–62, 1951, pp. 58–62.

Saetvelt, P. ECOLOGY OF THE GREAT HORNED OWL AND THE RED-TAILED HAWK (THE) (with Herb Tyler), *South Dakota Bird Notes,* Vol. 21, 1969, pp. 77–84.

Salt, Ray BIRDS OF ALBERTA (THE), 2nd Ed. (with A. L. Wilt), Alberta Dept. of Industry and Development, Edmonton, 1966.

Saunders, A. A. SOME NOTES ON THE NESTING OF THE SHORT-EARED OWL, *The Condor,* Vol. 15, 1913, pp. 121–25.

Schwartzkopff, J. ON THE HEARING OF BIRDS, *The Auk,* Vol. 72, 1955, pp. 340–47.

Scott, L. GREAT HORNED OWLS OCCUPY ARTIFICIAL NESTING SITE, *The Blue Jay,* Vol. 28, No. 3, Sept. 1970, p. 123.

Shaw, W. T. BIRDS OF WASHINGTON STATE (with S. G. Jewett, J. W. Aldrich, and W. P. Taylor), Univ. of Washington Press, Seattle, 1953.

Sherman, R. A. NEST LIFE OF THE SCREECH OWL, *The Auk,* Vol. 28, 1911, pp. 155–68.

Shoelds, M. ACTIVITY CYCLES OF SNOWY OWLS AT BARROW, ALASKA, *The Murrelet,* Vol. 50, 1969, pp. 13–16.

Shriner, J. NESTING AND FOOD OF THE BARN OWL (*Tyto alba*) IN HAMPSHIRE COUNTY, MASSACHUSETTS (with Elizabeth M. Boyd), *The Auk,* Vol. 71, 1954, pp. 199–201.

Silloway, P. M. A HANDSOME LITTLE OWL, *The Oölogist,* Vol. 18, 1901, pp. 85–87.

Simmons, G. F. ON THE NESTING OF CERTAIN BIRDS IN TEXAS, *The Auk,* Vol. 32, pp. 317–31.

Sindelar, C. R. BARRED OWL FEEDS ON CROW, *Wilson Bull.,* Vol. 81, 1969, pp. 100–1.

Smith, D. G. CLOSE NESTING AND AGGRESSION CONTACTS BETWEEN GREAT HORNED OWLS AND RED-TAILED HAWKS, *The Auk,* Vol. 87, No. 1, 1970, p. 170.

——— FALL NESTING BARN OWLS IN UTAH, *The Condor,* Vol. 72, No. 4, Oct. 1970, p. 492.

Soper, J. D. FLIGHT OF HORNED OWLS IN CANADA, *The Auk,* Vol. 35, 1918, pp. 478–79.

Sprunt, A. BARN OWL AT SEA, *The Auk,* Vol. 49, 1932, p. 86.

Stegeman, L. C. THREE-D SIGHT AND HEARING OF OWLS, *New York State Conservationist,* Oct.–Nov. 1959, pp. 10–11.

Stewart, P. A. DISPERSAL, BREEDING, BEHAVIOR, AND LONGEVITY OF BANDED BARN OWLS IN NORTH AMERICA, *The Auk,* Vol. 69, 1952, pp. 227–45.

——— MOVEMENTS, POPULATION FLUCTUATION, AND MORTALITY AMONG GREAT HORNED OWLS, *Wilson Bull.,* Vol. 81, 1969, pp. 155–62.

——— PREY IN TWO SCREECH OWL NESTS, *The Auk,* Vol. 86, 1969, p. 141.

——— WINTER MORTALITY OF BARN OWLS IN CENTRAL OHIO, *Wilson Bull.,* Vol. 63, 1952, pp. 164–66.

Sutton, G. M. INSECT CATCHING TACTICS OF THE SCREECH OWL, *The Auk,* Vol. 46, 1929b, pp. 545–46.

——— MEXICAN BIRDS: FIRST IMPRESSIONS, Univ. of Oklahoma Press, Norman, 1951.

——— RUFFED GROUSE CAPTURED BY A SCREECH OWL, *Wilson Bull.,* Vol. 39, 1927, p. 171.

Swan, C. WINTER NOTES ON THE SHORT-EARED OWL (with G. O. Hendrikson), *Ecology,* Vol. 19, 1938, pp. 584–88.

Swarth, H. S. SAGUARO SCREECH OWL AS A RECOGNIZABLE RACE (THE), *The Condor,* Vol. 18, 1916, pp. 163–65.

Taverner, P. A. BIRDS OF CANADA, *Nat. Mus. of Can. Bull.* No. 72, Ottawa, 1934.

——— CANADIAN RACES OF THE GREAT HORNED OWL, *The Auk,* Vol. 59, 1942, pp. 234–45.

Taylor, W. T. BIRDS OF WASHINGTON STATE (with J. Aldrich, S. Jewett, and W. Shaw), Univ. of Washington Press, Seattle, 1953.

——— FOOD HABITS OF SHORT-EARED AND BARRED OWLS IN TEXAS, *Texas Game & Fish,* Vol. 2, June 1944, p. 24.

Terrill, L. M. NESTING OF THE SAW-WHET OWL IN THE MONTREAL DISTRICT, *The Auk,* Vol. 48, 1931, pp. 169–74.

Thomsen, L. BEHAVIOR AND ECOLOGY OF BURROWING OWLS ON THE OAKLAND MUNICIPAL AIRPORT, *The Condor,* Vol. 73, 1971, pp. 177–92.

Tomich, P. Q. NOTES ON FOOD AND FEEDING BEHAVIOR OF RAPTORIAL BIRDS IN HAWAII, *Elapaio,* Vol. 31, No. 12, June 1971, pp. 111–14.

Tompkins, I. NOTES ON THE WINTER FOOD OF THE SHORT-EARED OWL, *Wilson Bull.,* Vol. 48, 1936, pp. 77–79.

Townsend, C. W. BIRDS OF LABRADOR, Boston Society of Natural History, Boston, 1907. (With G. M. Allen)

——— FINDINGS IN PELLETS OF BARN OWL, *The Auk,* Vol. 43, 1926, p. 544.

Tryon, C. A. GREAT GRAY OWL AS A PREDATOR ON POCKET GOPHERS (THE), *Wilson Bull.,* Vol. 55, 1943, pp. 130–31.

Tuttle, H. E. SCREECH OWL (THE), *Bird Lore,* Vol. 22, 1920, pp. 265–69.

Tyler, H. ECOLOGY OF THE GREAT HORNED OWL AND THE RED-TAILED HAWK (THE), (with P. Saetvelt), *South Dakota Bird Notes,* Vol. 21, 1969, pp. 77–84.

Urner, C. A. NOTES ON THE SHORT-EARED OWL, *The Auk,* Vol. 40, 1923, pp. 30–36.

Warnock, J. E. GREAT HORNED OWL NESTING IN A POPULATED AREA (with Edwin C. Franks), *Wilson Bull.,* Vol. 81, 1969, pp. 332–33.

Warren, E. R. SOME COLORADO HORNED OWL NOTES, *The Condor,* Vol. 13, 1911, pp. 153–56.

Weigand, J. P. FERRUGINOUS HAWK ATTACKS GREAT HORNED OWL, *The Auk,* Vol. 84, 1967, p. 433.

Wiggins, I. L. FORAGING ACTIVITIES OF THE SNOWY OWL DURING A PERIOD OF LOW LEMMING POPULATION, *The Auk,* Vol. 70, 1953, pp. 366–67.

Wilkinson, G. N. HORNED OWL KILLING A SKUNK, *Bird Lore,* Vol. 15, 1913, p. 369.

Willard, F. C. FLAMMULATED SCREECH OWL (THE), *The Condor,* Vol. 11, 1909, pp. 199–202.

Wilt, A. L. BIRDS OF ALBERTA (THE), 2nd Ed. (with W. Ray Salt), Alberta Dept. of Industry and Development, Edmonton, 1966.

Wilson, K. A. OWL STUDIES AT ANN ARBOR, MICHIGAN, *The Auk,* Vol. 55, 1938, pp. 187–97.

Wilson, R. E. BEHAVIOR AND POPULATION ECOLOGY OF THE BURROWING OWL IN THE IMPERIAL VALLEY OF CALIFORNIA, *The Condor,* Vol. 73, No. 2, 1971, pp. 162–76.

Wilson, R. R. SCREECH OWL AND MARTIN NEST IN THE SAME BOX, *Bird Lore,* Vol. 27, 1925, p. 109.

Wolfe, R. WESTERN HORNED OWL IN WESTERN KANSAS (THE), *The Oölogist,* Vol. 29, 1912, pp. 222–24.

Index

Acadian Owl. *See* Saw-whet Owl
Acadian Saw-whet Owl. *See* Saw-whet Owl
Adult, defined, 265
Aegolius acadicus, 56–65; *A. a. acadicus,* xx, 38, 56–64; *A. a. brooksi,* 38, 56, 60, 64–65
Aegolius funereus richardsoni, 39, 66–71
Aiken's Screech Owl, 55, 96, 119–20
Albinism, defined, 265
Allen's Barred Owl. *See* Florida Barred Owl
Alula, xxiv, xxv; defined, 265
American Barn Owl. *See* Barn Owl
American Hawk Owl, 166, 195–203; annual broods, nest, nesting habits, 200; beak length, 196; coloration, markings, 198–99; courtship, mating, 200; distinguishing features, 195; distribution, 202–3; ears, hearing, 198; ear tufts, plumage, annual molt, 198; economic influence, 203; eggs, 202; enemies, defenses, 199–200; eyes, vision, 196; flight pattern, 195–96; food, feeding habits, wastes, 200; general habits and characteristics, 199; habitat, roosting, 199; hunting, carrying of prey, 200; incubation, brooding, 202; individual wing length, 196; legs, feet, talons, 196; migration, 203; mortality, longevity, 198; other names, 195; scientific name, description, 195; sexual differences, 198; shape at rest, in flight, 195; tail length, 196; total length, 196; voice, 198; weight, 196; wingspan, 196; young, family life, 202
American Long-eared Owl. *See* Long-eared Owl
American Snowy Owl. *See* Snowy Owl
American Sparrow Owl. *See* Richardson's Owl
Anal area, defined, 265
Annual broods, xxii. *See also* specific owls
Annual molt, xx. *See also* specific owls
Arboreal, defined, 265
Arctic Horned Owl, 215, 224, 257–58, 260
Arctic Owl. *See* Snowy Owl
Arctic Saw-whet Owl. *See* Richardson's Owl
Arizona Pygmy Owl, 167, 204, 211–12, 218
Arizona Screech Owl. *See* Mexican Screech Owl; Saguaro Screech Owl
Arizona Spotted Owl. *See* Mexican Spotted Owl
Arizona Whiskered Owl, 134, 149, 154–55
Asio flammeus flammeus, 54, 83–95
Asio otus, 72–82; *A. o. tuftsi,* 72, 80–82; *A. o. wilsonianus,* xx, 39, 72–80
Asymmetrical, defined, 265
Auditory, defined, 265
Auriculars, xxiii, xxv; defined, 265
Axillaries, xxiv; defined, 265

Back, xxiii, xxv
Back of head. *See* Occiput
Barn Owl, xiv, xvi, 3–19; annual broods, nest, nesting habits, 16; beak length, 4; coloration, markings, 8–10; courtship, mating, 15; distinguishing features, 3; distribution, 18; ears, hearing, 6; ear tufts, plumage, annual molt, 6–7; economic influence, 19; eggs, 16–17; enemies, defenses, 12–14; eyes, vision, 6; flight pattern, 4; food, feeding habits, wastes, 14–15; general habits and characteristics, 10; habitat, roosting, 10–12; hunting, carrying of prey, 14; incubation, brooding, 17; individual wing length, 4; legs, feet, talons, 4–6; migration, 18–19; mortality, longevity, 8; other names, 3; scientific name, description, 3; sexual differences, 7–8; shape at rest, in flight, 4; tail length, 4; total length, 4; voice, 7; weight, 4; wingspan, 4; young, family life, 17–18
Barred Owl, xiv, 20–36. *See also* specific species
Barred Owl, Western. *See* California Spotted Owl
Barrings, defined, 265
Bastard wing. *See* Alula
Bayou Owl. *See* Southern Screech Owl
Beach Owl. *See* Florida Screech Owl
Beak, xxiv, xxv; defined, 265
Beak length, xviii (*see also* specific species); comparison tables, 264; defined, 265
Belly, xxiii, xxiv
Bendire's Screech Owl. *See* California Screech Owl
Bibliography, 268–73
Big-eared Owl. *See* Great Horned Owl
Bill. *See* Beak
Billy Owl. *See* Western Burrowing Owl
Birds as prey, 236. *See also* specific owls
Boreal, defined, 265
Boreal Owl. *See* Richardson's Owl
Breast, xxiii, xxiv
Brewster's Screech Owl, 71, 96, 123–24
Bristle, defined, 265
British Columbia Horned Owl. *See* Northwestern Horned Owl
Brooding, xxii (*see also* specific owls); defined, 265
Broods, annual, xxii. *See also* specific owls
Brooks's Owl. *See* Queen Charlotte Owl
Brush Owl. *See* Long-eared Owl
Bubo virginianus, 224–60; *B. v. algistus,* 183, 224, 244–46; *B. v. heterocnemis,* 183, 224, 246–48; *B. v. lagophonus,* 198, 224, 248–50; *B. v. occidentalis,* xiv, 198, 224, 250–52; *B. v. pacificus,* xiv, 199, 224, 252–53; *B. v. pallescens,* 199, 224, 253–54; *B. v. saturatus,* 214, 224, 254–57; *B. v. scalariventris,* 214, 224, 257, 258; *B. v. subarcticus,* 215, 224, 257–58, 260; *B. v. virginianus,* xvi, xx, 183, 224–44; *B. v. wapacuthu,* 224, 260
Burrowing Owl, xiv, 163–76. *See also* specific species

Cactus Owl, 182, 216, 220, 222–23
Cactus Pygmy Owl. *See* Cactus Owl
California Horned Owl. *See* Pacific Horned Owl
California Pygmy Owl, 167, 204, 210–11
California Screech Owl, 70, 96, 121–23
California Spotted Owl, 22, 37–43; annual broods, nest, nesting habits, 42; beak length, 38; coloration, markings, 39–40; courtship, mating, 42; distinguishing features, 37; distribution, 43; ears, hearing, 38; ear tufts, plumage, annual molt, 39; economic influence, 43; eggs, 42–43; enemies, defenses, 40–42; eyes, vision, 38; flight pattern, 37; food, feeding habits, wastes, 42; general habits and characteristics, 40; habitat, roosting, 40; hunting, carrying of prey, 42; incubation, brooding, 43; individual wing length, 38; legs, feet, talons, 38; migration, 43; mortality, longevity, 39; other names, 37; scientific name, description, 37; sexual differences, 39; shape at rest, in flight, 37; tail length, 38; total length, 38; voice, 39; weight, 38; wingspan, 38; young, family life, 43
Canadian Long-eared Owl. *See* Western Long-eared Owl
Canadian Owl. *See* American Hawk Owl
Canyon Spotted Owl. *See* Mexican Spotted Owl
Carpal joint, xxiv, xxv; defined, 265
Carrying of prey, xxii. *See also* specific owls
Casual, defined, 265
Cat Owl. *See* Florida Screech Owl; Great Horned Owl
Cattle Owl. *See* Florida Burrowing Owl
Cere, xxv; defined, 265
Chat-Huant du Nord, Le. *See* Northern Barred Owl
Chat-Huant Tacheté du Nord, Le. *See* Northern Spotted Owl
Cheek. *See* Malar region
Chin, xxiv, xxv
Chouette à Terrier de l'Ouest, La. *See* Western Burrowing Owl
Chouette Cendrée d'Amérique, La. *See* Great Gray Owl
Chouette de Reine-Charlotte, La. *See* Queen Charlotte Owl
Chouette de Richardson, La. *See* Richardson's Owl
Chouette des Granges de l'Est, La. *See* Saw-whet Owl
Chouette Épervière d'Amérique, La. *See* American Hawk Owl
Chouette Naine, La. *See* California Pygmy Owl
Chouette Pygmée, Côtière, La. *See* Coast Pygmy Owl
Chouette Pygmée de Californie, La. *See* California Pygmy Owl
Chouette Pygmée de Vancouver, La. *See* Vancouver Pygmy Owl
Chouette Rayée, La. *See* Northern Barred Owl
Cinereous Owl. *See* Great Gray Owl
Citrus Owl. *See* Barn Owl
Cloaca, xxiv; defined, 265
Clutch, defined, 265
Coastal Screech Owl. *See* Kennicott's Screech Owl
Coast Pygmy Owl, 182, 204, 212–14

migration, 55; mortality, longevity, 50; other names, 48; scientific name, description, 48; sexual differences, 50; shape at rest, in flight, 48–49; tail length, 49; total length, 49; voice, 50; weight, 49; wingspan, 49; young, family life, 54

Great Horned Owl, xvi, xx, 183, 224–44; annual broods, nest, nesting habits, 241; beak length, 226; coloration, markings, 230; courtship, mating, 240–41; distinguishing features, 224–25; distribution, 244; ears, hearing, 226; ear tufts, plumage, annual molt, 228; economic influence, 244; eggs, 241–42; enemies, defenses, 232–34; eyes, vision, 226; flight pattern, 225; food, feeding habits, wastes, 236–40; general habits and characteristics, 230–32; habitat, roosting, 232; hunting, carrying of prey, 234–36; incubation, brooding, 242; individual wing length, 226; legs, feet, talons, 226; migration, 244; mortality, longevity, 230; other names, 224; scientific name, description, 224; sexual differences, 228; shape at rest, in flight, 225; tail length, 226; total length, 225; voice, 228; weight, 225; wingspan, 226; young, family life, 242–44

Great Plains Screech Owl. See Aiken's Screech Owl

Great White Owl. See Snowy Owl

Gregarious, defined, 266

Ground color, defined, 266

Ground Owl. See Western Burrowing Owl

Guadalupe Screech Owl, 96, 144–45

Gular area, xxiv; defined, 266

Habitat, xxii. See also specific owls

Hammock Owl. See Florida Screech Owl

Hasbrouck's Screech Owl, 87, 96, 131–32

Hawk Owl. See American Hawk Owl

Head (see also Topography of an Owl): studies of varied owls, xvi

Hearing, xviii–xx. See also specific owls

Heel, xxv; defined, 266

Hibou à Longues Aigrettes, Le. See Long-eared Owl

Hibou à Longues Oreilles, Le. See Long-eared Owl

Hibou à Oreilles Courtes, Le. See Short-eared Owl

Hibou Blanc, Le. See Snowy Owl

Hibou des Marais, Le. See Short-eared Owl

Hill Owl. See Western Burrowing Owl

Hindneck, xxiii

Hind toe, xxv

Hoot Owl. See California Spotted Owl; Great Horned Owl; Northern Barred Owl

Horned Owl, xiv, xvi, 224–60. See also specific species

Horned Owl, Lesser. See Long-eared Owl

Horned Owl, Little. See Kennicott's Screech Owl

Hudsonian Owl. See American Hawk Owl

Hunting methods, xxii. See also specific owls

Immaculate, defined, 266

Immature, defined, 266

Incubation, xxii (see also specific owls); defined, 266

Incubation period, defined, 266

Inner toe, xxv

Iris, xxiii; defined, 266

Juvenal plumage, defined, 266

Juveniles (see also specific owls): coloration and markings, xx; defined, 266; portrait studies, xx

Kennicott's Screech Owl, 96, 97, 102, 106, 135–37

Kirtland's Owl. See Saw-whet Owl

"Knee." See Heel

Labrador Horned Owl, 183, 224, 246–48

Least Screech Owl. See Flammulated Owl

Lechucilla Llanera. See Western Burrowing Owl

Lechuza Barranquera de Wilson. See Long-eared Owl

Lechuza Mono. See Barn Owl

Legs, xviii. See also specific owls

Length, xvi, xviii (see also specific owls); comparison tables, 263; defined, 266

Lesser Horned Owl. See Long-eared Owl

Lesser wing coverts, xxiiiff.; defined, 266

Linear, defined, 266

Linear measurement, xvi, xviii. See also specific owls

Little Dukelet. See Eastern Screech Owl

Little Owl. See Eastern Screech Owl

Little-eared Owl. See Eastern Screech Owl

Little Horned Owl. See Kennicott's Screech Owl

Long-eared Owl, xx, 39, 72–80 (see also Western Long-eared Owl); annual broods, nest, nesting habits, 78; beak length, 73; coloration, markings, 76; distinguishing features, 72; distribution, 80; ears, hearing, 74; ear tufts, plumage, annual molt, 74; economic influence, 80; eggs, 78–79; enemies, defenses, 77; eyes, vision, 73; flight pattern, 73; food, feeding habits, wastes, 78; general habits and characteristics, 76; habitat, roosting, 76–77; hunting, carrying of prey, 77–78; incubation, brooding, 79; individual wing length, 73; legs, feet, talons, 73; migration, 80; mortality, longevity, 76; other names, 72; scientific name, description, 72; sexual differences, 74; shape at rest, in flight, 72–73; tail length, 73; total length, 73; voice, 74; weight, 73; wingspan, 73; young, family life, 79

Longevity, xx. See also specific owls

Lores, xxiii; defined, 266

Lower back, xxv

McCally's Owl. See Texas Screech Owl

MacFarlane's Screech Owl, 96, 102, 137–39

Maculate, defined, 266

Malar region, xxiiiff.; defined, 266

Mammals as prey, 236. See also specific owls

Mandibles, xxv; defined, 266

Markings, xx. See also specific owls

Marsh Owl. See Short-eared Owl

Mating, xxii. See also specific owls

Mature, defined, 266

Meadow Owl. See Short-eared Owl

Measurement, xvi–xviii. See also specific owls

Median (medial), defined, 266

Median line, xxiv

Median wing coverts. See Middle wing coverts

Melanism, defined, 266

Mexican Screech Owl, 71, 96, 124–26. See also Saguaro Screech Owl

Mexican Spotted Owl, 33, 37, 45–47

Mice as prey (see also specific owls): Harvest Mouse, 90

Micrathene whitneyi, xiv, 177–84; *M. w. idonea*, xiv, 151, 177, 183–84; *M. w. whitneyi*, 150, 177–83

Middle toe, xxv

Middle wing coverts, xxiii, xxv; defined, 266

Migration, xxii (see also specific owls); defined, 266

Molt, xx (see also specific owls); defined, 266

Monkey-faced Owl. See Barn Owl

Montana Horned Owl (*Bubo virginianus occidentalis*), xiv, 198, 224, 250–52

Mortality, xx. See also specific owls

Mottled Owl. See Eastern Screech Owl

Mottled Owl, Western. See Texas Screech Owl

Mountain Pygmy Owl. See Rocky Mountain Pygmy Owl

Mouse Owl. See Eastern Screech Owl

Names, xiv. See also specific owls

Nape (see also Hindneck): defined, 266

Nebraska Screech Owl, 96, 119, 145–46

Neck, xxv

Nesting habits, xxii. See also specific owls

Nests, xxii. See also specific owls

Nocturnal, defined, 266

Northern Barred Owl, 6, 20–32; annual broods, nest, nesting habits, 29; beak length, 21; coloration, markings, 23–25; courtship, mating, 28–29; distinguishing features, 20; distribution, 31; ears, hearing, 22; ear tufts, plumage, annual molt, 22; economic influence, 32; eggs, 29–30; enemies, defenses, 25–26; eyes, vision, 21–22; flight pattern, 21; food, feeding habits, wastes, 28; general habits and characteristics, 25; habitat, roosting, 25; hunting, carrying of prey, 26–28; incubation, brooding, 30; individual wing length, 21; legs, feet, talons, 21; migration, 31–32; mortality, longevity, 23; other names, 20; scientific name, description, 20; sexual differences, 23; shape at rest, in flight, 20; tail length, 21; total length, 21; voice, 22–23; weight, 21; wingspan, 21; young, family life, 30–31

Northern Short-eared Owl. See Short-eared Owl

Northern Spotted Owl, xx, 22, 37, 43–45

Northwestern Horned Owl, 198, 224, 248–50

Northwest Saw-whet Owl. See Queen Charlotte Owl

Nostrils. See Cere

Nuhl-Tuhl. See Great Gray Owl

Nyctale Boréale, La. See Richardson's Owl

Nyctea scandiaca, xiv, 151, 185–94

Oak Owl. See Florida Screech Owl; Pasadena Screech Owl

Occiput, xxv; defined, 266

Okpik. See Snowy Owl

Olfactory, defined, 266

Ontario Horned Owl, 214, 224, 257, 258

Index